More praise
Then They Starte

"Beautifully illustrates the way in which people (in this case children) actively engage with the experience of war . . . Highly original."
—*TIMES LITERARY SUPPLEMENT*

"Out of the horror of human cruelty in the Bosnian war comes a bright note."
—*FOREIGN AFFAIRS*

"Thought-provoking and readable."
—*LIBRARY JOURNAL*

"Careful, sensitive . . . a deeply intimate look into the emotional makeup of children of war."
—*KIRKUS REVIEWS*

"Absorbing . . . offers new insights into Bosnian Serb–Muslim relations through the eyes of children."
—*PUBLISHERS WEEKLY*

"Psychiatrist Lynne Jones, working in Bosnia, discovered a striking puzzle: most children exposed to the extreme trauma of war were not "mentally ill." This remarkable book not only contributes to social history—including our understanding of the genocide in Srebrenica— but also to psychiatry. Her astonishing work challenges the medical model in understanding human responses to cruelty."
—SIMON BARON-COHEN,
Professor of Developmental Psychopathology, Cambridge University, and author of
The Science of Evil: On Empathy and the Origins of Cruelty

"Part narrative, part analysis, part thoughtful reflection, this book belongs among the classic accounts of children and war."
—JENNIFER LEANING,
M.D., S.M.H., Harvard School of Public Health

"Lynne Jones brings to the extreme situation she describes a truly unique combination of hands-on, communally-oriented psychiatric help; sensitive research on the impact of war and upheaval on children; and an astute sense of the interplay of political policies and psychological behavior. . . . The book not only deepens our understanding of what happened in the former Yugoslavia but contributes greatly to our more general grasp of the consequences of death, loss, and dislocation, and the stubborn human persistence in the face of them."

—ROBERT JAY LIFTON,
author of *The Nazi Doctors: Medical Killing and the Psychology of Genocide* and *Witness to an Extreme Century*

"One of the most illuminating books to have emerged out of the embers of the Bosnian war. Few outsiders have acquired such an inside knowledge of the thoughts and feelings of ordinary Bosnians, on both sides of the wartime divide."

—NOEL MALCOLM,
author of *Bosnia: A Short History* and Chairman of the Bosnian Institute in London

"Lynne Jones is an internationally-known expert on the effects of war on children. Her description of the legacy of the savage war in Bosnia is a shattering but necessary read. . . . This book should be in the knapsack of every international administrator."

—BRENDAN SIMMS,
author of *Europe: The Struggle for Supremacy*

THEN THEY STARTED SHOOTING

*Children of the
Bosnian War and the
Adults They Become*

LYNNE JONES

BELLEVUE LITERARY PRESS
NEW YORK

This edition published in the United States in 2013 by
Bellevue Literary Press, New York

For Information, Contact:
Bellevue Literary Press
NYU School of Medicine
550 First Avenue
OBV A612
New York, NY 10016

Library of Congress Cataloging-in-Publication Data
is available from the publisher upon request.

Bellevue Literary Press would like to thank all its generous
donors—individuals and foundations—for their support.

Book design and composition by Mulberry Tree Press, Inc.

Manufactured in the United States of America.

1   3   5   7   9   8   6   4   2

ISBN 978-1-934137-66-6

For Asmamaw

CONTENTS

MAPS

The Balkans, 1990

The Balkans, 2013

Bosnia-Herzegovina, 1998

The Drina Valley, 1998

ABBREVIATIONS

ARBiH	Army of the Republic of Bosnia and Herzegovina
BiH	Bosnia and Herzegovina
EU	European Union
HDZ BiH	Croatian Democratic Union of Bosnia and Herzegovina
ICTY	International Criminal Tribunal for the Former Yugoslavia
IPTF	International Police Task Force
JNA	Yugoslav People's Army
NATO	North Atlantic Treaty Organization
NGO	Non-governmental organization
NSP	New Socialist Party
RS	Republika Srpska
SDA	Party of Democratic Action
SDP BiH	Social Democratic Party of Bosnia and Herzegovina
SDS	Serbian Democratic Party
SNSD	Alliance of Independent Social Democrats
SFOR	United Nations Stabilization Force
SRS	Serb Radical Party
UN	United Nations
UNHCR	United Nations High Commission for Refugees
UNICEF	United Nations Children's Fund
VRS	Army of Republika Srpska

THEN THEY STARTED SHOOTING

INTRODUCTION

IT IS THE RIVER THAT CATCHES YOUR HEART. I would wake to it every morning, stretched like a small sea below my bedroom window, reflecting the light of the sky and the mood of the town. My flat was upstairs in a comfortable villa overlooking the Drina, three minutes' walk from the center of Gorazde. This had been what Nerma, my landlord's fourteen-year-old daughter, called *the first front line* during the war. The house was neatly positioned under the line of hills to the south, from which Serbian troops could bombard the town with impunity. Nerma and her family had escaped for a few months to the town center and then returned to live downstairs. When they offered me the upstairs flat, it had a large shell hole through the bedroom ceiling, broken floorboards, shrapnel scars over all the walls, and no windows. Nerma's father took my rent money and repaired the damage in a week: putting in a new stove and helping me order wood for the winter. Beyond the front garden was an unpaved road followed by a stretch of reed bed and water meadow, where old people walked their single cows in the evening, or sat on the path for a smoke, watching the light fade on the newly reconstructed dome of the mosque across the river.

Gorazde is a small place. It has two main streets, one on each side of the Drina, connected by three bridges. Before 1992, it was one of the more prosperous towns in the area, with two industrial suburbs, Kopaci and Vitkovici, and an armaments factory in town. There were clusters of communist-style apartment blocks and increasing numbers of private houses built with wages hard earned in Germany. It had two primary schools, three high schools, and a large health center with a hospital in the neighboring town of Foca. A quarter of Gorazde's population was Serb, the rest Muslim. The different ethnic communities got along well.

Then war came. For Gorazde this meant four years of siege and bombardment, followed by a peace settlement that divided Bosnia between two political entities: the Federation belonging to Muslims and Croats, and

Republika Srpska, belonging to Serbs. Gorazde became an island of Federation territory entirely surrounded by Republika Srpska, connected to the Federation's capital, Sarajevo, by a yet-to-be-built road.

I arrived in late 1996, appointed by an aid agency to work as the municipality's sole psychiatrist; there had been none for the previous four years. The war had been over for a year, but the town was still half-destroyed, with roofless houses and shattered public buildings. Electricity had only come on that month, and there was still no running water. A continuing reminder of war was that non-Serbs who had been displaced from what was now Republika Srpska could not return to live there because local Serbs, particularly those in the town of Foca and the Gorazde suburb of Kopaci, were against it.

By the summer of 1998, the mood had changed. Many houses had been rebuilt and repainted in vivid colors. Around the corner from my flat was a new sports hall donated by the Dutch government, where Nerma would drag me to pop concerts and handball matches against visiting teams. Farther down the road was a street of cafés and small boutiques packed full of young people on warm nights. Displaced families were still living in crowded collective centers. Otherwise, the only obvious signs of war were the scaffolding walkway clinging to the underside of the central bridge, built to protect pedestrians from snipers, and the ring of burned, unoccupied houses on the edge of the town, whose Serb owners had still not reclaimed them after the war.

There were two completely gutted buildings next door to ours, where Serb families had lived. They had the appearance of having been burned from the inside, not hit by bombs. These Serbs had been good friends with Nerma's family and their other neighbors. One day Nerma's family heard gunfire. Thinking it must be coming from the hills, they climbed out the windows to escape. Then they saw that their Serb neighbors were shooting from their house. A short time later the Serb family took to the hills, leaving large piles of weapons and a short-wave radio in their living room. Not long before I moved in, one of the Serb women came back to visit her former best friend. *We asked why she didn't warn us*, Nerma told me, *and she said she wasn't responsible. Then she asked for a spade. We lent her one and she went and dug up some gold from her garden and left again.*

There was something striking about Nerma. It was not simply that she was intelligent and attractive. It was that despite having had her home, school, and community shelled from the surrounding hills for four years, and despite having lost friends and relatives, she was completely well. She told funny stories when she showed me where her family got spring water during the war. She said she would not mind if her Serb neighbors came back to live near her again. In break time and after school, she sat with her girlfriends under the cherry trees on a low stone wall beside the river outside the primary school. They gossiped, giggled, ate hamburgers, and ignored the admiring groups of boys. She was happy and full of plans for the future: exchange holidays in Spain, high school, medical school in Sarajevo. The war had begun when Nerma was nine and ended when she was thirteen. Yet there was no evidence here of the war-traumatized child so often portrayed by the media. Nor in six months of psychiatric practice in the town did I see very many others.

The war had come suddenly when I was living in Slovenia in the summer of 1991. Since that time, I had divided my life between aid work in the Balkans and training in child psychiatry in Britain. As the war moved south and gained ferocity, I had moved with it. I worked with adolescent refugees from Croatia and Bosnia in the summers of 1991 and 1992, worked in Sarajevo while it was under siege in 1994 and 1995, and arrived in Gorazde a year later. It was never difficult to find work. "War-traumatized children" attract public attention and funds, and any number of humanitarian agencies were looking for staff.

Yet through meetings with children like Nerma and her school friends, I came to believe that humanitarian programs and mental health professionals were approaching the subject of war trauma and children from the wrong direction. The largely unquestioned assumption was that large numbers of children would be traumatized—that is, made medically unwell—by war and would need psychological assistance. Such children were identified by means of questionnaires (filled out by the children themselves or their mothers) that established whether they had symptoms, and the symptomatic children then received psychological treatment. Regardless of whether they were Croat, Muslim, or Serb, regardless of their particular experiences—bombing, rape, or ethnic cleansing—it was assumed that "traumatized" children would manifest their problems in similar ways, and that the Western treatment methods adopted by most humanitarian agencies would help them. Other assumptions were that war was necessarily brutalizing and damaging to children's moral development, and that today's traumatized and untreated children were tomorrow's terrorists;

hence the need for "treatment." Underlying this approach was a belief that individuals' psychological worlds existed in a vacuum, completely separate from political and social realities.

But the majority of the children with whom I worked did not fit this picture. Some teenagers in Gorazde did have "symptoms"—poor concentration in school or nightmares—but often they did not see their symptoms as illness requiring treatment, but rather as normal reactions to horrifying events. They were angry, unhappy, grieving, bewildered, but not, in most cases, psychologically disturbed. They had complex and sometimes discomfiting moral and political perspectives, but certainly not stunted ones. Moreover, the most significant factors affecting their mental health seemed to be rooted in the immediate environment in which they lived, rather than in any traumatic events they had experienced.

As I explored the academic literature, I found much that supported my view. In conflicts studied around the world, 60 to 80 percent of children showed no psychological ill effects. Furthermore, their well-being was not necessarily related to the amount of violence they had suffered, but it was related to the way they made sense of their experiences, their subjective view of events. However, most of the large body of work exploring the effects of war on children focused on rates of illness and the identification of symptom clusters and "vulnerability" and "protective factors"; no one appeared to be examining the experience of war from the child's perspective. For all the children I had encountered, war had been a life-changing event, but it had not necessarily made them ill. If I wanted to understand the true impact of war on childhood, I had to step away from a medical model and the search for psychopathology and start to listen to children describing their experiences and their own understandings of the ways such experiences had affected them.

What happens if you are nine years old and you see your neighbors and school friends being forcibly evicted and half the town burned down? How does it make you feel, and how do you feel if those neighbors come back? What if your father or brother is killed on the front line? How do you make sense of that? Whom do you hold responsible? What happens if you are trapped in a city where the safest place for months on end is the basement? How does it feel to be imprisoned in your home by your neighbors? What is it like to fight over food parcels or to walk across mountains in the snow? How do children who have had such experiences view the future? After four years of war, how do they adjust to peace? Is there an enduring effect on their psychological health? I set out to learn from Bosnian teenagers themselves how they experienced war, how they made sense of it, and how it affected them. I did not want to confine myself to one side of the conflict: I would talk with Muslim young people in Gorazde and with their Serb contemporaries in Foca.

Foca is half an hour from Gorazde by road. Before the war, it was another provincial town on the Drina, rather similar to Gorazde. It had industry centered on timber; 55 percent of the population was Muslim and some 45 percent Serb, with good relations between communities and frequent movement, for work and other reasons, between the two cities. In April 1992, in the first three weeks of the war, Bosnian Serb forces, with the assistance of paramilitary groups from Serbia, took control of Foca, and the Muslim residents fled, were forcibly expelled, or were imprisoned. Many of the detainees were tortured and killed, while Muslim shops, homes, and mosques were destroyed. In the following three years, the Serb residents lived in considerable hardship, although there was no direct assault on the town until NATO (North Atlantic Treaty Organization) bombing destroyed its three bridges in September 1995. In the years following the end of the war, Foca remained relatively isolated from the outside world, and received relatively little in humanitarian assistance because its authorities refused to comply with the Dayton Peace Agreement of December 1995: They did not wish non-Serb residents to return to their homes, and a number of indicted war criminals lived in the town.

I visited Foca for the first time in the early summer of 1997. One of the local school psychologists had visited Gorazde for a seminar organized by some international aid organizations and had told me I would be welcome to visit her school to see how the students felt about talking to me. The weather that day was terrible, rain and wind dragging plum blossoms off the trees and whipping the Drina into brown foam. The road follows the river. After Ustikolina, the valley narrows and the rounded hills acquire more forceful and dramatic outlines. The only indication that we were crossing into another entity was the sudden dearth of traffic and an orange stick with a round disk like a lollipop stuck beside the road marking the inter-entity boundary line. This was closely followed by a large sign in Cyrillic announcing that we were in Republika Srpska.

We crossed into town on a Bailey bridge built by SFOR (the UN Stabilization Force) to replace one of those destroyed by NATO, and bumped along a cobbled street past a hillside covered with gutted houses. There was little sign of the shell damage so evident in Gorazde, but the town had a dilapidated, uncared-for appearance. The school looked much like its counterpart in Gorazde, one of those buildings that say public school the world over, with wide drafty corridors stretching in three directions, dirty paintwork, and unmarked doors. We opened one into a bare classroom where the children, sitting at double desks, rose politely to greet us.

I had been worried that because I had worked in Gorazde, teachers and pupils in Foca would not want to talk to me. I was completely mistaken. They were pleased that I wanted to talk to children on both sides, and one boy, Mladen, volunteered to be interviewed that day as a pilot for my study. We sat in the small library. He was a pleasant, articulate child who felt well and happy with his life, and like Nerma, he wanted to be a doctor. The fighting in town had scared him, as had the NATO bombing, but it appeared to have had no lasting effects. He told me unequivocally that "ethnic cleansing"—a term he used without embarrassment—had made Foca safe for Serbs to live in, because without it, he believed, all the Serbs, including old people and babies, would have been in danger of being killed in their beds by Muslim fanatics. Ethnic cleansing was not a crime but a defensive necessity, and ethnic separation was essential for Serb survival.

In a short journey up the Drina Valley, I had stepped through a mirror reversing all my previous understandings of the conflict. It was becoming clear to me that the lasting legacies of the war were not the psychopathological effects on young people, but their profoundly different understandings of why it had happened, what it had achieved, and what should be the relations between ethnic groups. These understandings resulted in quite different and incompatible wishes for the future. If I wanted to understand the war's impact on Mladen and Nerma, I would have to immerse myself in both their worlds.

That is what I did for the following year. For security reasons, I could not live full time in Foca. However, I spent three to four full days of every week there, and as in Gorazde, I interviewed young teenagers and their families at length about their experiences, their understandings of the war, and their psychological well-being. I spent time with the children, at school and at home, participating in the normal life of both communities, shopping, watching TV, going on trips and to parties and various festivals.

My intention was to come home in mid-1998 and spend the following year analyzing my findings and writing this book. Events overtook me. In Kosovo, a province of Serbia, Albanians had lived under a form of apartheid for the previous decade, although they were the majority. They had learned from their exclusion from the Dayton peace process that non-violent protest does not get the world's attention. By 1998, the province was at war. I was asked by an aid organization to go to Kosovo to set up mobile clinics and an emergency mental health program. A three-month commitment to set up a child and family mental health service in what had become a UN-administered area extended into three years. The book had to be put aside.

The delay created an opportunity. In four years my young teenagers had grown into young adults and their world had changed. Milosevic fell from power and was indicted for genocide in Kosovo, Croatia, and Bosnia at the International Criminal Tribunal for the Former Yugoslavia (ICTY) at The Hague. At the request of the UN, Kofi Annan produced his report on the town of Srebrenica, where despite its designation as a UN Safe Area, Serb forces had killed approximately seven thousand non-Serb civilians and expelled twenty-five thousand. The report criticized both the UN and the international community for failing to recognize what the war was about and to take action to stop it. He wrote, "Srebrenica crystallized a truth understood only too late by the United Nations and the world at large: that Bosnia was as much a moral cause as a military conflict."[1]

I went back in 2002 to explore whether that was how young people in the Drina Valley saw it. Had they recovered from the stresses and miseries of the war? What did they think about the crimes of the past and the possibilities of the future?

The first edition of this book was published in 2004. By then the name Yugoslavia had disappeared from the map of Europe. Milosevic died from a heart attack in 2006 while still on trial for war crimes at the ICTY, cheating all of his victims in the former Yugoslavia of any final reckoning. Dr. Radovan Karadzic was arrested in 2008 while hiding out as a New Age doctor in Belgrade and General Ratko Mladic was finally handed over to the ICTY by Serb authorities in 2011. Both of them are now on trial in The Hague. Bodies of their victims from the massacre at Srebrenica continue to be discovered: 520 newly identified bodies were buried at a memorial service outside that city in July 2012; thirty thousand people attended.

How the massacre at Srebrenica is understood and defined continues to be a signature issue for interpreting the Bosnian war as a whole. Both the ICTY and the International Court of Justice defined the event as genocide. In 2005, Boris Tadic, then president of Serbia, attended memorials in the city and apologized to surviving relatives. In 2010, the Serbian parliament issued a formal apology for not doing more to prevent the massacre. However, in June of 2012, the newly elected president of Serbia, Tomislav Nikolic, announced on Montenegrin state television that "there was no genocide in Srebrenica," although "grave war crimes" were committed.[2] Nikolic was once deputy head of the ultra-nationalist Serb Radical Party under Vojislav Seselj, also on trial at The Hague. His opinion is shared by Milorad Dodik, the current president of Republika Srpska.[3]

In the last few years Dodik has also challenged the peace settlement that ended the war and the existence of Bosnia and Herzegovina as a state. The internationally appointed high representative warned in his November 2012 report that "the leadership of the Republika Srpska (RS) has intensified its six-year policy of open and direct challenges to the fundamentals of the peace agreement. Statements uttered by senior RS figures, as well as actions initiated by them to erode the competencies of the state, raise profound doubts about the commitment of the current RS leadership to the most fundamental aspect of Dayton—the sovereignty and territorial integrity of BiH." Milorad Dodik's statement that "BiH is a rotten state that does not deserve to exist. BiH constantly confirms its inability to exist . . . BiH is definitely falling apart and it will happen sooner or later. As far as I am concerned, I hope to God it dissolves as soon as possible," was just one example.[4]

The high representative was also gloomy about the economic situation, stating that "the country is faced with a deteriorating fiscal situation, poor growth prospects, high unemployment, and accompanying social problems."

So how were the young people in my study coping with all of this? How did they feel about the nature and state of their country? In 2012, twenty years after the war began and 10 years after I had last interviewed them, I returned to Bosnia to try and find out what had happened. In the intervening decade, my respondents had grown up, developed careers, left home, and in some cases created families of their own. Helped by Facebook and my interpreters, I managed to track down fourteen (seven in each community) still living in their home towns or making regular visits. I was touched by the welcome they gave me, and their willingness to tell me about their lives, their well-being, and to share their thoughts on all that had happened in the previous decade.

This revised edition of the book is the result. In it, I recount my exploration of the way children in the Drina Valley, from both sides of the conflict, experienced and made sense of the Bosnian war as teenagers. I then follow a smaller group into adulthood and examine its longer-term impact. I set their experiences in the context of other wars, and suggest implications for our understanding of how children survive and develop in wartime and how such experiences affect adult life. The book is not a history of the war, though it includes a chronology of key events to guide the reader through the political context in which these children lived. History is written looking backward. Hindsight and the passage of time allow a broader and supposedly more objective view. Yet history is lived forward. All of us have a limited, partial, and subjective view of what we witness and experience. We grasp at selected events that have personal meaning, and we interpret them in the frameworks available to us at that moment. As we grow older, we create new stories that determine the way we remember and explain the past. It is the beliefs, attitudes, and feelings arising from these fragmentary perspectives that drive the future and that need to be understood.

The book is divided into four parts. In part one, I describe the war through the children's eyes. In 1998, I interviewed forty children and many of their parents, but for this part I have interwoven the stories of eight children whose experiences are particularly representative of the conflict on both sides. Children's perceptions of what happened, their concerns, fears, and preoccupations, are often startlingly different from those of adults. Their concerns focus on the domestic environment as much as the external one. The stories are presented exactly as the children told them to me in 1998, in their own (translated) words. This includes using the terms they themselves used to describe other groups. I have not extrapolated upon their experiences or guessed at feelings they did not share with me.

In part two, the focus shifts to the children's understanding of the issues raised by the conflict. I explore the way parents made sense of the conflict to give some idea of the world in which the children lived. I then examine the manner in which war crystallized ethnic identity and altered children's perceptions of themselves, their neighbors, their communities, and their country. The war in Bosnia did not arise out of deep-rooted ethnic animosities. On the contrary, these communities had spent most of the last half-millennium living harmoniously together. However, this last war, and in particular the settlement that brought it to an end, had an enduring impact on these young people's sense of themselves and their neighbors, which has significant consequences for the future stability of the region.

In part three, I examine the war's impact on the children's psychological and social well-being two years after its end. I begin by summarizing changes that have occurred over the past half-century in professional beliefs about the psychological impact of war on children, and how the changes have framed their assessment and treatment. I then explore the children's own perceptions of their psychological health, looking at the diverse responses to particular events such as the loss of a parent, or being bombed, or losing one's home; and the relationship between the children's well-being and the way they made sense of events. I discovered that in this war the specific interpretation of an event mattered less than whether or not a child chose to look for meaning. Children who avoided searching for explanations for past events appeared to have better individual psychological health than those who did not. Distancing oneself from the past can be protective, but in some contexts, it has costs for the community as a whole.

In part four, I explore the more enduring impact of war. I look at my respondents' psychological health and their shifting understandings of the conflict, first as older teenagers on the verge of leaving home in 2002, and then as young adults in 2012. In 2002, in the context of numerous arrests of war criminals, I explored their views about war crimes and how the past should be remembered. In 2012, I discovered that almost all of those I met were doing well, and I discuss what contributed to this resilience. I also discovered that the real world in which these young people lived was quite different from that described by the media and their political leaders, from whom they were profoundly alienated. Thus, despite the gloomy prognostications and the economic difficulties, ethnic identity was less pronounced and genuine reconciliation seemed more possible than it had a decade earlier.

For the reasons explained above, I could only track down a subsample of the original group on both visits. Apart from one individual, the 2012 group was a smaller group of those I interviewed in 2002. There is an obvious bias in this group: They are the ones who chose to remain connected to their home communities. Those who chose to move away or leave the country might have given a very different picture of both psychological health and political understanding. However, the young people within this subgroup were of both of genders and suffered a wide range of war experiences including flight, displacement, loss, imprisonment, and shelling. The group also included those who, as children, showed a wide variety of responses to such events. Some of them had been quite well in 1998, some quite unwell. Thus although one cannot generalize from their experiences and reactions, I hope the long period of in-depth follow-up will contribute to a richer understanding of the impact of war on those who grow up in its shadow.

There are some points to note about the text. Most of the interviews were conducted through translators. The children spoke an almost identical language, which they identified as Bosnian in Gorazde and Serbian in Foca. (In communist Yugoslavia, Bosnian and Serbian were considered to be separate dialects of Serbo-Croatian. The linguistic differences have been emphasized on both sides since the war.) My experience of working both in refugee mental health clinics and in the field is that the presence of a good interpreter from the local community (one who understands the work and has a few years' experience of speaking English) often leads to better interviews than those conducted in my own language in Britain. The presence of someone friendly from their own town seemed to increase the children's ease and confidence with me and freed me to pay attention to nonverbal language as well as verbal. Also, the interpreter could explain to me many cultural references the children took for granted. Perhaps most important, common language can give the illusion of comprehension when there is none. Not speaking the language made me take the time and trouble to clarify, to make sure I understood. I was lucky enough to be able to draw on the same interpreters in all my visits.

Quotations from my interviews and conversations with people in Bosnia, and from the children's written stories, are given in italic type without quotation marks. In these quotations, three unadorned ellipsis points mark the speaker's or writer's own pauses, while ellipsis points enclosed in brackets indicate places where I have omitted words or sentences. Other written or spoken quotations from textual sources are in normal type with quotation marks, and breaks in the text where sections are omitted are marked by three unadorned ellipsis points.

I use the term "Muslim" rather than the now officially sanctioned "Bosniak" for references to the Muslim population in Bosnia. It is the term all the Muslims I spoke to in Gorazde, adults and children, used (with the exception of some politicians). More important, young people made clear that it was their preferred choice on my second and third visits, by which time they had become aware of the official terminology and rejected it.

The names of almost all my respondents and their relatives and friends have been altered, along with personal details such as parental occupation, to provide anonymity. In a couple of cases, children asked me at the start to use their own names and I have done so. On my final visit, a few more respondents asked that their real names now be used. They know who they are.

The issues raised by the Bosnian War are, if anything, more pertinent today than they were 10 or 15 years ago. As I write, at least 2 million Syrian children are exposed to prolonged terrifying violence, famine, losing loved ones and homes, forced marriage, torture, rape, and forced recruitment. UNICEF (United Nations Children's Fund) again predicts a "lost generation,"[5] while the CEO of Save the Children warns of "layers and layers of emotional trauma."[6] Both call for something to be done to protect them, but the wars in Iraq, Afghanistan, Libya, and now Syria show that Western states have not solved the conundrum of whether or how to intervene. They continue to wrestle with the issues of how to address the cumulative damage caused by dictatorships to whom they previously gave support, how to reconcile differences in multiethnic states, how to balance competing needs for "justice" and "order," and how to help countries with young populations emerge from a long periods of tyranny and establish truly indigenous democracies. Yet the voices of those who must live with the consequences of such decisions are rarely heard.

The young adults of Gorazde and Foca have much to teach us. They bore no responsibility for the Balkan conflict, but they suffered its effects: deprivation and displacement, living with and witnessing violence, the wasteful loss of their childhoods, the deaths of friends and relatives, and the complete disruption of their common community. Their stories confront our stereotypes about war, identity, justice, and the way people react to traumatic events. For example, Bosnian young people challenge the monolithic and negative image of what it means to be a Muslim and the prejudices this has created. Their antagonism to the corruption and self-interest of politicians will resonate with many. They demonstrate that it is possible to grow up in the shadow of genocide and destruction and retain vitality and spirit. They continue to debate how to deal with the past, how to live in the present, and how to ensure a better future. Their stories also show that interventions of any kind, whether military, political, or judicial, that are ill thought out and halfheartedly applied, may prolong conflict rather than resolve it. As always, it is young people who will pay the price.

PART ONE

CHILDREN IN WARTIME

1

FIGHTING BEGINS

Foca, April 1992

Stojan knew something was wrong when he found his father's gun. His father was a teacher and had nothing to do with guns. He felt very frightened. When he thought about it, he realized that he had been frightened for quite a while. He was eight years old and enjoyed his life. He and his family had a nice apartment not far from the river, and he liked his teachers at school. He had wanted to be a football player when he grew up, but he had just discovered basketball and decided it was much more interesting.

Now there was fighting on TV, not movie fighting, real fighting. The army had been sent to a town called Vukovar in Croatia. The Muslims held a big meeting here in Foca, with people waving flags. The Muslims were fighting—well, not actually fighting, but wanting an independent Bosnia—and there was a Serb meeting too. He didn't understand. There was a Serb party, maybe they had given his father the gun, but his father wasn't interested in politics. Stojan decided to pretend he hadn't seen it. Maybe things would get better.

Over the next few days he became even more worried. There was more shooting on TV. Then without any warning or explanation, he and his mother were sent to Montenegro. That was fun. They could swim and he didn't have to go to school. He could still see things on TV, but it didn't seem so bad. He thought he understood what was happening. The Muslims wanted to be in control of Bosnia, and there was fighting in Sarajevo. But he didn't want to think about war anymore. They were going to stay with his grandparents in Belgrade.

Svetlana wished she could be in Belgrade. That was where her father was. Things were always better when her father was there, but he was usually away. Her mother said he was always away when things went wrong. Like the time Svetlana was really sick with her throat and had to go to the hospital. But it wasn't her father's fault. He was a builder and he had to work. If he went away, he got a lot of money. Sometimes he went to places like Iraq and Libya. Recently he had been home more, which was good because he could help with the work in their fields, but bad because everyone was worried about money. That's why he had gone to Belgrade, to see if he could find more work. Now her mother was worrying all the time about "war" coming.

Her mother was the kind of person who worried if there was a thunderstorm, but Svetlana was a little worried herself. She loved her home. There were three houses connected, belonging to her father, her uncle's family, and her grandfather, so she was never lonely. She was nine, had been in the village school one year, and had lots of friends, and the teacher was very kind. But now things were different. Her mother had started to worry and walk halfway to school with her, and then she had stopped her from going to school, so she had to stay home, and she couldn't see her friends or talk to them as her family had no phone.

People were talking about "Muslims" and "Serbs." She knew that both Muslims and Serbs lived in her village. Muslims had a holiday called Bajram and played music outside and made cakes. She had cried once because her mother hadn't made cakes too. But her family had Christmas, and their neighbors came to them. She was still not really sure who was a Muslim and who was a Serb because they all lived mixed up together. Now everyone together was "guarding" against any "outsiders" coming in. People were scared, she could tell. A neighbor had come around one night crying, asking what was going to happen, as if her mother would know.

They had the TV news on all the time. She didn't understand it, she was sick of it. Sometimes her mother was so nervous she just insisted they lie on the bed together. Then one day there was a football match on TV. Red Star, the Belgrade team, won, and immediately afterward they heard shooting outside. Her mother was really scared and said, *Come on, get dressed, we have to go, the war has begun*—but she was wrong. People were just shooting in the air, as they always did after football matches and weddings.

Then her mother said they were going to Belgrade. Just like that. Lots of other women and children from the town were leaving, and her mother decided they should leave too. Svetlana was glad because now she would see her father.

Ivana lived in a large house that her parents were building themselves. The family had moved around a lot in her life, and it had taken time to get used to the new house, but she was just beginning to feel that Foca was home.

It was a morning in early April. She had started school that year, but was still at home because she was in the afternoon shift. Her parents had just left for work. Then the shooting started. Ivana had no idea where it was coming from or who was doing it. Luckily, her mother came home quickly and seemed quite calm. She just said they should stay inside. Then her father telephoned and said he was coming home too.

I went to the clinic, her father said. *I thought I'd better get a sick note for the next few days, in case I can't get to work. Don't want to lose the job.* Ivana's father worked in a business in Gorazde; he had been at the bus station when the shooting started. *They wouldn't let me into the clinic at first, it was all locked up, and I think they thought I had come to shoot them! Then Dr. Mehmed saw it was me, and let me in. No problem giving me a note.*

The family spent most of the next ten days in the basement. There was not so much shooting in their part of town, so Ivana was allowed outside in the evenings. Not many people were out, and those who were behaved oddly. For one thing, Ivana noticed that Muslim people were not coming out of their houses at all, but Serb people could move around freely. Then one day she and a group of Serb friends saw the police go into a Muslim house and take the men out. The children stood and watched as the men were marched by. Someone said they were being taken to the prison to work.

Ivana's friend Asra lived in an apartment in the neighborhood. Ivana had not seen her for two weeks, so she decided to visit. Asra was really glad to see her. She told Ivana that no one in her family had left the house for fifteen days. They began to play, and then Asra started crying. Ivana didn't know what to say. Asra was mumbling about the police coming the day before and taking her father to prison, and that she wanted to see him, and she was going to see him. Ivana thought about the men she had seen being marched off in the street.

Suddenly there was a terrible banging on the door. The whole family leapt to their feet. Everyone looked terrified. Asra was still crying. Some-one opened the door and all these police came in. They started shouting something about looking for weapons. Ivana was really scared; no one seemed to be paying attention to her, so she ran out of the apartment and into the street. She felt bad for Asra, but what could she do?

Nothing was the same anymore. She was afraid to go back to Asra's. Anyway, it seemed that Muslim families were leaving town, some by them-selves, some sent away by the police. She saw people going into the empty houses and turning everything upside down, taking some things, ruining others. There were some empty shops and people were stealing from those too. She didn't feel scared for herself so much, but she felt sorry for all the people who had left their homes.

One night she couldn't sleep. There was a bright light across the river, so she got up to have a look. Her fourteen-year-old brother was up as well. They could see what it was: houses on fire. Her mother came and said, *Don't watch! It's not good to watch, go back to bed.* She was crying. *Maybe our house will burn like that someday.* Ivana felt scared again. Why would anyone want to burn their house? She did what she was told and went back to bed. In the morning, the houses were completely destroyed; only the walls remained.

A few days later her mother told her she had to go to Belgrade. *It's not safe here. People are getting shot. You could be killed.* Ivana cried all that night, she didn't want to be sent away, but her mother insisted.

Gorazde, April–May 1992

Serb children were leaving Gorazde, and Amela was jealous. She was nine and lived with her younger brother, parents, and grandmother in a Serb part of town, on the same side of the river as the health center and the post office. That spring it seemed as if all her friends left at the same time. When she asked their fathers, who had mostly stayed behind, they said, *Oh they are just away for the weekend*, but it did seem odd that they would all go away on the same weekend. She was bored. There was no one to play with. She asked her mother if she could go away for the weekend too.

But even before they left, her Serb friends were somehow different. They all stayed together and didn't want to talk to other children. They seemed angry without any reason, and when she phoned them to ask if they could come over to play as usual, their parents would say they didn't have time.

She loved school. Her dad hadn't wanted her to go. He said it was a waste of time and that she would be better off in the village. This second year he had refused to buy her schoolbooks. Sometimes if he saw her struggling with homework he yelled at her, *Why are you wasting time in school when you don't know anything?* Sometimes her mum tried to help. But he shouted at her mum, and sometimes he got drunk and beat her. Sometimes he hit Amela and her brother as well. When he was drunk and they were fighting, she wished she were dead. Sometimes she felt so frustrated she just banged her head against the wall until she couldn't feel anything at all. Once she ran off into the woods and hid there, just to be by herself and be quiet, then her mother came to find her. She really loved her mum and her little brother, so she came home.

Then one day she went outside and found a strange sign on their door. It was like a cross, with four Cs around it. She wondered if this was a new game: maybe some children were playing hide-and-seek and this was "home." They might have asked her first, she was a bit cross, so she started to shout, "Why are you writing on my door?" Then her dad came out on his way to work. He saw the sign and got mad and told her to go in and look after her brother. He told her she was never to phone her Serb friends again, and she was not to see them—not that any were around anyway— and did she understand that if she was with them, she could get killed. He was not drunk; he was really angry. Then he went off and she felt terrible. It didn't make any sense. She didn't think her friends were stronger than she was, or could do her any harm.[7]

She wondered if it was because he was angry with the fathers of her friends. They never spoke to one another anymore. Until just a few months ago, they had invited her dad around for drinks all the time. Now they never did. And they looked different. The father of one close friend had changed a lot since his daughter had gone. He now wore a hat called a "Subaru." He had stopped cutting his beard so it was long and dirty. He smelled so bad that she could hardly bear to talk to him. Almost all the men in the neighborhood were growing beards.

There was one old Serb lady who was still friendly, but she was a little crazy. Once she called Amela's grandmother to come over and give her a hand with something heavy. When her grandmother got there, she saw it was weapons! There were guns on all the couches. The old lady said they belonged to her two sons. Grandma was terrified and ran home as soon

as possible to tell them all about it. Grandma talked a lot about war. She
wanted to explain everything to Amela. She kept saying she understood it
all because she had lived through one war, and they should get ready for
another. Amela told her she would hit her if she didn't shut up about war.

Nina was ten and doing very well in third grade. She also noticed that her
Serb classmates were leaving. Every day there was a different reason: *I have
to go to the village. We are going to the seaside for a picnic. Please can I leave
the class?* She wasn't bothered, although things were a bit strange. Around
her apartment block people started guarding at night, she didn't know why.
Then they saw all these tanks go by on the train. She thought they might
be going to Slovenia or Croatia. She knew there was a war there. She had
seen pictures of houses burning and felt so sorry for those people, when
everything was so nice here. She was a little worried and asked if it could
happen here, but her mother promised it could not.

But now everyone had left the apartment block except the two or three
Muslim families who lived there. Then her mother's best friend phoned
from Belgrade and said, *You should leave, there is going to be a war.* Her
mother didn't believe her. So Nina was determined not to worry.

Narcisa's parents decided they would leave even though they both had good
jobs at the factory. Narcisa felt very upset. She didn't want to go. She loved
Gorazde, she loved her house, which her parents had built themselves, and
she didn't want to leave her parrot and her dog. A lot of people seemed
to be coming and going. She was in second grade, and when the spring
term started half the class was absent. Then all these new people came into
town. Then there were barricades in the street, and her parents stopped
her going to school. They said it was dangerous and they were going to a
friend's house in Visegrad. The Yugoslav Army had promised it was safe to
go there. They would travel on to Czechoslovakia.

Narcisa was standing in the living room when she heard a strange
noise, a sort of droning like a large insect, only louder. It felt really close
and everything began to shake. She was terrified. She ran outside just in
time to see an airplane flying really low over the town. Maybe it would
be better to go. *You see,* her mother said, *fighting has started; if we don't
leave we'll be killed.*

The friend's house was big, but there were too many people staying in it:

her grandparents, her aunt, uncle, and cousins, her parents, and her older brother. It was much more frightening in Visegrad than in Gorazde. On one occasion, she was nearly killed. She and her brother were playing in a field and he got hot and hung his sweater in a tree. On the way home he realized he had forgotten it, so because she adored her brother and would do anything for him, she offered to go and get it. She was just untying it when she heard something whiz past her head really close, then a small branch fell off and hit her on the head. She suddenly realized that someone was actually shooting at her. She felt sick with fear and ran home as fast as she could, clutching the sweater.

After that incident, she did not go out so much. But home wasn't pleasant either. You could sit on the balcony at night and hear shooting in the town. People said it was on the old bridge, the famous one that was in a novel. She believed them because you would hear screams, and then a sound like a body falling in the water. It was horrible. Her father, grandfather, and uncle mostly stayed away from the house. They were hiding because Chetniks—that's what everyone called Serbs now—were looking for Muslim men to put them in prison. Her mother said they might have to move again.

So they moved, all of them, but it was no better in the new house. The Chetniks came around almost every day, sometimes five or six of them, sometimes more. They wore uniforms and they had guns, so the family had to open the door. Sometimes they said they were looking for weapons, or they just came in and demanded gold and money and took anything they could find. They came one night and tried to kill the landlady. Narcisa was awake and saw them come in and point a gun right in the landlady's eye and say they would kill her. They kept asking where her husband was. All the men were hiding or they would have been killed. Narcisa was really scared, but nothing more happened. Then they came back in the daytime and pushed the landlady into a room by herself. Narcisa couldn't see what happened, but after the soldiers left the landlady was crying, and went to take a bath right away. Narcisa thought they had searched her and made her take off her clothes. She knew her mother and her aunt hid some money in their clothes, probably the soldiers knew that too. But she didn't think she should ask. The landlady was too upset.

The Chetniks came again. Her mother was in town, and all the men were hiding somewhere outside and Narcisa was terrified. They were screaming at the landlady: *Where is your husband, where is he hiding? Where is your son?* They got the Koran down from a shelf and started kicking it around the room. Narcisa had studied the Koran with her grandmother and knew it should be treated with respect. She wished her mother were there. Then the soldiers got bored, and left. She watched them go down the street, but they met her mother coming home, so they all came back and it started all over again, just like before. Except that this time they told all the women that if they stayed in the house it would be set on fire. So they spent the night in the field. Thank goodness, it was summer and not too cold. She wished she could see her father.

The next morning there was no sign of the soldiers, so Narcisa and her family went back to the house. No one knew what to do. People were coming into town all the time saying the Chetniks had set fire to all the villages. Some people were gathering at the fire station, but her family didn't want to go there. Narcisa thought they might get locked in. They decided to spend another night in the field; the house didn't feel safe anymore, so many houses were burning. Narcisa was more afraid every day. She wondered if they would be killed just like those people on the bridge. Her father and uncle and all the other men were hiding and preparing to go into the mountains to try and get back to Gorazde. Then some Serb men, including a priest, came over and read from bits of paper. They told all the people sitting outside that they had to go and wait in a certain place, and there would be trucks to take them to their own side. It was true, there were trucks, and people were being pushed on as if they were cattle. Narcisa got on with her family and the trucks set off. She wasn't sure where they were going. She was still scared to death.

She saw a road sign saying Foca, then some forests. Then the trucks stopped. Men yelled, *Get out, get down, be quick,* and pushed them onto the road. Narcisa could see woods ahead; someone said their own soldiers were there. They kept walking. The road curved and they couldn't see the trucks anymore, but suddenly there was shooting. Narcisa wondered if the Muslim soldiers would think they were Serbs and shoot them by mistake. She was so tired. Everything was confused.

All of a sudden there were lots of people and they were being told to go to a school. Then her mother said she must go and get some water, but Narcisa didn't want to let her go. It was dark now and there was always a curfew, it was dangerous, there were Chetniks. *Narcisa, there are no Chetniks anymore, these are our own soldiers, there isn't a curfew here. You are safe.* Narcisa looked around. Her mother looked exhausted, but she was smiling. So were the soldiers. Narcisa sat down at a table, buried her head in her arms, and burst into tears. She could hear the soldiers asking her mother what was the matter. They sounded very kind, but she wanted her father; she wanted her uncle and her grandfather. She missed them so much she could not speak.

Back in Gorazde, Nina had stopped going to school. Her mother thought it was too dangerous. After talking with some other relatives about the telephone call from Belgrade, they decided to leave. So everyone went to get photos and passports, and they set off for the family's house in the countryside. They had only been there twenty minutes when Nina heard shots in the nearby hills. Nina's mother was making coffee in the kitchen and Nina was playing outside. She rushed into the house calling for her mother. *What is it? What is it?* Her father went outside to listen. Everyone panicked and started talking at once. They decided to get in the car. Her parents said the greatest danger would be in the direction of Foca, and they should go towards Pale, so they drove up into the hills.

Amela's first feeling when she heard all the noise was curiosity. She had never seen grenades before, and although she was a little scared, she wanted to go out and see. But her grandmother told her to watch out because she might be killed. Then just after she and her brother went to bed, Dragan, their next-door neighbor, arrived. She liked him. He had always given her and her brother presents at Christmas, and he had not changed his appearance like the other neighbors.

She listened through the door. He was talking with her parents. He kept saying, *I am not going to hurt you or your children, but I don't know about others. You should go, take the children and go.* Then her mother came in and got them out of bed and made them get in the car with her father and her grandmother, with just their pajamas and their slippers on, nothing else. Grandma was going on again, about how they shouldn't worry because they would get through this. They had to leave their home and *resign themselves to fate,* and grandma knew all about it because she had lived through one war. Only this time Amela didn't feel like hitting her. Dragan hugged her mother and he hugged Amela and her brother as well.

He said, *don't tell anyone I helped you*, and they drove across the river to her aunt's house.

The house was cold and completely empty because her aunt had gone away to Germany ages ago, but you could see across the river to their own house. Amela went upstairs to have a look. It was strange; she could see a little fire. Maybe someone had started a fire next to the house. Why would they do that? She hoped her toys would be all right, and her bicycle and her harmonica. Her grandmother came and got her. *Don't watch*, she said. *It's better not to watch houses burning.*

Samir was playing outside when the shooting began—alone, because his best friend, Milan, had gone away some time before. He saw the shells in the air and bolted into the house. After that, none of the family was able to go out again. First of all, his father came home and locked the door. He seemed very nervous and worried. Then some neighbors came around and said, *Why lock the house? You are free*, so Father stopped locking it. The shooting was still going on, and they had hardly any food. Father wanted to go into town to buy food, but these neighbors, who were all Serbs, according to his father, stopped him. They said, *Stay at home, because this won't take long. We just have to deal with these extremists from Foca and Visegrad. It's not safe going into town. Your Muslim friends might mistake you for a Serb and kill you.*

Samir didn't really understand what it meant to be a Serb or a Muslim. The names were different. His friend Milan was Serb, and so were most of their neighbors apparently. He had thought they were all friends, but when his father asked one of them to get food for him, this man said he didn't even have any for himself. His father said this was not true because they were taking it from some of the shops. Then one of them shouted, *Get Alija to give you food! You voted for him.*[8]

Now these friends came around whenever they liked, and his parents were always polite and treated them as guests. His mother made coffee. He and his two sisters sat on the floor, keeping very quiet. But the Serbs were not polite at all, they had really changed. They carried rifles. They didn't hurt anyone, but they shouted, *Bring me the water! Shut up!*, and other impolite things. They stayed for hours, drinking rakia and having long discussions with Father. Not real discussions because Father never said anything, he just listened while they went on and on about history.

Samir couldn't understand it. It was all about what things were like six hundred years ago, how everyone was Serb before and then Turkish people came and somehow, some of them, the ones who were Muslim now, got Turkished. The Serb neighbors insisted that all Muslims were originally Serb. His father told him later that it wasn't true, but anyway it didn't matter because they weren't religious. He never went to mosque. But it seemed to matter to the neighbors a lot, as if they wanted to prove something. It felt as if the family were in prison in their own house. It was weeks since they had been allowed out.

Then the Serbs began to get more aggressive. Once a neighbor, one of father's old school friends, came and shouted at father to come outside, and when he did, the neighbor yelled at him, accusing him of shooting at the neighbor's brother. Father said he had no weapons and would never do such a thing. Then the old friend shouted, *You stay here and you have to obey us, and if something happens to my brother, I will kill you all.*

They came every few days. They said, *If you have any kind of weapons you'd better give them to us,* and when his parents said they had none, they would go through the cupboards and throw things around. Sometimes one of them would go out on the balcony and start shooting toward the hill. Samir knew that was where the Muslim soldiers were. Then they would shout at the family not to leave the house or they would shoot them. Sometimes they said they were going to kill them the next day anyway. Samir was more and more terrified. But his parents went on being very polite and offering coffee.

One afternoon two Serbs came to visit again. Samir knew them. They always pretended to be friendly, but he didn't believe them and neither did his father. Once one of them had said he would help them escape, but he had offered to take them to Rogatica, which was a town in Serb territory. Father said if they went there they might be put in a camp or killed, so they should stay here. Now Samir and his two sisters sat on the sofa together. His mother brought in the coffee. The other Serb was telling his father about the war in Croatia. He had spent a year there and was boasting that he had killed forty Muslims. Samir could see that his mother and father were unhappy, but they just sipped their coffee without speaking.

So, what do you think, what kind of weapon did I use to kill those guys? Father looked at the floor and stayed silent. Samir could see he didn't want to answer, but the Serb man insisted. *Come on, what do you think?*

Father lifted his head and looked at the man's stomach. There were two guns stuck in holsters; he pointed at one. The man laughed. *No, it's not this gun.* Father pointed at the other gun, and the man laughed again. He was enjoying himself. *No, it's not this one either.*

Father shrugged. *I really don't know what kind of weapon you used to kill them.*

Come on, I insist. Samir wondered if Father had seen the knife on the man's belt. He was frightened; it didn't feel like a game.

With that knife?

No, not with this knife. The man looked really pleased with himself. With a flourish, he pulled a small knife out of his pocket, the kind some men use as a razor. *This is what did the job, forty Balija, with this little knife.*

Samir felt sick. The men gulped their coffee, then the one who had said he would rescue them stood up. He looked straight at Samir and his sisters. *You better choose three knives yourself and kill these children of yours. Better to kill your children yourself than watch while some Serb does the job for you. Kill the boy first and then the others, they're just Balija.*[9]

The men left. Samir and his sisters sat frozen on the couch. Samir didn't want to speak, he was too scared. What would his father do? What was Balija? After what seemed like hours, he heard his older sister whisper, *Oh Father, it's not true is it? You won't kill us.* Immediately father hugged them and told them not to be silly. He would never do such a thing, he was there to help and protect them, he would always be with them, and never leave them.

Samir lost count of the days they were in the house. He was nervous all the time, about everything. He wished they could go away, but he was afraid to go anywhere. Then suddenly it seemed they had to go. More Serbs in army uniforms arrived. They kicked in the door and started shouting *Come out! Get out! Take your things with you, and come with us!* They shoved the family onto a truck with a whole lot of other people. Samir's mother tried to reassure the children, but he heard her say something to his father about camps and he could see she was crying. He thought maybe now the Serbs would take them somewhere and kill them. He was not going to cry. He would just keep quiet and try not to think about whether it was going to be good or bad.

The truck stopped and someone shouted at them to get out. They had to wait all night, then a bus came and they all got on, and a Chetnik explained that when the bus stopped they should get out and run. Samir was sitting near a fat guy called Edo. The Chetnik didn't like Edo, and threatened him with a knife. Then the bus started and drove an hour, with Samir keyed up, ready to run at any moment. Finally it stopped. The Chetnik wanted to keep hold of Edo, but he got away, and they all just ran and ran. Edo kept telling Samir to go faster, but he couldn't, he had a pain in his leg. So he ran toward a small stream. If anyone was shooting, maybe they wouldn't notice him.

No one was shooting. They all spent the night by the stream. Someone said there were Chetniks on another hill, but it seemed alright here. Samir slept.

2

THE WAR GOES ON

Foca, 1992–1993

Stojan's father phoned when they had been away a little more than a month. He told them they could come back because *Everything is finished*. Stojan was glad, even though he liked being in Belgrade. He had heard that their apartment was robbed and felt very upset at the thought of robbers sitting in his home drinking and having fun.

When he got back things were both better and worse than he expected. The apartment was alright, but a lot of things were missing. So many houses were burned around the town. It seemed to be mostly Muslim houses, although some Serb houses were burned too. He felt awful when he saw the damage. He knew that the town had been liberated very fast, and that most of those Muslim people had gone away on buses to Croatia or wherever they wanted to go. But what if they wanted to come back someday and found their houses burned down? He didn't think that could be right.

Even though there was no fighting in town, things still felt rather frightening. A lot of people were going off to fight, and some said there might be more fighting. At least his father was at home. He had a job in the army, but it was in town, so Stojan saw him every day. They stayed at his grandmother's house now. Sometimes there was no electricity, but they had water all the time because she had her own well.

In Dusan's house there was no electricity or water. It was an old house, large enough for his whole family including grandparents and uncles and aunts to live together. He hadn't seen any fighting because the family went to their house in the village before it began. But it had been very tense. Everyone talked about Muslims attacking. His older brother, Vlado had known there was going to be a war. Once he had told their mother, *All Muslims should be killed*. She was completely shocked and asked him, *Who put so much hate inside you? What about your Muslim friends?*

Mother, you have no idea, you don't go into town and you don't know anything, he had replied. *There are cafés where only Muslims go and the others where only Serbs go. That's how it is now.*

Dusan was eight and thought his older brother was one of the cleverest and bravest people in the world. His parents had told him not to worry, it was just some extremists. Those who wanted to fight could go out on the bridge and fight there, and it would be over in a few days. Then the shooting had begun, and the family decided they would go to the village, but Vlado had refused, he wanted to be with his friends. Father told him he was too young, and threatened to tell the authorities he was only seventeen. But Vlado had somehow got a ride back to Foca on a truck and lied about his age. So now he was on the line, along with his father and uncle. After a month, father told the rest of them to come back to their house. He said the war would be over very soon.

Dusan's neighborhood was completely changed. Nothing was there anymore except their house and their neighbor's house. Almost everything else was burned down. They saw another neighbor, who told them that Muslim Green Berets (SDA militia) had been burning houses. Dusan's next-door neighbors were Muslim. They had stopped Dusan's house being burned because theirs was connected to it and would have burned as well. Then Serbs came and started burning Muslim houses, but some Serbs had saved the neighbor's house to stop Dusan's from being burned. The only damage he could find was two bullet holes: one in the bedroom by the bed and another in the TV. He was glad his family had come home. When he looked out the window, he could see people going into the empty houses that were still standing and just taking anything they could carry: televisions, doors, windows. When there was nothing left to take, they threw a hand grenade and burned down that house too. Once Dusan saw some children running in and out of the empty houses and wondered if it would be fun to go with them. But his parents and his grandparents told him, *You never take things that don't belong to you.*

Dusan's Muslim next-door neighbors were gone. He didn't know where. They had not been very close friends. In fact, before they left for the village, his father and Dusan's uncle had looked out the window and had seen the neighbor with a gun. He hadn't been shooting, just standing in his yard. At the beginning of the war those same neighbors had asked his aunt, *Who sleeps in which room?* Looking back, everyone thought that was a strange question, especially after they heard that some lists had been found in some Muslim houses. Everyone said these were lists of the people they had planned to kill.

Dusan's family didn't have much food. Just before the war his grandfather had told them to store food for the hard times coming and his parents had laughed and told him he was being silly. Fortunately, they had home-grown vegetables, and flour given out by the Red Cross. He was a bit bored. There was no school because the teachers had gone to fight, but he couldn't enjoy the free time because his mother worried about unexploded bombs and all the drunken people around, so she made him stay in the yard. He was glad when his brother came home on leave. His brother was teaching him how to use a gun so he could defend himself.

Gorazde, 1992–1993

Amela decided that if she had to choose between cows and shelling, she would choose shelling any day: it was much less frightening. After they arrived at her aunt's house, Grandma became very organized. She seemed to know what to do. She had keys to a shop owned by a relative and she went there to get some food. Then she found a cow left by one of the departing Serb families, which she caught and brought back. Amela was terrified of all farm animals and could not bear to go near the cow. The family spent most of their time in the basement because of the shelling, but she was scared the cow might come into the hallway and jab her with its horns. This worried her much more than being hit by a shell, and she went on and on at Grandma to kill the cow so they could have some meat. Finally grandma did kill it, and then they swapped the meat for milk and cheese with another family for a whole month, and felt very well fed.

The front line was very close so they hardly went out at all. There was no possibility of going to school, but she didn't mind. She had all her dolls and made a small den under the staircase where she could play with them. She and her brother were allowed outside to pee in a basin, and then they had to come in. In quieter periods, her mum dressed both of them in white pants and white shirts and let them play close to the wall of the house, which was also white. The idea was that the snipers wouldn't be able to see them.

Amela loved feeling fresh air on her face. At night when it was cold, her grandmother made a wood fire in a pot. It kept them warm, but the smoke was terrible. Her mum was nervous when there was shelling, Amela could tell, but grandma wasn't frightened at all. *Nothing can hurt me*, she said all the time. Then one day a shell came right through the basement wall. There was an enormous "crack" as something seemed to burst above their heads. Amela bit her tongue, and then thought she would choke from all the dust. As it cleared they saw that grandma had been hit on the head by a brick. It had stunned her but she seemed all right. Amela started giggling. *That's good, now you know things can happen to you! Even you!* Mum had been cut too, but not badly. The worst damage was to the wall. It had a large hole in it.

Dad had gone to join the army and was back on the other side of the river. There was no way to cross, so they didn't see him for some months. Amela didn't know if she minded or not. It was nice not having anyone shouting at her, but time seemed to go more slowly when he wasn't there. She could see that her mum was worried about him, and her brother missed him a lot. He would walk up to strange men and say, *You're like my dad.* She would rather be beaten than have her brother calling strange men "Father."

Up in the hills above town Nina and her mother and sister were thinking about how they could get back to being with her father and brother. Both were based at a local defense unit down in their village. In four months, Nina had lived in three different villages, moving to avoid the shelling. She didn't mind. For some weeks, they lived in a village with four other families. She liked the garden and they had enough to eat, but the house was so old that she thought if it got hit by a shell it would just collapse. She could hear shooting in the villages below and she saw some houses burning. But no one was shooting at them and she was left to play with the other children. After a few weeks, her mother got worried about schooling, so Nina's sister, who was ten years older, gave her and some other children lessons under a peach tree. Then they moved to another house that had a basement, but her mother wanted to get back to their own house. It was concrete and she thought it would be safer, and the family could be together. So they decided to walk down through the woods.

The three of them set off in the morning, heading down through the trees to keep out of sight of snipers. Suddenly Chetniks began shooting at them. Nina could hear the bullets whizzing past everywhere. They got behind a big tree. Mother said, *Be glad they aren't shelling or we would all be dead.* Then she said *Run!* They ran so fast through the trees that Nina still felt she was running when they stopped at a small spring. They could still hear shooting, but it was above them at the big tree, so the Chetniks thought they were still there. They walked on. Nina was now too excited to be scared. She knew they were getting close to home, and she couldn't wait to see her father. Then she saw their cherry tree, full of bright red fruit, and she rushed to climb it, filling her hands and mouth with cherries. They had never tasted so good.

During the next few weeks there was more shelling. Two airplane bombs fell a hundred meters away, but no one was hurt. Nina learned to listen for the dull tone that meant a shell was coming in. If she heard that, she knew she had to lie down somewhere at once. The house felt very safe. It was behind a little hill and her father built a shelter in the underground garage, so that became their home. Their uncles and cousins joined them. She was glad to be with the family, although it was more boring than in the hills. Sometimes, for a change, she would sit in the car beside the house and try to teach herself to knit.

Sometimes she went to a neighbor's house to play with a friend. She was there one day when she heard the sound of a shell flying really close. There was no time to reach the garage so they crouched against the wall of the house. It fell so close she couldn't believe she was all right and was still checking herself all over when her father appeared, screaming *Where have you been? What have you been doing? How could you do such a thing?* They ran into the garage.

Father was still shouting at them when a strange woman appeared, crying and talking very fast: something about Nina's cousin. Nina had seen her cousin only ten minutes before, smiling and friendly, as he went to put grass in the barn. Her father and sister rushed outside. He was dead; a piece of shrapnel had gone straight into his heart. Nina's sister helped to lay him out in the yard. Then her uncle came back and when he found everyone crying, he guessed at once, even though they tried to tell him gently. They took the boy away to be buried. From that moment, Nina could not bear to look at the place where he had been lying.

That wasn't the only bad thing that happened. Once when they were all at home they suddenly heard screaming somewhere in the hills. The whole village went outside to listen. It was a little girl screaming, on and on. No one knew what to do. Nina didn't want to hear it. She hugged her mother. Later they found the girl. She had been raped and killed. Nina knew what that meant. She had known the little girl and cried when she thought of her.

A few days later Nina's father saw Chetniks coming slowly toward the house, down the hill, through the fields. He ran into the basement, shouting at them to run and hide. She and her mother hid in the field. Luckily, she was wearing an old fur coat which she kept on even though it was summer. It had a hood and she was sure it made her harder to see when she was lying down in the grass, so she felt safer. She thought about what had happened to the little girl, and whether it might happen to her. Then she made herself stop and did what she always did when she was scared: thought about other people who were worse off than she was, and how they were surviving, so she would too. She tried to think of the nice times they had spent at the seaside before the war and how they would do so again when it stopped. There were some shots. Then her father called them back. The Chetniks had run away. Her father and the other men were laughing. They said the Chetniks probably thought there was a big army unit here, rather than a few men with old hunting rifles, and that was why they left. The village could have been taken in an hour if they had tried.

Nina wondered if they were ever going to stop moving. The family decided to move back to the apartment in Gorazde because her father's and brother's unit were there. They had a terrifying journey in a truck full of all their food. She and her sister sat on sacks and they drove without lights, but even so the Chetniks saw them and fired at them. She could see the sparks and was really scared, especially when they crossed the bridge. She knew that one grenade would destroy them all.

Everything in Gorazde was different. There were strange people she had never seen before, the air smelled of smoke, and every building in the town seemed to have been hit by shells. There was no water or electricity, and the shelling never stopped. Nina hated being in the basement all the time; she preferred going outside even if it was dangerous. On one occasion, she and her sister were almost hit while they were getting water from the pump at the post office. They saved themselves by diving into an apartment building when they heard the whooshing noise. Each time something like that happened she vowed it was her last trip out, but it never was.

She was happier living close to her father and brother. Then her father decided he wanted them to get out of Gorazde, out of Bosnia altogether if possible. He said he couldn't bear being on the front line and worrying about them in the city, it would be easier for him if he knew they were safe. *Besides, the children might learn something good abroad.* So her mother finally agreed.

That was why in the middle of winter and in the middle of the night she was dressed up in five pairs of trousers, five pairs of socks, and three sweaters, carrying a small rucksack and walking with her sister, mother, and uncle in a long line of people through the snow.

They were going over a mountain called Grebak. The lines had been pushed back a few months earlier and people could get in and out of Gorazde this way. They were in two groups, and there were soldiers leading them. It reminded her of the old films about partisans and she felt quite excited.

After some hours, though, she began to feel exhausted. Sometimes the snow came right up above her knees, almost to her waist. The tea in the thermos had frozen, so all they had was some thick plum juice her mother had made. At one point, they were going along a stream, but her mother had stopped her from drinking the water. Then right by the stream, she saw an old man lying on the ground. He was all blue, and his eyes were open. Nina stared as she walked past; she knew he was one of theirs, and that he was dead. She looked back, keeping her eyes on him as long as possible. No one wanted to stop and close the man's eyes.

Sometimes they took little breaks to do some exercises to keep their circulation going, but no real rest. Then Nina noticed that her family was alone. They had lost the group. They had no idea of the way, but dared not stop with Chetniks all around, so they just kept walking, hoping and praying they were not blundering across enemy lines. She had never been so cold. She just wanted to sleep, but her mother kept nudging her to keep her eyes open. Then she saw a small house ahead. It was just beginning to get light and there was smoke coming out of the roof. *Mama,* she called, *I'm so cold, let's go inside and get warm, just for five minutes.* But as she got closer the house began to disappear. Instead there was a tree with wide branches. She wanted to weep. Her uncle pulled her along, promising chocolate and saying *Come on you can make it! I am going to tell your cousins in Zagreb how brave you are.* She just had to keep going a little longer. Now the sun was right up and there was another cabin, but perhaps this one would disappear too. It did not, and as they got close, they saw the sign for their own police force. They were on their own side. They walked in and there was a stove and a small bed. Nina went straight over to the bed and fell asleep.

Samir spent two nights sleeping in the hills before they managed to cross no-man's land to their own side. A group of them were sent in a bus to a town called Visoko. It was better than being trapped in their house in Gorazde, but people were not very friendly. They slept in the school for a month. Then they were given a room in a house whose Serb owner had left. There were still Serbs and Croats and Muslims living together in the town. Sometimes he thought the Muslims were the worst. He saw some of them selling humanitarian food aid in the shops, when lots of people did not have enough, but one of their Serb neighbors brought them oil and flour and was very nice. Then sometimes when his father was home on leave, local people who didn't know him would send the police around to say he should be on the line. Father had papers now to show what unit he was with, and where he should be, but it felt unfriendly. Other times people would ask, *You refugees, when are you going home?*

There was occasional shelling in town—one day Samir counted eight rounds one after the other—so you had to be careful. Once when he was walking home with his friend, a piece of shrapnel hit his friend in the leg right in front of him. But it wasn't as bad as Gorazde or Sarajevo. He could see how things were there on TV, with people dying all the time. Sometimes he and his friends played volleyball in the street. Some of them collected shell casings and bits of shrapnel, but he wasn't interested.

His father was on the line, but he got home every week. He managed to find some fruit and vegetables to sell to try and get them a little money because they had nothing. Samir started school again, having missed a whole year. The other children were friendlier than the adults and there was a sports hall where they could play games. There was a Hodza (a Muslim religious teacher) at the school, so he was starting to learn a little bit about being a Muslim. He decided to start going to mosque.

Narcisa and her mother were bused through three separate towns, including Visoko, before they found one that still had room for refugees. First, they were put in a school, then they were offered room in a house, but then some of the occupants made it clear they were not wanted, so they went back to the school. They shared a classroom with five other families.

They put mattresses and blankets on the floor, each family marking its own space. Narcisa didn't think it was so bad; she could get used to anything, except being without her father. One day she saw her brother Kemal take a picture of father out of mother's purse. He made a kind of frame around the picture and put it around his neck. When he thought he was alone he would take it out and look at it. He would talk to it very quietly, but when she came close he dropped the picture and pretended he wasn't doing anything. She thought they were all dead—father, uncle, and grandfather—she would never see any of them again.

At lunchtime one day a girl walked into their room and told Narcisa's mother there were some men from Gorazde asking for her. Her mother went out, saying there might be news, and the next moment everyone was shouting at Narcisa, *Your father came!* She couldn't believe it. She ran down the stairs and there was her mother, she had not realized how thin she was, but she was laughing and crying, and there was her father! Narcisa ran into his arms, crying and asking questions all at once: *How are you here? How is my dog? Is she okay?* Father was laughing and crying too, but he told her he was sorry, the dog was dead. She had been barking during the shelling and a man had got scared and shot her.

Where's Kemal? Father asked. Half the people in the room set off to find him. He came running up the stairs, carrying the tins of hot food he had collected for lunch, and when he saw father he just dropped everything on the floor and they were hugging, and both were crying. Narcisa thought that everyone in the room, everyone in the whole school, seemed to be crying with them. She had never felt so happy in her life.

They spent the next days talking and talking. Father had been in Gorazde. He said it was very hard in the city. There was shelling; there was no food and you had to climb to a place high in the mountains to buy flour or anything. You could get in and get out of the city that way, but it was a very long and dangerous walk, forty kilometers, and you had to walk in silence, at night, without lights.

Narcisa wanted to go home and all the family agreed, home was the best place to be no matter what. So shortly after Nina and her family walked out over Grebak, Narcisa and her family walked back to Gorazde along the same route. The house was still standing even though it was a mess with all the windows broken. As there was not so much shelling, she could go outside sometimes. All her friends were pleased she had come home.

Nina's family were weeks on the road. After sleeping in a bed with five strange children, traveling in a hot truck where people were packed so close Nina found it hard to breathe, her family came to a small town called Kiseljak, near Sarajevo. Nina could not get used to it. The war was going on only a few kilometers away and yet here were Muslims, Croats, and Serbs living together almost as if nothing was happening. The shops were open and you could buy anything—jam, chocolate, meat. It was as if you had walked into another world. Nina wondered if people had any idea that other people she knew were fighting and dying and suffering while everyone here was enjoying themselves.

She did not go to school. Her mother said there was no point when their visas for Germany might arrive at any time. They were staying with another uncle, and mostly she played with his two little boys. There was a large sports stadium opposite their house, but they couldn't go there. It seemed to have been turned into a prison. Sometimes Nina watched from her window. She saw that the Croats were in charge there. She wasn't sure if the prisoners were Muslim or Serb, but she saw them being taken from cars and left in the stadium. It was a freezing winter, yet the guards made the prisoners take off all their clothes except their underwear and run around in the snow. Nina couldn't understand it. Why make them run without clothes in the freezing cold? She found it hard to watch. It made her think of her father. Maybe he would be caught, and made to run like that? The thought was unbearable. Even so, she had noticed something about herself. At the beginning of the war, everything had upset her: the little girl screaming, people being hurt. Now after a year she didn't think anything could really shake her up. If she saw burned people, wounded people, dead people, she just felt cold, and she never cried any more.

After three months in Kiseljak, Nina's mother decided they had better move to Zagreb and try from there. So they set out on yet another journey. This one was the worst. It took days because they had to take a bus through Chetnik territory. Twice they got turned back and had to start again with another route. Nina thought she was living on buses. Sometimes Chetniks would get on and search and demand money, then the Croats refused to let her cross their border because they said her mother was planning to put her in school in Zagreb, and they didn't want that. Then they phoned some Croatian friends who came and got them by car and there was no problem.

Finally, after a bus journey to Split and another to Zagreb and another to Berlin, they arrived in Germany, and moved into the house of the pastor who had sent their visas. Everything was different. Nina had no idea if she would see her father again, and now she had to learn a whole new way of life.

Foca, 1994

Svetlana was tired of being homeless. She had liked being in Belgrade. They had stayed with relatives and she had gone to school and done well, even though some children had teased her for being a "refugee." But they had used up all their savings, and hadn't wanted to burden their relatives. When they got back to their village it was completely empty, everyone had run away. They didn't dare stay there alone, so they moved to Foca. Svetlana couldn't recognize it, so many houses were destroyed. They managed to find an apartment in town. Then the landlord wanted it for someone else and kicked them out. They found another empty apartment. They just moved in without getting permission, and one day, when Svetlana was at school, the police came and threw all their things out on the street. Only her little brother was home at the time and he was terrified. They called her mother at work and she ran home, but he was hysterical and wouldn't let her touch him. Then Svetlana came and tried to get close to him, but he screamed and yelled and refused to let her—the same with her father. It took hours to calm him down; she had never seen him like that. Now they were in another apartment. It was very old and the rooms were tiny, and who knew when they would be thrown out of this one. They had heard that their house in the village had been burned down by Muslims, so her father had the right to be given somewhere to live.

That was not the worst thing that had happened. First her grandfather had died. Not because of the war, he was quite old. But she missed him, she remembered him taking her for rides on his horse and how much she had liked that. Then her favorite uncle died on the front line outside Sarajevo. He was really young and had been so nice to her. She still couldn't bear to think about him or talk about him. If she did, she cried. If she looked at his picture, she cried. So she tried to avoid doing those things; everyone said that was best.

Both Ivana's grandparents died. Her mother phoned her in Belgrade to tell her and she cried. The grandparents had come to stay in Foca at the beginning of the war when Turkish people tried to attack their village. Grandma didn't like it because she wasn't used to sleeping up on the third floor, she was afraid she would fall down. Ivana and her brother thought this was terribly funny. Then the Turks left, and her grandparents wanted to go home, even though the village was empty. They were worried about their cows. So they went back, but the Serbian army had put mines around to stop Turks from coming back, and grandma stepped on one. Then when Grandfather was sick, he couldn't go to the hospital because there were too many wounded people there, and he died too.

Ivana loved being in Belgrade. All her mother's family was there. They were quite well off, had a big house, and lots more relatives came to get away from the war: an aunt and cousins got out of Sarajevo. There was another bad moment for them when Turks killed old people and children in a village called Josanice, near Foca. It was a horrifying massacre. They showed it on TV, and her aunt had relatives in that village.

When Ivana's mother came to take her back to Foca, she didn't want to go. She had seen what the town was like on television, with the center empty and destroyed. She told her mother she wanted to stay in Belgrade.

Don't be silly, her mother said, *don't you want to see your father? Things aren't so bad now. All the children have gone back to school.*

I don't want to go back.

Well, your brother does. If you don't come with us now, I can't tell you when I will be back to get you, maybe never.

Ivana was not sure she believed this, but her mother looked serious. When they got back to Foca it wasn't quite as bad as she had expected. There was no electricity. A lot of people appeared to be dying. She only saw her father one or two days a week. There were lots of children she didn't know. But they asked her which class she wanted to be in at school and she chose the one with some old friends from her part of town. They could play together, mostly hide-and-seek or ball games. The boys played war, hiding behind trees and killing themselves and one another. They were very aggressive and shouted and pushed, and she thought it was stupid. Asra and her family had gone, she did not know where. When she asked her mother, she didn't know either. Her mother could see she was upset. *They wanted to stay, but they could see people leaving every day,* she explained. *They were scared. It was us or them, my dear. Somebody had to go, or this war will never end.*

After the massacre in Josanice, Dusan's grandfather said, *Not a single Muslim ear should remain.* Father and Grandfather never minded when Dusan listened. Father seemed astonished and said, *But you were always telling me about "brotherhood and unity."*[10] Grandfather replied that he was eighty-five years old; he had survived three Balkan wars, the first, the second, and now this one. In his opinion the Muslims had betrayed the trust of the Serbs too many times in the last two or three hundred years. This was the moment when they should be destroyed.

The best times were when Dusan's brother came back, even though sometimes it was for friends' funerals. He was always filthy and exhausted, and then had to rush off again. He wasn't an ordinary soldier anymore. First, they had transferred him to heavy weapons, but he told Dusan the army was a big disappointment: Too many people just held the lines and didn't try to advance, they even ran away. There was looting from people's homes, and drunkenness. People took liquor up to the lines with them, or arrived there already drunk, shooting at random from the trucks as they drove up. Then they would fall asleep and get massacred.

Vlado thought there were too many cowards and he despised the corruption. He had got himself transferred to an "intervention unit." Sometimes they were in really close fights; he had to jump into enemy trenches. He brought home some Muslim guns he had taken, but he never talked much about what he did. Dusan knew they moved a lot. The lines extended all the way from Gorazde to Treskavica. His uncles, father, and brother were in completely different places and it was hard to keep track. They had the radio on all the time at home. There was no TV because there was still no electricity. The radio made everyone tense because sometimes the news was awful. Sometimes they sat up all night to hear how many people had died and who they were. He and his mother always wondered: Will it be one of ours?

Nothing worked normally in the town. All the shops were empty, people were hungry. There was humanitarian food aid, but not everyone got it. Father said smugglers and profiteers were taking it. Everyone seemed tense; sometimes people shot guns out the windows just to let off steam. His parents still didn't want him to go out much. Anyway school was not working normally. You would get there and find the classes canceled because there were no teachers. He and his friends played soldiers. Different groups had camps in different parts of the town, so they invaded each other's camps and tried to destroy them. Sometimes they built a fire. It was just like the regular army; girls did the cooking and cleaned the camps. Sometimes the boys collected bullets. When Dusan couldn't play, listening to music on the radio cheered him up. He liked the songs about the war; they made him feel brave and courageous.

Finally, his parents decided conditions were so bad that Dusan and his mother should go to Serbia. There would be more food. He could go to school properly. They could live in an old house belonging to a relative. It had no running water or inside toilet, but it would be better than here. Father promised Dusan he could come back to Foca for visits.

Gorazde, 1993–1995

There was a man calling Amela's name as she walked up the street. The shelling had eased off and she was enjoying being outside. She looked around and saw a thin, bearded, very dirty man. He looked just like a Chetnik. She thought of running, but before she could, he caught up with her. He was laughing and put his arms around her. He smelled just like a Chetnik too, disgusting!

Amela, it's your dad, it's me. Don't you recognize me?

She stared at him, pulling back and stepping away. *Okay, so if you're my father tell me something about us that only Dad would know, from when we lived together. Then I'll believe you. But don't come near me until you have!*

All right, how about the time you ran away to the woods when you were a little girl? As he was speaking, there was a sudden crack and a bullet shot over his head, so that he dived toward her, clutching her again. *Do you believe me now?*

She roared with laughter. *Scaredy cat!* It was her dad, and despite the beard and the smell, she was really glad he was back; it was more than a year since she had seen him.

Walking home, he told her he hadn't had a razor for a year, let alone a place to shave, so he had chopped at his beard with a knife. He had bad news as well: *Dragan is dead, and his family, I think.*

What happened?

I don't know exactly. I'm told that our lovely neighbors burned down his house with him inside.

Amela couldn't believe it. She remembered Dragan hugging her before she got in the car. She remembered his two little children and the presents given every Christmas. What about Andrija and Diana?

I think they might be dead too. I'm so sorry, Amela. He didn't want to join in their dirty war, but he couldn't get away. They put gasoline around the house, I think he was tied up inside. Maybe his family tried to help and it was too late.

Amela had a vivid picture of the girls frantically trying to untie their father as flames leapt around the doors and window frames. She started to cry. They were almost the same age as her, one a year older, one a year younger. Her dad told her that their own house had also burned down completely, and all her toys were gone. Of course that was awful, but not as bad as what had happened to Dragan and his family. She had to stop and pull herself together. They were almost home. Her dad seemed to stiffen a little.

They were using the whole house now that there was less shelling. Amela pushed open the front door into the living room. Her dad walked in, and stared at her mum. *So you're not dead then?* Amela wasn't sure she had heard right. Maybe he was joking, but he looked completely cold. Oh poor Mum, to wait a year for this. All the warmth Amela had begun to feel disappeared in a rush of rage. Dad sat down and called Adem, her brother, to sit on his knee, but Adem shrank into a corner, scared by this strange, rude man. Grandma started crying, asking him if he had any feelings for his family.

Put a sock in it, you stupid old woman! he shouted. He stretched out on the sofa, his hard military boots still on. Grandma looked at him and retreated into the other room, slamming the door. Mum was crying, and then she bent and kissed Adem on the head. He stayed stuck, frozen in his corner, staring at his dad and refusing to speak. Mum made the coffee and tried to make things normal as she always did. Dad lay with his eyes closed. Amela wondered if he was drunk. He obviously wished they had all died. She wished he had as well. After a couple of hours, some of his colleagues came and banged on the door to get him to go back to his unit on the line. She was not sorry.

That was how it continued. Now that he was on their side of the river, he could come home quite often. He came back for meals, demanding the best food in the house. He would question her mother about what food she was using when he wasn't there and shout at her if she didn't keep the best stuff for him. Then he would go out to coffee bars with his friends.

Sometimes he was away for weeks and would say he had been on the line, but Amela knew it was not completely true. She had heard he was spending time with other women in town. She saw her mum slaving away for him, accepting everything, and for what? She knew she should try to help, but how? Amela couldn't understand why her mum put up with him. She could see he didn't love her mum anymore, he just saw her as a house-keeper. He still beat her, and he hit the rest of them, even Grandma, or he kicked them. She didn't think he loved her anymore either.

It was worse than before the war, and she wished she could run away, but there was nowhere to run. Sometimes it was slightly better. When she was alone with him, he sometimes seemed to want to be friends with her, give her advice, or just chat. It felt as if he had two faces. Maybe the war had made him sick with his nerves. Maybe she upset him because she was always on her mum's side. Well, someone had to be, and her brother was always on Dad's side now.

One day after a really horrible fight, Amela's mum told him they had to separate and she would take the children. He stormed off. Now he was back on the line again, farther away, so he was not coming home much anyway. Their aunt came back from Germany, so they had to move to an abandoned shop near the mosque in the center of town. The shelling got worse again. The Grebak route closed and you couldn't get food that way anymore, so they began to get really hungry. Still, Amela felt better than she had for a long time. She was getting to be really grown up and could help her mum with everything. Sometimes it felt as if her mum was her sister or her best friend.

Some food came in on the airdrops. You could never be sure where it would land, but sometimes they were lucky. One night Amela and her mum waited in the wrong place for an hour before someone said, *No, go there.* They were crossing some woods when they saw the pallets drop-ping from the planes and were terrified they would get hit by one. So they started running. When Amela thought about it, it was pretty funny: running away from "lunch." Then she crouched under a tree and lost her mother. Still she couldn't miss the chance. She grabbed two large cartons. Everyone around her was doing the same. She opened one and started to stuff the small packets into her backpack. It was getting lighter and people were hurrying to get away. You weren't actually supposed to get the food yourself. If the police found you, they would take it. Mostly it was supposed to go to the army.

Amela lugged her cartons and her backpack down toward a little stream, filled the rucksack to the top, and hid the other cartons out of sight. Then she changed her mind and decided to try to drag them home. The hill was very steep, but somehow she managed to pull them along behind her. When Amela finally got home, her mother opened the door. She had obviously been crying. The police had grabbed her stuff and hit her with a gun handle, and she thought Amela was injured or lost. Then she saw Amela's bags, and then Adem came down all sleepy. When Amela started to pull sweets out of her backpack, Adem was ecstatic; he didn't know what to take first. *When my sister is alive I'm not afraid of anything!* he shouted. He stared at Amela. *I will never forget what you did, Sister, until the end of my life.* The next night they went out and loaded up again. Dad came home once and immediately had an argument about it, telling Mum he didn't like her going out, it was not her job. *I have to, because you don't want to*, she replied. *Someone has to feed our children.*

Amela started going to school again. They dug some trenches for protection from snipers, so children who lived farther away could walk in them. There was still some shelling, but she was so used to it that she really didn't mind too much unless she actually heard it overhead. That was scary. And if the Chetniks saw you take cover in a building they might shell it.

Then the shelling got really bad again and they were back in the basement. Sometimes it felt as if they had spent all their lives in the basement. She didn't know what year it was or when her birthday was anymore. It was impossible to sleep for long with the constant noise. Her mother was frightened all the time. Amela tried to play games with her brother to stop herself from thinking. Then Mum would shout at them to be quiet because she was listening to which way the shells were coming, as if that could keep them from falling on the house. Sometimes it was impossible not to listen; you just sat silently wondering if you might be hit. The best thing was when Grandma told stories. She had very funny ones about how when she was young, she was the troublemaker in the house, and how she had started work at fifteen and met their grandfather and built a house with him. Grandma knew this was the best way to stop the fear, just to keep on talking. It was great that she was there.

Narcisa thought the heavy shelling was boring. Her parents had made her and her brother a den in the center of the house. They had everything they needed there: they could play and sleep and it felt very safe. She had her harmonica. If it was a little quieter, they played in the yard and ran indoors when the shelling began again. In the days when it was really heavy, they just stayed inside. She and her brother invented a new game around counting the grenades; it made a change from playing cards. Her father was very clever and had found a way to make electricity by putting a wheel in the river. The water turned the wheel and generated electricity, so sometimes they could even watch a video. Neighbors came to watch with them and brought more food and drink.

When the shelling was less intense, she sometimes went to find her father. He managed to come home every three or four days, but in between she missed him. At one point, he had a position near the house. She and her brother would put food in a basket and take it up to him. There was a small path up the hill that they could use. If a grenade came over, they just flattened themselves on the ground. But he was only there a short time, and then he moved to another position, then another. Then they would sit listening to the radio waiting for the lists. There was always that moment when they announced that someone was hurt or dead, then the relief when it was not her father's name.

Less shelling also meant that she could go to school. Sometimes it started on the way there or back. One day she was at mekteb, the religious school, where she went to study the Koran. She came out, and as she put on her shoes she noticed two other children and their mother going past. She and a friend started walking. The familiar whooshing came, followed by an enormous crash ahead of them. Narcisa could guess what had happened. She started to pray the prayers she had learned in mekteb. There were people running by talking about bodies. Her heart was pounding, but there was no other way to go to get home. She and her friend turned the corner and there they were, three mangled bodies lying in the street: the woman and two children, although you could no longer see their faces. One body seemed to be hanging over the street, another lay blocking her way. It was so horrible she thought she would be sick. The blood was thick and she had to step through it and over the bodies. Later she couldn't get the pictures of cut-up bodies out of her mind. They kept coming back, especially when she went past that spot again.

Amela started having bad dreams after her friend was killed. They were walking near the house, when her friend suddenly fell over, hit by sniper fire. Amela started yelling but no one came to help and there was nothing she could do; she couldn't even move her friend's body. So she ran home to tell her mother. This wasn't the first person she had lost. The strange thing was that although she sometimes felt frightened, especially in the dark, and although she had bad dreams about blood and shootings, she didn't feel so very sorry for anyone's death. Eight relatives and friends had died. It was hard to have any feelings such as real sadness when you had no idea if you yourself would be alive the next day. So she had not cried. Maybe she would when the war was over.

Foca, 1995

On New Year's Eve in Serbia, children played with firecrackers. Dusan felt that celebrating with things that flashed and banged was rather strange, and didn't enjoy it very much. His mother had found work in Serbia, and he was doing all right in school. Finally, his father let them come back home for the summer holidays. His grandfather had died a year ago, so he slept in his old room, alone. Then he woke up, and the oddest thing: there was someone right next to him, with his head on his pillow. *Hello, little brother*.

Dusan gave a shout. It was Vlado! He always liked playing jokes. He had just arrived from Treskavica and come in especially to see Dusan. They would talk about everything in the morning. Dusan went back to sleep happily, but when he woke his brother was not in the same mood. He had no time to talk. There was some kind of emergency and he had to go back to the line right away, but not to worry, he would be back very soon.

Vlado was killed two days later, while heading home. Dusan was the first to hear because only he and his aunt were there when the news came. They had been going off the line and a grenade had fallen between three of them. Vlado and another man had been killed instantly, the third wounded. Dusan couldn't believe the news; it was impossible that his brother was dead. Then he wanted to cry and cry, but as he listened to what people were saying about his brother, to all the stories of how brave he was, some of the pain began to turn into pride. This was his brother they were talking about: a good soldier, always first into action, even though he was usually the youngest; always clean; no raping or looting; not corrupt; a great Serb, fighting for a Serb country.

As the days and weeks passed, though, he couldn't always hold on to these feelings. His father had returned from the Front and was completely devastated. His mother could not stop crying, and Dusan couldn't bear to see it. He felt as if his whole family had died; no one could talk or think about anything else. Dusan knew he had to be very strong and keep his feelings inside so he could help with the funeral. That was not so difficult because a lot of the time he just felt empty; he didn't feel like doing anything, so he just did what had to be done. Other times he felt again that it couldn't be true, there had to be a mistake; Vlado would just walk in with his jokes, as he had in the past.

After the funeral, Dusan and his mother went back to Serbia. His father insisted. He didn't want to go. When he got there, he felt worse than ever. He couldn't stop thinking about his brother, so it was impossible to concentrate at school. Anyway, he had no interest in schoolwork anymore. Sometimes he felt afraid for no reason because after all nothing bad was happening in Serbia. Dusan knew he wanted to be with his family in his own house. At least he had the video of the funeral. It comforted him to remember how well people thought of his brother. He wanted to be as much like Vlado as he possibly could.

Back in Foca, Ivana was twelve and had settled into a new year at school. The higher up you went the more homework there seemed to be, so she sat up in the evening doing biology. There was some talk of "bombing" and some people at school were nervous, but a neighbor phoned her mother and told them not to worry.

They just want to frighten us, her mother said. *It won't happen.*

Why do they want to bomb us? Ivana asked. She wasn't quite clear who "they" were. *They want our army to move from its positions*, her father explained. *If they don't, then they'll be bombed.* This still didn't make much sense. At 9:30 she decided to go to bed, leaving her mother standing on the balcony watching the river.

A moment later her mother was shaking her to wake up. *Get up, get dressed, they're bombing us; we have to go to the shelter.*

Ivana just wanted to sleep, but she could hear sirens going. She dragged herself out of bed and went down to the cellar with her mother and brother. It was dark because there was no electricity, and completely full of neighbors. People kept going outside to see what was going on, and coming in again if there was any sound of planes. She wanted to see too. Her brother yelled at her to come and look at the planes. *Crazy guy, those planes drop bombs and they can fall on us!*

But she joined him in the doorway. Suddenly there was an enormous thud and the door fell out of the frame, hitting both of them and knocking them back into the cellar. Ivana got up and checked herself. She was all right. Her mother yelled at them to come in, and they retreated to the lowest level. Ivana was really afraid now and she couldn't stop shivering. The last time she had felt like this was the first day of the war. They had sat in the cellar then, too. She could hear shells falling and got as close to her mother as possible. She felt exhausted. She wished she could sleep, but she was much too tense. What would happen to them all? She couldn't bear it if anyone else was killed; losing Grandma was bad enough. Around 2:00 in the morning it grew quiet, so everyone went back to bed. Next day when she woke up, she didn't feel frightened at all.

NATO bombed off and on for the next few days. Ivana stayed indoors with her mother and brother. The radio was on all the time so they could hear what was happening. All the bridges in town were destroyed, and when they had TV they could see planes bombing Pale. Ivana heard that the Serbs shot down a plane and local people found the pilots and beat them up. She wasn't surprised. Everyone was angry. Sometimes at night her fear came back, but it was not so bad. She didn't think they wanted to bomb people. All the same, if the Serb army didn't move, they might bomb more places.

On the other side of town, Svetlana also had trouble waking up. She heard her mother shouting at her to go down to the cellar. So she blundered about in her bare feet, still half asleep, and then a window fell in and she cut her feet. That woke her up. There was blood everywhere. Her mother tore off part of her trousers to bind it and then they sat in the cellar. Svetlana could tell her mother was terrified, she was muttering to herself, saying she wished she had died before the war began. A lot of people were crying and moaning. They all seemed scared. Oddly, Svetlana didn't feel frightened at all. She just wanted to sleep.

Stojan was really scared. He woke up to the sound of a plane going over, and at first he couldn't make sense of the noise. When he went to the window, he could see a fire on one of the bridges, and then he saw a plane flying in that direction and dropping something that looked like a rocket. It felt like a movie, but when he heard the explosion and the sound of glass cracking, he knew it was real. He stood rooted to the spot, shaking with fear. Then his mother came to take him down to the cellar. It was freezing and full of people. All Stojan could think about was: Were they going to bomb people as well as bridges? People were saying it would start with bridges and then go to factories and shops, then houses.

After two or three days the bombing stopped, although planes still flew over the town. This made everyone nervous. Ivana still couldn't go to school. All the school windows had been broken, so they had to wait until they were repaired. Nobody in Foca had been killed by NATO bombs, but people were still dying. One day Ivana was sitting alone in the house when she heard the most terrible sound, a little like singing, but more like wailing. She went onto the balcony. The woman next door was crying, making a high moaning noise. Her son had just died. Ivana phoned her mother to come right away, as the woman was her friend. She felt miserable. The worst thing was that her own brother was supposed to join the army in just a few days. What if this happened to him? She just wanted the war to be over, and people to stop bombing and dying.

3

ADJUSTING TO PEACE

O N December 15, 1995, I was in a convoy of vehicles trying to get into Sarajevo. There was deep snow and the journey up the dirt road from Mostar had taken almost twenty-four hours, rather than the expected three. Now we were stuck in our minivan, on the wrong side of Mount Igman, along with French non-governmental organization (NGO) trucks carrying seed and food for Gorazde, and UN and NATO personnel in a variety of military vehicles. Supposedly, there had been a cease-fire for the previous two months, brought about by the combination of a successful Bosnian and Croat ground offensive and NATO air strikes against the army of Republika Srpska (VRS). Presidents Izetbegovic of Bosnia, Milosevic of the Federal Republic of Yugoslavia, and Tudjman of Croatia, meeting in Dayton, Ohio, had reached an agreement on November 21. It maintained Bosnia and Herzegovina as a unitary state and divided that state into two entities: Republika Srpska and the Federation of Bosnia and Herzegovina. It also stated that all refugees would be allowed to return to their homes, and that those responsible for war crimes would be arrested and tried. It set a series of dates for the transfer of various parts of the country from one entity to the other, to conform to the agreed-upon boundaries.

The agreement had been signed on December 14 with great ceremony in Paris, but here on the ground there was no sense that the war was over. Serbs still controlled the suburbs of Sarajevo and were angry that these suburbs would be given back to the Federation over the next few months. Shots had been fired that morning, and no one was sure if it was safe to move. Gorazde was still cut off to all but authorized aid convoys and International Forces. It was now an island of Federation territory, only accessible through Republika Srpska.

Welcome to Sarajevo, my friends said when I finally reached the foggy, snowbound city that night and we sat huddled over an oil stove. *You see, no gas, no electricity, no water, and the shelling continues. There won't be peace until we can cross Igman, or walk in Ilidza without danger.* The war trickled to an end. There were no victory parades. I saw no dancing in the streets. Gorazde remained isolated and completely dependent on humanitarian aid. Many of the Serbs who did not want to live in Federation territory headed for Foca. Not surprisingly, it was hard to get a sense of how or when the war actually ended for the children.

Foca, 1996–1997

Ivana heard that Serb forces had left their positions and an agreement had been signed. She was relieved that her older brother would not have to go to the front line and that the shooting had stopped. Both of her parents found jobs in the town, although for very little pay. She went to visit her aunt in Serbia for a holiday, glad to be in a city where no one talked or thought about war, and where people had nice things. When she came home, she settled down at school, got good marks, and enjoyed her life.

Stojan did the same. He was glad they could move back to their old apartment. He had a video player and enjoyed watching action movies like James Bond. He had his own room back and stuck posters of his favorite basketball heroes on the walls. He planned to be a sports star himself, and he did well at school. Sometimes he wished they could travel more, the way they had before the war, and that the town was a bit more up-to-date, but he enjoyed life in most situations. There was no reason not to do so now.

It was not so easy for Svetlana. Her family had moved again, to yet another abandoned Muslim apartment. They had no legal standing, so it felt very insecure. The Dayton Agreement meant the owners could come back at any moment, although there seemed little chance of that. Svetlana could think of nothing nicer than for everything to return to the way it was before the war. She longed to see all her old friends again, but knew it was impossible. The war had destroyed everything. There were lots of new people in Foca, and everyone had changed. There were often fights at school. The atmosphere in town was depressing, and at home her mother was just as nervous as before. Both her parents worked, but neither of them got paid much so they had hardly any money. The war was over, but it didn't feel like it. She was fed up with the endless news on TV. She hated it. Everyone always seemed to be arguing, and she worried that the fighting could start all over again.

She was not doing very well at school. Her mother said it was just laziness, but she knew it wasn't. She just found it hard to sit still and concentrate. She felt nervous and everything bothered and upset her, even little things. If her mother asked her to wash the dishes when she was trying to draw a picture, she felt like screaming. She thought she might pick up the plates, throw them across the room at someone, and then burst into tears. She found some ways to escape, listening to music, doing the things she was good at like art or karate training. Talking to her closest friend was the best; they were like sisters and understood each other perfectly.

Dusan came back to Foca with his mother. The town was now called Srbinje, but his father said that Vlado had died fighting for Foca, not Srbinje. Dusan saw that his parents were completely exhausted. Luckily, people wanted to help. A friend set them up in a small business, so they were very busy and that gave them less time to think. He tried to concentrate on doing well at school to please them. He knew things would never be the same as before.

He hardly ever stopped thinking about Vlado. He visited the grave every week, looked at photos, and thought about all their times together. He liked talking about him with his parents. The conversations made him feel that in some way he was keeping Vlado alive, at least in his memories. Dusan could think of nothing better than trying to be exactly like his brother. But sometimes it was very painful, and when he was alone he let himself cry. Sometimes he would play with his dog or go for a ride on his bike or play with his friends. That helped him to forget for a while. Sometimes he thought he had no feelings at all.

Physically he was fine, he slept and ate well, but there were still times when he wasn't interested in anything. He felt bored and cut off from everything. Nothing would ever make him happy again. Other times, when he thought about the war, he felt angry. His brother had fought against violence and for Serbia, to save them from living under Muslims, as they had done for five hundred years. He had learned in history class how bad that had been. Now it felt as if his brother had fought for nothing. The family had been pleased about Dayton at first, but nothing was settled. The countries were not separated yet, and foreign forces were pushing in the wrong direction. He knew it was foolish to try to put Croats, Muslims, and Serbs in one country. It would humiliate all those who had died in the war, fighting for separate nations. Anyway, if Muslims came back to Foca, what would happen to the Serb people in Muslim houses? Where could they go? It wasn't right.

He thought there would probably be another war in the next ten, fifteen, or twenty years. After all, his grandfather had lived through three. Whether it was Balkan people or outsiders who wanted a war, they always had it here. Ordinary people never had a say; it was always politicians. When there were no proper laws and when people had no money and no food like now, then there were wars.

Gorazde, 1996–1997

Samir worried that there might be another war. Sometimes he talked about it with his mother, and she said she couldn't bear to go through all that again. He and his family had returned to Gorazde in 1997. They could not go back to their house; it was almost completely destroyed. But his father said, *You should spend your lives in the place where you were born.* Samir didn't want to live in the old house. If he went inside, he remembered the man talking about three knives and felt scared. They had two rooms in a big hut for displaced people. He liked it. They had a TV; he had his own bed. He knew his parents were very worried; they had no money and couldn't get their old jobs back because the factory was closed. Father said the authorities should help them.

The town was getting better. They had rebuilt the school and the sports hall. The trouble was that it didn't feel completely safe. Gorazde had declared itself an "Open City." This meant Serbs could come back and live there and the police would not search them anymore. Recently, there had been two Serb men in their area, and someone said they were armed and had shot a dog. On the radio, Samir heard angry Serbs say that if they didn't get a town called Brcko, they might take Gorazde by force. He didn't like or understand politics, but these things worried him. He felt very confused about Serbs. He thought everyone should be able to go back to their own homes, which meant Serbs should be able to come back too, but not if they cursed or had guns, and not the ones who had wanted to kill his family.

His biggest worry was school. In Visoko the teachers had been patient and explained if something was unclear. It wasn't like that here, and he got so nervous when they asked him a question. And there was so much homework to do. He felt a bit lonely. He had always been shy, but since coming back to Gorazde, it felt harder to make friends. He had a couple of good ones, but he would have liked to be part of a crowd.

Another trouble was that he still remembered things from the war, like when he and his family were imprisoned in their house, and then he would just start shaking. Sometimes the memories made him angry; sometimes he just felt really tense and cut off from his friends. It could happen out of the blue: one moment he would be feeling fine and the next he would be afraid. It was getting better, so he didn't tell anyone; he wanted to forget everything to do with the war. Even so, his father knew he was still a little nervous and was going to take him to a local woman who had a special method for taking fear away.

As far as Amela was concerned, the end of the war meant things just got worse. Her father was back, as bad as ever. As usual, her mother put up with everything. One night he came home really drunk with a hand grenade and started yelling, *Get out of the house, or I'll kill you, it doesn't matter if I die too.* They ran to the police station, but the police wouldn't do anything. Amela knew some of them were friends with her father. She thought he gave them money. They spent the night there anyway and then went back home. Another time he threatened her mother with a knife, and Amela tried to stop him. She was terrified that her mother might die; it would be the end of everything. One night she felt so miserable she decided to take all her grandmother's pills. If she were dead, there would not be all this fear and pain and arguing. She fell asleep, and woke up late the next day feeling sick, drowsy, and amazed and angry to be alive. No one seemed to have noticed, so she decided not to tell anyone. There didn't seem any point in trying again.

Then one day her father hit her mother so hard he broke her jaw and she had to go to the hospital in Sarajevo. The period that followed was one of the worst of Amela's life. They had to stay with her father's mother, who let them go hungry. Meanwhile, her father continued to drink and see other women who Amela thought were ugly and stupid. She went to school and tried to work, but it was difficult to concentrate on what the teachers were saying. Often her head would be full of pictures of her father shouting at them. She didn't tell anyone, she was ashamed. She didn't want anyone to know that things were different in their house. Anyway, she knew that lots of people had suffered in the war much worse than she had.

When her mother came home from the hospital after four months, she went straight to court to ask for a divorce. Amela felt as if they spent the next three months sleeping on the court benches. Father fought to keep Amela and her brother. Amela didn't want to leave the courthouse until she was sure she would be with her mother. Sometimes it was horrible; her father would curse and swear in court. But her mother was really tough. Other times, her father cried. He said things like *I had everything for thirteen years. I didn't appreciate it, and now I have nothing, and I realize what I have lost.* That was the hardest moment. She thought she might cry too, but she was determined not to.

Finally, everything was resolved; Amela and her brother could go home with their mother. They all left the courthouse and walked down the main street. Dad was just ahead. Suddenly he turned to them. *Let's all go and have a drink together! Come on, for old times' sake.*

Amela looked at her mother, who just stared at her father and then burst into tears. *We don't want to drink with you,* Amela said. *When we needed to sit and drink together, you weren't there.*

He looked at her. *Don't ever call me Father again.*

Then he turned back to her mother. *And you just remember who I am, I am a man from Montenegro, and you will remember me. Until the day I die, I won't let you forget. I'll find ways to remind you.*

After that, things did get better. They moved to a tiny, damp house. Mum said she didn't want his money and could manage by herself. That meant she had to work all hours, so Amela did the housework and took care of her brother after school. She didn't mind. It was better than the fights. Sometimes, to her surprise, she missed her father. She even felt sorry for him. He seemed to be drinking less and was lonely, so she went to visit him and helped with his laundry. Sometimes she wished they could be together, but she knew he didn't want to live with her mother.

As for the war, she tried not to think about it, although every time she turned on the television it made her nervous. There always seemed to be arguments. She was glad about Dayton and about having international troops in the town, but she was still afraid the town could be taken, or swapped for another town, if the troops left. Maybe they would all have to move. That numbness she had felt during the war had gone. She missed the relatives who had died, and thought about them a lot. Sometimes she had nightmares. She had always been afraid of the dark, now it was worse and she couldn't sleep alone. She felt very edgy a lot of the time. She would just yell at her brother for no reason. That wasn't fair, but it was hard to stay calm. Other times even the funniest book was boring. And her memory was still bad. Her mother teased her that sometimes she didn't know what day of the week it was or what she had had for breakfast. At the same time, there were things in the past she wanted to forget, but they wouldn't go away.

As soon as the Dayton Agreement was signed, Nina was eager to get back home, she missed everything so much. She had spent three and a half years in Germany, living in an apartment in the house of the pastor who had invited them. They were the only Bosnian refugees in the small town. Her father and brother had tried to join them, but couldn't get out of Bosnia. But they called often and she exchanged letters with her friends through the Red Cross, so she knew how things were at home. She liked Germany and settled in well, learning German, going to the local school, and getting top marks in every class. She made friends and loved their host and his family. Her older sister married another Bosnian refugee. Her mother always tried to be happy about their success, but Nina knew she hadn't stopped thinking about Bosnia for one moment. She never turned the radio off, even going to sleep with a small transistor beside her. Nina told her that when the war was over and they were back in Bosnia, *You will never turn that radio on again.*

When the time came to leave she felt glad and sad all at once. She felt she was leaving her own family. All their friends came over the night before for a party, and when they returned in the morning to say goodbye, she cried and cried. Finally, after a long bus journey, they arrived in Sarajevo. The bus was hours late, so no one was there to meet them. Her mother called her father, and then they sat on plastic chairs and waited. Nina watched her mother watching every person who came in. Nina had often thought about her father in Germany, wondering if she would ever see him again, and if she did, how she would feel. She had heard stories on the journey home, people saying her father had found another woman. She didn't believe it; she knew there were many false rumors.

There is your father, her mother said. Nina ran toward him and stopped in front of him. She could see he didn't recognize her, and he looked a bit strange too, his teeth were odd.

Nina? Nina? Is it really you? Why you're completely grown up! Then her mother came up and they were all hugging, and everything was all right.

The next day they drove the car over Grebak, a long, bumpy, potholed dirt road that went back over the mountains, almost the same way that Nina had walked out nearly four years earlier. It took five hours, but it meant they could avoid driving through Republika Srpska, and Nina didn't mind. They came to the curve of the road from where you could look down and see the Drina, flat, bright, like metal in the sunlight. Nina loved the water; now she knew she was coming home, she was bursting with excitement, her heart beating really fast. Finally, they got to the apartment, and there was an unrecognizable older brother running toward them from a café and hugging them and declaring how grown up she was; she knew everyone was happy because they were all together again after three and a half years.

That evening she went out to walk around the town with her brother and his wife. Her friends had all changed physically, so none of them could recognize her or she them, but it didn't matter, she was so pleased to be back with them. It was strange how in Germany she had felt like a child and hardly ever gone out at night, but now she suddenly felt very adult. They stayed out late to give their parents time to be alone together and catch up. When they came home, Nina knew right away that something was wrong. It was a two-room apartment; her mother was in one room making up a bed; her father was nowhere to be seen.

What's happened? Where is papa?

He went for a walk, her mother said in a flat odd voice. This made no sense to Nina—why would he go for a walk alone on their first night back? Why not take her mother with him?

Why did he go for a walk?

He just left. I don't know . . .

Mama, what's wrong? Is something wrong?

Nothing . . . there's something wrong with your father, he is not alright.

Her mother wouldn't talk anymore; she wanted to sleep. Then Nina's brother explained: it was true, her father had met someone else during the war, and he no longer felt the same about her mother.

Nina couldn't believe it. How could this have happened? They were one of the happiest families in Gorazde. Everyone knew that. She remembered leaving Gorazde. Her father had stood by the door and cried. It had been the worst day of her life. She knew his feelings for them, for her, so how could he do this?

The next year was horrible. Her father promised to stop seeing the other woman if her mother moved back to the village to take care of *his* mother, who was blind. She agreed. Because of school, Nina stayed in town with her brother and his wife. Whenever she went home, she saw how bad it was: her mother did everything her father wanted, but he was different; it was not a normal marriage. There were always arguments. He was never home on time, and when her mother asked him where he had been, he put on this serious face and said, *Who are you to ask me where I was? I can do whatever I want.*

School was not easy at first. Nina had lost a year in Germany because of having to learn the language, so now she was a year behind her contemporaries. But she worked through the holidays and caught up.

After a year, her mother had had enough. She told Nina she was leaving her father if he didn't change. *What kind of a life is that? Why take care of someone or clean up after them, when they don't love you?*

There was no change, and her mother moved into Nina's brother's house; her father decided to have nothing to do with them. He had been seeing the other woman all the time. Nina hated her. The woman looked nothing like her tall and elegant mother. She was small and had children of her own, but she had done something incredible to Nina's father because he had never been like that before. Nina had heard people say there is some force that can change a man and make him crazy. She knew many men had seen other women during the war. But they had always gone back to their families. Her father had not. What also made her angry was the thought that the money they had kept sending from Germany had gone to that woman. If her mother had known, she wouldn't have sent a penny.

Sometimes Nina felt that losing her father in this way was worse than anything that had happened during the war. It was almost as if he had died. She cried much of the time and became very thin. Sometimes she felt so bad she thought, *I'll kill myself, what am I doing here?* She knew that was just something silly in her mind. She would never do such a thing. She wrote everything in her diary, and she talked a lot to her mother and her best friend. She couldn't say everything, but it helped. She also talked to her father. He had started coming around once a month to give her money, and she told him how angry she was. She cried in front of him too, asking him why he had left and why he didn't come back. He still didn't want a divorce, and he sometimes said, *Anything is possible.* Then she realized nothing would change and decided she just had to carry on with her life. After all, lots of people were divorced or separated. She was all her mother had left now that her brother and sister were married, and her mother had been so brave.

She finished eighth grade with top marks and passed the exams for secondary school. She was pleased she had done what she had set out to do. She had many friends and enjoyed her life. Sometimes she thought about her life in Germany, but that whole period had a dreamlike quality. This was her home again now.

Narcisa knew she was lucky. She had not lost any close relatives, her father had come home safely, and their house was still standing. Her mother didn't have a job anymore and her father didn't get paid much, but they managed. She was beginning to enjoy herself again. She loved school and did well in every subject. She never seemed to have free time because she belonged to a singing group, helped run a school newspaper, played basketball, and went to mekteb. The worst thing the war had done to her was damage her eyesight. She blamed her need to wear glasses on all that reading by candlelight and worried a little that it would mean she wouldn't get boyfriends. That was her biggest concern and she knew it was silly. Sometimes, walking down the street where she had stepped over the dead bodies, she remembered. Sometimes she thought of taking another route, but she never did, and now the memory came less often.

In some ways, she didn't want to forget. She thought it was important to remember all the suffering of the last four years. As far as she was concerned, the war had helped them understand what was what. They had seen the real faces of all those people who had once appeared to be such good friends. The mass graves had taught them a lesson. When she thought about what she had been like before the war, she couldn't recognize herself; she hadn't even understood that there were any differences between people. Even now, she knew that not all Serbs were terrible, but the trouble was that the ones who had done the killing gave the impression that all were the same. She knew the Serbs had to be allowed to come back to Gorazde; everyone had to be able to go home. But she would not be friends or mix with them in the same way. She would not forget and she could not forgive.

Most of the time she gave no thought to such things. The war was over and she wanted to get on with her life. She decided to become a lawyer. The war had made her realize there was a lot of injustice, here in Gorazde and in the world. She wanted to change that.

PART TWO

UNDERSTANDING WHAT HAPPENED

4

WHY DID WE FIGHT?

Bosnia is a formidable, scary place of high mountains, brutish people and tribal grievances rooted in history and myth born of boozy nights by the fire. It's the place where World War I began and where the wars of Europe persist, an ember of hate still glowing for reasons that defy reason itself.

—Richard Cohen, *Send in the Troops*, 1995

Did you know what nationality you were before the war?
Tatiana: *No. Actually, one day in the schoolyard, they asked me whether I was Serb, Muslim, or Croat. And I thought it sounded nice to be a Muslim, I liked the sound of the word, so I said I was Muslim.*

—Fifteen-year-old Serb girl, Foca

Milica was fourteen, pretty, dark haired, soft spoken, and shy. She and her family had decided to leave the small town of Ustikolina after the war ended, when the Dayton Peace Agreement allocated the town to the Federation. She sat in the bleak classroom in the primary school in Foca, answering my questions politely, with the slightly bewildered air of one discussing the obvious.

Why wasn't it possible to stay?

How could I stay—there were Turks there?

Did someone say you had to move, or did you want to move?

They told us we had to move, on the news, because the Turks who had lived there were supposed to come back.

Ustikolina was not Milica's original hometown; her family had moved into an empty Muslim-owned house there early in the war, after fleeing

81

from a village near Gorazde. She had happy memories of her old life. Her father had built their house himself, and the family had a small farm with a cow, pigs, sheep, and chickens. She helped her mother by watching the sheep. Her father worked in a factory in Gorazde. The families in their village were Serb, although there were a few *Turks* living there and the neighboring village was *Turk*. This was the term she now used for her Muslim neighbors. At school, her teacher was *Turk* and her friends were of all nationalities. When the shooting began, all the mothers and children ran away, leaving the fathers to defend their houses. Her father left a few weeks after that. Later they heard that the house had been burned.

After the war, Milica was angry with the returning Turks for making them move again, and she missed her old home near Gorazde. Sometimes she thought it would be nice to go back, but she knew it was impossible.

Why? I asked.

Because Gorazde will never be Serb, it will always be theirs.

Gorazde will always be Muslim?

Turk.

Can you imagine ever living with Turks again? I decided to stick with her definitions.

No.

Can you explain to me why not?

She was silent for a while. *Because I don't want to live with them.*

Why is that?

Because I don't like them.

Why don't you like them?

I don't know why . . . because they're Turks, that's why I don't like them.

But she found it hard to specify the differences between Serbs and Turks. She knew she liked Serbs, and she thought Turks looked different, although some of her girlfriends in the village had been Turks, and they had looked and behaved just like her.

Did you like Turks before the war? She was silent again. This time the silence continued until I broke it. *Did you know who the Turks were before the war?*

No.

So it's only since the war?

Yes.

So what has made Turks since the war so unlikable?

Another silence. *I don't know. Serbs look better to me, umm, and I have more Serb friends now.*

Do you hate the Turkish friends you had before the war?

No! Why? They didn't do anything to me. She looked astonished.

Would you ever like to see those friends again?

No.

Because?

I don't know why.

But later in the conversation it became clearer. She was convinced that *Turks hate Serbs*, although again she had no idea why.

On another afternoon I visited Milica's parents. The family now lived in another Muslim-owned house, an old two-story building close to the river in Foca. We walked through a door in a high stone wall into a paved yard with fruit trees. Wood was neatly stacked against the wall. I pulled off my shoes, placing them as usual with the other pairs outside the door. Milica's mother ushered me in. She was a pleasant-faced, sad-looking woman with graying hair loosely pulled into a bun, wearing a long skirt of printed material. Her husband joined us in a neat front room that doubled as a kitchen. I was seated on a shiny plastic-covered sofa, while she poured Fanta into glasses, and started grinding coffee with a small hand grinder. When I said that I wanted to understand how things were now and how they had been before, Milica's mother burst into tears. She continued to cry as she talked of her old home, the animals left behind, and her husband's inability to find work in the town. *It was better than now*, her husband said. *It was good until the war.*

Admira was a Muslim thirteen-year-old who had also lived with her family in a village near Gorazde before the war. They shared a house with her grandparents; each family had a separate floor. They kept cows and horses. She went to school in the suburb of Kopaci, and had no sense of difference between herself and her Serb friends. The only way she could tell was by names. Then the war came and her father was killed in the first year of fighting. Two years later, as Serbian forces attempted to take Gorazde, she fled into town with her mother and her older sister, Jasmina. Now they lived seven floors up in a flat vacated by Serbs and allocated to them by the municipality. She wanted to go home to the village. The whole family felt the same. *I would like to live together, if that's possible*, Jasmina said.

Yet again, I was sitting shoeless on the sofa as the mother ground coffee, and we drank Coca-Cola from glasses. *Could you live with the people who killed your husband?* I asked Admira's mother.

Well, it wouldn't be the way it was before but we have to try . . .

Many families I talk to in Foca say, "If we live together again we'll all kill each other. So we have to live separately."

Jasmina laughed. *They know we wouldn't kill them. They pass through this town safely, nobody stops them. But when we go through Rogatica, they stop you all the time.*

Admira thought it would be much safer if everyone went home: *If they don't come back there's a possibility of war.* I asked her to explain. *If they were together with us, they wouldn't start a war.* She couldn't say why she thought that, it was just how she felt.

I would like it to be so that everyone could forget everything that happened, said her mother. *Friends. I mean before the war Serbs and Muslims worked in the same factories together, they were sitting in the same cafés, they were using the same buses, I mean my husband was a driver, he was driving Serbs—*

Jasmina interrupted, *Why couldn't we try to do that even now?*

I don't know, her mother replied. *With some nice things everything could be forgotten, you have to go on living.*

There is a story told about the war in Bosnia. It has variations, but the central theme remains constant: Balkan peoples have always fought; they are tribal, primitive, and barbaric; and the animosity between them stretches back not just centuries, but millennia. The hatreds were temporarily frozen in the ice chest of communism, but after Tito's death, the age-old animosities emerged intact. This story was useful to the domestic elites in Serbia. They used it to support their claim that they had no part in the fighting in Bosnia and that this was a civil war arising out of unresolved long-term grievances. The story also had a powerful hold on the public imagination in the West. It was used to justify Western neutrality and the policy of nonintervention championed by the British government.[11]

Yet the story bears no resemblance to the lived experience of any of the families I got to know in either city. On the contrary, their descriptions of prewar life were not of unspoken tensions and repressed hostility, but of what now seemed like a halcyon period: when hard-working young families had just begun to feel prosperous, when almost everyone earned good wages and few gave much thought to the nationality of their neighbors. As winter turned to spring in 1998, I drove up and down the Drina Valley, past the burned-out houses to which no one had returned and the convoluted piping of the chemical factory that no longer functioned, listening to words and phrases that became very familiar. The recollections took on an elegiac quality: mourning for a period of lost grace.

Everything was good then. When you could earn enough to build a house in two years, that was good.

It was wonderful, we were free, the children were healthy. We could live like normal people. We could go to the coast, to the mountains.

I don't think it will ever come back.

They brought us eggs at Easter; we all ate cake at Bajram.

We used to go to work together. And at every holiday, I used to get a big piece of roast meat like a Christmas present.

We were so close to each other.

I had more Serb friends than Muslims and I never thought that my colleagues would shoot me.

My best friend was my Muslim neighbor and we were in the same class.

I didn't know then who was Muslim, who was Serb. All my friends were the same for me.

They were always helping us whenever we asked.

I did not feel that I was in danger.

His first teacher was Muslim and he was great in the school.

It was much better while we were together.

We were all together somehow before the war. There was much more company then than there is now. And I think we were all honest, and everything we did, we did it together.

It would be wrong to dismiss this as retrospective nostalgia. In any careful reading of history, Bosnia is notable for the half-millennium in which four different faiths (Orthodox, Catholic, Muslim, and Jew) lived together remarkably free from violence. The conflicts that had occurred prior to the most recent war were no more frequent than those between other European nations, and were largely instigated by outsiders.[12] Intermarriage, though still rare in rural areas, was accepted and increasingly common in cities.[13] According to a survey on national tolerance carried out by a consortium of Yugoslav sociology institutes, in 1990 Bosnia had the highest index of tolerance, 3.88 on a scale from 1 to 5. This was well above average.[14]

This war, far from arising out of ancient animosities, actually created them. Families who formerly shared many aspects of a way of life and celebrated their differences now felt that they had been dispossessed. Children who previously had no strong sense of ethnic identity and no feelings of enmity toward their neighbors now knew who they were, and many perceived the other ethnicity as a threat to their safety.

So what happened? I wanted to discover how the families made sense of the events that led to the shift in neighbor's perceptions of neighbor. Most of the children were not aware of anything different until actual fighting began in their community. Their parents thought the changes began a little earlier. It was the parents' understandings, whether spoken or not, that helped to shape their children's worlds.

Foca

National parties, Nikola's parents told me. A university-educated professional couple, they had their own book-filled apartment in a high-rise by the river in Foca. *Everyone started to separate. Nobody asked you to join. Everybody joined his own people. The Muslim National Party was created first, then the Croat National Party, and then the Serb National Party was formed.*

Simo Mojevic, headmaster of one of the primary schools in Foca, had previously been head of the primary school in Ustikolina. He had gone to the founding meeting of the Stranka Demokratske Akcije or Party of Democratic Action (SDA), the party predominantly supported by Muslims, held in Ustikolina's youth club. He was the only Serb present, invited as a guest. *I suddenly realized that Muslim people were not satisfied with Yugoslavia,* he told me. *They all talked as if Muslims were in danger! Some uneducated people started to shout things about not sleeping together, about separating the children, making separate kitchens. Someone even said that Serbs who didn't want to be killed should go to Montenegro. I think I understood then that Yugoslavia would be divided. Serbs started doing the same, but a month later.*

Anyone who gave it any thought knew that the evil was coming, said Nikola's father. *Television had an enormous influence.*

Everyone I met in both cities had TV sets, no matter how impoverished they were or whether or not they still lived in their own homes. The set occupied a prominent position in the living room or kitchen and was invariably switched on. Before 1992, families in Foca could watch television stations from Sarajevo and from Belgrade. They could also buy the main Serbian daily newspaper, *Polityka*, and a number of magazines. For the three years before the war, Serbian TV and newspapers told the same disturbing story: Serbs were in danger and under attack all over Yugoslavia. Serbian families in Foca saw "Albanian separatists" beating Serbs who were protesting for their rights in Kosovo, and watched Serbian President Milosevic promise, *No one will beat you again.* They heard horrifying accounts of the rape of elderly Serb women in Kosovo, and of attacks on Serbs by Croatian militias using the same flag as the Ustashe, the Second World War Croat fascist regime. Finally, many thought, the truth about Serbia was emerging: the historical facts that had never been properly discussed, such as how many Serbs had been killed by Ustashe in concentration camps or massacred by Muslim SS collaborators during the Second World War. It seemed that Serbs had sacrificed a great deal, and for what? Milosevic reminded them that Serbs had never been conquered or exploited by others; they had always liberated themselves and tried to help others do the same.

Serbs were always for Yugoslavia, and maybe the biggest Serb tragedy was in 1918 when they let Yugoslavia be created instead of a Greater Serbia, Dusan's father told me. He had been a Communist Party member for seventeen years, even though it was the party that had put his own father in jail. No one wanted communism anymore. He thought Tito was part of the problem. Tito was the architect of the 1974 constitution that benefited every nation except the Serbs, at Serb expense. Muslims, for example, had been given national status, and yet everyone knew they were Serbs who had converted to Islam when the Turks came.

It was a euphoric time, there were so many people on the streets, Ivana's mother recalled, discussing the period before the war. *Now we know that those people in power were just communist Serbs, and now they are radical Serbs, the same people, just changing places. Muslims and Serbs simply thought that those who got the most votes would be in control. It was just the same between Croats and Serbs in other places.* She and her husband did not vote. They hoped it would all die down.

Svetlana's mother was not so hopeful. *That was the end of everything, I was terrified. My neighbor said how good it was to have national parties and asked why I was frightened. How could not I be afraid when two people start a fight? I couldn't see how so many people could make peace between themselves. Maybe they knew something I didn't; they were all going to meetings. I didn't know anything.*

Her husband was more confident that there would be no war. *Because we lived together so nicely, we had good relations. I had worked twenty years with Muslims, I couldn't imagine us fighting. My Muslim friends felt the same.*

By the summer of 1991, everyone felt uneasy. The three national parties had all won proportions of the votes that reflected their constituencies and formed a coalition government with a rotating presidency. Dusan's father hoped this was a continuation of "brotherhood and unity" without communism, but most Serbs in Foca did not trust it. They watched as Slovenia and Croatia went to war against Serbs and Yugoslavia. Serbs in Croatia defended themselves by forming their own autonomous regions. Radovan Karadzic, president of the Srpska Demokratska Stranka or Serb Democratic Party (SDS), said that Serbs in Bosnia should do the same, and called for a united Serb state that would bring Serbs from Croatia, Bosnia, and Serbia together. That sounded sensible to some. Dusan's parents saw that "brotherhood and unity" was over. Alija Izetbegovic had told parliament he would sacrifice peace for the sake of an independent Bosnia, and what kind of Bosnia would that be? They knew that Izetbegovic had dedicated his entire life to creating an Islamic country with only Muslims, no Serbs or Croats. That was why he asked for Bosnia-Herzegovina to join the "Organization of Islamic Countries." He had gone to prison years ago for writing a statement that said as much. Dusan's father wished they had never let him out.

There was a strike at the Foca Trans bus company. Stojan's father explained it to me. The Muslim director had been accused of corruption. For Stojan's father the issues were clear. The director had been smuggling wood to Italy, and all the workers went on strike against him, but when Muslim politicians came down from Sarajevo and took the director's side, the Muslim workers went back to work, and the abandoned Serb strikers were fired. So they had no choice but to set up their own bus company. A few years earlier, when a close friend had married a Muslim, Stojan's father had been best man at the wedding, but now he realized that he and his Muslim friends interpreted every event differently, so it was hard to be together anymore. The whole town seemed to be going the same way. He knew it was ridiculous; this was the late twentieth century, and yet Serbs and Muslims took separate buses and drank in separate cafés.

Things that had not seemed significant in previous years suddenly seemed to matter: that wedding, for instance. Both sets of parents were religious and were against it, particularly the Muslim parents of the bride, although they had always been very friendly to Stojan's father. There was a big fight about what to call the first child. The girl's parents wanted a Muslim name, and the boy's parents wanted a Serbian name. After all, it was normal for a child to be named after the father's family. The couple decided on something completely neutral, and asked him to help them make peace between the grandparents, but it was not a friendly occasion. The girl's father kept saying that he couldn't forget that Chetniks had killed his brother in the last war—even though it was fifty years before.

What's that have to do with your son-in-law when he was not born then? Stojan's father asked. *He lives with your daughter. They have a son. Why should it spoil their life?*

No, the girl's father said, *I cannot forget.*

After we left my Serb friend's father said, "Did you see that Balija?" That's a bad name for Muslims. You use it if you want to insult them. Because there were some Muslim units in the Second World War, called Ballist Units, which collaborated [with the Nazis]. My friend's father went on, "I was sitting in the corner." Then I realized he had spent the whole time sitting in a corner so that no one could sit beside him. He was just waiting to be attacked. He had a gun with him! And he told me, "If that Balija had come toward me to attack me, I would have killed him." Stojan's father laughed as he told me this story, but it was clear he thought it significant. None of his generation had been interested in all the stories their parents had tried to tell them about the past, but now the memories seemed more important. Those experiences had become relevant.

Then there were the rallies. The SDA held a large one. Muslims came from all over Yugoslavia: Kosovo, the Sandzak (the area of Serbia with a predominantly Muslim population), waving green flags and talking of building an enormous mosque, as if the town didn't have enough mosques already. *It's not just a coincidence that that big SDA rally was here*, Stojan's father explained. Foca was a key point on the "Green Road." If that road was cut, Muslims from Bosnia would be separated from those in the Sandzak and Kosovo, so of course Muslims paid special attention to Foca. The Serbs believed it was the bridgehead for any putative Islamic Front driving up from the southeast. *When someone comes from another republic with a Turkish flag and walks around town provoking people . . . if it was just a Muslim town okay, but it was half and half. Every country has its own flags, so if someone comes with other flags . . . It's a wonder someone didn't throw a bomb.*

In August 1991, Mojevic arrived at work one morning to find the monument in the schoolyard destroyed. It commemorated a partisan killed by Chetniks and Italians in the Second World War, and it had stood in front of his office, surrounded by roses. A note on the shattered stump was addressed to him. It said, *You will finish in the same way.* Mojevic decided to join the SDS. *I said to myself that I have to join with my people. I was afraid for my physical safety, I had no other choice.*

The coalition government, with its joint parliament, was not working. Serbs resented SDA support for Slovene and Croat attacks on Yugoslavia, at a time when they believed Serbs risked extermination in those countries. Karadzic suggested peaceful ethnic separation. Dusan's father hoped it would work, but the Muslims rejected the idea. Serbs knew Muslims wanted their own country, which they could dominate. So in November, when the SDS held a plebiscite for Serb voters only, on whether or not to "remain in Yugoslavia together with the Serbs of Serbia, Montenegro, Krajina, Vojvodina, and Kosovo," most voted yes.[15] If Muslims wanted to leave Yugoslavia, let them, they had that right. Serbs also had the right to refuse to go with them.

None of the Serb families I knew voted in the referendum on Bosnian independence the following February. Stojan's father hoped it was a joke. By now, Ivana's mother had begun to feel out of place when she went to

Gorazde. She knew she was not a nationalist, not like some of her Serb colleagues. She had a close Muslim friend, but couldn't seem to talk to her anymore. After that "Muslim" referendum, she noticed a real change. She could see that it was a *great moment* for the Muslims. They seemed proud, as if they finally had their own country. An experience at the bus station told her which way things were going. She met an elderly Muslim gentleman and said "dobar dan"(good day) as she always had, and a young Muslim man turned around and said in a very threatening way, *After today you cannot say "dobar dan," you have to say "merhaba."*[16] She had never given any thought to how she greeted another person before. Suddenly she was afraid; it felt as if there was no more tolerance or life together.

In the few weeks before the fighting began, all the Serb families could see that both sides were arming. The national parties were giving out guns. One day Headmaster Mojevic saw a Muslim colleague wearing two pistols and a rifle. The colleague told him he was a hunter and liked collecting weapons. Mojevic knew the hunters' club was legal, but he was sure it was a cover for gathering weapons, just the same as the Serbs were doing. He was worried because in his area there were 70 percent Muslims and only 30 percent Serbs. The good thing was that the Serbs did have better weapons, real ones, not just hunting rifles, although they had had to buy them. Nothing came free, but he was determined to defend his homeland and his people.

He hoped they could avoid a fight. He continued to behave perfectly correctly in school. However, he remembered what had happened to some local Serbs in the Second World War. The Muslims had tricked them, disarmed them, and said they were sending them to work in Germany. But they had hanged them on trees by the river. The widows and orphans survived to this day in his village. The day before the war started, he warned a Muslim colleague at a funeral: *This time you won't cheat Serbs. You won't stand on Serb land. And you won't have the chance to put any Serbs in prison.* He was not planning to fight a war, just to defend his home and his family if they were attacked.

Dusan's mother respected and admired her son's Catholic teacher, but she was disappointed that now the teacher seemed to award marks on the basis of nationality rather than merit. And there was an incident with a little Muslim girl who wore a crescent moon around her neck. One day she made nasty remarks about Serbs to Dusan, and he got in a fight with her. So the teacher slapped him, quite unjustly. They had always been a religious family, but they believed religion was a private matter. There was no need for anyone to wear symbols and no need to show off who you were by singing national songs. That was what they had always taught Dusan.

Some families still did not believe there would be a fight. In Svetlana's village, Muslims and Serbs kept watch together. Mirko lived high in the hills above the town on a small farm. In his village, the SDS came around and offered all the men guns, for "defense." Mirko's father thought it was completely unnecessary; he couldn't imagine his Muslim neighbors attacking him or he them. But the SDS insisted it might be necessary, just in case the neighbors did attack. So he accepted the weapons. Some families were warned. Bojan's uncle told his family to go to their grandmother's house because there would soon be fighting. Then a man came to give out guns and told Bojan's father to start keeping watch. A courier came and ordered Jovan's parents, *When the war starts, take whatever you can and leave.*

As I listened to these accounts, I could see how things appeared to the speakers. I could look down from the school psychologist's apartment to the garage where she said she had seen her Muslim neighbor handing out rifles, and imagine how disturbing that might be. I could sit in a midtown café and picture the streets full of people shouting and waving foreign flags. I had been similarly discomfited, walking through Belgrade in the summer of 1990, when suddenly surrounded by a running, angry, flag-waving crowd yelling *Kill Albanians! Give us guns! Kill Albanians! Give us guns!* I was pushed into the street, and people swirled past, unseeing and uncaring. It was my first direct experience of the frightening indifference and power of a mobilized crowd.

I would drive back to Gorazde, swinging around the curve of the river where the name "Tito" was still marked out in stone, prominently visible on the hillside, even though sheep grazed on the uncut grass and no flags flew from the poles. I thought of Nina telling me how excited she had been to be made one of Tito's "pioneers" in first grade. That was in 1990, and she was the last of her kind. She wore a white shirt, a blue beret with the red star, and a blue scarf. There was a procession from school and a ceremony and they all sat in chairs and listened to speeches. Led by *some old man,* they repeated an oath to respect professors and parents and protect the country. Then there was a party at school and *everyone was happy.*

Gorazde

Families in Gorazde did not talk so much about the distant past, although they lamented the loss of the immediate one. Narcisa's parents, like Nina, had been Tito's pioneers at school. They had believed in the oath. Milosevic's meetings in Kosovo had disturbed them. They heard him in 1989, at a rally of nearly a million Serbs, threatening that Serbs might have to fight to protect themselves—even though no one was attacking them! *The non-National parties weren't strong enough. We all thought if we chose something else, we would lose protection, security. And we believed that nothing would happen to us.*

Fikreta's father was a cook. He had worked away from home most of his life, in Germany, Libya, Sarajevo. They lived in an old house in town, with a garden. His wife looked after their children well, but it was tough. He thought that after forty years there was no point in voting for the communists, who just offered old ideas with new names. The new parties might give them a better life, but having been born a Muslim, he did not see how he could vote for the Serbs or Croats, they wouldn't want him. Samir's father thought the SDA was for everyone, Serbs and Croats as well as Muslims. When he realized it was just a National party like all the rest, he knew things were going wrong.

If anyone had a reason to join nationalist parties, it was Bosnian Muslims, said Elvira's father. He ran a business in Gorazde and we were sitting in his office. *We didn't have the same rights as others in Yugoslavia; we weren't even able to declare ourselves as Muslims or Bosnians for a long time. . . . Seventy-eight percent of the officers in the JNA were Serb. And look at things here in town. Serbs were 27 percent of the population but they had more than 90 percent of the administrative jobs and occupied more than 70 percent of the state-owned apartments besides. When the national parties formed . . . Serbs felt they were losing some of that power . . . they felt jeopardized, so of course we were in conflict immediately.*

Personally, he had hoped war could be avoided. He and some other professional people, Serbs and Muslims, set up a citizens' group, an association of people with good intentions who wanted to be between the National parties. But it was difficult, they were only a small group and there was pressure. Serbs in the SDS criticized the Serbs; the SDA bullied the Muslims. He thought the national parties appealed more to people from the villages than to those from the city.

In her village, Admira's mother felt bewildered. She was a Muslim; her husband's parents prayed regularly, but her generation hadn't bothered so much, just observed the customs. Her Serb neighbor always came to her house for coffee at Bajram and her family returned the visit at Christmas. Admira went to mekteb, where she learned that there were different ways of worshiping God. No one made problems. Admira's mother had traveled all over Yugoslavia and loved each part equally. Everyone was always welcoming, and even in Belgrade she could drink that special kind of Bosnian coffee. She was proud of their army, the JNA, their flag, and their generals. When it came to voting, she circled all the parties, Serb and Muslim.

Families in Gorazde anxiously watched what was happening in Slovenia and Croatia. If those republics left Yugoslavia, they couldn't imagine how Bosnia could stay. Milosevic had made it clear he wanted Yugoslavia to be Greater Serbia. They had watched him send tanks into Kosovo, declare martial law, close the Albanians' parliament and university, stop them from using their language, and sack them from their jobs. If Muslims stayed in Milosevic's Yugoslavia, they would be treated like Albanians, they would be second-class citizens without any rights.

There were some big rallies in Foca, both Serbs and Muslims. Not many people from Gorazde went to the SDA rally. It was people from the Sandzak, all protesting about how badly they were being treated in Serbia. That showed how things might go for Muslims. You just had to listen to the president of the Serb party, Karadzic, calling for the creation of a unified Serb state. The Serbs did not want the government to work. They kept walking out of parliament. They wanted to control their own areas of the country, but that was ridiculous because everyone lived completely mixed up together. There was no way to separate nationalities without forcing people to leave their homes. Then Karadzic made a horrifying speech saying that if Bosnia did not stay in Yugoslavia, all the Muslims would be killed and disappear. In January 1992, he actually declared a separate Serbian state in Bosnia. It looked as if he and some Serb extremists were determined to divide up the country.

People in Gorazde knew there were tensions in Foca. There was that affair of Foca Trans, when some experts from Sarajevo tried to calm things, but the Serbs started their own bus company. Yet even with all this madness and stupidity, Muslim families in Gorazde could not imagine that a war could happen in their town. Everyone got along too well. Neighbors were all talking to each other, the children were happy in school. People were sure that if the worst were to happen, the army would protect them. The JNA would never allow Bosnian people to be killed.

The Bosnian government held a referendum on independence on February 29, 1992, open to all citizens of the republic. It asked, "Are you in favor of a sovereign and independent Bosnia-Herzegovina, a state of equal citizens, constituted by the peoples of Bosnia-Herzegovina: the Muslims, Serbs, Croatians, and members of the other peoples who live there?" Gorazde's Muslims all voted for independence. *In Foca, they can't understand why you didn't want to stay with them in Yugoslavia,* I said to Fikreta's mother. *They see that referendum as a declaration of war.*

Never mind what they say, she responded briskly. *If they wanted to live with us, if we lived together as well as they said, why didn't they vote to stay with us in an independent Bosnia? We didn't want a Muslim Republic of Bosnia. Anyway, Milosevic would have tried to create a Greater Serbia whether or not we were independent.*

Samir's father thought he was voting for all the nationalities to live together equally in Bosnia, as the referendum stated. He thought it was the best solution because Yugoslavia was broken. Muslims could never have any say if they stayed in Milosevic's Yugoslavia, or any important positions. He wanted one country that would be equal with all the others, and where everyone in it would be equal, so anyone could be president: Serb, Muslim, or Croat; he didn't care.

After the referendum, the Gorazde police split into Serb and Muslim forces. Hasan's father was in the police reserve and it made no sense to him, but the Serbs insisted. This was happening all over Bosnia and there was no way to stop it. President Izetbegovic was determined to show that there was no threat from the Muslim side. He told the territorial defense forces to give all their weapons back to the JNA, so they tried to cooperate. The police divided up the automatic rifles among them. Now Serbs were checking everyone all the time and they seemed to have heavy weapons as well. Hasan's father assumed they had obtained those from the JNA. He had seen loaded trucks arrive at the Ministry of Internal Affairs one day and then drive off around the town.

His family had just finished building their house. He had been in the

Communist Party all his life and thought it a good system. He hoped that with time all the crazy people who created the national parties would just disappear. Meanwhile, he went on going to work in Kopaci. Most of his colleagues were Serb. When he asked his workmates what was going on, they said they had no idea, but not to worry, nothing would happen here.

None of the other families in Gorazde recalled being given weapons before the war, although they thought some party activists might have received some. *The Serbs had a plan,* Elvira's father told me. *It was to make a Greater Serbia. They had had it for seventy years. I wish we had had a plan, then we would have been ready for this war and fewer people would have died. Our national party did nothing for their own people. They got us into the war but they didn't prepare us. So we defended ourselves with our bare hands and made our own weapons.*

Muslim families did not receive any warnings from couriers. Even so, when I arrived six years later with the hindsight of the nightmare that followed, I found it almost impossible to comprehend why, in April 1992, with non-Serbs being killed and driven out of cities all over northern and eastern Bosnia and refugees arriving with harrowing tales from Foca and Visegrad, Muslim families in Gorazde still believed their own city could avoid war.

Some families noticed a change in their friends and neighbors. Armin's father saw that the Serb staff members at his factory were holding a lot of meetings. He got fed up with all the partying, the shooting of guns in the air, and the singing of Serb national songs near his house, so he thought they should move to his parents' village for a while. Their next-door neighbor, who was his wife's best friend and a Serb, had not called around, or come to work for two months. Yet no one believed there would be a war. Every day you said, *No, it won't happen, it won't happen,* Elvira's father told me. They looked at all the Muslims who had come to Gorazde from nearby towns, and thought there were far too many people in town for a war to start. And if the worst happened, Samir's father said, *We thought that the world would stop it.*

5

WHAT BECAME OF OUR NEIGHBORS?

We put to fire the Turkish houses,
That there might be nor stick nor trace
Of these true servants of the devil!
From Cetinje to Tcheklichte we hied
There in full flight the Turks espied;
A certain number were by us mown down,
And all their houses did we set ablaze;
Of all their mosques both great and small
We left but one accursed heap,
For passing folk to glance their scorn.

—Petar Njegos, *The Mountain Wreath*, 1847

I'd never been aware how beautiful my house is
until I saw it burning.

—Goran Simic, *"A Scene, After the War,"* 2003

Foca must once have been a beautiful town. There was a city here in pre-Ottoman times, lying on the trading route between the Mediterranean port of Dubrovnik and Constantinople. The Ottomans took a liking to the place, endowing it with mosques and other public buildings. The oldest part clustered on a hill in the V where the Cehotina joins the Drina. Here was the Orthodox church, with its cobbled yard and its white-plastered monastery; a marketplace and a mosque; an Ottoman clock tower; and a cluster of small shops with wooden shutters and tiled roofs. Steep flights of steps led down to the newer city with its public buildings and apartment blocks. They were of no particular charm, but stood in tree-lined streets and parks beside the river, alongside the graceful sixteenth-century Aladza mosque. More villas were spread out downstream along the Drina toward the prison and the hospital, and upstream toward the timber factory. These were three-storied affairs with gardens and balconies to catch the sun and the view of wooded hills: houses built or bought with hard-earned wages by both Serbs and Muslims, to hold whole families. Before the war, just over forty thousand people lived in the municipality, 52 percent of them Muslim, 45 percent Serb.

When I arrived in the autumn of 1997, it was a dispiriting place. Coming upriver from Gorazde, I would pass the Serbian police checkpoint and cross the Bailey bridge constructed by the UN Stabilization Force (SFOR) to find myself in Donje Polje. This had once been the predominantly Muslim part of town. The mosque had been destroyed, but the villas were still there. Arson does not have the same impact on a house as shelling. When a shell hits, the walls are destroyed or collapse inward from external impact. Brick buckles and crumbles into rubble. The steel of reinforced concrete protrudes. Kerosene and matches have a different effect. The outer walls usually remain standing: an empty, windowless, and roofless box. Each villa now had its own small wilderness, roses blooming in tall grass, lavender struggling with nettles. Here and there were signs of new occupancy, plastic over windows, a freshly dug vegetable patch, hens in a coop. Mostly there was silence.

In the center of town, things were slightly livelier. People were sitting on the terrace of the Hotel Zelengora, an ugly 1960s high-rise, whose residential portion had the heavy lines of laundry indicating refugee occupancy. In the marketplace, traders sold synthetic clothing, portable radios, bright plastic satchels, and the cheaper brands of athletic shoes, along with local chocolate, cigarettes, and peppers. There were few customers, and half the stone trestles were empty, as were most of the small shops that lined the street curving up to the top of the hill.

The whole town felt neglected, deserted, and disjointed. There were too few people on the streets, and too many oddly placed spaces like the one beneath the old watchtower: a large sunlit area of rubble, lined with the shells of burned-out or blown-up shops. The Aladza mosque, with its slender fourteen-sided minaret, its motifs of roses, carnations, and pomegranate flowers, and its colored wall paintings, had gone without a trace. The site it had occupied was indistinguishable from the surrounding park, with only a few turbaned Muslim tombstones leaning askew amidst the litter. The fourteen other mosques that had graced the city had also disappeared, although one shattered dome still stood near the watchtower.

In another unkempt public garden farther along the road, in front of another shattered building, there was a monument, a plain white piece of marble that read: "This is to thank Marshall Tito and the people of Foca for liberating the town and helping to found the Socialist Republic of Yugoslavia." Something metal that had stood in front of the plinth had been ripped away. The marble was scratched and damaged, the listed names almost obliterated by graffiti. *How sad*, I remarked to Gordana, my translator. *If they died fighting for something, they still deserve remembering.*

I agree, she said. *And the same with this war.*

Gordana's parents had moved here from Sarajevo after the Dayton Agreement. They had felt unable to stay in what they perceived as a Muslim-controlled city. Gordana's mother did not know Foca well, and like most of its newer occupants called it by its new name, Srbinje. She was not sure what the destroyed building with the monument had been, though later I learned it was a school, named after a Croatian partisan hero, Ivan Goran Kovacic. It was his statue that had been ripped away. The school had been knocked down to make room for a yet-to-be-built Orthodox church. The town was full of spaces about which people were either not quite sure or altogether silent.

At the beginning of my study, I asked children aged thirteen to fifteen to write stories about "What war means to me and how it has affected my life." They wrote them at school, during class time, supervised by Gordana and me. The exercise was voluntary, no one had to do it—but 127 young teenagers did. We collected their stories, unsigned, with their authors identified only by age and gender. When we read them, the texts appeared to contain the same spaces and silences as the town itself.

The children had plenty to say. Some were dissatisfied with a mere forty minutes of class time and took the stories home to finish. Understandably, for the most part they focused on their own worst experiences. A quarter of the young authors wrote movingly of losing a close friend or relative in the war, and a similar number wrote of the pain and anxiety of separation from people they loved. A few had experienced atrocities at first hand and wrote vividly of them. (I will return to these in chapter 9.)

For the majority, the worst experience was the NATO bombing of Foca's bridges in 1995. Accounts of this event often revealed anger at NATO (in phrases like *American killers*), pride in Serb courage and sacrifice (*since they existed, Serb people have fought for their survival; they fight to defend the dignity of the Serb people*), and the belief that *Muslim terrorists, Ustashe,* and *powerful foreign people* were to blame for starting the war. In some, the bitterness toward the other side was palpable. One fourteen-year-old boy wrote, *I had to run to cellars or shelters to hide from those threatening, hostile warriors who killed and slaughtered without mercy. They raped innocent girls. They did not care if it was a boy or a girl, baby or child; they enjoyed [killing], as if it was their hobby. They did different genocides and sometimes even drove trucks over innocent souls and killed them.*

A number referred to the *defense, stabilization,* or *liberation* of the town, or more vaguely to their current freedom and the situation being calmed down. One boy wrote, *Our town was full of grief, but it departed with our enemies. When the town was liberated, everything was easier and more cheerful. Although we grieved for the towns that were still occupied, since their liberation, only scars remain from those difficult times.* All this was to be expected. Yet the stories were almost completely silent about what achieving this "liberation" and "freedom" had entailed: the total disappearance of half the town's population, some twenty thousand people—their neighbors and schoolmates.

There were plenty of unspecific references to the destruction of the town, and to burned houses: *I cried when houses were burning,* wrote a fifteen-year-old girl. *I do not know why. I just found it difficult to watch a house burning, when people had put so much effort and hard work into it. Well, it was someone's house.*

But most stories gave no clue as to whose houses were burned. A few stated that most of the burned houses belonged to Serbs, although only three Foca children mentioned their own houses being burned (a loss of such significance one would expect it to be mentioned if it had occurred). In contrast, many lamented the destruction of the bridges by NATO. A thirteen-year-old girl wrote, *The black birds were making circles in the sky like hawks searching for prey. Why do they do that? Don't they ever think about their children? But it seems that children are the greatest victims of this war [. . .] blood and sweat with which our fathers built the bridges, they were no more, and all my memories were destroyed with them.* An older girl wrote, *I was waiting for the day when Father would take us back to Foca. I considered it the most beautiful town in the world. Then the bombing came. The awful roaring of planes and the destruction of bridges. I cried, not from fear, but because I felt sorry for the bridges on the Drina.*

Children referred to the bridges with poetic eloquence as the *spine of my town*, and as being in need of protection because they *connect people*. In contrast, only one story mentioned the destruction of a mosque. Many of the young writers described having had friends of all nationalities before the war, and missing friends in general. Only one hinted at what had occurred in the town and specifically mentioned Muslims being driven out. *But some didn't have anywhere to go, and they had to watch and listen to all those massacres, blood, shooting. It was awful. After a while, Muslims were expelled from Srbinje. Serbs came back to Srbinje.*

Although all of these young writers had been in school for at least six months when the war began, and a third of them had had two-and-a-half years in ethnically mixed classes, the majority did not mention missing Muslim schoolmates. The handful of exceptions was striking. A thirteen-year-old girl wrote:

> *Daddy explained to me what war really means. I asked him when we could go back home. He said we could not come back immediately because the town was destroyed and some houses burned down. We came back to the town and I thought all my friends would be there. My father and mother told me that I had lost my best friend, Lejla. I started to cry. I was sad because she would not be with me in school. I remembered Lejla and I still do. War took my best friend. It took my joy and happiness. Today I am happy, but I will never be like before the war, awful war. It destroyed all my nice dreams and everything I hoped for. I thought I would never lose Lejla, but it is all for nothing. Lejla is gone. I can still remember her face. She is still in my heart.*

But for the most part, it was as if, like the mosques, the Muslim population of the town had never existed.

By 1997, the ICTY had indicted nine individuals for their involvement in the ethnic cleansing of Foca. The charges included crimes against humanity, grave breaches of the Geneva Conventions, and violations of the laws or customs of war. The indictments and a Human Rights Watch report, all publicly available at that time, gave a different picture of what had happened in the town. I sat in my room beside the Drina, trying to tie together the dry language of the reports with the children's stories.[17]

Before the outbreak of war, the community had begun to split along ethnic lines. Bosnian Serbs formed a crisis committee, similar to those formed in other Serb autonomous regions in Bosnia, to plan and carry out the takeover of Foca. They inherited heavy weaponry from the JNA, which had withdrawn from Bosnia, and they organized assistance from paramilitary troops and reservists from neighboring Serbia and Montenegro. Many of these troops were thought to be under the control of Zeljko Raznatovic, also known as Arkan, and the Serbian Radical Party politician Vojislav Seselj, both notorious for other brutal mass murders and ethnic cleansing campaigns. Muslims also formed a crisis committee and armed themselves with light weapons. Between April 7 and April 17, 1992, Serb military forces occupied and took over Foca and rapidly defeated the lightly-equipped Muslim forces. Surrounding villages remained under siege by Serb troops until mid-July 1992.

The occupation was immediately followed by the destruction of Muslim shops, homes, and mosques, the forced expulsion of thousands of non-Serb inhabitants, and the detention of thousands of others. Most detainees were Muslim civilians, who had not been charged with any crime. Muslim men, including the ill and the handicapped, were kept in Foca prison, commonly known as the KP Dom, one of the largest prisons in the former Yugoslavia. Women, children, and the elderly were held in houses, apartments, and motels in Foca or in surrounding villages. Many of those detained were kept in inhumane conditions and terrorized, tortured, and beaten. Many died, or were summarily executed by Serb forces. Women and girls as young as twelve were systematically sexually assaulted.

The majority of detainees were exchanged or released during 1992 and 1993, but the KP Dom remained a detention facility until October 1994. Between 600 and 1,000 men were detained there, and 354 of them were still missing. Former prisoners told harrowing stories: "There was one guy hanging a meter off the floor at the wall. Ropes held him up there and on one side there was hot water falling on one of his shoulders and on the other side there was cold water and he was crying . . . It was really hot water and he was really suffering and he was screaming."[18]

Other prisoners watched guards carrying what seemed to be human bodies in blankets and dumping them in the Drina. A woman reported seeing, on repeated occasions, a yellow minivan driven out to the Tito sign above the river. Serbs then led out small groups of men, forced them to strip and hand over money and identification, and then murdered them with knives and threw their bodies into the Drina. Many Muslim residents of Foca fled to the hospital, thinking it would be safe. However, it had been taken over by Serb irregular forces, and the staff had to work in harsh conditions with little food or supplies. Muslim patients and staff were in effect imprisoned there, and many of the male patients were transferred to the KP Dom, from which some disappeared.[19] The Partizan Sports Hall near the police station in the center of town, and the high school where I now worked, had both been used as "rape camps":

> Many of the female detainees were subjected to sexual abuse during their detention at Foca High School. From the second day of their detention, every evening, groups of Serb soldiers sexually assaulted, including gang rape, some of the younger women and girls in classrooms or apartments in neighboring buildings. . . . The soldiers threatened to kill the women or the women's children if they refused to submit to sexual assaults. Women who dared to resist the sexual assaults were beaten. . . . The detainees lived in constant fear. Some of the sexually abused women became suicidal.[20]

Serb soldiers came every night. They told the women, aged between twelve and sixty, to strip and chose the ones they wanted. They often chose a mother and daughter together. One woman watched five soldiers rape an eighteen-year-old and was selected twice herself. While she was being raped by two men, one said, "You should have already left this town. We will make you have Serbian babies who will be Christians." Another was gang-raped in an outdoor stadium by soldiers: "I counted twenty-nine of them. Then I lost consciousness." Sometimes the girls were not brought back: "When they take you away they may kill you. So if you are raped, you feel lucky. At least you're alive."[21]

The stories seemed endless. Human Rights Watch reporters found Nihada in a refugee camp, lying sick on a cot, with bandages on her arms and inner thighs. She was a widow with three daughters between eleven and eighteen. They had lived near Foca. They had hidden in the forest for four months, but they had gone back to their house to get food when a soldier arrived with a piece of paper and said he had been ordered to kill her and her children. He put a grenade on the table and started loading his gun. "He then said 'Listen closely to what I am going to tell you. I am going to cut a Serbian Cross into your face and throw salt in your face.' I told him that he couldn't do that, and then he said he would tattoo me 'with sixty-four letters.' I told him he was crazy. He then got angry and said he was going to kill my children, that he was going to cut the fingers from my children's hands and make a necklace out of them. I got scared and I let him tattoo my body." Nihada removed the tape and showed the interviewers the hastily made tattoos saying "Rade—husband" and "Rade—don't forget me." After tattooing her, he had tried to shave a Serbian Cross on her eleven-year-old daughter's head.[22]

In September 1997 Radovan Karadzic was wanted by the ICTY for genocide and crimes against humanity. His picture was plastered all around the town. But these posters said, "Don't touch him," a warning from the current inhabitants of Foca to the international community not to arrest their wartime political leader. Not that any arrests seemed likely at that time. The French SFOR troops who patrolled the town had not arrested even one war criminal, although several lived and moved freely in the community. Dragan Gagovic, one of the first to be indicted for rape as a war crime, owned and ran the Krsma bar, where "Tuta," also known as Janko Janjic, one of the most notorious leaders of a paramilitary gang, regularly drank coffee. Tuta was filmed on the Hotel Zelengora terrace next door to the International Police Task Force (IPTF) headquarters, bragging of his crimes and showing off the hand grenades on his belt, while French NATO officers drank coffee nearby.

Others who had played leading roles in creating an "ethnically pure" municipality also retained their influence. Petko Cancar, who had arrived in Foca in early April 1992 and had led the crisis committee to, in his own words, *stop the threat of Islam* on the Drina, became mayor during the war and continued in that position until April 1997. Velibor Ostojic had been Karadzic's minister of information. Three days before the takeover in 1992, he had demanded at a public meeting that all the Muslims give up their weapons and concede that Foca was Serb territory. He told them to leave for a concentration camp at nearby Jabuka mountain "or else the last Muslim seed will be destroyed in Foca." In September 1997, he was made head of the commission for human rights in the Bosnian parliament. (Dusan's family told me this; they found it uproariously funny.) The literature professor Vojislav Maksimovic had apparently told local Bosnian Serbs that if they would not take up arms and start shooting Muslims, he would call for reinforcements from Serbia. He had been responsible for supplying weapons, training SDS members, and coordinating the irregulars. Now he was rector of the University of Republika Srpska. He kept a house in the Foca woods, an apartment in the town, and his influence in the local SDS.[23]

Neither Karadzic nor the SDS were particularly in favor by 1998. Unemployment in the town was running at 99 percent and local people were fed up with the increasingly visible corruption. They turned in large numbers to the Serb Radical Party (SRS), led by Vojislav Seselj, another tribunal indictee.

In the first months I spent in the town, I too was silent about these matters. There were many reasons for this. I wanted to hear about the children's own war experiences, their suffering, their losses, and the disruption of their lives, without putting them on the defensive. Their initial hostility toward me as a citizen of a NATO country was made clear in the messages a few attached to their stories: One child drew a hideous picture of a figure of indeterminate sex saying *I am a war criminal, the more Muslims the better.*

Somebody survived war and then you bombed us. Why? Dusan wrote. *You think that we suffered so little fear and grief, that you should give us more. Muslims, Croats, and Serbs took part in the war. Why did you bomb only us? Could you answer our questions?* Then at the bottom, he printed in capitals, SERB PEOPLE FROM REPUBLIKA SRPSKA ARE AGAINST WAR BUT ALSO AGAINST PEACE WITH SFOR. WE ARE FOR PEACE WITHOUT SFOR, WITHOUT PEACE STRANGERS, and finished it off with a diagram of the Serb symbol of the four Cs and *God protect the Serbs.* Interestingly, Dusan was keen to be interviewed. I knew that if I wanted to learn how these young people felt about ethnic cleansing, I had to let them take the lead.

Some of them did. They spontaneously mentioned the *liberation* or the *stabilization* of the town, and I asked them to explain what this was. With others, I asked open questions such as *What happened here?* Or the topic came up indirectly through discussion around related themes, such as whom they held responsible for the war or what they thought the war had achieved.

I began to notice that there were two quite distinct groups of children. Those in one group were curious. They took an active interest in these sorts of questions. They wanted to discuss why the conflict had taken place and what it had been about. Svetlana *just wonder[ed] why this happened. I ask myself, but I don't know the answers.* When Dragoljub Kunarac, one of those indicted for rape, handed himself over to The Hague that spring, she talked about it with her friends and asked her father what Kunarac had done. *He said he didn't know because he wasn't with them.* Mirko knew that all the Serbs were *fighting to kick out the Turks from the town.* His brother-in-law had told him the Turks wanted to kick out the Serbs, but the Serbs were stronger. He had seen *special units* come and burn down houses in the Turk village opposite his. He asked his father why the shooting and shelling had started in the first place. His father didn't know either and just told him, *It was stupid, it was a war.*

The children in the other, larger group distanced themselves from these events. They often discussed their personal wartime experiences in moving detail, but through verbal and nonverbal language they made clear that questions about what had happened in the town and why, were boring and unimportant. The distancing took different forms. Some were completely uninterested. Milica had no idea why the war had started, or for what her father had been fighting. She never discussed it with her parents and had no interest in doing so. She liked living in Foca, liked her new friends, and hoped things would get better. Ivana, despite having witnessed what happened to her friend Asra, told me she never spent time wondering why it happened. Nor did she appear very curious about Asra's fate.

Some, when asked, were able to give quite well-worked-out answers as to how they made sense of things, but were untroubled by gaps or inconsistencies in their knowledge and made clear that they had other things to think about. Stojan said he didn't know much because he wasn't in Foca during the war and didn't understand, but he thought the town had been *liberated very fast.* When I asked him what *liberation* meant he explained that the Muslim people were transported wherever they wanted to go by bus. He thought that was best for them because once they were defeated, there was nowhere in the town to which they could retreat. He had no idea what might have happened to them if they had stayed. *Maybe they signed this kind of a peace; they saw that a lot of people left, so that's why they left too*. All the same, he thought the town had been *better before*.

Marko had spent the war evacuated to a village. He had been in third grade then and was in high school now, a pleasant, diffident boy who wanted to become an engineer. He had returned to Foca six months after it was already *liberated*. I asked what he meant by liberated. *Everything was burned down. Everything was destroyed.* He felt awful, although his own house and his predominantly Serb neighborhood were undamaged. He noticed that it was mainly Muslim houses that were burned, including those of all his Muslim friends. They had already left.

How did you feel about that? I asked.

I don't know . . . I felt safer because there wasn't a threat anymore that somebody could meet you on the street or something . . .

What did you feel threatened by?

Well . . . He was silent.

Did you feel threatened before you left for the village?

No . . .

But when you came back you felt safer?

Yes.

Seeing that I was confused, he explained that he had not known he was in danger until he came back to Foca and saw what had happened. When he saw all the destruction, he realized that Muslims could have done the same to them, and then all of the Serbs would have been without their houses.

So were you pleased the Muslims had gone?

Well, I don't know.

Did you miss any of your friends?

Well . . . partly. Later it passed.

Fifteen-year-old Susana lived near the center of town. Her parents were professionals and she was doing well in high school. She liked listening to music and told me her favorite film star was Richard Gere. She wrote in moving detail of the death of her cousin:

I can still remember some moments I experienced in that awful war. It is as if I am watching now: my mother crying when she heard the

*words, "Your cousin Mihajlo has been killed and his remains could
not be removed from that furious battle." I felt grief in my heart. To
know that he would not come again, with wet shoes, which my mother
would have dried carefully, made some special food, and taken care of
him like a sister for her brother. It was both difficult and painful.*

Susana made a clear distinction between these kinds of details from the
war, in which she took an interest, and those in which she had none. She
watched war stories on television, particularly when they were about people who lost close relatives. But she had no explanations for, and no interest
in, what had happened to Muslims in Foca. *I don't know. They didn't like
being together, they wanted something,* she responded vaguely when I asked
how she made sense of the war. *It's all finished. They wanted to separate.*

Everybody wanted to separate? I asked her.

I guess so. I didn't follow that.

She never discussed such questions with her parents or her teachers or
followed the topic on TV. The news bored her. She preferred movies and
soap operas like the one about an Australian high school. There were no
tensions or troubles in school before the war. She had had friends of both
nationalities, as was *normal.*

Did you have a best friend? I asked.

I had Vasvija. She's Muslim; she's not here anymore.

At the beginning of the war, there had been a panic and everyone had
left. Her family had taken her to the village for ten days and then they had
come back.

When was the last time you saw your best friend? I asked a bit later.

*It was in the school. She wasn't my best friend. I also had the other friends
. . . all those who were Muslims left, but it didn't stress me or shock me.*

Do you know why they left? I could see from her expression that Susana
was already a little bored with the conversation.

I didn't.

So can you explain it?

Susana looked incredulous. It was as if I had asked "What color is but-
ter?" I apologized. I was an outsider, I said, perhaps these things were
obvious to her, but I didn't want to rely on what I read in newspapers and
reports. She gave a little laugh. *Because they were other nationalities. We
just split up, separated.*

How was it when you came back to Foca?

Two houses next to mine, Muslim houses, burned down. Actually one, and then when I came back, the other one. She had watched the second one burn. *I could see other places, houses, burning. Every night some house was burning.*

She did not know who had set her neighbor's house alight—probably outsiders who had come from somewhere else. She had heard about the house burning when she was in the village, so she had expected to see it when she returned. *I wasn't very upset.*

Did you know the neighbors who owned that house? Did it matter?

Yes, I knew them. They were our next-door neighbors. But they had left at the beginning. So I knew they wouldn't come back. She had particularly liked the small girl, who had visited her often. But before the war the girl's parents and grandparents had stopped her from coming around so often, and when she had come, she had talked about the SDA. Nothing unpleasant, just stuff about political parties that Susana thought the family must have told her to say.

So it didn't matter that the house was burned down?

No.

You didn't care?

She gave another small laugh. *No.*

How would you have felt if it had been your house that had been burned down?

I would have felt sorry. Everybody is sorry when their house is burning.

Not all the Muslims had left by the time Susana returned to Foca. *Those who stayed longer, they were forced to leave.* She did not know how. She had not seen.

Susana had not found the NATO bombing particularly frightening because she knew they were aiming at military targets. She had been far enough away, and felt secure enough, to watch from her windows. She thought the destruction of the bridges made the town *awful*. I asked if it was just the bridges, or if the earlier destruction had upset her as well.

It was mostly Muslim houses that were burning.

And mosques presumably?

Yes.

Was that a problem? Did you mind?

No.

When it came to discussing the question of responsibility for the war, a pattern began to emerge. The teenagers who had shown the most curiosity about events were also the most evenhanded, tending to hold both sides, or no one at all, responsible for the conflict. Svetlana did not blame anybody and was not angry with anyone. Some of the disengaged teenagers, in contrast, tended to see Muslims as more to blame. Milica was sure that Turks had started the war, although she had no idea why. Stojan believed *Muslims wanted to have the power, to have the president of Bosnia.* Others blamed outsiders, such as the West, who they believed wanted to weaken Yugoslavia or destroy it.

Almost all told me they had worked these things out for themselves by *watching television* or *listening to adults talking.* When the more curious children had tried discussing the war directly, they had received unsatisfactory answers and given up. Some sensed that it was not something to be discussed. Divac, a high school boy who had moved from Sarajevo in the first year of the war after his father had been injured on the line, said he *listened and overheard things; I thought things out for myself. I didn't consult anybody or ask anybody. My parents didn't want to worry me with that and I didn't ask them.* Others wanted to protect their parents. The war had taken Jovan by surprise. His parents had a shop in town, and they had sent him to the village when the courier came to warn them. He had asked questions at first, *then I didn't want to ask anymore. I knew this was hard for them. . . . They have their own problems.* He hadn't wanted to upset them. Similarly, Stojan said, *They don't want to talk about that.* Dusan was an exception in that he and his parents had often had lengthy discussions. But as time passed, he too was concerned with protecting his parents and himself from distress: *I don't want to remind my parents and I don't want to remember what happened.*

Their parents agreed. They wanted to protect their children, or thought the children were not interested and had other worries. *We don't wish the children to see what we saw,* one father told me. *She isn't interested, she is interested in books.* Another, contradictory explanation was that *the children know everything* because *they saw for themselves.*

This mutual silence covered an unspoken, shared understanding of events. Svetlana's mother sounded as bewildered as her daughter: *It's hard to explain. I don't even know myself how I explained things to her.* Ivana echoed her mother's experience at the bus station with the elderly Muslim man when she said the problems had begun *with people not respecting each other, they were not saying good afternoon to each other.* She shared her parents' view that it was *us or them.* Her father had fought to prevent Foca being *their territory, to stop them occupying it so we would have to move from here.* None of the families denied that some terrible things had happened to Muslims in Foca, although many felt that the Muslims and the Western media had exaggerated events or had not understood the danger faced by Serbs that had precipitated the conflict. All were convinced that *kicking Muslims out,* as Jovan's mother put it, had made them safer. *If we stayed together, no matter whether it was Serbs or Muslims, it would be more dead people,* Ivana's father said. *That's how it is: Muslims are running away from here, somewhere else it's Serbs, somewhere else, Croats.*

The parents, like most of the children, distanced themselves from these events in a number of ways. Many told me simply that they had not been present when the worst excesses occurred. Women were with children out of town, men were on the line in another area. They thought the real crimes were committed by *outsiders, criminals,* and *psychopaths.* Many described personal assistance they had given to help friends escape and the danger involved in doing so. Many Muslims had left of their own accord right at the beginning, Nikola's parents assured me, and it was only those with nowhere to go who had stayed. They themselves had helped a family get to Montenegro and intervened to get the husband of one of the daughters out of prison.

Why were most of the men put in prison? I asked.

I don't know how it was regulated; men were in prison. The same as Serbs were in prison in Gorazde and they don't know why they were in prison.

So were any Muslims actually forced to leave?

They knew how they would live if they stayed here, Nikola's father replied.

Nobody trusted anyone, his wife added.

I asked how those who did stay had been treated, but they said they only knew about the ones they had protected, who had therefore been alright. It had been very dangerous to protect people, so no one knew about it.

Nikola's mother had worked in the hospital. She told me that things had carried on there *just like before the war. We worked together. My boss stayed there. Every night we had dinner together, we were drinking coffee, laughing together. When he left, he was crying.*

Why did he leave?

Because he was Muslim. But nobody touched him in the hospital.

He had to go, Nikola's father explained. *It was safer for him.*

But the staff treated him fairly, Nikola's mother said. *Everyone got along well, he didn't have to go because of the staff. He had absolutely no fear of me.* They were anxious that I should understand and continued to speak in turn:

It was not an organized army.

Nobody knew what night could bring.

Or who could come into an apartment with a knife. We criticized the Serbs who stayed with the Muslims, and they criticized Muslims who stayed with us. Asking them why they were staying, why don't you come to us? Muslims, Serbs, Croats. It was like a nightmare.

Dusan's father felt aggrieved that the West had not recognized the Serbs' restraint. *Serbs could have liquidated all the Muslims on that road if it had been to their advantage. You drive from Ustikolina to Foca all the time. It's ideal for destroying people on foot. Two guns and nobody would have got to Gorazde alive. But the Serbs had nothing to gain. . . . To be honest, it's a pity they didn't do it because they shouldn't have let them reach Gorazde. To be honest, I think it's a great mistake that we didn't exterminate them. We had the possibility, but the commanders and the people in power, parliament didn't let us. And now they are called war criminals!*

All the families set the ethnic cleansing of Foca in the context of what they perceived as a completely symmetrical war. *It was us or them*, I was told repeatedly. If Serbs had not acted preemptively, Muslims would have attacked with equal brutality. As evidence of this they mentioned the occasions when Muslims were known to have attacked and committed atrocities, such as the concentration camp of Celebici near the town of Konjic, which was run by Bosnian government forces and held Serb prisoners, and where, according to Human Rights Watch, "prisoners were bestially beaten in the Celebici barracks and many died as a result." There was the execution of around sixty civilians in the village of Bratunac near Srebrenica. And after Bosnian government forces had partly lifted the siege of Gorazde in 1992, they had attacked several hundred Serb civilians who had left the town by bus. Three hundred were alleged to have been killed by Muslim machine-gun fire.[24]

Many families had experiences that confirmed their view of an entirely equal conflict. Stojan's relatives in Sarajevo had been unable to get out of the city, and were forced to do manual work on the front line. His father did not believe many Serbs had stayed willingly in that city. Dusan's uncle had been imprisoned by Muslims and had seen his house burned down in Foca at the beginning of the war. If the Muslims had not been pushed out of the town, he would surely have been killed. Four of the children said their own homes had been burned. The most horrifying event was the massacre of at least sixty-five Serb civilians, mostly elderly people and children, in the neighboring village of Josanice. Some were relatives or friends of the families I interviewed.

In early 1998, while I was still in Bosnia, the Bosnian press accused Foca's primary school headmaster Simo Mojevic, in his role as a member of the Ustikolina crisis committee, of having supervised the ethnic cleansing of Ustikolina and of involvement in the disappearance of fifty Muslim men. There were two witnesses, and the charges were repeated in the Human Rights Watch report.[25]

Throughout my stay in Foca, Mojevic had done everything possible to help my work. No international agencies were working in the town at that time except the bureaucracies of the Organization for Security and Cooperation in Europe (OSCE) and the UN. A youth club run by foreign aid workers had been closed down by the local authorities. However, the headmaster told me that he ran an *open school*, even if Foca was not an *open town*. He provided space for me to work, encouraged parents to meet with me, and gave class time to parts of the project. He confirmed the heterodoxy of his views by boldly displaying a calendar with a photo of Biljana Plavsic, a hard-line nationalist and a former close colleague of Karadzic who had just been elected president of Republika Srpska. She was being courted and supported by the West for her apparent support of the Dayton Peace Agreement and for her criticism of her former colleagues. Many in Foca despised her for bringing disunity to the Serbs yet again.

The headmaster invited me to his house for the evening. He asked if I believed the accusations against him. I said I felt quite unable to judge, and that it was not my job to do so. He wanted me to hear his story of what had happened in the war, and he poured it out over rakia. It was a long and complicated tale of killings by Muslims, betrayal of Serbs in the Second World War, and massacres by Serbs in response; of deals done and broken between local units on opposing sides and corruption and self-interest by all parties during the recent war; and of criminal profiteering and self-interest since then. He was convinced that outsiders—Americans, the CIA, the Vatican—had started the war for their own interests. Perhaps Milosevic was even an American agent? Why would local people want to break up the land of his grandfathers? He wanted to make clear that his only concern had been to defend his homeland: Yugoslavia.

Mojevic distanced himself from the ethnic cleansing of the region in the ways that I had begun to find familiar. I had made a list:

> *Minimizing:* it was not as bad as people said
> *Scapegoating:* others were responsible
> *Absenteeism:* I was not there at the time
> *Equalizing:* they were just as bad, guilty, and criminal as we were

He did not deny that atrocities had occurred. Over a few days, he had watched old people and children fleeing Foca: *Everyone who could move was going in carts or walking to Gorazde.* He had seen Serb soldiers join in the looting of Muslim houses in Foca: *It was a rich part. Because Muslims didn't take everything.* He thought the accounts were exaggerated: *They said people were killed, butchered. . . . Something happened, but not even 10 percent of what people said in fear. Probably frightened people made things up because it's difficult to leave your house, especially for older people.* He blamed Muslim journalists for exaggerating the threat, for saying things like *a thousand Chetniks are coming.*

When the main atrocities were perpetrated in Ustikolina, he said, he had not been present. *It was paramilitaries and irregulars from Serbia or Montenegro. People released from prison or from hospitals for the insane. They killed the best people who wanted to live with us.* He thought it was *the greatest tragedy. They also killed Serbs who wanted to protect those people.* He had sent a group of women, including his oldest sister and a few cousins, to protect his neighbors, but they had been threatened as well, so he was unable to do anything. There was no command or organization so everyone did what they wanted without telling anyone else. *They burned all the houses. . . . They killed innocent people inside the houses, and they took truckloads from the houses they robbed. Mosques fell down. The extremists came out on both sides.*

He told me he had ensured that no atrocities occurred under his command. On the section of the road where he was in control, he had forbidden his men to shoot any fleeing civilians. On one occasion, he had helped a group of elderly Muslim people trapped in a village to escape. On another, he had saved two Muslim boys. Like all those I interviewed, he set these events in the context of all the equally terrible things that had happened to Serbs in the war, such as at Josanice, and the brutality and treachery of some Muslims.

Instead of just listening as usual, perhaps from weariness or too much rakia, I challenged him, pointing out that while no one denied the atrocities committed by Muslims, this insistence on the symmetry of the war was hard to accept, given that Serbs had taken control of 70 percent of the territory in the first two months of fighting. During that time approximately a million people had been displaced from their homes, and several tens of thousands of people, mostly Bosnian Muslims, had been killed. The headmaster replied that this was simply because Muslims had not had enough guns, because of President Izetbegovic's foolishness in removing Muslims from the JNA. This rather undermined his earlier insistence on symmetry, but he did not appear to notice.

I told him there was no equivalent on the Bosnian side to what had happened during the fall of Srebrenica. The headmaster's wife, who had been listening to our conversation in between serving enormous quantities of food, interrupted asking me exactly what had happened in Srebrenica. So I told her of the organized murder of at least seven thousand men, by soldiers under the command of General Mladic, and the forced expulsion of the rest of the population, some twenty-five thousand people, from the town. She and her husband both listened quietly, and when I had finished she looked deeply upset. *If it is true, it is terrible,* she said, and I had the sense that she was hearing this story for the first time. *We lived very near to the Partizan Sports Hall,* said the headmaster. *Believe me, we knew nothing of what happened in there.* Then we had to stop talking because Red Star was playing a football match on TV.

The more time I spent in Foca, the more I became aware that the war had reduced each family's world to their immediate neighborhood: relatives, friends, how to survive, with no attention to anything else, not even what was going on in the house next door. The media continued to play a key role. In England, I had been able to watch or listen to reports on the entire war from almost every part of the country. After the takeover of the local transmitter at the beginning of the war, families in Foca could only get Serbian radio (and Serbian television when there was electricity). This always showed Serb forces as fighting for freedom and to protect themselves from Muslim forces. Muslims were fighting a religious war and were intent on forcing Serbs to belong to an Islamic state. The Serb side never attacked: *The Muslim authorities are holding Sarajevo under siege from within* was typical. A single broadcast from Foca in August 1992 mentioned *Alija's wanton hordes, Ustashe chauvinists, Islamic chauvinists, and Islamic fundamentalists.* There was no discussion of the strategic goals of the war, no maps to show who controlled what, no pictures of the destruction inflicted by Serb forces, and the only victims ever shown were Serb.[26]

So it was not surprising that many Serb children believed the Serbs had suffered the most violence in the war, in places such as Josanice or Celebici. The majority had no idea what had happened in Gorazde, just up the road. *How could I know?* one asked me in some irritation. When a child had first-hand knowledge and did not depend on adults or the media, this made a significant difference: Jovan told me, *I was only watching one side,* but went on to say that he thought Gorazde had suffered more. A gun emplacement near his house had been used to shell Gorazde, so he knew that *there was the shelling of the town,* and that *in the Muslim part I know they had very bad living conditions, they didn't have food for some time.* He did not know why they were shelling.

The war was not symmetrical.[27] There was no organized ethnic cleansing of Gorazde. The prewar population of the municipality was approximately fifty-seven thousand, of whom 70.2 percent were Muslim and 26.2 percent Serb. In the city, there were about ninety six hundred Muslims and fifty six hundred Serbs. Gorazde was of crucial strategic importance in any attempt to create an ethnically homogeneous Serb area in eastern Bosnia. It lay on the main road between the cities of Foca and Visegrad, both of which were rapidly and effectively "cleansed" of their non-Serb populations in the first months of the war. Gorazde also possessed a large armaments factory, located in the western half of the city. The majority of Bosnian Serb residents left Gorazde in the weeks and days before the outbreak of fighting. They believed the local Serb leaders' assertion that they faced an Islamic takeover and would be killed if they stayed. As in Foca, most Serb families sent women and children out of the town immediately prior to the fighting. At the beginning of May 1992, Serb men withdrew to prearranged positions and began shelling the city. Bosnian Serb forces hoped to take the city as rapidly as they had taken neighboring Foca and Visegrad. Then Serb families would be able to return.

They miscalculated. First, unlike the situation in Foca and Visegrad, there was no place to which Gorazde's non-Serb population could retreat. Second, although poorly armed, the Muslim population included a larger number of men of fighting age because of the influx of refugees from the neighboring areas. And third, in the previous weeks the less-trusting local authorities had refused the offer of JNA "protection." Thus, indigenous Bosnian Serb forces at this point lacked JNA support. The "siege" continued for three and a half years. For the first four months the bombardment was intense, then in September 1992 the Bosnian Serb forces were pushed back and a narrow corridor was created over the mountains (the Grebak route), allowing communication between Gorazde and Sarajevo. Shelling and sniping continued throughout the four years and further offensives occurred intermittently. The worst offensives were in the spring of 1993 when the Grebak route was lost, and in 1994 when General Mladic attempted to storm the town. Bosnian Muslim fighters also launched offensives out of the enclave. On occasion, they were responsible for serious abuses of human rights, such as the destruction of villages and the massacre of civilians. Human Rights Watch states that these actions appear to have been perpetrated by individuals, rather than as part of a premeditated plan.[28]

After the closing of the route over Grebak in 1993, the town of Gorazde became completely dependent upon its own resources and what could be obtained from airdrops. Convoys carrying humanitarian aid over land were repeatedly blocked by the Serbs. Electricity, which had come from Foca, was stopped, and the fresh water supply was disrupted by shelling. Around seventy thousand people were trapped in the city, all subject to the same harsh living conditions.

The Serbs who remained were those with nowhere to go, those who had not managed to get themselves exchanged and those who did not wish to join the Bosnian Serb nationalist enterprise. Regardless of the reasons, many of them suffered at the hands of neighbors and some sections of the local authorities, particularly during offensives against the city.[29]

Sladjana and her mother stayed because they could not make up their minds about going, and because they had no money and no offers from anyone to take them to safety, whereas it seemed that many of their neighbors had both. Sladjana's mother found it difficult. She felt attacked by both sides. When the shelling was particularly intense, one neighbor said she was going to kill them. Another threatened her in the shelter, saying *If there are any Serbs in this building we should kill them.* She had no desire to quarrel. *None of our neighbors helped.*

How can you say that, Mum, when neighbors came with food and coffee? Sladjana said.

That was not help! That was not saving my life!

Sladjana turned to me. *We never had any complications, and they never mistreated us. They just didn't like making conversation because of what was happening.*

That is mistreatment, her mother interrupted.

But some Serbs were kicked out of their homes and put in some kind of prison, weren't they? I asked. This was what I had heard.

Refugees came, Sladjana replied, *people who had suffered and been kicked out themselves and seen death. Some of them wanted to take Serb flats by force. I found some people I knew and we took them in, but I could see by the way they looked at us that they wanted us to get out and give the flat to them. There were around twelve people here for two years. Then they found another place.*

She explained that the authorities had warned the Serbs in 1992 and 1993 that it was not safe to stay in their homes and had moved them into collective centers in town. Their own neighbors, though, had insisted they stay in their flat. Others had moved, leaving their property vulnerable to takeover, looting, and burning. Furthermore, many Serb houses had been in the area that Serb forces recaptured in 1994. These soldiers were not local and in ignorance had burned Serbs' houses.[30] I knew the area, a pretty rural suburb on a small road on the eastern side of the Drina, winding up to Cajnice, with the same overgrown unkempt gardens and the same deserted silence as in Donje Polje.

Savo Heleta's family chose to stay because they "refused to believe that people who had grown up together in peace and friendship, had gone to the same schools, spoke the same language and listened to the same music, could overnight be blinded by ethnic hatred and start to brutally kill one another." Unfortunately, this did not protect them from the anger of vengeful neighbors or brutal mistreatment by officials. In a disturbing memoir about his childhood in Gorazde, Savo described how his family and many other Serbian ones were sacked from their jobs, threatened with execution, made to do forced labor, and starved.[31] Savo's father was clear as to the reason.

> Everyone in this city is suffering, but we are also seen by Muslims as the enemy. Muslim extremists, hit squads, and even the police and government officials have threatened to kill us. The only reason we are oppressed is because we are Serbs. Many innocent people have already been killed just because they were Serbs and remained in their homes.

Savo described how a drunken local Muslim called Rasim

> . . . interrogated my parents for more than four hours; my sister Sanja and I remained silent and still between our mom and dad on the couch. Dressed in a green camouflage uniform, Rasim sat on a chair, smoking one cigarette after another. His machine gun rested near him on the dining room table, the gun barrel pointed toward us. I watched his hand move toward the AK-47 whenever an answer didn't satisfy him. Fondling the barrel, sliding his finger toward the trigger.

Rasim kept insisting the family had weapons and were spies, signaling the enemy. "Better you admit guilt now, rather than later. I know people who are ready to take you to the river. A bullet in the head, they roll you into the Drina, and then you float all the way to Serbia."

Just like Samir, imprisoned by Serbs in another part of the city, Savo had many moments when he was sure they would all be killed. Yet with remarkable empathy, he recorded what was happening to those around him. For example, in response to NATO air strikes against Serb forces in the spring of 1994, "the Serbian forces, incensed by the NATO attack, went on to brutally and indiscriminately bomb the city."

> The Serbian snipers often shot at everyone—women, children, and old people—even though they were located on the hilltops

not far from the city center and could probably distinguish
between civilians and soldiers. I saw with my own eyes old
women getting shot while scurrying across the street with water
canisters in their hands.

Veljko, who had worked as a factory manager, had also chosen to stay.
His experiences were somewhat different. He voted in the Bosnian government referendum in February 1992 because he wanted a unified Bosnia.
He was convinced that from the outset, Milosevic was bent on the division
of Bosnia, and for him the choice was simple: a divided Bosnia or a unified,
independent one. Some fellow Serbs called him and said that if he voted he
would be killed. He thought it was intimidation like this that had stopped
most of his fellow Bosnian Serbs from voting. *They went into Serb homes
and said if you vote you will get shot. The only people who mistreated me
were Serbs.* He showed me two repaired walls that had been destroyed by
shells, and the holes of more than 250 sniper bullets. In the 1994 offensive,
Serbs called him by name from across the Drina, saying they were coming
to get him. But he acknowledged that many of his Serb neighbors suffered.
He estimated that some two to three hundred Serbs had been murdered.

The children I interviewed in Gorazde were not silent about their Serb
friends' leaving. For many of them, the mysterious disappearance of children from school in the month before the war was what first made them
aware that something was not right in their town. *One day two Serb children would be missing, the next day another one, until all of them escaped,*
Suada recalled. She had been in third grade. Nedjad, another third grader,
had had a Serb best friend: *He said he was going to visit his grandparents
and he would be back in a month. I didn't see any change on their faces. All
of them left just before the war.* Jasmin had also had Serb friends in that
class. He had noticed no tension, but *they left. They ran away [. . .] before
the war started. They didn't say anything.* Ten-year-old Iris, like Amela,
had been jealous: *They said they were going on vacation, and I said "Oh,
why couldn't I do the same thing?" I didn't understand why they were leaving.* Iris was in her second year of primary school. *My teacher was a Serb
but I really loved him very much, regardless of his nationality. He stayed
until the day before the war and then suddenly he just seemed to disappear.*
Iris's parents were professional people living in the center of town. Serb

neighbors warned them: *It was strange because almost all our Serb friends said to my father, you should leave, but they didn't explain anything. Why should we go? Actually, we were supposed to leave, but then my father decided not to go, and I didn't want to leave either. I couldn't imagine living somewhere else. Mother's family came to stay with us and they were refugees from Foca, so we couldn't just go and leave them.* The relatives brought tales of their experiences. *In the area where they lived in Foca, they used to come to their house every night to look for weapons. And they threatened them, if you don't leave, something like that, we will kill you, and then the shooting started there, and so they left. When it started in Foca, I knew the same thing was going to happen here, and sometimes I thought maybe it would be better if we went somewhere else, but anyway it is best to be at home.* Senad's aunt had a Serb friend who warned her that there would be a war. His parents sent him out of the country to Spain with the aunt and her children. They thought of going too, but they had good jobs in the factory and delayed until it was too late.

Many of the Serb adults had simply departed like the children. Jasmin's neighbors suddenly got in their cars and disappeared. Then he noticed Serbs building barricades behind his house. *Then I heard that some young Serbs left Gorazde and went to the hills; only old Serbs stayed in my neighborhood. Then the war started. They started shooting. We started to take shelter. They started to shell. It was like that all through the war.* The shelling was so intense in the first months that *we couldn't move, we couldn't go on the streets, and that's why, to protect the center of the town, the Muslims drove them far away from the town.* The siege of the city was lifted on September 18—*the date of the liberation of Gorazde,* Jasmin called it—the same day that his father was killed in the fighting.

In contrast to the situation in Foca, where Serb children had returned to a relatively calm city, *free* of Muslims, for Muslim children in Gorazde, the departure of their Serb neighbors from town did not signify the disappearance of Serbs from their lives or the end of fighting in the city. On the contrary, they now discovered that the parents of their former school friends were the ones shelling them from the hills.

As in Foca, I asked a large sample of children aged thirteen to fifteen to write anonymous stories for me; 155 children did so in Gorazde. The vast majority gave graphic and powerful descriptions of being shelled or shot at. Most of these described witnessing death or injury, often of more than one person, often of family or friends. Almost a third of the children told of losing a close relative or friend. More than a quarter wrote of being displaced. Many wrote of the harsh living conditions. Ten recounted having been wounded themselves. A few, like this thirteen-year-old boy, wrote of their personal experiences of imprisonment or ethnic cleansing.

> *In 1992, I was a prisoner in Rogatica. I was imprisoned with my mama, sister, grandma, and grandpa, who were killed near the house. My father ran away so they could not catch him. He fled to the forest with his friends who had no guns. The Serbs drove us down the street, which was full of people from that street. They took all of us to the priest's house. We did not eat for three days. On the fourth day they brought us beans that were not cooked very well, just water and beans. We were there for ten days. Then the Serbs came and told us we were going to a school where there were lots of people from Rogatica. In that place they raped girls and women, separated children from mothers, brothers from sisters. . . . We got in a bus and were driving along. As we were driving, we went past the street that would have taken us to that school. Then the driver told us we were going to be exchanged in Zepa. That was easier.*

There was an interesting silence in many of these stories as well. Foca children, although mostly absent during the initial fighting, had mostly been present when NATO bombed the town, and usually identified the perpetrator by name, accompanied by understandable anger. However, although the majority of Gorazde children were in town throughout the bombardment, only a third of them mentioned an aggressor, often in the matter-of-fact manner illustrated above, and half of these simply used the term "aggressor" without identifying the person as Chetnik or Serb: *The war started in 1992. My family and I went into the basement. We only came out during the night. The aggressor from the hills was shooting a lot of projectiles around the town and people.*

Most of the stories were dominated by concrete descriptions of horrifying events that seemed to come out of nowhere: inexplicable and bewildering catastrophes. They started abruptly: *One morning grenades woke me up . . .*

They often mentioned injuries and multiple losses, as this thirteen-year-old girl did.

The shell fell suddenly when I was in front of my building with my friends. One of my friends was killed and the other and I were wounded. We were in the hospital a long time. When I came out of the hospital, I visited my friend Mirela. I saw she was without her leg. I was so sad. I heard some shelling on my way back. My father told me some time later that one shell hit Mirela's flat and she was killed. I was so upset because she was my best friend. We had been together in school, at the same desk. I was sad for a long time. I wish she were alive and we could be together now. But that is destiny. I will never forget that day. It is always on my mind.

Or, like this thirteen-year-old boy, they mentioned witnessing terrible events.

One day the war started in my town. There were a lot of shells falling down. There were many dead people who were killed on the street next to me. I was on the street one day when the shooting stopped a little bit, with my best friend. [. . .] We were playing the game Ganje. My best friend was killed by a sniper on the way back. I and the other friend were next to him. We took him in our arms and we put him behind the house, trying to hide ourselves. We were very sorry for our friend. Then we went home. [. . .] I was wounded at the same place a few days later. I was wounded in my leg. It was very painful for me and I thought about my friend who was killed next to me. The war impressed my life with many sad things.

In at least two-thirds of the written stories, the children made no mention of the perpetrators of these actions. I would suggest three reasons for this silence. First, the events themselves are so numerous and overwhelming that describing them filled the allocated time and was given more importance than explanations of responsibility. Second, one child mentions "destiny." Such mentions were not frequent in either the written narratives or the interviews, but stoical acceptance of death is part of Muslim culture and faith, and was mentioned quite often by parents. Third, this silence makes sense in the context of the Muslim families' complete lack of preparedness for the war. In their anxiety to prove that they had no aggressive intent, the Muslim officials in the tripartite government had constantly reassured their own people that there was no danger and would be no war.

Even after Karadzic famously threatened the Muslim population with annihilation, on the night of October 14, 1991, Izetbegovic said, "I want to tell the people of Bosnia-Herzegovina not to be afraid because there will be no war. . . . Therefore, sleep peacefully." Many Gorazde families, when I talked to them six years later, saw this as a great failing on his part. It was the main reason why they held their own politicians equally responsible with the Serbs and Croats for the conflict.[32]

The writer Mark Thompson suggests that the Bosnian state media, particularly RTVBiH (Bosnian state radio and television), strongly influenced by its hard-line communist past, was determined to play an "impartial" role in covering both the wars in Slovenia and Croatia and the events leading up to the Bosnian war. Being impartial meant presenting all parties as equally responsible for the descent into violence without analyzing the context or the details of their positions. The journalist Zlatko Dizdarevic noted in his Sarajevo diary for June 1992: "Journalists from the International Press Center want to know 'when will Bosnia-Herzegovina's television start to use a terminology about this war that describes what is actually taking place?' (In the interests of moderation, Bosnian TV journalists have avoided naming the aggressor or any of the parties involved in the conflict.)" Thus in contrast to the Serbian media, which had for the previous three years been warning Serbs of an Islamic threat and reminding them of their unresolved historic grievances, the Bosnian state media had left Muslims psychologically unarmed.[33] This explains Narcisa's family's readiness to trust the JNA guarantees about security in Visegrad despite refugees' experience to the contrary, and the disbelief that anything could happen in Gorazde. It also explains the perception, revealed in many of the children's narratives, of an anonymous "war" that erupted out of nowhere. This perception altered with time and hindsight, as my interviews with the children made clear.

When I discussed responsibility and explanations for the war with the Gorazde children, I could distinguish two groups, as I had in Foca. Those in one group were curious and wanted to understand more about the conflict, and those in the other group were less interested in these questions and distanced themselves. Here, in contrast to what I found in

Foca, the distinction between engagement and distancing appeared to be related to the amount of violence the children had suffered during the war. The children who had not been present during the worst of the siege, because they had been refugees abroad or living in a safer area, had more distance. The children who had experienced the most violence were the most engaged in trying to make sense of what had happened to them. Moreover, again in contrast to Foca, the children in the distanced group were much more evenhanded about assigning responsibility for the war, while those engaged in looking for meaning ascribed greater responsibility to the Serbs.

Suada, for example, left for Germany with her family a few days after her Serb neighbors disappeared, and returned a year after the war was over. In Germany, she had watched television news and worried about her grandparents and friends. Now back in Gorazde, she was not interested in discussing the war at all. She was friendly and happy to talk to me, especially about her current life. I tried all sorts of approaches:

When you try to make sense of what has happened, what explanations do you come up with?

I don't know really.

So how will you explain it to your children when you're grown up?

I don't know.

Nor was she very interested in other people's explanations: *Nobody really says anything about that, but the Muslims say the Serbs are guilty and Serbs say the Muslims are guilty.*

And do you have an opinion on that?

No.

Do your parents?

I don't talk to my parents about it.

Because? You're not interested?

I'm not interested in that.

In contrast, the children with the worst experiences were the most interested in making sense of them. Amela, who had escaped from her house thanks to the decency of her Serb neighbors, then spent most of the war being shelled, and had lost close friends and relatives, thought it would be best if people forgot the war, but she herself wanted to understand why it had happened. Her explanation was that *Serbs wanted to live by themselves [. . .] because they don't like living together. I don't know why.*

But I also blame both sides because our people killed their people also, as well as them killing us. However, she thought the Serbs had begun it: *Well at least they started the shooting, I don't know about politics.*

Admira, who had fled her home and whose father had been killed, thought a great deal about why the war had happened. *It's interesting because if you look at the purpose of the war, I mean you wouldn't like to have it again.* She thought that *Serbs wanted us to be under their religion, and they wanted us all to be only one nation, they didn't want to have Muslims and Croats and other nationalities who live in Bosnia. [. . .] Those who would accept their religion, they would keep them, and those who wouldn't accept being Serbs, they would kill them.*

Why would they want to do that? I asked. But as with most Gorazde children, the logic underlying this plan escaped her.

I don't know, she replied.

As for Muslims, according to Admira, *Muslims wanted peace and freedom. [. . .] They wanted to be free and not to have war; they wanted the situation to be as it was before the war.*

Did they want Serbs to become Muslims?

No.

Admira had worked things out for herself. Gorazde children did not discuss the war very much with their parents. *Nobody wants to talk about that subject,* Amela told me. Those who wanted to know more listened in on adult conversations and the news, but avoided asking direct questions, for the same sorts of reasons as had children in Foca. They did not want to bother their parents or remind them of unpleasant times. Nedjad said, *Maybe they wouldn't know how to answer me exactly because I think the war came like a surprise for them too.*

Parents agreed that they did not know what to say. Samir's parents told me that he sometimes asked about his Serb friends, but they didn't know how to answer. *I mean I really don't know where his old friends are and what happened to them,* his mother said. Like quite a few other families in both cities, they underrated their son's curiosity. *I never explain to him, and I believe he doesn't know,* said his father, who thought it *better not to talk about that, so that he doesn't hate all the Serbs or all the Croats. Because I admit that there were some good Serbs and Croats in the war. I mean I don't want to create any hatred toward these people.*

Many parents felt that their children already knew as much as they needed to know. *They were old enough to see everything that happened, and they know who was attacking, so we don't need to explain anything to them,* Armin's father told me. There were more important things to do than discuss the past. Now it was time to move on.

6

WHAT COUNTRY IS THIS?

We urged . . . that the country be called, simply, "Bosnia and Herzegovina" . . . "Giving up the word Republic is giving up nothing" . . . Owen told Izetbegovic. The second point was more difficult. "That name [Republika Srpska] is like the Nazi name," Izetbegovic said. We replied that the name meant nothing, and that the governing—the overriding—sentence was the preceding one that recognized Bosnia-Herzegovina as a country "with its present borders"—that is a single country of which R.S. was a part . . . But I regret that we did not a make stronger effort to drop the name Republika Srpska. We underestimated the value to Pale of retaining their blood-soaked name.

—Richard Holbrooke, *To End a War,* 1998

When people say "What country are you from?" what do you say?
Susana: *Republika Srpska.*
Is that part of any other country?
Susana: *I think it's independent.*
So what is Bosnia-Herzegovina? Does it exist?
Susana: *I think not.*

—Fifteen-year-old Serb girl, Foca, 1998

What's the name of this country?
Narcisa: *Bosnia-Herzegovina.*
And what does it consist of?
Narcisa: *It's broken, [only] some towns.*

Have you heard of something called Republika Srpska?
Narcisa: *I think that is Serbia.*

—Fourteen-year-old Muslim girl, Gorazde, 1998

Stojan and I sat in his room in Foca. It was a comfortable teenage boy's room, computer in the corner, posters of basketball stars on the wall. He told me that he wanted to go to America to play basketball profession-ally because they had the best leagues. Then he remarked that if he was in a competition he would say he was from Yugoslavia because nobody had heard of Republika Srpska. *Why not Bosnia-Herzegovina?* I asked. Because he didn't think Republika Srpska was part of Bosnia-Herzegov-ina. He knew it was not really part of Yugoslavia. Apparently, Republika Srpska was in a strange no-man's-land called "the former Bosnia-Her-zegovina." *The Federation calls the part that it got Bosnia-Herzegovina,* he explained. He knew that people in the Federation included Repub-lika Srpska in the country of Bosnia-Herzegovina, but he did not agree with that. *Serbs don't include themselves in Bosnia-Herzegovina.* Seeing my puzzlement, he said he would prefer to be called Yugoslav because only Serbs lived in Yugoslavia and *In Bosnia-Herzegovina they are mixed.* Coming from Yugoslavia would give him a clear ethnic identity. Living conditions were better there as well, he added as an afterthought.[34]

As I talked to Stojan, I realized that the quickest way to get a grasp of these young people's sense of identity was to ask them where they thought they lived and how they felt about sharing their part of the country with others of a different ethnicity. Their answers were revealing, but under-standing those answers requires a brief diversion to explain the Dayton Peace Agreement.

The Dayton Peace Agreement that ended the war was formally signed in December 1995 by the presidents of Yugoslavia, Croatia, and Bosnia and Herzegovina (a lineup that clearly demonstrated the importance of outside players in Bosnia's war). The agreement appeared to be the win–win solu-tion of which conflict resolvers dream: taking something from everyone, and providing something for everyone. The Muslims got the multiethnic, independent country for which they had fought. This would be a sover-eign, internationally recognized, unitary state, in which a central tripartite government would have control of foreign policy, a central bank, a single currency, and a constitutional court. They had to give up part of the country's name. It would no longer be the Republic of Bosnia and Herzegovina, just Bosnia and Herzegovina.[35] The Serbs gained political control of a large proportion of the territory from which they had expelled the non-Serb population. This was achieved by dividing the country into two entities, each with its own parliament and its own security forces. The Bosnians and Croats would share 51 percent of the territory as one entity called the Federation of Bosnia and Herzegovina. The Serbs would get the other 49 percent of the territory as an entity whose name included the crucial republican prefix that Bosnia and Herzegovina itself had lost: Republika Srpska.

The Western sponsors of the agreement insisted that this was not de facto partition and thus a reward to the Bosnian Serbs for their brutal campaign of ethnic cleansing and terror, because Dayton also ensured the right of all residents to return to their homes, freedom of movement, and the possibility of voting in democratic elections in one's own hometown even when not physically present. These provisions would restore the status quo ante, an integrated Bosnia with an integrated population. How this was to be achieved given the continuing presence of the political and security forces who had conducted the campaigns of terror in the first place remained unclear. The newly created International Police Task Force (IPTF) was only there to monitor and train local police and had no mandate to act in the face of any abuses of human rights. The international military presence, the Implementation Force (IFOR), later to become the Stabilization Force (SFOR), was there to enforce the military aspects of the agreement, with no obligation to enforce civilian aspects such as freedom of movement or right of return. They had the authority to arrest war criminals, but again, they were not obligated to do so.

Some aspects of the agreement were achieved rapidly. International troops poured into Bosnia, local forces pulled back from the front lines, and after almost four bitter years, the fighting stopped. The agreed reallocation of territory between entities proceeded on the agreed dates. Yet even in those early months, the contradictions and weaknesses in the agreement were apparent.

In March 1996, I went to Banja Luka, the new capital of the new Serb entity, to discuss my proposed research with Dr. Kuzmanovic, the deputy minister of health. He believed the Serbs had won the war. He was delighted that the world had finally recognized that *Serbs want to live alone* and had given them Republika Srpska. He explained to me at length that the world had tried to use the Serbs to destroy Bosnian Muslims to stop the spread of Islam, but that all the Bosnian Serbs wanted was to live alone in their own land. He was very pleased with their success in achieving this, and assured me they would be good neighbors. The West would also appreciate that they would be *a dam against Islam*. We had blundered in making an *Istanbul of Sarajevo. It is going to be a bomb from which every evil will spread to Western countries.*

It felt as if little had changed. Dr. Kuzmanovic was sure the Federation would fall apart: *Islamic extremists cannot live with Croatian fascists, but everyone enjoys living with Serbs.* The remark contrasted oddly with the views he had just expressed about Muslims, and with local events. Only a few days previously, a thousand Serbs had demonstrated violently at a nearby village to stop three Muslim families from returning to their homes, a harbinger of things to come. Moreover, he saw little chance that the twenty thousand Muslims forced out of Foca could return home, as Foca was full of Serbs who had just left Sarajevo.

In the first months of 1996, there was a massive exodus of the Serb population from the suburbs of Sarajevo when these areas were handed to the Federation under the terms of the agreement. Yet again the Bosnian Serb leaders had convinced Serbs that it would not be safe to live with Muslims, and that they would be traitors if they did so. They had been helped in this endeavor by the actions of some Muslims, harassing and intimidating Serbs who had thought to stay in Ilidza, the first suburb to change hands.

That March I witnessed the effect of those actions and the propaganda during the handover of Grbavica, another Serb-controlled part of Sarajevo, to the Federation. This area above and around the Jewish cemetery had been controlled by Bosnian Serb forces from the beginning of the war. The steepness of this hill in the center of the city had given the Serb gunners, camped out in the ruined fortress that was the partisan memorial from the Second World War, a full view of much of the riverside and the center of town. They had turned these areas into a shooting gallery. The Brotherhood and Unity Bridge had been a front line marked by barbed wire, tank traps, and sheets of metal and old buses that gave some cover from snipers.

By March 1996, this detritus of a divided city had been pushed aside and you could walk across the bridge. Most of the buildings not damaged by shelling had had doors, windows, and roof sections carefully removed. I watched as residents loaded them into cars and vans already stuffed with furniture and miscellaneous household goods: a bathtub sticking out of a car's trunk, a child's blue mattress strapped with dining chairs to the top of a small Yugo. Some people had only what they could carry. I met an elderly woman struggling up the hill weeping, weighed down by four large carrier bags, one on each shoulder and one in each hand. They contained what looked like clothing, shoes, and light fixtures. The woman was a primary school teacher who had taught Muslims, Serbs, and Croats all her life and had never known the differences. She had escaped to Belgrade and hated it, had come back home, and now was walking four kilometers to Lubavica, the first village in Republika Srpska. She could not stay in Grbavica, she said, she was terrified. She had heard it was not safe. On another street tired-looking elderly people, waiting for a bus to take them they knew not where, told me it was impossible to live with Muslims: *I would rather live under a tree than in Sarajevo with Siladzic* [Bosnia's wartime prime minister] *and Izetbegovic,* an old man told me. *If it was possible to live with Muslims we would not have had this war.*

At the police station, the Serbian police sang their national anthem, then ceremoniously lowered the Serbian flag and rolled it up. Dignitaries lined up to kiss it and the deputy minister of the interior made a speech about how special units had raised the flag in 1992, but unfortunately, according to Dayton, a region that had been Serb for centuries must now be given to the other side. (In fact, the ethnic composition of the pre-war population of Grbavica had been mixed.) The ceremony was accompanied by explosions. Fifty meters away a house burst into flames, and smoke rose in plumes from the remains of others similarly gutted. What the Serb community could not keep, they were reluctant to leave for others. Italian troops arrested three Serb teenage boys with grenades in their pockets, pushing them, hands splayed, against the wall and searching them. It looked tough, but IFOR could only detain them for seventy-two hours, then they would be handed over to their own police. They knew they would be released in a couple of days.

Not all the Serbs left. Eleven thousand stayed in Grbavica. The relatives of friends of mine had lived through the war in a mixed apartment block where all had acted collectively to protect their Muslim neighbors. They were determined to stay. In the days leading up to the handover, the Serbian police visited them regularly to ensure that they were leaving. The family devised a strategy to avoid harassment. They pointed out two packed suitcases placed near the door as a symbol of imminent departure. Dr. Kuzmanovic felt sorry for such people. They and any other Serbs who remained in Federation territory, he said, were likely to be *hunted down and killed like animals* by *Islamic fundamentalists,* and no one would be able to help them.

In failing to prevent this exodus, the international community and the Bosnian government contributed to the ethnic separation and consolidation of both entities. The exodus also highlighted the inherent weaknesses of a peace agreement that did nothing to challenge the mind-set of the domestic elites who had gone to war for ethnic separation in the first place.

Over the following years, these weaknesses became ever more apparent. Instead of something for everyone, Dayton became nothing for most people. Far from reversing ethnic cleansing and creating an integral, functioning democratic state, Dayton gave legitimacy to leaders who still trumpeted the benefits of an ethnic separatist project built on paranoia, murder, and forced expulsion. The lines of ethnic partition were frozen solid. Indicted war criminals retained their prestige and influence, and corruption was rampant. Biljana Plavsic described Republika Srpska, of which she was then president, as "a state in which the budget does not actually exist, where police are involved in smuggling and stealing from their own state, and where a majority of the population live in abject poverty."[36]

These contradictions were particularly apparent in the Drina Valley. Gorazde was the only enclave in eastern Bosnia to hold out against the Bosnian Serb assault. Dayton designated the municipality as Federation territory except for one suburb of the town, which had previously had a Muslim majority, but went to Republika Srpska. The Serbs called this suburb Serb Gorazde; the Muslims called it by its old name, Kopaci. Gorazde was supposed to be connected to the bulk of the Federation by a new highway, constructed on a corridor of Federation land over the mountains between Sarajevo and Ustikolina. Three years on, the promised highway was still lines on a map, and a potholed dirt track still switch backed over the mountains, four hours of choking dust in summer, impassable in winter. Those who took the main road, which went through Republika Srpska, risked assault and kidnapping.

When I first arrived in Gorazde, one year after Dayton, it still wore the war like an old winter coat. The footbridge to protect pedestrians from

snipers still ran under the central bridge. Homemade waterwheel genera-
tors still floated in the Drina, and almost every house was pitted and cra-
tered by shrapnel and blast damage. Many were shattered and roofless. The
roads were treacherous with potholes. Every untended garden, every field
in the surrounding countryside carried the risk of mines and unexploded
bombs. There was no power, no running water, and no phone connection.
Women still did their laundry in the Drina.

Over the following two years, I watched the town come to life. Electricity and clean water were reconnected, buildings roofed and repainted. The
schools were re-equipped and a new sports hall built. There was a cultural
center running local TV and radio shows. On summer evenings, the streets
and cafés were full. The energy in the town was in marked contrast to the
gloom and quietness of Foca. Even so, Gorazde still felt as if it was economically and politically under siege. Local businesses struggled to pay the
exorbitant costs of transporting goods through risky territory. Local professionals felt isolated. Despite projects to restart local factories, there were
few real jobs and young people just wanted to get out. They recognized that
Gorazde was an island. In a divided Bosnia of monoethnic communities,
the town made no sense. An appendix, one friend quipped. It was an appropriate metaphor: easy to inflame and not difficult to cut out.

The international community pushed through the first municipal
elections in 1997. More interested in finding an exit strategy from the
region than in building a democratic state, they ignored the fact that the
conditions for holding elections were neither free nor fair. Large numbers of displaced citizens, the majority of them Muslim, still lived in
squalor and uncertainty far from their original homes, and freedom of
movement was still a myth. These elections did nothing to contribute
to democratic change. Not surprisingly, given the continuing insecurity,
most people voted for the national parties that had fought the war on
their behalf. In Kopaci, the local Serb authorities, recognizing that a vote
reflecting the composition of the prewar population would throw them
out, discouraged and intimidated displaced Muslims who wished to vote,
and registered large numbers of nonresident Serbs to ensure their own
victory and consolidate their hold on the area. (About three thousand
five hundred people registered to vote, although the maximum prewar
population was estimated to be two thousand.)[37] I sat in a shrub-fringed
lay-by, one warm September afternoon in 1997, counting the many buses

and cars with Serbian number plates, as they brought in the suddenly enlarged population of this rural suburb to cast its votes.

In Foca, the votes of displaced Muslims did succeed in returning some of their own politicians. They had to be given protection to travel there, and council meetings were usually deadlocked by disagreement between the ethnically-based parties. Three years after Dayton, not a single non-Serb had returned to live in the town. Visits by former Muslim residents to relatives' graves were organized and protected by international police and still met with hostility from local Serbs. The community oriented itself politically and culturally eastward, toward Yugoslavia. Many local people preferred to travel the single-track dirt road to Montenegro, and then drive for four hours to Podgorica to go shopping, rather than travel for an hour on a reasonable highway to Sarajevo. Local businesses used Yugoslav dinars. Television in Republika Srpska still referred to Bosnia-Herzegovina as "the former Bosnia-Herzegovina" and put all news from the Federation in the "foreign" news. (This ended when SFOR took over one of the television transmitters in November 1997). The local Serb authorities were still closely associated with those who had organized the terror and ethnic cleansing of the town in 1992.

Because of this noncompliance with Dayton, the international organizations continued to refuse to release aid to the town. This left local Serbs confused and impoverished. I spent part of Easter in 1998 visiting a teacher and friend living in the hotel-cum-collective center in the middle of town. She had fled from the fighting at the beginning of the war and now lived in a small room containing one cheap dresser and a bed, with all her possessions piled in boxes around her. She had no hot water and cooked on one electric ring. She had invited me to learn how to decorate Orthodox Easter eggs, so the ring now warmed a saucepan of melting wax. We sat on the bed and the one chair while she deftly painted the red wax onto the eggs and talked.

She hated Foca. *They are horrible to refugees in this town. There is no collective spirit. No one cares. People know my situation, but no one asks me to eat, or even for coffee. They know I don't have hot water. Do they ever offer me a bath?* The tirade went on and on. Given her unhappiness and obvious discomfort, I asked if she would consider returning to her hometown in the Federation. Under Dayton she had a right to reclaim her house there, and even to receive some assistance to get it rebuilt if it was damaged. She had told me how much she loved it before the war. *Absolutely not!* She looked at me in bewilderment. *Why did the West give us our republic if they want to make everything the way it was before?* In a few words, she had identified the contradiction at the heart of Dayton.

The teenagers I interviewed in Foca may not have known the political and physical geography of the new country, but they grasped the psychological reality of Dayton completely. Although the interentity boundary line (IEBL) was only fifteen minutes up the valley from the center of town, more than half of the children thought Republika Srpska was not part of Bosnia-Herzegovina. They avoided the word Bosnia and were uncomfortable if pushed to use it. When I asked Ivana where Republika Srpska was, she replied *On this territory where this country is, where war was.*

Okay, I said, *I'm not being clear in my questions. Is Republika Srpska inside any other country?*

I don't know, she responded, then definitively: *No.*

Is it inside Yugoslavia?

She hesitated. *Maybe.*

Well, where is Bosnia-Herzegovina? I asked, finally giving up the hope that she might mention it herself.

She paused, and then laughed. *I guess on Turks' territory.*

And is Republika Srpska inside Bosnia-Herzegovina?

No.

Many of the children thought that Bosnia-Herzegovina had ceased to exist. Dusan thought that Republika Srpska was independent. He was uncertain where Gorazde was, but thought it might be in *the Federation*: *That's the name of the country of the Croats and Muslims.* Svetlana was sure that Republika Srpska was inside Yugoslavia, and that there was no more Bosnia.

Half of the Muslim teenagers in Gorazde also believed that the Federation and Republika Srpska were not in the same country, and had a similar vagueness as to where Foca was located. Their descriptions of the country were both more confused and more complicated than those I heard in Foca. They believed Bosnia-Herzegovina existed, but many did not think Republika Srpska was part of it. Some thought that Serbs still had parts of Bosnia, such as Serb Sarajevo and Serb Gorazde, and consequently these were no longer in Bosnia. *There were a lot of towns that were in Bosnia*

before and now they are not in Bosnia because they were taken by them [. . .]
they're in their territory. [. . .] That territory is in Yugoslavia now, and before
they were in Bosnia, one boy explained, firmly and nonsensically placing a
suburb of his own town in a completely different country. Narcisa thought
Republika Srpska was in Serbia. Foca was in Bosnia, she said, but it was
occupied by Serbs from Serbia, not Bosnian Serbs. Samir thought Republika
Srpska was *down in Belgrade* and not part of Bosnia-Herzegovina at all.

The children's ideas about where they lived connected to their ideas about
with whom it was possible to live. Sara thought her town, Foca, was now in
Serbia and Yugoslavia. Sara's family had just finished building their house
in the town before the war. Her best friend had been a classmate who was
the daughter of her Muslim next-door neighbors. When the friend fled
three days before the war, Sara had already left for a village. Her father
was badly injured driving over a mine, but had recovered. She missed her
friend and wanted to see her again, but still thought it was better to live
separately. She had heard adults talking about Muslims hating Serbs and
Serbs hating Muslims: *If they hate each other, they can't live in the same*
town. She worried that if Muslims returned there would be another war
because we were together before and war happened then.

Almost all the Serb children were opposed to non-Serbs returning to
Foca, and those who had been displaced from cities within the Federation
had no wish to return home. It was not because they felt personally antagonistic toward Muslims; many liked the idea of seeing their old friends and
did not hold them responsible. But living together would be dangerous.
Their logic was simple: They had lived together before, and there had been
a war, so if they lived together again, there would be another. *They're start-*
ing to come again today, Susana told me in her usual slightly offhand manner, shortly after former Muslim citizens of Foca made an arranged visit to
the graveyard. *I think everything will be the same as it was before.* She didn't
mind, she didn't hate them; but she thought there would *probably be a war*
because we are together again.

Another concern was that people living in the entity belonging to
another ethnicity would be treated as second-class citizens. Helena had
come to Foca from Sarajevo at the beginning of the war. She had loved
Sarajevo. They had an apartment in a predominantly Muslim area; her
mother worked in a public company, and had deliberately not had Helena

baptized in case she chose to marry someone of another religion. When the war began, Helena's father did not want to join the Muslim militia on their street. He hoped to avoid the fighting by moving to a village, but he was called up by the VRS, and killed on the front line in the first month of fighting. Despite this terrible experience, Helena was not angry with Muslims. *Only one man killed him. Not all of them. They are not all guilty.* She thought she would like things to be as before because they had been so good, but she also worried that living together would lead to war because there was likely to be discrimination and jealousy. *For example, if in some factory the director is a Serb, maybe the Muslims will only get bad positions.* Jovan had seen on local television that some Serbs who had tried to return to the Federation were not able to work on their own land and were treated badly.

Many felt that even if ordinary people could get along, the extremists would cause trouble. Divac had shared a shelter with Muslim neighbors on his street in Sarajevo at the beginning of the war; when Serb forces took control, his father had acted to protect those neighbors. Divac said he would go back to Sarajevo the next day if only others felt like him. But bad people on both sides would destroy the situation, the same if Muslims returned to Foca, and there would be war again. Nothing could be done about such people. Everyone should get new houses and live separately. Helena's mother had very similar attitudes to her daughter. She was still grieving for her husband and spent much of our time together in tears, but kept insisting *I don't hate anybody.* All the same, she wanted to live separately from Muslims because she was afraid *they will have some laws which will make us lower-class people.* She had friends who had returned to Sarajevo and could not get jobs. *At this moment, I don't think it is possible to live together. We can't find a common language.* The problem was not with people like her, but with extremists.

Can't you do something about extremists?

It's impossible, only the law could do something, and who believes in the law? [. . .] We ordinary civilians can't do anything. Even a lot of us together can't do anything. [. . .] I don't believe democracy can live here. We are the kind of people who need to be told what to do. She had been watching the RS assembly on television and found it ridiculous. *I think the intelligent people left and only the uneducated ones are still here. How can people who only went to high school be in parliament?* She had possessed a passport in 1992 and now wished she had had the courage to emigrate so her children could have seen *somewhere civilized.*

Others believed that no matter how good relations had been before, the war had generated so much hatred that living together now would be impossible. One thirteen-year-old boy in Foca wrote: *The war caused me great pain because my family was killed. That's why I hate Islamic criminals. Because of that I would never live with those cretins, jerks, Ustashe, and merciless people. The news about what those heartless people did in Josanice upset me the most.* Dusan could not imagine how he could live next door to the Muslim neighbor they had seen with a gun. *His son died, too,* Dusan's father said, *so how do you think we can live together? We will see who can throw the other in the Drina first. I'm younger, so probably I will manage. I won't let him do it.*

Even children who had not suffered personal losses told me it was impossible to go back. Radmila had lived in a mixed village where her mother worked the land and her father had a factory job. It was not an easy life, but relations with her Muslim neighbors were good. She told me that after the Serbs had *kicked out* the Muslims from Foca, her family had feared reprisals and had moved in with Serb neighbors on the other side of the river. Her Muslim neighbors had done nothing to threaten or harm them; they were afraid and had fled as well. After fleeing the fighting a number of times and being bombed by NATO in Ustikolina, Radmila ended up on a farm formerly owned by Muslims. Her family had managed to keep their own animals and take them along. Their relatives were in neighboring houses so it felt like home. Radmila liked it much better because it was easier to get into town and see friends. She did not want to see her prewar Muslim friends because the war had changed everything.

I think they hate us.

Do you hate them?

I do.

Why?

Because they are a different nationality.

She said she did not hate other nationalities on principle. Normally she thought all kinds of people could live together. But Muslims were different from Serbs in ways that she could not define. She was worried that they might attack. This was the same discussion I had had with Milica. Both girls now hated Muslims, based on a new perception of difference and a belief in the others' hostility. Their hatred had arisen because of the war. Radmila was clear that it was the war itself that had made her feel like this.

The most significant argument against living together had nothing to do with the children's feelings of safety. The war had been fought so that Serbs could live alone. If Muslims came back to live in Foca and other parts of Republika Srpska, it would make the effort meaningless. A fifteen-year-old boy in Foca wrote, *Some people dear to us gave their lives for our liberation. [. . .] When everything was liberated my town got a new name: Srbinje, that name presents the face of our town and the determination of its people to fight for Serbs and unity. [. . .] Now they are trying to take from us that for which we gave our young lives, our sacred country, Republika Srpska, but they will not succeed, however hard they try. While there is one Serb in this area, they will stay forever.*

Like my friend in the hotel, this boy had touched the heart of the contradiction within the peace agreement. When the international community stated that it wanted to return refugees to their homes, it was in effect saying that the creation of Republika Srpska through territorial aggression and ethnic cleansing was an unjust and criminal project that should be undone. Yet by creating an entity called Republika Srpska, albeit reduced, and at present within the confines of Bosnia-Herzegovina, it appeared to be telling the Serb community that this had been a goal worth fighting for.

Some children wrestled with the complexity of this issue. Vesna had been driven barefoot from her village near Sarajevo by Croat and Muslim forces. Her family had moved to a relative's home in the Sarajevo suburb of Ilidza. They had not wished to leave after the Dayton Agreement handed it back to the Federation. However, the Muslims who took over the police and local authorities had done nothing to make Serbs feel welcome. Every day more neighbors departed, more Muslims moved back, and they heard stories of other Serbs being attacked, so they felt *there was no place for Serbs. I don't know who set the terms. We just had to move out. Everybody was saying it is much easier with your own people.*

Vesna had cried when they left Ilidza and did not particularly like their new home in a village near Foca. She had a loving, close-knit family and was one of the brightest children in her class at high school. She planned to be an engineer. I asked her how she thought things could be healed after the war.

We have to help each other, she immediately replied. *People have to help each other. Nobody can live alone.*

Do you mean people should go back to their homes?

I don't know, it would mean that the war was for nothing. Why did we fight if they come back?

She was clearly uncomfortable with her own conclusions. She was not sure that separation achieved by war was a good thing: *I don't believe things can be separated like that.* But letting Muslims return to Foca would mean the war *was for nothing because after the war some people left their homes. Probably they were forced, and now if they came back . . . Why were those people fighting if they are . . . Why did they separate it at the beginning if they are coming back? Why did so many people die just to be together again? Because it can happen again. I never thought about things like this.*

When telling me about leaving her original village, Vesna wept. It was the first time she had talked about it in detail for six years. She was surprised at her own reaction and insisted on continuing. Later in our conversation, again on the edge of tears, she assured me that she did not want to return to her old home, nor did anyone she knew because nothing would be the same. I wondered how much her own certainty on this point, combined with her obvious distress, had to do with feeling a need to give meaning to the sacrifices her own people had made, even as she sensed the moral ambiguity of the separation project as a whole.

Dusan felt his brother had fought and died *for nothing* because the countries were still not properly separated. The international community was wrong to force Croats, Muslims, and Serbs into one country. *It is humiliating for so many people who died during the war.* They had fought for separate nations. *I think Muslims should live in a Muslim country, Croats should live in a Croat one, and Serbs should live in Republika Srpska or a Serb country. Later if people want to, they can mix. I think it's awful that Serb people who moved into Muslim houses should have to leave because of Muslims who want to come back.* Anyway, he did not think many Muslims genuinely wanted to return; they were being pushed by their politicians.

Many children expressed the feeling that the return of Muslim neighbors would make a mockery of the sacrifices of the war, and would mean that Serbs had fought for nothing. Perhaps another, unvoiced reason was that such a return would also require meeting former friends and hearing firsthand the means by which separation had been achieved. A painful essay written by a fifteen-year-old boy hints at this:

> *I imagine how things would look if this war had not occurred. I imagine people who are not here anymore. I tell myself that it would not be better, I am deceiving myself, but it doesn't matter because it helps me look at the present in a different way. The present is here and it cannot be changed, and that is why we have to accept it. The Muslims want to live with us again, they ask "Who did this to all of us?" We have to accept the present time, but not with them. I don't want it. It is true that we talk the same language, listen to the same music, write the same way, but they are completely different and I do not want to erase that difference. There is no more peace and no BiH. We can look at each other only through gun sights and be together only in the Olympic Games. I was educated to love and not to differentiate people on the basis of religion. But I cannot love someone who does not love me. Many of my friends were Muslims before the war, we never had a fight, and I remember them, but the question is what our meeting would look like now. I don't have the courage to think about that meeting and also I don't want to because who knows what it might bring.*

Not all the children in Foca were totally opposed to return. Svetlana said that she would *love* to have her Muslim friends and neighbors come back and saw no danger from that. *They are people; they are human beings just like us.* Ivana thought the best way to make peace was for everyone to go home. *Everybody should live their own life and not interfere with other people.* Some children were ambivalent. Helena did not care which entity she lived in or what it was called. She wanted to go back to Sarajevo and live with her Muslim friends again. She also felt Muslims had the right to come back to Foca. Her conversation slid from saying that living together would be dangerous, to wanting to do so *but without war*, to deciding it *would be the best to stay like this, Serbs on one side and Muslims on the other.* I could sense the difficulty the issue caused her from her sighs while answering.

These three girls had had very close contacts and friendships with non-Serbs in their own childhoods. As with other aspects of their understanding of the conflict, there appeared to be a pattern. For the most part, it was the children like Svetlana and Helena who were trying to understand what had happened in Foca, who were more enthusiastic about living with Muslims again. Children like Milica, Radmila, and Susana, who distanced themselves from what had happened in the town, were also more forthright in their opposition to Muslims' return. Disengagement and distancing allowed for certainties; curiosity could lead to openness, but sometimes to confusion and distress.

The families in Foca assured me that Muslims in Gorazde were equally opposed to living together. If I was told differently, it would be because they were lying or manipulated by their politicians. A few of the Gorazde children's written stories did make such feelings clear, such as this one by a fifteen-year-old girl:

> I've lost my father, my life changed a lot with his death. I was very happy when he was alive [. . .] four years have passed, but every day it's just worse and worse. [. . .] I wonder very often why he had to die. Why? But I know I will never get an answer to this question. I just know one thing, he is not here anymore. I will never be able to live with the people who gave me all this pain. I cannot stand the fact that they will return to Gorazde and live as before the war. I am not scared of them, but I just hate them from the bottom of my soul.

Gorazde had changed by the summer of 1998. Many of those who had been refugees abroad had come back. The international community had finally clamped down on illegal checkpoints and imposed a unified number plate policy. This meant that it was no longer possible to identify the entity from which a car originated, so it was safer and easier to travel through Republika Srpska to Sarajevo and the rest of the Federation. Visiting sports teams came for matches. More small shops and cafés opened. Young people commuted home on weekends from Sarajevo University. Most significantly, in November 1997 the local authorities had decided to make Gorazde an Open City, committing the municipality to facilitating the return of non-Muslim refugees and protecting them from any abuses. This was pragmatic. Local officials knew they would be rewarded with more international aid. They also knew that someone had to break up the peculiar game of musical chairs in which the different ethnic communities appeared to be engaged. If Serb returnees were offered their homes back in Gorazde, the mayor of Serb Gorazde could no longer argue that the Serbs in his town needed the houses that belonged to their Muslim neighbors. There had been a steady trickle of visitors and former inhabitants ever since, as well as cars driving through from Visegrad to Foca. It was not surprising, therefore, that the majority of children and their families to whom I spoke in Gorazde were in favor of living together again, although some were ambivalent.

The ambivalence was most evident in the children who had been in Gorazde through most of the siege and who had had some of the worst experiences. Their uncertainty focused on two issues. One was the same question raised by Foca children: If one had suffered directly, how could one live with the people who had inflicted the suffering? Iris thought living separately was better. *Most of my friends have lost fathers, sisters, they can't imagine living with someone whose parents were killing their families.* Later she said that if things went back to the way they were before, without misunderstanding, *I don't know, in a way they should return, in a way they shouldn't, I don't know. And probably all the people who did the killing during the war wouldn't return.* But as it might not be possible to distinguish the innocent from the guilty, how could one live with any of them? Armin thought families who had lost someone might want revenge and then take it out on the wrong people.

A second issue was a feeling of personal insecurity. This was not the Foca children's fear that another war might arise automatically if the two communities mixed. In Gorazde, all these children repeated, almost as a mantra, *Everyone has a right to their home.* They knew this meant allowing Serbs back into Gorazde. In contrast to Foca, they almost all felt that living separately would result in another war, while living together would foster long-term security. However, direct encounters with particular Serbs had created anxiety for some.

Amela demonstrated all these contradictory feelings. She told me about an incident that had scared her. A Mercedes with Serbian plates had parked in front of her house, a short distance out of town, and a somewhat aggressive man had asked the way to Gorazde. She had helped him and he had driven off leaving her feeling *unsafe.* She had been afraid the man would hit her. She could not say why, simply that he was an impolite stranger and she wondered why he had picked her. Even so, she said, she would help the next Serb who asked, and she did think they should come back, as long as things went back to the way they had been before the war, when the only distinction was religious belief. She was not afraid of life together. *It will be easier if we are all together, sharing the life we had before. [. . .] If we go on living separately I think it will be a disaster. . . . Because there are a lot of Bosnian areas in their hands, so if they came back, Bosnians could go back to their towns.* She thought Gorazde would look better if Serbs repaired their houses. She had also noticed that many of the factory managers were Serbs, and she was worried that the Bosnian Muslims lacked the education and skills to restart the economy by themselves.

In a later meeting, Amela repeated her wish *to continue the life we had before the war.* She thought the solution to any difficulties was for no one to talk about the war. *Even if we can't forget it, I don't want to mention it.* She still felt that living together was the only way to avoid another war. But she had been watching television and listening to adults talk and had heard that Serbs still wanted a town in northern Bosnia (Brcko), and that they still wanted Muslims to leave Gorazde and wanted to take it for themselves.[38] This horrified her. She thought the Serbs were making impossible demands.

I told her that many Serb children in Foca believed living together was not safe. *Then maybe it will be better. . . . It would be better if they don't want that, then it would be better. . . .* She looked very sad and sighed. *They don't want to live together with us. And we want that. Just to avoid the war. If our people try to do something by force, to live together again, then it is war again. Well maybe that is impossible. But maybe the way is to forget everything that happened. Let's all forget everything that happened.* Then she came full circle again: *But I think it can't work because everybody talks about the war. So I think we can't live together.*

All the children in Gorazde distinguished between war criminals and others. No one wanted the criminals to come back. There were also stories of Serbs who had actively assisted them, while other Serbs were seen as ordinary soldiers because they had no choice. Samir said *My father has . . . had, a good friend, Serb. He didn't fight in the war. He had a house at the seaside and he went there. If some Serbs didn't have enough money to pay to go, they had to go and fight, even if they didn't want to, they forced them to. They were saying, "We'll kill all your family if you don't go."* The solution arrived at by most ambivalent children was usually that Serbs should come back and live in their own homes, but that they personally would have nothing to do with them. *Gorazde is an Open Town,* Nina said. *And by law everyone can live in it. And I don't care, I don't really mind. I have my own friends to socialize with, so it doesn't matter if they come back.* She wanted a normal country like Germany or America where people lived together.

The children who unequivocally favored the return of their Serb neighbors were those who had been some distance from the worst of the siege. They did not think things would be the same as before; they wrestled with the dilemmas of whether they could or should forgive and forget what had happened, but they felt that normal life and security meant living together. Fikreta put it in bald pragmatic terms: *Everyone should go back to their own homes because if they don't return the Muslims won't return to Foca and to Visegrad.* She did not think she would have any problems living with Serbs again. On the contrary, she found it hard to imagine life without them. *I learned that in school, and my parents taught me—because we have to be with others and we can't live alone because, for example, if now our neighbors are Serbs or Croats, we have to be with them because how can we be alone in the house and not be with anybody else? How can we not talk to them and not spend time with them?*

Fikreta felt as many did that a mixed life was the best one. As in Foca, I found that children's views were similar to those of their parents. Fikreta's mother told me that if Serbs and Muslims did not return to the towns from which they had fled during the war, *we will never have peace, it will never be good, nobody is for that.* She believed that living in a monoethnic state carried its own risks. Although religious herself, she had no desire to live in a *Muslim Republic of Bosnia. I don't want to go covered; I don't want to live in Iran. I will go and live in Republika Srpska,* she said, laughing, *but I will not have a cloth on my face. I don't have to be dressed completely to be Muslim.* Living together with other groups was a protection against the extremism of one's own.

Other parents thought a multiethnic society was a better guarantee of democracy. Armin's father was helping an aid agency rebuild Serb-owned houses. *Just Muslims* was not a good way to live: *They will rob their people and ours will rob our people. [. . .] There are a lot of poor people here and there are also a lot of poor people there.* Of course there might be *some fear, some period of silence maybe.* But with time, everything would be okay. *Because before, Serbs and Muslims were always helping each other,*

Samir's father told me. *If only Muslims ruled there wouldn't be any democracy because only their families would be on the top.* He believed that in a monoethnic society some families would be privileged at the expense of others, whereas in a mixed one Serbs and Muslims would protect each other's rights. If Serbs and Muslims had real equality, there would not be another war. *The Bosnia I fought for was multiethnic, not dependent on Croatia or Yugoslavia or Serbia.*

Gorazde and Foca felt much more than thirty minutes apart. Foca's Serbs had fought for ethnic separation. A generation of young Serbs was now growing up convinced that ethnic cleansing had been a defensive necessity, and that the only way to avoid future war was to live alone, in squalid poverty if necessary. The return of Muslims would mean that Serbs had lost the war and their parents' struggle and sacrifices had been for nothing. Down the road in Gorazde, Muslims had fought for life in a mixed society, so whatever their anxieties about meeting their former neighbors, for them, only a unified and mixed Bosnia could signify victory. Young Gorazde Muslims were growing up in a town whose isolated population had no viable existence outside a multiethnic state. But the different perspectives were not just the result of a flawed peace agreement. Serb and Muslim children's different aspirations regarding future living arrangements also related to the very different ways in which they thought about themselves.

7

WHERE DO THEY COME FROM?

Although the existing name [Foca] is pretty old and etymologically contains our roots, in its adapted pronunciation it has acquired the form of a Turkish name, and that with an overtone that was bound to irritate us Serbs since it continuously reminded us of the centuries of slavery under the foreign Islamic oppressors. [The name Srbinje] contains at its root the word which distinguishes our national name and essence. In this war, the fighters from Foca and from the [surrounding] region were worthy defenders of Serbianness and Orthodoxy. Therefore, they have merited that their regional capital and the entire region carry a name with an emphatically national hallmark.

—Vojislav Maksimovic, former mayor of Foca, 1994

It is a tragic illusion that war, ethnic ideologies and the fixing of boundaries are necessary for the realization of the self, through the production of a pure culture and a return to roots ... This approach leads only to the use of force and a falsification of history, past and present. Its advocates and propagandists do not realize how dangerous it is to their own pure culture and much loved nation, for it is a process that leads nowhere except to a ghetto mentality, to cultural stagnation, and eventually death.

—Ivan Lovrenovic, Bosnia: A Cultural History, 2002

There is a saying, "If you respect yours, you respect others," and it says in many books, and my father told me as well: If you respect your own nation and your own religion, then you respect other religions and other nations.

—Muslim mother, Gorazde, 1998

I had never been aware I was a nation
until they said they'd kill me.

—Goran Simic, "A Scene, after the War," 2003

History Lessons

Ask the Muslim people, "Where do Muslims come from?" Igor said to me.

I will if you like, but my question to you is "Why does it matter?"

It doesn't matter to me, said Adriana, Igor's wife.

It matters because it's a source of tension, it was a problem in the past as well, Igor replied.

Igor and Adriana had invited me to their tiny apartment because they wanted me to understand Foca better. Neither was happy with the city at that time, the winter of 1997. Adriana, who had loved her university life in Sarajevo, missed the past. Igor was bitterly disappointed in the present and the hopes of the promised future. They thought of emigrating. As usual, the television played in the corner much of the time. The evening news appeared to consist mainly of Republika Srpska politicians attacking each other in the run-up to the entity elections. Srbinje TV offered either Biljana Plavsic in Banja Luka castigating the corruption of her former friends, Karadzic and Krajisnik, in the Serb Democratic Party (SDS), or the leader of the Serb Radical Party (SRS), banned in Banja Luka at that time.

Gordana, my translator, despised and distrusted Plavsic for being a turncoat, interested only in power for herself, and for dividing Serbs yet again. Adriana despaired of them all. She saw the SDS as a party that had forced impoverished and uneducated people to fight while the leaders' own children were out of the country. The SRS were the same as the SDS: *Serbs, Serbs, and again Serbs.* All the parties were the same as in communist times; only the names had changed. *They pay more attention to religion and ethnic identity but we can't live on these things.* She wanted *a party that would open us up and take us to the West.*

Igor had just come home from an SRS political meeting. He liked the SRS because its program offered *discipline, work, and order.* He could see I looked a little startled at this phrase and, perhaps recognizing the resonance, immediately added, *not work as in Arbeit Macht Frei, as in Aus-chwitz. Our program is based on tradition, history, culture, and environ-ment.* I asked why he admired the radical Serb politician Vojislav Seselj. *Because he wants to build our country without criminality and corruption, to bring us back to Serb traditions and the history of the Serb people, which we all shared. He would never let Albanians in Kosovo use a different language. They would all learn Serbian.*

My friends in Foca would like you to tell me where you think Muslims come from, I said to the school psychologist in Gorazde a few days later. *I have no idea. Does it matter?* he replied. *I can answer that question,* said Hasan's father. *I was born in Foca, but I came here forty years ago, so origi-nally I am from Foca.* I often encountered this problem in these indirect exchanges. Both communities used me as a kind of carrier pigeon, wing-ing messages and questions to their former neighbors on the other side. However, the conversations frequently became derailed because the start-ing points and basic understandings were not the same, particularly when it came to questions of ethnic identity, origins, and history.

Origins and history mattered to the Serbs in Foca, both adults and chil-dren. They were clear about their own identity and its roots, and the town echoed with historical references. Some of these were newer than oth-ers: The name of the primary school had been changed from Ivan Goran Kovacic, a Second World War antifascist hero, to Sveti Sava. Saint Sava was a member of the Nemanja dynasty that had created the short-lived medi-eval Serbian empire, which at its zenith in the mid-fourteenth century had stretched from the Danube to the Peloponnese. Sava founded and headed an autonomous Serbian Orthodox Church, had his own royal family sanc-tified, and was canonized himself after his death. We celebrated his saint's day with a special service in church, a holiday from school (although as the teachers were on strike for lack of pay this did not count for much), a visit and blessing from the priest, and a lavish breakfast of roast meats and plenty of rakia in the staff room.

Children learned in third grade about Prince Lazar, whose portrait watched over their classroom. Lazar had lost that same medieval king-dom at the battle of Kosovo. Sara, a seventh grader, told me that Prince Lazar and Milos Obilic, who had reputedly assassinated Sultan Murat during the battle and lost his own life doing so, were the kind of Serbs *who fight for everybody.* They should be distinguished from those *who only want power for themselves,* like the Serbian traitor Vuk Brankovic, whose betrayal of Prince Lazar had allowed the Ottomans to begin their occupation of the Balkans.

They also learned about the origins of Muslims. In their seventh-grade history textbook, they discovered that under Ottoman rule some Christians converted to Islam for a variety of reasons, but mostly to retain their property. The majority of Islamicized Christians were in Bosnia-Herzegovina. During the Ottoman years they read that most Christian Serbs, were "feudal tenants," while most Muslims were landowners or privileged because of their religion. "Christian feudal tenants had bigger obligations than Muslim feudal tenants. . . . Christian citizens and clergy could never have the top positions in a Muslim state."[39]

We learn that they took children, Sara told me, referring to the Janissary system in which, according to her textbook, the sultan had Christian boys kidnapped and sent to Turkey to be Islamicized and trained in the military. *Children became Turks so they could have more soldiers, and all Serbs who became Turks were made into leaders.* This was bad because *those Serbs who became Turks were against Serb people. They were raised to be warriors. Then they took other children, and killed some of them.* Sara had read Ivo Andric's famous *Bridge over the Drina.* It had bored her, but she remembered the part where *some Serb who became a Turk built a bridge and he put two children into the bridge.*[40]

Helena knew that Turks had *enslaved Serbs and plundered and looted* from them. Jovan similarly had absorbed the message that *Turks were bad.* When I asked if Turks and Muslims were connected, he said he thought they were. *They are the same religion, and they are similar. They spoke the same language. Turkish warriors killed people.*

I asked Ivana why she mostly used the term "Turk" for Muslims, as many of the children did.

Well, if we are Serbs, they are Turks, Croats, and so on.

So, what is the connection between Muslims and Turks?

They are the same I guess.

I asked if everyone in her family used the term and she seemed embarrassed, mumbling quietly that she didn't know. She had never used the term about her best friend, Asra, nor had she heard Muslims use it about themselves. She knew they would not like that, she told me with a disarming smile. But history lessons about *the fights for Kosovo* had taught her that Turks and Muslims were connected.

Adriana and Igor talked about this connection. *People always learned that Turks lie,* said Igor. *They say one thing and do another. And now we feel the same about Muslims.*

You do, not me, Adriana corrected him.

I do, he agreed.

Eighth graders learned from their textbooks that "besides the aboriginal Serb population, this territory [Bosnia] was settled by Albanians and Turks. The Serb population was oppressed by Muslims who had come as settlers from the countries which Turkey lost in 1878, as well as organized Albanian groups influenced by the Turkish government." Muslims were either Serbs who had given up their real identity for material gain and benefited at the expense of their poorer Christian neighbors, or incoming colonizers. In the Second World War, as on previous occasions, they behaved perfidiously, siding with the Germans and the Croatian Ustashe, forming their own SS unit, and killing hundreds of thousands of Serbs. Jovan's teacher told students that the Croats created concentration camps in the Second World War, and that *the same thing happened in this war.*

Yet Serbs, Dusan's father told me, had continued to act with extraordinary generosity and forgiveness. They had agreed to give up their own national interests and to form a common state with Croats and Muslims, who as Islamicized Serbs, were not a people. *First of all, they don't have their own land, they don't have their own alphabet, and they don't have history.* They had their own religion, but no unique culture or customs. The heart of the problem, for him, appeared to be the Muslims' failure to understand and recognize their Serb roots, their treachery in turning on their own ancestors through the centuries, and Serb generosity in ignoring this for so long. *We were good to them, they used it.*[41]

Children now learned in school that Muslims had supported a system that had oppressed Serbs for half a millennium. It was to prevent a reversion to such a system that Serbs had gone to war when Bosnia became independent. Dusan told me his brother had *fought for Serbs against violence* because of the danger of being *like it was before, to be under Muslims. Because Muslims wanted to make their country in these areas [. . .] I know that from a story my grandfather told me, and now I know from history that we were under the Turks.*

In Gorazde, neither parents nor children were particularly interested in disputing the historical points. Fikreta's mother laughed and said she did not care where she came from. She had been very impressed when a prominent Bosnian Muslim politician recently said on television that he had Croat ancestors. Fikreta's father echoed his wife, *I don't ask where Serbs come from [. . .] they are people like us, Serbs, Croats, different religions, but I don't see any difference. I've never wanted a Muslim republic here in Bosnia.*

Most of the Gorazde children saw their differences with their neighbors as religious and cultural and had not thought about ethnic origins. Samir agreed that Muslims might have been Turks originally. Narcisa made a terrible face when I made the suggestion, but then thought about it and said *maybe before the Turkish Empire*. It wasn't a problem for her. The relative indifference was perhaps not surprising, given that Samir's and Narcisa's parents had been taught in the Tito period from textbooks similar to those Serb children still used in Foca in 1997–1998. *It's very confusing*, one teacher told me. *I learned that Princip was a hero, and the Austro-Hungarian Empire bad. Now children [in the Federation] are taught that Princip was a terrorist and the Austro-Hungarians good.*[42]

Postwar Federation textbooks certainly attempted to create a new awareness of Bosnian national identity and its roots. A far larger proportion of the new history text was devoted to "Bosnian history" than to South Slav or Yugoslav history. I had a sense that the primary school textbooks had been written rather fast, patched together from previous materials with new sections pasted in and old ones rewritten. While the narrative message that came across in the Serbian books was a long struggle for Serbian self-determination against the odds, with outside powers that acted to further their own ends, the Federation narrative message focused on the attempt to define a specifically Bosnian state, first within the Ottoman Empire, and then within the Austro-Hungarian Empire. While Serbian texts stressed the "anarchy, corruption," and "economic, political, and cultural backwardness of the Ottoman empire and the Turks," Federation texts emphasized the political and religious tolerance of the Ottomans and failed attempts at reform.

The Federation texts included the nineteenth-century attempt to define "Bosniak" as a multi-confessional national identity linked specifically to the region, and the growing importance of a secular Muslim identity. They presented Serb rebellions as having failed because of internal quarrels or despotic leadership, or as having succeeded because they had co-opted other "Bosnian Christian" reform movements.

Serb successes were linked with plans for expansion and domination by Serbia, as in the first half of the nineteenth century: "Serbian attempts to exert influence on the situation in BiH were evident. In these plans the proposed union of Bosnia with Serbia was dominant." Or as in the proposed Serbian national program of the late nineteenth century, in which "Serbia would include the greater part of Slav countries in the Balkan Peninsula (BiH, Montenegro, North Albania, Macedonia, and Bulgaria)."

The most significant difference was that Federation textbooks included attempts to destroy or exterminate the Muslim population. Seventh graders in Foca learned that the Balkan wars liberated Serbs from Turkey and the feudal system "increased Serb confidence," and left Muslims "confused and surprised." Seventh graders in Gorazde learned that during the Balkan wars Muslims "were executed, exiled, and converted to Christianity by force. The aim of Serbian and Montenegrin policy was the extermination of everything non-Orthodox by terror."

It was these attempts at extermination, rather than stories of historical origins, that stuck in the Muslim children's minds. A number of them told me of *six genocides* against the Muslim people. *The first one was in 1610,* Narcisa said. *The organizer of everything was the Orthodox Church and Serbia and Montenegro.* She felt that her own experiences helped her to understand how it was for people in the past. *Not everything is the same, but in some lessons there is some connection with this war. [. . .] Because it already happened, so we can have some picture in mind of how it was before.*

If claims to territory are based on a blood-and-soil discourse of what group was there first and what was their racial ancestry, then identifying origins, proving one's own historical continuity and the discontinuity or false claims of others, becomes important. The Serbian textbooks gave a clear picture of a people with a long historical pedigree struggling against colonizers and traitors for a unified state in which all Serbs could live together. There was another message as well: Attempts to create a Bosnian state, whether by imperial (Austro-Hungarian) or communist design, had been futile. Muslim children, in contrast, learned about the continuity of the Bosnian state rather than of a particular people, and about themselves as members of a collective that included multiple ethnic identities: Muslim, Croat, and Serb. Yet here too one could trace a contradictory message of ethnic exclusivity in the references to the victimization and oppression of Muslims and to the long-standing expansionist and genocidal tendencies of the Serbs.

I saw both these strands of thinking in a seventh-grade history class in Gorazde. They were discussing the Congress of Berlin in 1878, when according to their teacher, a weakened Ottoman Empire allowed Austro-Hungary to *occupy* Bosnia-Herzegovina, while Serbia and Montenegro gained their independence. The favored method of teaching in both cities was by rote learning and recitation. Grades were awarded for the capacity to memorize and recite the selected text. As I watched children stand up, either confident and word-perfect or nervous and tongue-tied, in scenes reminiscent of Dickens's *Hard Times,* it often struck me that the most useful reform would be to teach and reward them for questioning, arguing, and seeking answers for themselves. Then the content of their textbooks would matter less.

The teacher of this class told me he favored a more Socratic approach, but I sensed that the child pulled to the front of the class to join in "the dialogue" knew what answers the teacher expected.

What does occupation mean? The teacher asked.

To take over someone's country by armed force.

So we, Bosnia, were some object, given to anyone, first to the Ottomans then to Austro-Hungary, it was unfair and imperialistic. But who benefited?

Serbia and Montenegro.

And who was helping Serbia the most?

Russia.

And who is helping Serbia now?

Russia.

So all the changes in the world are made by the Great Powers.

The primary school where this class took place, a large, graceful, and solid building built by those same Austro-Hungarian occupiers, had largely withstood the shelling. It had been beautifully refurbished by a Swedish relief agency. It too had changed its name, from Nikola Tesla, the Serbian inventor, to a local religious intellectual, Husein Efendija Djozo. In Foca, meanwhile, as the primary school switched Croatian partisan for Serbian saint, the high school retained Nikola Tesla. The ghosts of the past were also moving to their "ethnic homelands."

The modern scholarly consensus is that Bosnian Muslims and Bosnian Serbs are both of somewhat mixed origins, like most of the peoples of Europe today. Prior to the Ottoman period, indigenous Bosnians were Slavs, and the region was dominated by the Catholic Church. However, the remote mountainous landscape, the distance from Rome, and competition with the Orthodox Church all allowed for the development of an independent church and various forms of folk religion. In the two centuries after the arrival of the Turks, many Bosnians converted to Islam. The conversions don't appear to have been forced: they included large numbers from all classes of society, and Christians who did not convert could keep their land. The Muslim population was also boosted by slaves captured in various Ottoman wars, as conversion meant freedom, and by Islamicized Muslims who had retreated with the withdrawal of the Ottoman Empire from areas such as Hungary and present-day Croatia.

Bosnian Serbs, particularly in the Drina Valley that borders on Serbia, are part of the indigenous Serbian Orthodox community. This group also includes those who assimilated and converted over the centuries, such as the non-Slav nomadic Vlachs, Catholics, and colonizing Greeks and Albanians. Paradoxically, the arrival of the Ottomans in the fifteenth century seems to have assisted the expansion of the Orthodox Church in Bosnia, through both conversion and colonization. During much of the Ottoman period, the Turks maintained a strong alliance with the Orthodox Church, to the benefit of both in their fights with other Christian powers.[43]

The Ottoman era, for all its contested symbolism, was outside the living memory of the families in both cities. The Second World War was not. Every child had grandparents (living or dead) whose memories and personal stories of that time had acquired significance since the most recent war. The power of the period to produce strong feelings was brought home to me by the incensed commentary on a Federation textbook from one of my Serbian translators. She was most upset by "the game with numbers"— by what she saw as Muslim attempts to reduce the size of the crimes against Serbs and to exaggerate the harm done by them.

There is no doubt that the Second World War was a horrifying and desperate period in Balkan history. There were at least four wars going on in the region. There was an initial war between Germany and Italy and the Yugoslav state, and a second war between the Axis occupiers and the various Yugoslav resistance movements. There were also two civil wars: one between the Croatian fascist regime, established by the Nazis, and the Serb population of Bosnia and Serbia; and another between the two main resistance movements, the royalist Chetniks led by Draza Mihajlovic and the communist partisans led by Tito. Almost a million Yugoslavs died, most of them killed by other Yugoslavs. The Serbs lost the largest number (209,000 in Bosnia alone) and the Bosnian Muslims the greatest proportion (8.1 percent) of their respective populations.[44]

People of all ethnicities fought on all sides, and some changed allegiances during the course of the Second World War. This was especially true in the Drina Valley, which at different periods was the headquarters of Tito's partisans or under Chetnik control. There was a Bosnian SS division. There were Muslims who either acquiesced or actively collaborated with the Ustashe. Muslims also protested against Ustashe atrocities against Serbs and Jews. There were leading Chetniks who advocated the creation of a homogeneous Serbia from which all non-Serbs should be removed. There were Chetnik massacres of Muslims, for their collaboration with both Ustashe and partisans, and Muslim massacres of Chetniks in retaliation. Muslims and Serbs fought together as partisans, and even Muslims and Chetniks cooperated on occasion. From this dismal period, one could find evidence to support every perspective and to justify every new outrage of the recent war.[45]

In schools in both towns, children were learning to play the history game, with the selective use of facts. *In the Second World War,* Marko in Foca told me, *Germany wanted to put everything under their control, and now maybe Muslims want it. They [Germans and Muslims] were together in the same army fighting against the Serbs.* In Gorazde, Jasmin learned that Muslims had protested on behalf of Serbs against the Nazi policies of extermination, and that the Chetnik leader, Mihajlovic, had wanted to annihilate Muslims. *They were on the same side but Serbs wanted to destroy Muslims [. . .] because they always wanted to govern all of Bosnia, and they couldn't stand Muslims living in Bosnia, and they are still bothered by Muslims.*

Many of the Muslim children used the term "Chetnik" as a disparaging way to refer to Serbs. Unlike the term "Turk" when used to describe Muslims, this is not always a term of abuse. Some Serbs use it with pride because of its historical associations: Its original use was to describe heroic Serb bandit fighters who struggled against the Turks in earlier times.[46] Iris said she usually called *those Serbs who were in the war Chetniks, but I can't call a Serb child a Chetnik.* Nor could she use the term for Serbs who had stayed in Gorazde during the war. She reserved it for those who had been *involved in this aggression against us.* Samir told me it was the term for those Serbs who called Muslims Balija, and for criminals. He would not use it for a Serb friend because a friend would not call him Balija either.

Identity and Belief

It was Ramadan, the month during which Muslims fasted during the day. Narcisa, who had always been the most devout member of her family after her grandmother, was fasting, as she had done since she was quite small. Her father and brother were abstaining from alcohol out of respect and support for her. I asked them, *What does it mean to be a Muslim?*

Believe me, I don't know, her father replied. *I was brought up a Communist; Tito was Allah for all of us . . . especially Muslims. He gave us a nation in 1971, so of course we are glad about that.*

How do you define a Muslim?

People who believe in Allah.

So can you be a Muslim?

He grinned at me, seeing the contradiction. *Yes.*

Although you don't believe?

I am almost an atheist.

And still a Muslim?

Well, I can't be an Eskimo.

War had made him more aware of his specific identity as something different from other national groups. *You know what—if you were in Foca, Visegrad, Zvornik . . . The Muslims there were slaughtered because of the hatred. [. . .] All the Serbs in Gorazde ran away from here, they wanted to get out of this hell.* But even before the war, he had been quite clear that being a Muslim was his heritage and tradition because that was how his parents and grandparents had defined themselves. *My parents were religious. It was my choice [not to be].*

If both parents are Muslims then it is natural to be a Muslim, Narcisa's mother explained. *I respect my mother because she respects Islam. I'm not religious myself. During that period [after 1970 in communist Yugoslavia], I*

had no need to go to mosque and my parents never made me. It was qualifi-
cations that mattered. We celebrated Bajram in both families.[47]

Why not? her husband interjected. *Lots of baklava and cakes!*

I didn't have time to learn about religion, Narcisa's mother continued. *I*
just celebrated because I belong to my people.

They said their daughter's more serious approach to religion had
always been her free choice. *We aren't worried about it. We see that besides*
school she has lots of other activities. She's not especially religious, it doesn't
preoccupy her.

This conversation, typical of many that I had in Gorazde, brought home
to me how soft-edged and fluid Bosnian Muslim identity was. There were
no references to the distant past, to land, or to historic origins. People were
Muslims because their parents and grandparents had been; it made them
part of a community and represented what they saw as a good way of living, with particular moral and cultural practices they valued. It did not
necessarily entail religious belief, and for many of the parents born in the
1950s and 1960s it had not done so because religious belief was not com-
patible with Party membership. The sense of community arose from established traditions, such as Ramadan and Bajram, which distinguished them
from their neighbors.

They enjoyed their neighbors' different traditions as well. Elvira's father,
a Muslim married to a Croat, said, *The customs we have as Muslims are*
very good and very practical. He took pleasure in wearing new clothes and
visiting for Bajram as well as for Catholic and Orthodox Christmas. It was
this sense of belonging to a shared country—Yugoslavia, then Bosnia—and
at the same time enjoying differences that was the striking feature of the
Bosnian Muslims' identity. Their sense of themselves was inclusive, and it
depended in part on living with others who were not the same.[48]

Tito seems to have recognized both the inclusive and the soft-edged
aspects of Muslim identity. He clearly hoped to make use of this identity
in his construction of a second Yugoslavia out of the ashes of the Second
World War. At the outset, although the Final Resolution of the Antifascist
Council for the National Liberation of Bosnia-Herzegovina (1943) recognized the "equality of Serbs, Muslims, and Croats" in their "common
and indivisible homeland," Tito denied Bosnian Muslims the possibility
of identifying themselves as a people (*Narod*) in the same terms that were
available to both Croats and Serbs.[49] His plan was a centralized state with

a new Yugoslav identity, into which he hoped Muslims would be the first to assimilate. By the late 1960s, he recognized that while a centralized policy benefited the more geographically dispersed and numerous Serbs, it caused tensions with all the other ethnicities. He moved instead to promoting diversity, in a more decentralized federal state, as a way of balancing national interests and retaining control. This culminated in the famous 1974 Constitution, now despised by the Serbs for undermining their interests, but welcomed by the other nationalities for increasing their power and standing within the Federation. Over this period, Bosnian Muslims rose higher on the complex ladder of categories of national identification within Socialist Yugoslavia, and from 1971 they could define themselves as a "people." This was one reason Narcisa's parents and many other Gorazde families saw Tito as their champion.

The sense of inclusiveness and multiplicity appeared to have survived the war and been passed to the younger generation in Gorazde. When I asked the children how they identified themselves, most used multiple categories. Alma had been a refugee abroad during the war and had told her schoolmates she was *Bosnian, and then they asked me my nationality and I would say Muslim.* All agreed that being Bosnian meant being a citizen of a multinational state which included three nations: Muslim, Serb, and Croat. They regarded the distinctions between these as religious, and for some like Senad and Samir, it was being Bosnian that mattered most. Senad wanted Serbs and Croats in Bosnia to use the terms "Orthodox" and "Catholic."[50] The state had also tried to grasp this nettle of the double meaning of the word "Muslim" and had recently introduced the term "Bosniak" so that Muslims had a nonreligious way of defining their national identity. The term had not caught on in Gorazde when I was there, and seemed to be a source of confusion. It produced fury in some families in Foca, who felt that the only distinguishing aspect of Muslim identity was religious practice, and that this new terminology was one more attempt to create something out of nothing.

The children in Gorazde were sometimes rather vague about Muslim religious practice. Admira said she was a believer, but was not sure what it meant. When I pushed her, she said, *I know that it's a belief in Allah, and we just believe in him.* She no longer bothered to go to the mekteb she had attended before the war. Children from more religious families, like Fikreta, were clearer. In mekteb, Fikreta had learned that *we Muslims have to pray to God. For example, people of other nationalities, they usually go to the churches and they also pray to God, like we go to mosque. I mean they do the same thing, but in another way.* Fikreta had worked out who she was by looking at others who lived beside her and did things differently.

I finally began to understand why despite all that had happened, many of the Gorazde families still felt they should live with their Serb neighbors once more. Part of being a Bosnian Muslim depended on living with others who were not. Differences were valued because they helped people to define themselves. Fikreta asked, *How can we be alone in the house and not be with anybody else?* No one in the Muslim families wanted to live in a monoethnic state. Again and again, I heard, *In the whole of Bosnia-Herzegovina there is no life, life would be without any sense* if Muslims lived alone. "To be Bosnian was to have a feeling for otherness, for the different, as part of the daily reality of one's most personal environment. It was this experience of the different that made it possible to be Bosnian," Ivan Lovrenovic wrote in his cultural history of Bosnia. He also lamented that "the new territorialization" and "the poison of chauvinism" had destroyed this "crowning glory" of Bosnian social life and turned Bosnians into Bosniak Muslims, Serbs, and Croats. Yet this feeling for otherness did not seem to have completely disappeared in Gorazde.[51]

Some Gorazde parents told me that the war had made them more aware of what being a Muslim meant and more curious about their religious roots, but I had no sense that the war had created increased religiosity or chauvinism in any of the children or their parents. Those who were religious had always been so. Those who were not had not changed. All the children said they believed in God, but for the majority this did not involve much in the way of religious practice, such as regular attendance at mosque or mekteb. Senad, whose grandmother had been a bula (a religious teacher), believed in God, *but I don't learn about it.* He thought it excessive to have to *pray every day, five times a day.* He also rejected the teaching in school that his own religion was best: *All people are the same, no matter what religion they are.*

For these families, actions like fasting for a few days during Ramadan were ways of showing that they belonged to a particular community. Hasan fasted *because of the tradition.* Hasan's mother was pleased that there was now religious teaching in school, but this had more to do with Hasan learning about his own customs than with devotion. She had been ashamed when as a refugee in Germany, she had not known the dates of her own religious festivals and a German woman had. She wanted her son to learn the things she herself could not teach him. Other parents thought religious teaching should be confined to the mosque and not take place during school hours. The reason for this again came down to sharing living space with other groups. Islamic teaching in the schools would make it difficult for children of other nationalities to come back to Gorazde.

This moderation contrasted with the new assertiveness of some of Gorazde's Muslims. The Mufti (Muslim jurist and religious leader) had tried to have a Serb woman, who had lived in the town throughout the war, dismissed from running the kindergarten. He gave me a variety of reasons, including *loose morals* and a father who had fought on the Serb side, but he was most upset by the idea of Muslim children being taught by a non-Muslim. He also made various pronouncements that the war might be related to Gorazde citizens' lack of godliness. Many families seemed uncomfortable with his behavior and distanced themselves from it. *Everybody has the right to believe what he wants,* said Narcisa. *People who believe in Islam should be treated no differently than Catholics and other religions.*

New female bulas had arrived in Gorazde from Zenica. They gave classes in a private house. Fikreta had gone because she was curious. These new bulas wore headscarves, and she was irritated because they had told her she could not wear tight clothes and miniskirts and should wear a scarf over her head. *I can pray,* she told me, *I can pray to God, but I won't accept having that scarf over my head.* She preferred the *real mekteb,* run by locals, which she attended regularly. *There are some Arabians and their women are usually wearing those and . . . I don't like it. My mother wouldn't accept it either, and no one in Gorazde and no one in Bosnia wears those scarves.*

She was also unhappy with their teaching about other nationalities:

> *They tell us that people who have other religions are not religious at all and that we shouldn't have any contact with them. But I don't think that is true. Like Serbs and Croats, that we shouldn't have contact with them. These people from Zenica, they're Arabians you know, and they teach us these sorts of things, but in our real mekteb they*

only teach us about our religion and how to pray. Our real hodza in our mekteb, he teaches us about Suras, that's a kind of lesson from the Koran, and how to pronounce things. And in this Arabic mekteb they teach us about Christians and about Jewish people, and how they didn't respect these books God sent them.

She did not argue when she disagreed with the bulas. *When I have to study these lessons, I just study them to get a good mark, but I don't try to keep them in my mind. My mother wanted me to go to the real mekteb and not to go to them anymore because they don't pray to God in the same way that we do.*[52]

Like the interviews, the children's written stories indicated that living in a specific and much loved place, being a citizen of a particular country, was more important than the ethnic or religious identity of victim or aggressor. Terms like *sacrifices for our Bosnia,* or *the good spirit of the Bosnian people,* or *our brave town, Gorazde,* were common. One fourteen-year-old girl wrote, *War is the worst experience that could happen to me and all the people in Bosnia. I heard that some people wanted a country where only one people would live and other people had to suffer because of that.*

The sense that their country was still inclusive came through even in the angriest of texts—as in this one from a fifteen-year-old girl:

And those who wanted the war are not human beings; they just look like human beings. Their hearts are made of stone and through their veins runs dirty blood. How could they do it? How could they ruin a country which belonged to them as much as us? The country had room for everyone. How could they kill the children of their friends, friends who sat beside them at school? Only wild people could have done this, those who lived in the forest, but what could be done? [. . .] I think that Bosnia-Herzegovina will be the same as it was before and that the people who deserved will live in it without those who have ruined and killed it.

Again, *the wild people* are unidentified. The headmaster of the high school in Foca saw this Muslim habit of talking about unspecified aggressors, and of teaching children that Serbs from Montenegro and Serbia had fought in Bosnia, as profoundly dishonest, a way of denying that Muslims and Serbs had been equally involved in a civil war: *The graveyards are full of Serbs and Muslims born and killed in Bosnia. So Serbs were aggressors on one side of the street and Muslims who lived on the other were defending themselves? Who kicked Serbs out of Zenica?* Dusan's father asked, *How can I be an aggressor in my own country?* My unspoken answer was only by refusing to share it with those who regard it as a common home. I could see that from the perspective of the Muslims who wanted to rebuild this common home, talking about an unidentified aggressor or using the term "Chetnik" in preference to "Serb" did make it possible to separate the cause of the conflict from local Serb neighbors, so that those *who deserved* could still be included in a joint state.

The problem was that young Serbs in Foca did not want to be included in the Bosnian state and did not believe it existed. There were no fluffy edges to Serb children's sense of themselves. They knew who they were, and they knew they were not Bosnian. For many of them the war had helped in this crystallization.[53] Some parents lamented the loss of the old identity: Bojan's mother mumbled sadly *I was born in Bosnia and I am still in Bosnia.* She obviously did not like the topic much, and was almost whispering when she added that she was *Serb, I don't know what difference does it make. We say Serbs, it was Bosnia before. . . . What do I know?* However, her son Bojan told me confidently, *I am Serb because I am not other nationalities, it is important for everybody.* Ivana's mother said proudly, *I am still Yugoslav,* but Ivana was sure she was Serb. Dusan had always been Serb. It was *not just my nationality, but also the nationality of my grandfather and great grandfather.* Even those who had understood the complexities of the Dayton Agreement, and knew that Republika Srpska was an entity within a country called Bosnia and Herzegovina, were quite sure they were not Bosnian. Vesna had called herself a Bosnian of Orthodox religion before the war. She was still *Orthodox,* but now a *Serb.*

Again, there was a small disaffected minority in Foca. They were all girls, and belonged to the group of children who were curious about the war and more open to their Muslim neighbors' returning. Helena did not care what nationality she was and did not understand the differences: *I don't know if there are differences between Muslims and Serbs; maybe in religion but not life.*

The distinctiveness of Serbian identity showed up most clearly in written stories. Many Serb children used a poetic and rhetorical style reminiscent of their own national epics, and quite absent from Muslim scripts. One fourteen-year-old boy wrote, *War [. . .] turned our dreams into nightmares. [. . .] War is a monster who wanted to seduce people of different religions and bring them to bloodshed. [. . .] Hostile warriors left trails of grief behind them. [. . .] Instead of laughter there is grief, instead of a hand, an artificial limb, instead of a healthy body, many scars. [. . .] I would like it if war never happened again and we could live in our Republika Srpska, which is small but dear in our hearts.*

Several raised questions of land ownership and origins. A fifteen-year-old girl wrote: *The Muslims were responsible for starting the war. I do not say this because I am a Serb, but because it is obvious. They started the war because they wanted to create their own country in areas which were always ours. Everybody knows that Muslims come from Serbs, and they did not have the right to start a war and endanger our childhoods. They had no reason to do it.*

Even the youngest children set the Serb victory of achieving an "independent homeland" squarely in the context of the Serbs' historical experience: their victimhood through the centuries, their exploitation by others, and their strength and virtue. A thirteen-year-old girl put it this way:

War brought unrest to our hearts. Many people gave their lives defending their homeland. Serbs survived a lot of suffering, misfortune, and annihilation through the centuries. Many families left their homes to start a new life with bundles in their arms. Everything that happened and happens to us reminds us that history repeats itself. Is it fate? Only Serbian people could handle all this because they are used to pain and suffering. We got used to fighting for someone else's interests without thinking. We did not realize our own strength.

Sometimes Serbian identity was connected to a feeling of being misunderstood and isolated by the rest of the world: *The entire world is against Serbs,* wrote another thirteen-year-old girl, *but I don't understand, we are human too. I hope that we can prove it; truth and justice will emerge. Why does the world separate Serb children from others. We want peace, love, and joy; we don't want shooting and war.*

Vesna Pesic, a sociologist and politician from Belgrade, describes this kind of thinking as resentful nationalism. This is an identity built on frustration (at failed historic projects such as the re-creation of the old empire), feelings of inferiority and jealousy (from lagging behind Europe), and anger at the undeserved ill feelings of others, combined with selective blindness to behaviors that might have created resentment in the others. Sometimes this blindness was striking. Stojan's father asked me in amazement one day why Muslim children had any problem with reading Njegos, the nineteenth-century Montenegrin poet whose epic *The Mountain Wreath* celebrates the conversion—or massacre and expulsion—of Turks from Montenegro. The idea that lines like "No single seeing eye, no tongue of Turk, escaped to tell his tale another day! We put them all unto the sword" might be troubling to Muslims, whom many Serbs still called Turks, had not crossed his mind. Pesic argues that resentful nationalism is the basis of all identities in the Balkans. I could not find this symmetry in the Muslim community in Gorazde; indeed, it was this failure to think within a similar framework that generated some of the Serbs' anger and their frequent assertion that Muslims lied.[54]

The school psychologist in Foca suggested that children wrote in this way to gain approval and that it did not necessarily represent their true feelings. This may well be true. At one point, I thought of working in Visegrad, and asked a group of children there to write stories. In this case, the stories were written under the eye of their teacher and handed back to me. This one by a fifteen-year-old girl is typical:

Many Serb heroes are deep in their graves, deep in the black ground, proud because they gave their lives for their country. Certainly, it was not what they wanted. They wanted to walk freely around Republika Srpska. But they had to stop those who want to harm Serb people, someone like you. Serb Sarajevo is no more, thanks to people like you. You were not on the Serb side during the war and now you come to test fifteen-year-olds? Are you not ashamed? How dare you, how do you have the courage to come now in Republika Srpska, now when we do not need you? [. . .] Now we live in a collective center. Serbs do not trust anyone, especially those who were our enemies. Serbs, those proud people, now only believe in themselves.

The hatred directed at me was fair enough, but in Visegrad, story after story was written in a similar manner with little reference to personal experiences. Many used identical phrases such as an appended *P.S. First you bombard us, and then you test us.* It seemed as if strong suggestions had been made to the children as to what to write. I was not able to discover how much they believed their own statements, as I felt unwelcome and unsafe in Visegrad and did not return.

Social identity theory suggests that all identity is fluid to a degree. Mother, daughter, housewife, doctor, partygoer, churchgoer, citizen of a nation— we can be all or any of these and shift between them depending on the social role we need to fulfill and the situation in which we find ourselves.[55] In Foca, the children wrote their stories in the schoolroom. They were unsupervised by their own teacher, but writing for a stranger from the "aggressor country" probably increased the emphasis on national pride and defensiveness. When I got to know some of the children and their families, the rhetoric disappeared and I discovered some of the same Bosnian moderateness that I encountered in Gorazde.

This was evident in religious practice. Foca, like Gorazde, was experiencing a religious revival. I attended packed church services on various holidays with the crowd pushing in the door toward the singing, incense, and light beyond the ancient painted screen. At Easter, I went to a mass baptism. The families and attendant relatives were in their best clothes, one mother resplendent with bright red hair and tight red short skirt, holding her baby in a blue flounced dress. There were two more babies, some embarrassed-looking teenage boys, and a cluster of six- and seven-year-olds. The occasion had a rather routine, businesslike feel: One priest wrote at a desk, while the other sang. The children lined up with the sponsors behind them; babies were held in their sponsors' arms. The priests took it in turn to sing and chant at speed, questions were thrown out and answered, the lined-up children were anointed, then had water splashed on them, then were anointed again. People wandered in and out of the church. I felt as I always did at Orthodox ceremonies: Overwhelmed by the mysterious beauty, but coming from a rather participatory Protestant tradition, bemused by the passivity of the congregation. There was a feeling of magic being worked rather than of promises and relationships being made.

When I told Dusan's father, who had always been a believer, about the baptisms, he responded *Humph . . . it's kind of a fashion.* He liked the idea that Serbs were returning to the church, but feared it was not real, and had less to do with piety than with the conformity learned under communism. Dusan told me he was *not that religious, but I believe in God.* Almost all the children expressed similar views. Some were baptized, some not. For most, celebrations such as the family saints' days (*Slava*), Christmas, and Easter were important as traditions that showed one belonged to a family and an ethnic community. They resented the intrusion of politics into these matters.

The Serbian Orthodox Church had played a significant role in the mobilization of Serbs' anxieties about Islam before the war, warning that it was caught between "two powerful religious internationals [Islam and Catholicism]" and that "the national and ethnic survival of the Serbs is in great danger." The same writer had called for "the expression of an exclusively Serbian nationalist ideology" and declared that "Serbia must of necessity be formed within its ethnic boundaries." The church had added legitimacy to the use of force to achieve such an aim. Another article in an official church publication just before the war had accused the "partisans of peace" of being "champions of treason and defeat" and of having helped "the evil forces that are opposed to God (and by the same token to humanity)." "In our present Armageddon," the article continued, "they are on the side of the destructive Gog and Magog (the mythical personifications of enslavement and tyranny)."[56]

The young priest who taught religious studies at the school in Foca felt it was disrespectful to have destroyed the mosques, but pointed out that some of them had once been churches taken over by Muslims. He opposed rebuilding them, just as he opposed Muslims' return to the town, for reasons of security. The president of the local SRS assured me that there was no extremism or politics in the Orthodox religion, and then explained how his party's symbol, the double-headed eagle, represented the unity of spiritual and secular power. He thought Milorad Dodik, the newly elected prime minister of Republika Srpska, was *a Satan* for suggesting that religion might be taken out of school. *Has the Orthodox Church ever called for war? No!* he said. *But Islam always calls for war. That is the tragedy of those people.*

None of the children in Foca shared this disparaging view of Islam as a religion. They all said people had the right to believe and worship as they wished. Nikola's parents hoped that religion might have a role as a cultural alternative to nationalism, something enjoyable to express who you were, rather than identifying you with a political party. But they feared it was not working out like that. *The way they teach it, children are starting to hate it.* Nikola's father worried religion might replace Marxism as the most onerous and boring subject in the curriculum. Jovan's father was all for getting religion out of school.

Children were not preoccupied with national issues in either town. Getting good grades at school, relationships with friends, sports, and the lack of things for young people to do in their town (particularly in Foca) were what concerned them most. When I first asked them to describe themselves in an open-ended way, only two children spontaneously mentioned national identity. I had to ask about it directly to learn how they identified themselves.

In some children, I could sense the tensions and contradictions created by a pluralist and inclusive upbringing followed by living in a community that lauded ethnic separatism. Divac, who had grown up in a mixed apartment block in Sarajevo thinking of himself as Yugoslav, held *Muslim separatists* responsible for the war. He missed his old life, and still did not understand why Muslims had wanted to destroy it. My suggestion that they might have felt uncomfortable in a Serb-dominated Yugoslavia was roundly rejected. *They wouldn't be minority if they were Yugoslav. They're supposed to be Yugoslav.* This is the argument the English have with the some of the Scots and Welsh over their reluctance to see themselves as "British." Even the most cosmopolitan citizens of hegemonic nations tend not to notice the degree to which the interests and values of a multinational country can become enmeshed with the interests and values of the most numerous and widespread group, if that group is their own. I had tried:

If Yugoslavs are mainly Serbs, I asked Divac, *you don't think that might be a problem for people who aren't Serbs?*

Why would it be? Because we were all Yugoslavs in my opinion.

They would say, "Look at how the Yugoslavs have treated Kosovar Albanians, who are supposed to be Yugoslavs, but are not treated equally."

I don't know, I heard on TV that many Albanians came to our country without citizenship, they were just sent there without visas.

Never mind. The main point was that before the war Divac had an idea of himself as belonging to something multinational and inclusive. Since the war, this had disappeared. *Of course it's changed. It's not that I have a different opinion from before the war. I have to adapt to the surroundings. [. . .] I didn't know that I was Serb. But we are not living in Yugoslavia any more. We are living in Republika Srpska.*

Is being a Serb an important part of who you are?

Now it is, he replied.

Just how much he had adapted became clear when I switched off the tape and we were discussing how depressed and hard things were in Foca. He said he wanted to leave Republika Srpska and Yugoslavia as quickly as possible. *I will try to go somewhere, anywhere there is a better situation.* He asked me why the international community was blocking aid to the town, and I explained about the failure to hand over indicted war criminals or allow Muslims to return home, and he suddenly changed. The easygoing, open young teenager, whose father had protected his Muslim neighbors, was suddenly an ardent nationalist talking to a representative of a NATO aggressor state, defending Serb pride from outside pressure and interference. *Maybe there are things we don't want to do. These people [Karadzic et al] are national heroes for us. Maybe we prefer not to have people come back. If you make that choice then there is a price to pay. Maybe we prefer to pay that price.*

The war had not been caused by conflicting perceptions of national identity, but it had certainly created them in this younger generation. All the Serb children now thought of themselves as Serb, and half of them said if they could vote, it would be for a Serb party. But the war had also produced a feeling of not having "a country," confusion as to the nature of the state in which they lived, and alienation from their current home. Although most said they would fight for Republika Srpska if it came to another war, half of them did not want to live there or vote at all. Like Divac, they just wanted to get out. Many wanted to go to America because it was a *developed and modern* country, never mind that it was the enemy that had so unjustly bombed them.

As for the Muslim children in Gorazde, war had given them a country: Bosnia and Herzegovina. They too were prepared to fight for it in any future war, and unlike the children in Foca, they wanted to live in Bosnia in the future. They also had a stronger sense of Muslim identity than before the war, but for them ethnic identification was not paramount. When I asked them whether they would vote for a Muslim party if they could vote, the majority said no, just a decent one.

"The Serbs began it. On 28 June, they shot the Austrian Crown Prince Franz Ferdinand and his wife Sophie . . . everyone says the Serbs want war in order to maintain their independence and Russia will support them." Thus began twelve-year-old Piete Kuhr's diary on August 1, 1914. Piete was German and lived with her brother and grandmother in eastern Prussia, eighty miles from the German-Russian front. Her first few pages were filled with excited patriotism. She was moved to tears at seeing military uniforms brought out of storage. (Her grandmother had a different response, which reminded me of Amela's grandmother: "I have lived through this twice before . . . why can't people live in peace?") At school, Piete learned it was her patriotic duty to stop using the French "adieu" and start saying "auf Wiedersehen." "The girls are pleased that Germany is entering the field against its old enemy France. The most pleased of all are the teachers. We have to learn new songs that glorify war." She wrote these out:

> God save our precious fatherland
> Our ancient swords serve as of yore,
> Lasting as long as iron ore
> To save us from another's yoke
> Preserving the heart of German folk.

On August 5, 1914, she wrote:

> In our geography lesson we were again concerned with Serbia. I myself had quite forgotten where exactly its frontiers ran and had difficulty pointing it out on a map. We now have a great hatred for this little country and shout "Down with Serbia!" No one in my class can say what flag Serbia has or what its inhabitants are like, for example what religion they have. I said in school today, "Princip is better looking than Archduke Franz Ferdinand." I couldn't have done more to stir the hornet's nest if I had said that our Emperor Wilhelm was a traitor.[57]

Piete had no real concept of who the enemy was until the conflict began. I watched a similar process at work in Britain during the run-up to the Falklands War in 1982, when suddenly the public, which had taken no interest in the horrors inflicted by the Argentinean junta in its dirty war upon its own population in the 1970s, was preoccupied with the evil nature of the "Argies," and eager, as a popular newspaper headline said, to "bash" them.

The social psychologists Muzafer and Carolyn Sherif conducted some famous experiments with eleven-year-old boys in the 1940s and 1950s. In one, children who had camped and played together for a week were then divided into two groups in a way that deliberately cut across the friendships formed. The researchers discovered that even with such an arbitrary division and no previous history of conflict, the new group identities overrode all previous relationships. Before the split, 60 percent reported that their best friends were among those who were later placed in the other group, but only 10 percent still claimed those friendships after the separation. Those who tried to sustain friendships were ostracized, branded traitors, and sometimes physically abused.[58]

The need to categorize ourselves and feel we belong is so deeply embedded that even when groups are newly created on a completely random basis and participants are not acquainted with members of either group, they tend to value the members of their own group and devalue those of the other. In a different experiment, Henri Tajfel gave participants the chance to maximize material gain for their own group, or to gain less, but increase the differential between their own group and the other group. Most participants chose the second option: They would rather that their own group gained more at the expense of the other than that both gained more overall. Overt conflict exacerbates such tendencies, but does not cause them. Once separated and placed in competition, the eleven-year-olds in the Sherifs' experiments rapidly developed group identities, insignia, and codes of conduct, as well as derogatory stereotypes about the other group.[59]

There was no need to resort to any history of ancient antagonisms or supposed warlike habits to explain why two communities in the Drina Valley, which had lived intermingled and closely together for almost forty years and then were separated by war, became antagonistic to each other. My surprise was rather that in both communities, two years after the war, one could still sense the significance and impact of that joint life. At times, I felt quite bewildered as to where I was. It was not just the similar arrangements of furniture within the rooms, the almost identical clothes, the same rituals and courtesies of hospitality. It was also the phrases the families used when they talked, their aspirations and their values, their moderateness regarding excesses within their own religious communities. When I asked parents what values mattered for their children, they always gave me the same lists: *not to lie, not to steal, to respect elders, to value learning, not to abuse or mistreat others, whatever their beliefs or the color of their skin.* I had the sense of living in a common moral community with many shared values, where differences had only recently come to symbolize danger.

War creates its own dynamic, and the Serb leaders clearly hoped that their campaign of terror would lead to reprisals and create the interethnic hatred that had not previously existed. The justification of "mutual animosities" would then become a self-fulfilling prophecy. Tell people to go to war because their neighbors are planning to kill them, expel those neighbors with such brutality that some will strike back with equal nastiness, and then express astonishment, as Karadzic did, that "the international community should want people who hate each other to the point of extermination to live together again."[60]

War had created a sense of threat on both sides. For Serbs it had made sharing territory and daily life with Muslims almost inconceivable for the present. Reconciliation with Muslims was seen as a weapon that the West continued to use in its war against Serbs, forcing them to live with people who hated them after they had sacrificed so much to free themselves. War crimes trials were perceived as another one-sided injustice because the majority of defendants were Serb.

One night I drove Gordana to a party in Gorazde. My translators and the local staff members of international organizations appeared to me to be the main hope for Bosnia. Unlike the children I interviewed, they were old enough to remember good friendships with the other side, and unlike those children's parents, they were young enough not to have done any fighting themselves. Most were university students; many had been abroad. They moved easily between the communities, with access to all the media and all opinions. But when Gordana came to my flat to change for the party I sensed an edginess, and when I answered a seemingly innocuous question about Gorazde, she suddenly launched into an angry attack. I and the West would never understand, she asserted, because we relied on video and newspapers and these were manipulated, and who did I think had started the war? Serbs had been totally bewildered at the beginning, not understanding why there was shooting, and the JNA had taken away all the weapons so that Bosnian Serbs had to buy them back to fight and were treated like "shit" by Serbia, and Dayton was a complete disaster and tragedy for them—*and what about the concentration camps?*

What concentration camps, what were their names?

I can't remember, but you must know our history—and we were back in the Second World War. There was no arguing with her. All this while she changed into party clothes and did her hair and complained about the cold.

I HATE Muslims for what they did to us! Why did they start this? You know why I want to get my apartment back in Sarajevo? So I can sell it and leave! That's what we all want, we DON'T want to live with them and they don't want to live with us and anyone who tells you differently is lying. When they say they don't hate us, they are lying.

Gordana, why is it so important to prove to me that they hate you?

Because it's true, and the worst thing is they come from us, they are Serbs.

Are you sure you want to go to this party?

Yes—are you sure you want to take me?

Of course.

So we went; she ate and drank and seemed quite comfortable with her Muslim colleagues from Gorazde. At one point, she argued with Sean, an American friend who worked for the UN High Commission for Refugees, about why the United States thought it should be "world policeman."

It should be, Sean said, *but unfortunately, it isn't. Because it's the most powerful nation. If it lived up to its responsibilities, the war would have stopped far sooner.*

And why, Gordana countered, *isn't Izetbegovic at The Hague?*

He's an incompetent man, but not a criminal. Karadzic was responsible for Srebrenica. That happened, you aren't responsible, but your leaders are.

Izetbegovic had concentration camps, he shot soldiers with snipers.

None that I know of, and sniping is a legitimate act of war.

If you take Karadzic to The Hague you are saying we are all guilty.

On the contrary, Gordana, I interjected, *the point of arresting him is to release others from guilt. What I want to know is why you support him.*

Because he was our leader. The Germans supported Hitler. This was certainly an interesting parallel.

But now they're ashamed of that support, I replied.

But it took twenty years and we will need that time.

It's not the justice of your cause, the right to autonomy, but the brutality with which your leaders pursued it that was the crime. Anyway, I added, *now you have your territory.*

Yes, we have "Africa," they have "Europe." They have the cities.

But Muslim people mostly lived in cities before, said Sean.

Yes, exactly, and why? Because the Turks gave them power and wealth, and us nothing! We were back with the Ottomans.

But that doesn't make driving them out of the cities or bombing them in the cities right, does it? I asked.

In Srbinje we put them on buses, they were not hurt.

But Gordana, they had the right to stay, I responded.

How could they stay? They would have been killed. Just like the children, Gordana saw busing people out of their hometown as a humane action.

I was so often told that Muslims hated Serbs and that they lied when they said otherwise that I began to realize that the Serbs needed to believe this because only the existence of this Muslim hatred could justify and neutralize the forced expulsion of their Muslim neighbors. It was possible to find hatred and similar distrust in a few of the Muslim families, but war had not extinguished their desire for a joint life, even if it had made them feel life together could not be the same. The tragedy was that the Dayton Peace Agreement, through its inability to undo the logic of separation that had led to war in the first place, was continuing the de facto partition.

David Shipler studied Arab and Jewish communities in Israel in the mid-1980s. What he found regarding children's perceptions of one another makes depressing reading. Jewish children had stereotyped images of Arabs as fearsome, violent, strong, duplicitous, and cowardly. They also thought them fanatical, brutal, and primitive. (These stereotypes were reminiscent of some Serb writings about Muslims.) These images were reinforced by school textbooks. For example, a text about Arabs and Islam, produced by the Israeli ministry of education, focused on war, thievery, and conquest, rather than on Arab contributions to medicine, science, or architecture. A picture of a line of Arabs riding camels was captioned: "An armed group of men. It is possible they are heading for a robbery raid." Bedouin women were described as unfeeling: those "who lose their sons or husbands in battle receive the hard news without weeping or cries." Some Serb women had similarly complained to me of the unfeeling nature of Muslim grief because of the lack of tears, while some Muslim women had told me that Serbs were *hysterical* and *exaggerated* their feelings. Children's literature emphasized Arabs' hatred of Jews and their wish to destroy Israel.

Shipler points out that all these images were reinforced by the absence of personal contact between Israeli Jews and Arabs since 1948, when Arabs disappeared from most Israeli lives except as hired labor. A 1980 survey found that 51.6 percent of Jews thought the majority of Israeli Arabs (Arabs who were Israeli citizens living within the 1967 borders) hated Jews. Many Jewish children favored expulsion of all Arabs. Shipler quotes an Arab teacher and politician's description of a typical discussion class: "What you hear in the questions is terrible. For example, 'Why do you have to settle here? This is our country; you have to be expelled outside the country. You have a lot of land, and we have a very tiny piece of land. This is for Jews, so you have no right to stay here, and if we let you, you have to thank us for that.'"[61]

Arab stereotypes of Jews showed a remarkable symmetry, the most prominent being "the aggressive, brutal Jew, who embraces violence without remorse." The stereotypes became more pronounced as contact between the two groups decreased. Israelis were seen as Zionist aggressors, and their supposed plan for an enlarged Jewish state was emphasized. Literature and schoolbooks were full of nostalgia for the lost homeland, praise for Arab military resolve, and descriptions of Jewish cowardice. For example, a junior high school textbook said Jews were able to fight only when they were protected in fortified villages or shielded by warplanes.[62] Shipler's book is even more pertinent today in light of the renewed conflict between Israel and the occupied territories. It can be seen as a warning about the possible consequences of "solutions" based on partition, ethnic separation, and failure to confront the difficult issues raised by forced expulsion and refugee return.

Yet this bleak picture is not the only possibility. Piete Kuhr's grandmother ran a Red Cross soup kitchen at the railway station as the First World War dragged on. Piete encountered the full horror of war as the wounded, dead, and dying poured through her town on troop trains from the Front. A prisoner-of-war camp, with its ever-extending graveyard, brought home the suffering of her "enemies" on the other side. By the end of the diary, her patriotic fervor had been transformed into empathy for others of all nationalities, a profound hatred of war, and cynicism toward those responsible: "We have clearly perished from a surfeit of victories. And to what purpose, to what purpose? How can a child understand it?" [63]

I found that same hatred of war, the same wish for it never to recur, and the same profound cynicism about political leaders in every child I interviewed and in almost every story the children wrote. The empathy for the other side was less visible, unless expressed in the most general terms of sympathy for all the children in the world. If the goal is to create empathy and trust for certain others, there is no substitute for lived experience of those others. Separation and silence, like uncharted waters on medieval maps, leave a space where myths can flourish: "There be Dragons."

PART THREE

PSYCHOSOCIAL CONSEQUENCES

8

WAR AND WELL-BEING

DURING A PARTICULARLY SEVERE AIR RAID in Bristol, England in May
1941, several high-explosive bombs hit the children's hospital. Dr.
Frank Bodman, who was on duty at another hospital nearby, rushed over
to assist with the evacuation of the young patients. Later he described what
he saw: "Soldiers were crunching through a litter of broken glass, fallen
plaster, and blown-in blackout material picking children out of cots and
beds, and tucking them under their arms, running down the steps and
dumping them pell-mell into a lorry. The hospital was in darkness and
the only light came from the fires raging in the city below. A very heavy
barrage was in progress and heavy high-explosive bombs continued to fall
quite close to the hospital."

Fifty-four children between two and twelve years old were transferred
to Dr. Bodman's hospital that night. None had suffered any physical injury
in the raid, but the severity was such that Bodman noted, "I still feel a little
frightened myself when I recall it." After some months, Bodman decided to
see how the children were doing. He traced all but three of them. Seven had
died of infectious illnesses, including meningitis and diphtheria, an indication of the physical vulnerability of children in war. But, to the doctor's
surprise, only five of the forty-four children he contacted had any lasting
psychological symptoms that could be attributed to the raid.

Most of the children had been disturbed for the first few weeks after
leaving the hospital, with responses that differed according to age. All but
one of the youngest infants was quite untroubled. The toddlers were jumpy
when sirens sounded and ran to safety. Slightly older children had a period
of pretending nothing had happened and then started discussing it either
with their dolls or in their games. Those aged seven to eleven found the raid

exciting and interesting, and the oldest children also showed concern for younger ones. Those children who experienced further raids were untroubled when they occurred. The few children with persisting problems were all young (between one and five years), and most were no longer living in dangerous areas. Their problems varied: They wet or soiled themselves, continued to scream or jump if they heard a siren or saw a gas mask, had bad dreams at night, or were frightened of the dark. Bodman believed his findings demonstrated children's extraordinary toughness and flexibility in threatening situations.[64]

Anna Freud and her colleague Dorothy Burlingham, who ran a nursery for infants in north London, echoed Bodman's emphasis on resilience. They noted that children as young as two had some understanding of what was happening: They knew that bombs knocked down houses and killed people, understood why one had to take shelter, and could even judge how safe a shelter was, according to its depth. What children found difficult to understand and accept was being separated from their mothers. Although Freud had expected "traumatic shock" in response to air raids, something similar to the war neuroses of soldiers who served in the trenches of the First World War, she saw none. Like Bodman, she noted children's calmness and curiosity. She also made a careful delineation of what she regarded as normal fear and anxiety. This wore off if the child was allowed to ignore the threat and was not reminded of it by over-anxious caretakers. Indeed, she noted that after a week or so many children were bored or irritated by raids. She believed that the "quiet manner in which the London population on the whole met the air raids" was "responsible in one way for the extremely rare occurrence of 'shocked' children."

There were some disturbed children. Most of these had mothers who were extremely anxious, such as the five-year-old whose mother made him get dressed and stand beside her, holding her hand, as she trembled at the door whenever there was a raid. Or they were children who had lost fathers and for whom raids seemed to serve as reminders. But the most distressed and disturbed children were those who had been sent to the countryside for safety while their families remained in the city. "The war acquires comparatively little significance for children so long as it only threatens their lives, disturbs their material comfort, or cuts their food rations. It becomes enormously significant the moment it breaks up family life and uproots the first emotional attachments of the child within the family group. London children, therefore, were on the whole much less upset by bombing than by evacuation to the country as protection against it."

Separation from the mother, even if she was not a very competent one, appeared to be far more damaging than living in the unhygienic squalor of bombed-out buildings and the London underground. "Our own feeling revolts against the idea of infants living under the condition of air raid danger and underground sleeping. For the children themselves during the days or weeks of homesickness, this is the state of bliss to which they all desire to return."

Freud also paid attention to how children coped. Regressing to the behavior of a much younger child with thumb-sucking and bed-wetting was common. Children played war games without fear, in imitation of their daily experiences, and Freud predicted that they would shift to peacetime games when the war was over. Their make-believe battles were different from the compulsive repetitive play of a child whose father had died. Like Bodman, Freud noticed that most of the children did not talk about their losses, or their frightening experiences, for months or even a year; then they might suddenly recount the events as if they had happened yesterday: "In all these instances speech does not serve as an outlet for the emotion which is attached to the happening. It is rather the other way around. The child begins to talk about the incident when the feelings which were aroused by it have been dealt with in some other manner."[65]

In 1949, Dr. Charlotte Carey-Trefzer followed up more than two hundred children who during the Second World War had attended the Great Ormond Street Clinic in London with any form of war-related distress. She noted that although air raids produced "the greatest number of reactions," it was evacuation without parents that created "deeper and more persisting damage." Like Freud, she found that the persistence of children's reactions to air raids related more closely to their mother's reactions than to the seriousness of the raids. For example, Sylvia was nine when her house was hit by a bomb and the whole family was buried while in bed. "The parents made no fuss; they all got out without major injuries. After that Sylvia showed general anxiety and was backward at school." However, the condition cleared up of its own accord after the family was rehoused. When Sylvia was seen eight years after the event, she had done well at school and had a good job. Sonja, in contrast, was four when a bomb fell behind her house. Her mother, always a nervous woman, was scared stiff and Sonja wet the bed and stammered from that day on. When she was seen again, her mother was still "highly strung," distressed by all that had happened in the war, and Sonja was "spoilt and self willed" and still stammering and wetting the bed.[66]

It appeared from these findings that children largely overcame the shocks and stresses of war if they were in the company of their mothers or other family members who were coping well. Children's own first-hand accounts of the Second World War seemed to confirm this. Dirk Van der Heide was a twelve-year-old schoolboy when the Blitzkrieg began in Rotterdam in 1940. His diary shows excitement and curiosity, rather than terror:

> The air raid shelter was full of people, all our neighbors and some people I didn't know . . . Keetje [his younger sister] began to cry and Father whispered something to her and kissed her and she stopped. Finally, she went to sleep in his arms. We waited about two hours. At first most people thought the noise was only practice. All the time people kept running outside and coming back with news. It was war alright and the radio was giving the alarm and calling all the time for all men in the reserves to report for duty to the nearest place. The radio said this over and over. It was very exciting. The bombing kept on all the time, boom-boom-boom, and everyone said they were falling on Waalhaven, which is only five miles away. [Later I] got up a game with several other children playing soldiers and bombers. We took turns jumping off the high back steps holding umbrellas and pretending we were parachutists, but we had to quit this because the grown-ups said it made them nervous.

As the war continued, and as people he knew and loved began to get killed, Dirk recorded his sadness and how "awful it is to watch people standing by their bombed houses." He began to be afraid, particularly one night when his mother was absent: "I did cry some while the bombing was going on, but so many other little children were that no one noticed me, I think. I just got into bed with Keetje and hid my face. I was really frightened this time." Then he learned that his mother had been killed, and later the same night there was another raid. Overwhelmed by his sense of loss, he found the next raid much more frightening:

I can't believe Mother is dead and that we will never see her again.
. . . I cried almost all night and I am ashamed of what I did in front
of everybody. I tried to run away from Uncle Pieter after he told
me about Mother getting killed. I tried to get out in the street to
fight the Germans. I don't know what all I did. I was crazy. I was
alright until the bombs started to fall around midnight and then I
couldn't stand it. I know I yelled and kicked and bit Uncle Pieter in
the hand but I don't know why. I think I was crazy. I went to sleep
later but I don't know what time it was.

Dirk and his sister and uncle then made a terrifying escape through
minefields, across the channel to England, and when the Blitz started there,
to New York. He recorded his nightmares about running away from bombing, his fears on the boats because he could not swim well, and his misery
at the occupation of Holland. In school in New York, he found it hard to
concentrate and got poor marks. A doctor told him that he was nervous
because of the bombing, but that he would get better with time. "Sometimes when airplanes go over I want to run and hide. One night when it
was raining, I woke up and heard the rain on the glass and was frightened.
I thought I was back in Holland and that what was striking the window was
pieces of bombs."

Though his uncle wanted him to forget the past, Dirk knew he would
never forget the war, "or forget the Germans and how Mother died." But
despite his experiences and his acknowledged fear, one has no sense that
Dirk regarded himself as badly disturbed or sick. Moreover, he made it
clear that the reactions of others were important to his well-being. He
wrote of the moment when the battleships that had accompanied their
boat to New York turned and left: "When the boats all turned back we
could see how frightened everyone was. That's what made us frightened.
We weren't frightened before." Then a zeppelin appeared and accompanied them into the harbor "and people have been watching over us ever
since and there haven't been any bombings. Not one. And that is why
Keetje and I are happy now."[67]

The emphasis on children's resilience began to change in the 1960s and
1970s. Some psychologists writing about the conflict in Northern Ireland
argued that children were facing psychological genocide, or that constant

exposure to violence was producing a "lost generation" who would continue with violent and antisocial behavior when peace returned. Others argued that one had to consider context when looking at children's behavior—that, for example, although in England truancy was associated with later delinquency, high truancy rates might mean something quite different in an area where parents were afraid to let their children go to school. (In fact, the rates of delinquency and crime were lower in Northern Ireland than in the rest of the United Kingdom and there was no indication that they were rising.) However, although these authors argued about the long-term behavioral consequences of living with violence, there was still agreement that other psychological effects, such as fear and bed-wetting, were short lived, particularly if the parents were coping well.[68]

In the 1980s, the tone of the discussion changed. Professionals began to talk about lifelong psychological scars and enduring symptoms in large numbers of children. Elissa Benedek captured this shift in mood when she wrote in the mid-1980s of "an inability for professionals to accept that traumatic events, caused by fellow humans, in the lives of children might color and shape their lives for years to come." Gone was the admiration for stoicism and lack of complaint that characterized the authors of the Second World War. Enter the new world where those who could not acknowledge their own pain and the hidden pain of others were in unhealthy denial.[69]

The shift seemed to be the result of a number of converging developments in psychiatry and the wider world. These included the "discovery" of post-traumatic stress disorder (PTSD) and its establishment as a legitimate diagnosis in the third edition of the American Psychiatric Association's *Diagnostic and Statistical Manual of Mental Disorders* (*DSM-III*; 1980). The disorder was defined by four key components: a precipitating event, which had to be outside the range of normal human experience, such that it might produce an abnormal reaction in anyone; recurrent memories of that event; physiological arousal such as jumpiness and increased alertness; and avoidance of memories of the event through an emotional shutting down called numbing. Remembering could take a number of forms: nightmares, vivid and intrusive thoughts, or the feeling of re-experiencing the event as if it were happening again (flashbacks).[70]

PTSD was the only disorder in the manual for which there was a specific precipitant that had to be present before the diagnosis could be made.

Its inclusion was in part the result of powerful advocacy on the part of psychiatrists working with returning veterans from the Vietnam war. They felt that the standard classifications of personality disorder, depression, anxiety, psychosis, and substance abuse did not properly encompass their clients' experiences, but left them stigmatized, alienated, and even more vulnerable to "self-medication" with drugs and alcohol. Those advocating the inclusion argued that in fact PTSD had always been around. Charles Dickens, for example, had suffered "rushes of terror" and what today would be called flashbacks after surviving a serious railway accident. The "shell shock" and "combat stress" of the world wars, and the more recently discovered "survivor syndrome" in which some Holocaust survivors found themselves depressed and anxious, cut off and emotionally constricted, with frequent nightmares, could all be reframed as PTSD.[71]

PTSD appeared at a time when biological psychiatry was gaining importance. The discovery of effective medications for previously untreatable mental conditions led to calls for more rigorous, standardized methods of research to establish the existence of specific diseases and the validity of treatments. PTSD lent itself easily to formulation by means of a symptom checklist: Patients who could tick the appropriate number of boxes had the disorder; those who could not did not. Meanwhile, the new cognitive psychologies provided explanatory scripts both for the failure of memory processing and for its treatment. The cognitive model suggested that the brain, unable to assimilate terrible events, somehow became stuck in replay mode, continually revisiting the events. This state of responsiveness to remembered catastrophe was painful, so the mind tried to shut down, hence the emotional numbing and forgetfulness. The attempted repression was not always successful: flashbacks and intrusive memories could break through, especially if there were triggers to the memory such as particular sights or sounds, hence the avoidance of such reminders. Therapy would depend on helping the patient confront the memories and assimilate them.

The newly defined affliction of PTSD began to frame both public and professional responses to disaster. Meanwhile, increasing media coverage of deadly events both publicized the diagnosis and allowed people far from such an event to feel emotionally connected to it. In Britain, when a crowded football stadium in Bradford caught fire in 1985, millions watched the fire on television and identified with the families of those who died. The emergency services used the term "post-trauma stress" for the first time and set up an outreach program to offer clinical help to survivors. Within a few years, the term was well established, and media reports of catastrophes routinely included the phrase "professional counselors are in attendance." This sent two messages: First, help was at hand; and second, the televised distress was a matter for professional assistance. The professionals were available: A new field of "traumatic stress" studies had emerged with its own society, journals, and scientific papers. And there was now a "social movement" of specialists—psychologists, social workers, and psychiatrists—who wanted to both understand and assist the victims.[72]

Globalized television brought global disasters. Now not only the shocked survivors of stadium fires or sinking ferries, but the civilian victims of war moved into living rooms around the world as staples of the TV news. This was particularly true of the media-accessible Balkan wars. Civilians were increasingly the deliberate targets of late twentieth-century conflicts, and PTSD became a recognized medical consequence of civilians' exposure to violence.

By the mid-1990s, PTSD was regarded by Western professionals and public alike as a serious psychological disorder, and as the most likely response to a wide range of traumatic and stressful events. The suggestion was that it was often unrecognized, even by the sufferers themselves, because of repressive reactions in the victims and avoidance of distress on the part of carers. This needed to be overcome, as PTSD required early intervention involving some kind of re-exposure to the traumatic event, through talk or play, to prevent lifelong damage. Children were considered to be among the most vulnerable. UNICEF stated in its yearbook for 1996 that millions of children had been psychologically traumatized by war in the previous ten years and that (without treatment) "time does not heal trauma."[73] By the end of the 1990s, most large humanitarian agencies had trauma programs. In most conflict and postconflict areas of the world, one could find mental health professionals using symptom checklists to assess the level of pathology, training local residents to identify PTSD, and setting up counseling services to encourage the working through of feelings. Psychological trauma and its treatment often appeared to take precedence over other medical and material problems.

"Surviving under what is arguably the most draconian embargo in modern times, trauma which could usually be expected to lessen with time is intensifying because of hunger and deprivation. Iraqi children have given up playing games because the games remind them of dead playmates," Felicity Arbuthnot wrote in the *Guardian* in 1994. Note that she did not suggest that the lack of interest in games might be due to hunger, although she continued, "In July 1993, the UN Food and Agriculture Commission noted with deep concern the prevalence of several commonly recognized pre-famine indicators." Having pointed out the damage that sanctions and consequent malnutrition were doing to Iraqi children, she ended, not with a plea to lift sanctions or to provide more food aid, but rather with "All Iraq's children need counseling so that normality and childhood can be restored."[74]

In Sarajevo during the siege in 1994 there were seven NGOs running counseling programs. *You know 80 percent of our psychological problems would disappear tomorrow,* a weary social worker told me one day, *if you could persuade your government just to lift the siege of the city.* Unfortunately, counseling programs were much easier to achieve than changes in political policy. A focus on individual psychopathology allowed for spurious professional neutrality, creating the illusion of attending to need, while avoiding advocating other social and political interventions that might have a direct impact on the collective mental health of the community.[75]

Meanwhile, the diagnostic concept expanded. The fourth edition of the American Psychiatric Association's diagnostic manual, DSM-IV (1994), no longer required the events to be outside the range of normal human experience. All that was necessary was that the suffering individuals should have experienced, witnessed, or been confronted by an event that threatened them or others they knew with death or injury or damage to their physical integrity, and they must have reacted with a subjective feeling of intense fear, helplessness, and horror. The new criteria allowed for an even wider use of the diagnosis. Apparently, one could now be "traumatized" by losing a pet, hearing obnoxious sexual jokes in the workplace, surviving a hurricane or violent rape.[76] It was very hard to understand how such a varied range of experiences could produce similar psychopathology, quite apart from demeaning and trivializing serious suffering. Meanwhile the dividing line between what was appropriate human responsiveness and what was pathological became even harder to determine.

This was even more the case when humanitarian organizations exported the concept abroad, particularly to countries disrupted by war, where the breakdown of families meant that normal culturally protective practices, such as appropriate mourning and burial of the dead could not take place. Never mind that in the local culture the manner in which intense feelings such as fear or sadness were expressed might be quite different from that in the West, or that ideas of how to deal with pain and suffering might not involve the ventilation of feelings or the sharing of intimate histories with professional counselors. In this situation people borrow what is on offer, especially if the framework is one that gains significant attention from aid-providing organizations. PTSD became a signifier not just for the whole realm of psychological pain after a disaster, but for suffering as a whole.[77] This was brought home to me at a conference in Sarajevo in 1996, when a psychiatric colleague, visiting for the first time, mildly suggested that rates of PTSD might not be very high. *How can you say that?* a local doctor responded in rage. *Have you any idea what we suffered in this city?* It was as if to suggest that residents did not have PTSD was to impute that they had not had terrible experiences, or were not sad, angry, grieving, and suffering. Yet it seemed to me that to use a singular diagnosis in this way had exactly the opposite effect. It minimized through simplification. How can one assume that children who survive the sinking of a ferry boat will make sense of their experiences in the same way as children who live through ethnic cleansing or bombardment? Nor does it seem likely that war experiences will have the same meaning to children whose families are on opposite sides of a conflict.

By the turn of the millennium, there were increasing challenges to the hegemonic position of PTSD in defining the well-being of survivors of political violence. The voices were disparate and not always in harmony with one another. Some anthropologists and historians suggested that PTSD could be seen as a culturally specific response to the needs of a particular group at a particular time. In many periods and places, moral responsibility for disaster and catastrophic evil could be placed outside the individual by means of explanations based on witchcraft or religion. In the secular world of Europe and America today, they pointed out, PTSD had a significant role to play in creating moral order. It allowed victims to identify and place the source of suffering outside themselves, and to be compensated. For those whose victimhood was questionable, the diagnosis could be transforming. Thus for Vietnam veterans returning from a war that their own community regarded as morally dubious and in which they themselves may have been perpetrators, the diagnosis turned them into soldier-victims, just as deserving of compassion, treatment, and compensation from the state that had sent them to war as the victims of natural disasters or terrorist actions.[78]

Some criticisms came from within the psychiatric profession itself, arguing that the diagnosis lacked specificity and had not as yet proved to have a distinctive biological profile or effective treatment. They challenged the need for what they argued was just a repackaging of aspects of other diagnoses, such as the ruminations of depression, or the arousal of anxiety and panic disorders, or the avoidance that occurs in phobias.[79]

Others, myself included, worried that the preoccupation with PTSD and trauma programs by donor and humanitarian agencies led to the neglect of other serious mental health problems in war-affected areas.[80] I experienced this directly working in Kosovo in the aftermath of airstrikes in 1999. A large international donor, knowing I had been working with children in the conflict area and in refugee camps in Albania over the previous year, asked me if I would like funding to set up a "trauma service" for children. What my Kosovar colleagues and I agreed was needed was a children's mental health service that would serve the entire range of children's mental health problems. But to get the funds we were encouraged to highlight children's predicted traumatic responses in our proposal.

As the decade wore on, the debates around the diagnosis showed no signs of abating. Researchers continued to search for trauma-related symptoms in conflict zones around the world and continued to find it, although with extremely variable results. A study of genocide-affected Cambodians found rates of 15 percent, while another of genocide-affected Rwandan children found that 53 to 62 percent of respondents met criteria for "probable post-traumatic stress disorder (PTSD)." This researcher suggested that 100 percent of those with greater exposure had "probable PTSD." He concluded gloomily that "extreme catastrophic man-made violence extinguishes psychological resilience." Others looking at this same data interpreted it differently. They suggested that as the study was conducted in a context of continuing mass displacement, cholera outbreaks, with a continuing threat of renewed violence, the high levels of symptoms could as easily be interpreted as appropriate reality-based normal fear and distress rather than mental disorder.[81]

There are many problems with a symptom checklist approach. Those filling in self-reports may not understand the way the question is framed. They may overreport to be helpful to those conducting the study or because they believe positive answers will help them access assistance.[82] But even if the symptoms are truly present, one cannot assume that just because the same symptom turns up in two quite different parts of the world, it means the same thing to the people experiencing it. This is what the anthropologist Arthur Kleinman calls a category fallacy. Intrusive repetitive nightmares might be pathology in one culture or helpful messages from the dead in another.[83] Symptoms such as scanning the environment for threat, feeling jumpy and alert all the time might suggest a mental health problem in a British child in peacetime, but might serve a useful adaptive function in a city under siege. Symptom checklists used on their own, when they have not been properly validated for a culture, cannot distinguish psychopathology from temporary and normative adjustment to stress, nor can they reveal cultural meanings.

The child psychiatrist Steven Weine interviewed Bosnian teenagers who had survived ethnic cleansing and emigrated to the United States. He discovered that while many of the children had vivid and intrusive memories, "they did not view having these memories as being abnormal or pathological but as an understandable response to tragic occurrences," nor did they regard themselves as victims of isolated singular traumatic events but of a collective assault on their people. They were enjoying their new lives, liked by teachers and others, and doing outstandingly in school. The political meaning they gave to their traumatic experiences, and their sense of collective identity, meant they did not regard their symptoms as a problem.[84]

Psychiatrists working in the occupied territories in Palestine found that the most common symptoms in children exposed to house demolition and shelling were "identifying the event as 'extremely stressful,'" difficulties in sleeping and concentrating, and "avoiding reminders" of these sorts of events. These children were also frightened of high, dark, and closed places, afraid that things would collapse, as well as frightened of things they knew could not hurt them. Children living in safer areas had more "symptoms of anxiety." Most commonly, they felt alone even when in company, they worried much of the time, and they worried when going to bed at night.

Could these responses be defined as the "normal fear and anxiety" reactions observed by Anna Freud in the London Blitz? The researchers thought not. Although in studies of the impact of the earlier Intifada these same authors acknowledged that high rates of symptoms dropped dramatically in peacetime, by the time of the study quoted above, they regarded these high symptom rates as indicative of clinical psychopathology.[85] On this basis, they would certainly have diagnosed Dirk Van der Heide as having severe PTSD. We do not know how the Palestinian children themselves made sense of their fears and feelings. Perhaps staying awake, and being afraid of high, dark, closed spaces, and collapsing walls, are entirely appropriate, and indeed possibly lifesaving, responses when your home is at risk of being demolished by a tank? It does not seem surprising that children found such events stressful and had trouble concentrating, or that others living in safer communities, but watching what was happening to their neighbors on TV felt lonely and worried more than usual, especially at night. Is it helpful to define such responses as mental illness?

What is significant is that a substantial proportion of the Palestinian children in this study had relatively few symptoms of psychopathology, even in the middle of a prolonged conflict, when living under curfew, subject to daily deprivations, and rarely able to attend school.

By the end of the decade, most methodologically sound studies were finding the same thing. The majority of adults and children exposed to traumatic events do not develop mental disorders, regardless of whether these are singular disasters or more profound chronic adversity like war. William Copeland and his colleagues analyzed data from a longitudinal community study of children and teenagers in the United States. Fourteen hundred and twenty children from the Great Smoky Mountains area of North Carolina aged nine, eleven, or thirteen years on entering the study, were followed up every year until they were sixteen. Such studies are invaluable because they do not select a particular group of children or rely simply on children's recall of the past. The annual reviews with questionnaires and diagnostic interviews allowed the researchers to see how many children experienced a traumatic event, how many of these then developed mental health problems, and when these problems resolved. The answers were surprising. Exposure to traumatic experiences was common, but PTSD was not. Two-thirds of the children had experienced at least one event by age sixteen: Less than 0.5 percent of those exposed developed full blown PTSD, while 13 percent developed post-traumatic symptoms after exposure, but these mostly resolved rapidly. Apparently, time does heal trauma. They also found that symptoms of other mental disorders such as depression, anxiety, or behavioral problems were just as common as post-traumatic symptoms.[86]

Youth exposed to armed conflict have higher rates. A review of the soundest studies, that is, those that used random samples and diagnostic interviews rather than symptom checklists, showed rates of 15.4 percent for PTSD and 17.3 percent for depression in conflict-affected populations.[87] A follow-up of 143 children in the Lebanon study found that PTSD, major depression, overanxious disorder, and separation anxiety disorder were not uncommon in war-affected children in first months after exposure to a stressor: 24.1, 23.6, 24.9, and 17.9 percent, respectively. However, rates of self-recovery were high and the prevalence of PTSD, depression, overanxious disorder, and separation anxiety decreased to 1.4, 5.6, 5.6, and 4.2 percent, respectively, after one year.[88] We found something similar when we opened the child psychiatry service in Kosovo. In the first year, 21 percent of those coming to the four clinics in towns across the country had stress-related problems, but by the second year (2001), this had fallen to 4 percent.[89]

So the wheel has turned again. The emphasis is back on resilience. Once more the question is why do some children who live through terrible and horrifying events come out unaffected while others suffer badly?[90]

The most important answers are the same as sixty years ago. Family matters. The discoveries of Freud and Carey-Trefzer have held true: If you are with parents who care about you and are coping well, you will probably do the same.[91] If on the other hand you are on your own, evacuated to another city, spending anxious nights listening to the radio for news from home, you may be safe, but very unhappy. Parents that are anxious or beat you or fight with each other are not much protection either. In both the United States and the Lebanon studies, children who came from punitive or conflicted family environments had more symptoms. Similar results were found among the Palestinian children.[92] Such findings are not really surprising given that family violence is a form of traumatic experience in itself. Many studies also show that the more traumatic experiences a child suffers the more likely they are to have problems (the so-called dose effect).[93] Copeland also found that being older and having a history of anxiety made traumatic symptoms more likely. Similarly in the Lebanon study, preexisting disorders contributed to more post-conflict PTSD in children.

The word resilience—that capacity to bend and bounce back after adversity—is now as popular as the word trauma. As the studies pile up, a consensus is emerging. Resilience is not a "thing" that you have or not, something that can be worn like a protective amulet around the neck. It appears to be much more fluid, composed of aspects that are integral to the individual self: age, gender, constitution, temperament, and personal history; and others that are part of the world in which the individual lives: the family, the school, the values and beliefs of the surrounding community. Most importantly resilience depends on the constantly changing interactions between these things.[94]

For example, some brain imaging studies suggest those with smaller hippocampi—a particular part of the brain that is involved in the stress response and the processing of memory—are more likely to have post-traumatic symptoms after a stressful event.[95] But it is not as simple as saying some people have a biological vulnerability that will show up at times of environmental stress. There is also evidence that vulnerability in some contexts may be strength in others. Neurobiological factors, including differences in brain architecture and neuroendocrine responses to stress, make some children particularly reactive and sensitive to adversity. In contrast, there are other children who tend to keep an even keel, whatever is thrown at them. The interesting thing is that these same sensitive children may also be more responsive to positive changes in the environment and do better than the "even keel" children when such changes occur.[96]

Understanding that resilience is dynamic helps make sense of contradictions in the research. In some contexts, being younger might be protective, perhaps because younger children are more likely to be kept safely at home, and may not understand the dangers. But in other situations, greater maturity and better understanding may add to a feeling of security. An older child knows, for example, that an absent father is not "gone for good" or that conflicts do come to an end. Similarly, the findings on gender are not consistent. Mostly they suggest that girls do worse, but this may be because girls are better at acknowledging emotional distress, especially on symptom checklists, and boys are more likely to hide it. However, the first Intifada gave girls from a normally restrictive and patriarchal society a chance to take on new roles and gain status, and this may have actually improved their mental health. Boys, in contrast, suffered from the lack of structure, rules, and supervision, and so may have had more behavioral problems.[97]

Individuals and families live in communities. Well-being can be affected by how connected a child feels to wider network of support beyond the family.[98] Communities with shared values that both feel supported and can offer support may do better, even if they have suffered more. When a researcher compared rates of PTSD in two Chinese villages nine months after an earthquake, he was surprised to find much lower rates in the village that had suffered the most damage. He suggested it was related to the fact that these villagers had received more assistance, whereas in the less damaged village the feeling of being neglected and abandoned had resulted in higher rates of disorder.[99] Religious belief also helps. Buddhist religious practices such as meditation, reciting the five precepts, reading character stories appeared to promote resilience in war-affected orphans in Sri Lanka. These practices created meaning, empathy, and structure in an otherwise chaotic and disturbing time.[100]

Unfortunately, for the most part the resilience literature is still focused on the issues of individual psychopathology, even if more attention is now paid to its absence rather than its presence. Shared values and beliefs, sense of identity, community, and social support are all examined and acknowledged as contributing to individual resilience, but there is little exploration of the reverse relationship: How does individual resilience contribute to communal well-being? What is the wider impact of individual well-being on shared values and social relations?

Meaning matters, both individual and communal meanings and they interact with one another. Psychological trauma cannot be looked at as a mechanical event, equivalent to a bullet hitting bone, where caliber, velocity, and bone strength can predict the amount of damage. Children are not the passive recipients of experience. They are actively engaged in making sense of their environment, and acting to change it, from an early age. They gather meanings from what is around them, first from their parents or caretakers and then from the world beyond—friends, school, community—as well as from their own previous experiences. War touches every aspect of children's social worlds, including their history and values, and they recreate those worlds. The changes in sense of identity, feelings of trust and security, and connection to others that I found in the Bosnian children seemed likely to be profoundly related to their sense of well-being. These changes might not manifest themselves as "symptoms" that could be counted, but rather as "ways of living" that I needed to observe and discuss with the children themselves.

9

DAY AFTER DAY

War is no longer declared,
but rather continued. The outrageous
has become the everyday. The hero
is absent from the battle. The weak
are moved into the firing zone.
The uniform of the day is patience,
the order of merit is the wretched star
of hope over the heart.

—Ingeborg Bachmann, "Every Day"

*I heard some shooting when I woke up one morning. I asked my mum
"What's happening?" and she told me that the war had started. [. . .]
When it got dark, me and my family ran away to a safer place. When
we got there, my father had to go and fight against the Chetniks. [. . .]
He visited us just one night. They told us that my father had been
killed a few days later. That was so hard for me, and also the house
we lived in didn't have any windows or doors. [. . .] A shell hit the
kitchen one day when all of us were inside. There was so much dust
we didn't know where we were. But anyway, we stayed in that house.
There were thirty-one of us living there. Eight shells hit the roof of that
house. There was a basement where we hid. We stayed four months
and then we came back home. That was the happiest day of my life.
The war went on for another four-and-a-half years. Peace coming
made no difference to me. But I was free to go to school.*

—Fourteen-year-old boy, Gorazde

I feel very sad because I have seen frozen children in deep snow.

—Thirteen-year-old boy, Gorazde

Wars, unlike plane crashes and hurricanes, continue day after day. In Bosnia, it went on for four years, and many children experienced a whole series of catastrophic events, one after the other. We know from children's accounts of other wars that different kinds of events have quite different effects.

Krystyna Stankiewicz, who lived in Lodz, Poland, began a diary in 1941 when she was five-and-a-half and kept it through the next four years. There were bombings, round-ups, and shootings of civilians, but as a small child in a kindly, extended. middle-class family she was scarcely touched by these events and recorded them in a matter-of-fact manner: "22.6.41: We had a boat ride on the Vistula. We have started a blackout because of the war. We are frightened of bombs." Her main preoccupation was food. "26.10.43: Twenty people have been shot. We are laying in stores for the winter." But then her mother was arrested (for carrying money for the Resistance). "19.1.45: Mummy will not come back till after the war: The Germans have taken her to Germany. We miss her terribly and I cry all the time." Krystyna became depressed and irritable, although she went on getting good marks at school. The theme of missing her mother came up in every diary entry until the war ended and her mother was released.[101]

R. J. Street, who was a teenager in London during the Blitz, recorded in his diary the excitement of his first air raid: "The gunfire was very heavy, and when it was some way off we watched it and saw it disperse the planes. It was raining shrapnel and after the raid there were scores of children scouring the place for souvenirs." One month and 110 raids later, after four raids in one night, he wrote:

> I told Mum to duck and she dived under the table, but I did not have time to do so, so lay flat on the floor to be out of the way of the glass, but the first landed some way off, and we were OK. I got under the table for the second, which whistled even louder. And landed 150 yards away, it must have been a big one. . . . The continual strain and all these bombs near me and those two while I was out made me let down the good reputation of my fellow Londoners and I was horribly sick. I was not very well for some time after.[102]

If a child loses his home, his father gets killed, and he is crowded into inadequate shelter and repeatedly shelled, a symptom checklist cannot sort out the specific effects of these different events. Yet in discussion, children can make subtle distinctions between different feelings and explain how these fade, change, or endure over time. I did want to see if children had symptoms, so in addition to asking children to write stories, I gave out standard symptom checklists to 334 children aged thirteen to fifteen, more or less equally divided between Gorazde and Foca. These checklists had been culturally validated for a Bosnian population to measure traumatic reactions, depression, and anxiety.[103] I then asked the twenty children, with the highest levels of symptoms, and twenty children with the lowest levels of symptoms in each town (forty in total) if they would meet with me. If they did not want to, the child with the next score down was asked. I had long conversations with each of those that consented, and with most of their parents and teachers. I also gave the symptom questionnaires to my respondents' parents. (The school psychologists assisted with the mechanics of the selection process so that I could avoid knowing whether a particular child had high or low levels of symptoms when I did the interviews. This meant that I was not biased toward looking for distress in some children.) In this way, I gained a picture of children's well-being both in symptomatic terms and on the basis of their own and their parents' understandings of how their experiences had affected them. During the interviews, we discussed the child's life history, their war experiences, their pre- and post-war life and their understandings and feelings about events. I administered a questionnaire to record the quantity and details of their violent experiences, to get a measure of exposure, and also used nonverbal tools like the lifeline (see figure 1 in chapter 12): This is an adaptation of an instrument developed to explore how young people construct the past.[104] Each child was asked to put a dot on a grid, anywhere between feeling 100 percent "wonderful" and 100 percent "awful," for each year of their lives from five years old. The dots were then joined to produce the line.

This method allowed the less-articulate children to express subtle differences in feeling and relative differences between years, and helped to provide a basis for discussion. The children were then scored based on the position of the final dot: 1 = completely well; 2 = equivocal, i.e., a less than 25 percent drop from pre-war well-being; and 3 = less well, i.e., a more than 25 percent drop.

I thus ended up with two measures of well-being: a conventional quantitative one derived from the summated symptom scores and a qualitative measure derived from four components: the child's subjective assessment, nonverbally expressed by the lifeline, my impression drawn from interview and observation, parents, and/or teachers view, and school marks as a measure of function. I gave particular importance to a negative subjective view expressed by a lifeline score of 3. If children categorized themselves as "less well," this was accepted regardless of other measures. If they categorized themselves as "well" on the lifeline (1), they were only categorized as "less well" overall if they came across as less well on least two of the other three qualitative measures. Thus, poor school marks, parental anxieties, or researcher impression, on their own, were not enough to classify a child as "less well" from a qualitative perspective.[105]

The first surprise was that equal numbers of children in both towns felt unwell two years after the war, no matter whether well-being was assessed quantitatively or qualitatively. Given that Gorazde had suffered far more violence during the war than Foca, it appeared that interpretations of experiences and the effect of current context were just as important as the dose effect. The second was that although the girls had higher symptom scores than the boys in both cities, when well-being was assessed qualitatively, there were no gender differences. Girls were not sicker; they simply found it easier than boys to acknowledge symptoms in questionnaires. Third, in almost a quarter of the children I interviewed, the symptom checklists and the qualitative measures produced contradictory results. This suggested a problem with trying to define well-being simply in terms of the presence or absence of symptoms. You could end up labeling children as sick who thought of themselves as well, and missing children who did feel unwell, but did not express that feeling in symptomatic terms.

Their perceptions were subjective and retrospective. Sometimes the importance and meaning of an event shifted from one conversation to another, as did the amount of detail recalled, suggesting that children's current lives and concerns were important in framing their understanding of their war experiences. However, some distinctive patterns emerged.[106]

Losses

The greatest disaster that could happen to children was to have someone close to them injured or killed. Death and injury, including extraordinary near misses, came up repeatedly in the written stories and were often the most precisely recalled events. More than half (twenty-seven) of the children I interviewed had lost a close friend or relative during the war. Many had fathers who had been injured, most of them on the front line; the children had enduring and vivid memories of being told about these events. Sometimes they could recall all the details of a relative's injury or death as if they had witnessed it (see Dusan's account of his brother's death in chapter 2).

Very often, these losses were multiple. A fourteen-year-old Serb girl who lived in Sarajevo at the beginning of the war fled to Foca with her family because of the shelling. She wrote in her story, *I sat in the car and cried. I was looking at my house for the last time.* Then she heard that an uncle (her mother's youngest brother) had been killed. *Everyone was crying, especially my mother, I was with her, we cried together.* Her father joined the army, and later he came to see them in Foca.

> *He was in a good mood. I remember he taught me how to sing some Serbian songs, as if he knew it would be his last night in his apartment. The sun shone the next day. I was in my room getting ready for school. Suddenly someone was banging on the door. Mother opened the door and saw my uncle was crying. He said to her "R. is dead." It was my father. I heard my uncle's words. I fell on the bed and started to scream. I cried as much as I could. My mother cried also. Our neighbors asked what happened. My uncle told them. We went to the funeral. My mother and grandmother fainted and it seemed to me that everyone was spinning around me. When the funeral was over, we went home. I did not leave home for three days. A week passed. One rainy day I was returning from school. A friend of mine ran up to me and told me my mother had gone in tears to my aunt. I dropped my bag and started to run as fast as I could. I arrived. Everyone was in mourning clothes. I asked my mother what had happened. My uncle had committed suicide. I asked her "But why?" Mother told me: "Because of your father." Those were our worst moments.*

In the Gorazde stories there are frequent accounts of shelling and shooting, but almost always this is background detail to the loss or injury of someone the child knows. The stories bring home the relative significance of these events. It is the loss that is upsetting and remembered. A thirteen-year-old boy wrote:

> *My friend and I were playing marbles; our parents went to my grandma. We had only two marbles and we played. The bullets whizzed around us, but we didn't want to leave the game because it was interesting. We played for half an hour and then we came indoors because the shooting was very strong. One shell hit our building a few minutes later and the mother of one of my friends was wounded and her father was killed. The second and third ones hit my room where my bed and my comic strips and other games were. When I came into the bathroom, I saw my friend lying down without his hand. Then I went out and called some people to help him.*

Note that bullets whizzing around had no significance until people the boy knows are wounded and killed. Five of the children I interviewed had lost immediate family members, and four of them were actively grieving two to six years after the event. They responded and coped in very different ways. Admira remembered the exact hour when her uncle called and told them her father had been killed by a grenade. She went to the hospital with her family and saw that he was dead; but at first she still thought he would come back, so she was not upset. It took two weeks for her to understand that he had gone forever. After that she cried a great deal and was very sad. She stayed indoors all the time, watching the funeral from a window. Later she visited his grave, but the visits had to stop when Serbs took the territory.

The sadness was enduring. When I interviewed Admira six years after her father's death, she still felt it intermittently, although she could not always pin down the cause. Sometimes she forgot he was dead and then remembered suddenly. Sometimes she felt he was watching her. Although she could conjure up happy memories of her father, which she found comforting, she also had frequent unpleasant dreams about both him and the war. She would wake suddenly from dreams of people being killed; the dreams frightened her and sometimes stopped her from wanting to sleep, so she would watch TV until she felt better. Her appetite was poor, she could go two or three days without eating, and she sometimes felt frightened without any reason.

Admira talked freely about these difficulties, and despite them, she was doing very well in school, with consistently high grades. She had friends and was able to talk about her father with them and her family, although she did not always want to. She found that the best way to feel better when upset was to visit a friend and play on the computer. Her mother, despite complaining of loneliness and worries about money, came across as a warm, practical woman who had made a cheerful home.

The atmosphere in Edin's flat was quite different: immaculately tidy, sparsely furnished, and cold. His father had been shot in the first weeks of the war and their own house completely destroyed by shelling. Edin's mother initially refused to allow him to be interviewed, worried I might label him as disturbed, when she felt that he had *no problems.* She herself seemed immensely sad and very tense. Any remarks about her loss were brushed away with a reference to fate and the will of God.

Edin was polite, nervous, and monosyllabic in interviews. He was almost in tears as he described how his father had been shot by a sniper on the line early in the war. He had cried when his mother had told him, and had been unable to sleep. He had gone to the funeral, and the family were able to visit the grave, although that made him cry, and his mother had said, *If you cry, you won't go.* He still cried whenever he thought or talked about his father, but he tried to avoid doing this, as it made his mother cry and he wanted to do anything he could to stop her from being upset.

He was now the man in the family and had responsibilities. He had also lost a cousin his own age and his grandfather, both from shelling. He missed all of them. Like Admira, he sometimes forgot his father was dead and thought he might come walking in, and he too had comforting memories. Sometimes he felt angry. He insisted he had no problems, although he was doing badly in school, and his marks worried him a bit. His way of coping was to play the accordion his father had bought. He had avoided it at first, and then found he enjoyed it and was quite good.

Helena's father was killed in the first weeks of the war (see chapter 6). Immediately after his death, she asked her mother to promise never to marry again and then did not talk about her father again. This was despite her mother's encouragement to do so, and in contrast to her little sister, who mentioned him a lot. Tense, argumentative, and a perfectionist before the war, Helena cried for weeks after the death, and became irritable and difficult, refusing to help in the house, saying her house was in Sarajevo. However she was getting top marks in school.

She cried when she talked to me about what had happened, and told me she preferred not talking, as she was a very private person. Her mother respected this, but worried about her, and was still very depressed herself. She felt very isolated in Foca and worn down by the need to work hard and appear strong for the children. She too cried through our interview, saying she wished she had more real friends in the town.

Dusan had suffered the most recent loss: his brother had died in the last year of the war. His feelings of sadness, emptiness, and desire to identify with his brother are described in chapter 2.

The sadness of these four children was compounded by their parents' feelings, and in the case of the two boys, by a need to take on new roles in the family to compensate. The two who talked about their dead relative with friends or family were managing best. Although they cried when discussing the death, they were otherwise cheerful and articulate and open about their feelings. Helena's desire for privacy seemed in part a way of differentiating herself from her mother, but it came at a price, as did Edin's stoicism. None of these children regarded their feelings as indications of ill health; they viewed them as what should be expected when you lose someone you love, and a familiar home, in a war. All felt they were slowly improving with time.

Interestingly, Dusan and Helena both denied having any symptoms whatsoever when filling in the symptom checklists and had low scores. For Edin, however, the safe space of an anonymous checklist was the only place he felt able to express how bad he felt. Besides being objectively unwell throughout our conversations, he had the highest symptom scores of any boy in Gorazde, with marked feelings of depression and PTSD—yet he insisted to me that he felt fine and had put his post-war lifeline at 100 percent.

Do you feel that you shouldn't have symptoms and that's why you say you don't? I asked.

Yes, he answered very quietly.

All four felt they were coping. They had found ways to deal with sadness when it overwhelmed them, mostly through the distractions of physical and intellectual activity, games, and friends. They all wished that there were more recreational activities for young people in their towns, and that their parents had easier lives, but they all rejected offers of additional psychological assistance, and although I regarded all four as unwell, it was unclear whether giving them a pathological label such as clinical depression or PTSD would have benefited them in any way. On the contrary, it might have further stigmatized them at school at a time when they were all desperate to fit in. It seemed more important to reinforce the normalizing strategies that three of the families had adopted, of open communication if it was wanted and respect for privacy if not, and to encourage such strategies in the one family where they were lacking.

Witnessing Death and Injury

One fourteen-year-old Serb girl wrote of being captured by Muslim soldiers with her family (the site was not named, but was almost certainly Josanice). She woke up to find her house on fire: *What is the feeling when you wake up and find you are burning and dying?* She and her family got out, but she saw her best friend lying with her throat cut, alongside the friend's younger brother and sister. She could see they were not quite dead. The soldiers took her family's money and released them after some hours. Whenever she was reminded of the event, she dreamed that *I am in their hands, but this time they won't let me go . . . then I wake up with a wet face.* However, when awake she rarely cried because she felt her own losses were small compared with those of others. Even so, she often saw *pictures,* [heard] *sounds, voices crying,* [saw] *pictures of dead bodies. [. . .] The graveyard reminds me a lot, those pictures on the monuments . . . names . . . But I don't complain. I have my mother, father, brother, the most important in life. I have those who love me, but I would erase the memories if I could.*

Children who had witnessed death and atrocities usually continued to have vivid and intrusive memories. Elvira in Gorazde had bad dreams almost every night. She lived in the center of town where the bombing had been intense, and she had seen a number of people die. Three soldiers who had taken shelter in the anteroom of their basement were hit by two grenades:

> *They got stuck on the door because they were rushing forward looking for help, so there were three of them, you know, on the door. And my mother just got close and she didn't know whom she would help first. And the man she was laying down next to, S, his face*

it was totally gone. He was probably turned toward the door, so he got one piece off on his face. And when he started bleeding the blood came right out on us. And my mother just threw something like a blanket over us, so we could not see that. And he was asking for water and my mother wanted to give him water. She got lost again because she didn't know how to give him water because this man didn't have a mouth anymore. [. . .] Later my father arrived and they brought a car for this guy. They couldn't put him on the wheelchair because he was completely full of holes. He was really screaming and we really got scared.

That same night another neighbor was killed in the same spot. *I came down to the basement with my mother and I was holding a candle for her, and this woman was asking my mother to take her belt away because it was too tight around her waist, and when my mother tried to do that, this woman didn't have a stomach at all.*

On another occasion, a grenade narrowly missed Elvira and hit three of her friends. Two died instantly. She stood frozen, staring at her third friend until a car came to take them away. *She didn't have her leg and her head was completely bloody. I couldn't see which part was which mostly. [. . .] I just stood and she cried. I heard, "Help me, Father, it hurts here, it's painful here and there."*

She told these stories calmly, saying that she had never cried, at least in the daytime. Yet she continued to dream about these events almost nightly and wake up afraid and in tears. Often it would be the same event, but with her mother, brother, and sister in the place of those who had actually died. She was frightened of the dark, and her mood was very up and down, depending on how she was getting along with friends and at school. She marked these violent swings on her lifeline, putting herself at a low point at the time I interviewed her. She also had some of the highest scores on the symptom checklist.

Elvira and the Serbian girl who was captured had experiences of a particular intensity that seemed to contribute to painful and enduring symptoms and resulted in both children feeling unwell. In these cases, a diagnosis of PTSD was appropriate. Strong sensory stimuli such as smell, sight, and sound are thought to be associated with more intrusive traumatic symptoms.[107] But not all children regarded intrusive memories as indications of illness. Nina could not forget the frozen dead man she had passed on her journey over Grebak. Narcisa had memories of the muti-lated bodies she had had to step over in the street. She wrote, *Now, when it's peace, I always see the picture of the cut-up bodies when I pass by this place. I think that I will always have that sight in my memory. I hope that we will never have war in our country again because this war was enough. The consequences of the war will never be wiped out. Four years of suffering and worry are over, but we shouldn't forget them!*

Both Nina and Narcisa regarded their memories as isolated occurrences that were decreasing over time and had no impact on their general well-being. Narcisa clearly also felt she had a duty to hold on to some of the memories because they might inoculate her against future war. Many chil-dren in both towns wrote of the wish to forget and the difficulty of doing so, but Gorazde children also wrote of a duty to remember, *I remember a lot of things from the war which I wish to forget, but my conscience does not let me,* one wrote. Another wrote, *I am trying to forget everything, and also, I am trying to remember it in some way. [. . .] although I do not tire myself with memories because I want to know about everything else happening in the world because I lost enough time in four years.*

Shelling

The greatest difference between the two towns was in their responses to shelling. Gorazde had been shelled intermittently for four years; at times, the bombardment had been so ferocious that residents had to stay in their basements for days. Yet most children in the town did not regard shelling as their worst experience. They seemed to go through the same cycle of adaptation that Amela experienced (see chapters 1 and 2).

The initial reaction was of curiosity or even excitement. This was fol-lowed by fear as they learned that the explosions could kill and injure. Almost all the children I talked to remembered being frightened during the early stages of bombardment. Elvira told me *I didn't know what it was, at all. And later when I was a bit more grown-up, we wanted to go out; we just didn't want to stay in the house. But when some people died in our basement, then we got scared.* Later the children felt more confident: *When we heard the sound of the grenade flying above us, we just kept play-ing because we knew it was flying over us, that it was not going to . . . but when they fired the grenades—you hear when they fire it—and when you don't hear that sound any more you just lie down because you don't know then where it's going to fall.* And finally there was the boredom that had reduced Narcisa and her brother to counting the grenades (chapter 2). This indifference often put children at risk, as when Nina and her sister, wanting to collect water in town despite the danger, were nearly hit by a shell. Feeling vulnerable partly depended on how intense and close the bombing was and how personally exposed they felt. Nina was most frightened when two shells landed close to her in the fields; Elvira saw soldiers and her friends killed before her eyes.

Many of the children found the shelling toward the end of the war more frightening because by then they had heard stories of what happened to Muslims in towns taken by Serb forces. In 1995, most of them had some idea of what had happened in Srebrenica. Nedjad told me, *All of them were saying they would take Gorazde as well. I thought the same. I was sure that Gorazde would fall. I was afraid, really afraid that they would catch us and the same thing that had happened in Srebrenica would happen to us.*

How did you cope?

My brother and I stayed in our room. He's older, and he kept telling me "It never will happen, not to us." But I was sure he knew . . . that would be the end. Mother told both of us, "It will never happen." She told us in any case, whatever happened, we wouldn't be separated, we would stay together.

As in the London Blitz, children felt safest in shelters with people they knew, with people who did not panic, and when they had games to distract them. One mother told me it had been hard to get her children to understand that if they were caught in a raid it was better to take cover with strangers than to try to run home. As children still often tried to get home, parents would go out to find them and make them safe wherever they were. How parents themselves coped mattered. Armin's mother said that during the 1994 offensive she had lain awake every night, terrified that the town would fall. *I just thought how I will kill first the children and then myself because I didn't want the Chetniks to take us alive.* She knew her children were aware of her fear: *They noticed the difference and they knew everything.* Armin told me, *We got used to it. But I was always on guard.*

Some children never grew accustomed to the shelling and remained frightened all the time. Either these were children like Edin—who had already lost his father and who said *It was awful; it was very bad; I was afraid; it was always hard*—or they were like Iris, who shared her home with relatives who had escaped from Foca. Her aunt, who had been detained for a year, told her terrifying stories of young girls being raped. Iris lived one street from the Serb line in Gorazde and endured periods of intense shelling throughout the war. Every new bombardment felt threatening: She thought it would kill her directly, or the town would be taken. Unable to sleep, she imagined that Serbs would come into the basement to slaughter them, or that something undefined but terrible would happen to her. *Nothing was as bad as that. I mean you were waiting all the time, you were so tired, and finally you lay down, and then you heard grenades again. . . . I really longed for sleep. It was no better at school: you went to school if the shelling was less. There were sandbags under windows as some kind of protection. But the lessons were so short I didn't have time to learn anything. All I could think about was whether I was going to stay alive.*

She described one raid:

> *It was a Bosnian-language lesson and I was actually answering a question, when by chance I heard something coming down. I don't know why we thought the bags on the windows would help us, but . . . we all just jumped through the door of the classroom. You can imagine how it was with the whole school rushing out of all the classrooms. There was panic and screaming, crying. [. . .] You didn't think of other people in these moments, you just thought of yourself, how to save yourself. [. . .] We just lay on top of one another. All the other pupils were on the floor. You know how it feels: you hear the glass breaking in town, the shooting, grenades, then you just shake because of all those explosions. [. . .] I prayed, and I tried to hug myself, to make myself feel better. I didn't think of talking to anyone. I cried a thousand times; I could lose my life a thousand times.*

In contrast, Foca was bombarded only briefly at the end of the war, when NATO's aerial attack destroyed the town's bridges. The bombing began abruptly and continued for a few days. Many of the children in Foca did regard this as their worst experience, but not all were frightened. Those who believed the bombing was targeting them were scared; those who understood that the bombing was aimed at military targets were not, even if they did not know why they were being bombed. Jovan took refuge with his parents in the cellar. *I didn't know exactly what it was for, and I still don't know. I didn't feel so secure, but I don't know how to explain, I wasn't scared. [. . .] We didn't think they would bomb civilian targets; I knew I wouldn't be hurt because they didn't have anything to shoot at here. They were just destroying bridges and some military buildings.*

Nikola's apartment was close to the bridge, and a piece of shrapnel flew in through the window close to his head. *I didn't cry, but I was out of it. I closed my ears; I didn't talk at all.* He believed they could *all be destroyed.* A fifteen-year-old girl wrote, *Everyone was in a panic and they did not know what was happening.* Not surprisingly, she was *screaming and crying.* She went on, *My fear was so great it took over my body bit by bit. Our building had no shelters, so we were terrified and expected the worst.* However, as in Gorazde, even in this short period children adjusted. The same girl added, *The other days were also awful, but not like the first. It was as if we got used to it and it became part of our life.*

Most of the children who believed the NATO air strikes would endanger them had parents who shared this belief. Helena's mother told me she was terrified because she was convinced they would bomb people as well as bridges. Helena had the same fear, *I thought they would drop bombs on the lines and the Muslims would come into our country. They would send us away somewhere.* Bojan's mother was scared, his grandmother was crying, and his aunt was worrying about her nephew out in the town. Bojan grew more and more frightened as the night went on. There were also some children like Svetlana, who was accustomed to her mother's chronic anxiety and so was unaffected by it. It was almost as if her mother's worry about the bombing made it less threatening because her mother worried about everything.

Most children used forms of distraction to cope with the bombardment. They played with toys or friends, or talked. Like the children in Anna Freud's nursery, they were uncomfortable only if their parents drew their attention to the shelling, as Amela's mother did on occasion (chapter 2). But some, like Iris, found the shelling impossible to ignore. In the first year, Elvira coped by blocking her ears, humming, and rocking herself. Similarly, a thirteen-year-old girl wrote:

When there was shelling I had to cover my ears with my hands and everyone made fun of me because of that, but even if I tried not to, I couldn't stop. It was as if I had some radar that connected to the shells, so that I had to put up my hands and cover my ears whenever I heard the whistling. I know it's strange, but even now I can't listen to the sound of planes, the sound of a helicopter, or thunder, I have to cover my ears. It's automatic.

Being Uprooted

The effects of evacuation and displacement depended on where children went, why they went, and with whom they lived. Few of the Foca children were separated from both parents because in that town, evacuation was organized in advance of the fighting. Children usually traveled with their mothers to relatives in villages or to Montenegro or Serbia, so that it felt little different from holiday or weekend trips in the past. Only children like Ivana and Tatiana, sent away from both their parents to relatives in Belgrade, missed their families and found it hard at first. *The worst thing that happened to me was being separated from my parents,* Tatiana told me. *When I was in Belgrade, I couldn't wait to come back, I missed them so much.* But after a time the pleasures of living in a big city compensated for the loss, and both girls found it difficult to return to Foca.

In Gorazde, the war took families by surprise, and many children suddenly found themselves left with grandparents. Fikreta wrote about how it felt:

> *We stayed at our grandparents' house for four years. Our parents couldn't visit us because the roads were controlled by the Serbs. I cried often because there was a lot of shooting there [Gorazde], so I was afraid something could happen to my parents. We spoke to our parents after a long time by an army radio operator. When I spoke with them, I started to cry as soon as I heard their voices. Days passed, I was sad, and nothing could make me happy.*

Living in relative safety and being with her grandparents could not make up for her fears about her parents' safety, and contributed to her feeling unwell after the war.

Senad, in contrast, was sent with cousins and an aunt to Spain. He found the journey and his life there so exciting and interesting that it compensated for missing his parents. On arriving in Barcelona, he felt like a hero: *When we came out of the airplane, people had gathered as if they expected some president, and they all applauded us and waved to us and we waved to them. Everything was so comfortable. Then we caught a bus, and there were so many people in the street, trying to see what was happening, as if it was someone very important.* The Spanish took care of their housing and food, keeping groups of Bosnians together. Senad was fascinated by everything and made Spanish friends. He kept in touch with his parents by ham radio. The hardest time was when he thought they were in real danger. He cried after Srebrenica fell: *We prayed to God not to have the same thing in Gorazde because we really wanted to see our parents again.* Nina, evacuated with her mother and sister, found parting from her father incredibly painful, but still thrived in her new life in Germany.

Two years after the war, a third of my interviewees were still displaced inside Bosnia, and their feelings about this depended very much on the security and attractiveness of their current accommodation. Svetlana was simply waiting for the next eviction, and missed her old home in her village a great deal. Milica and Radmila both liked their new homes in Foca much better than previous village life. This was partly because of their conviction that "Turks" now hated them so much that they could not live together again (see chapter 6). It was also because city living meant no sheep to mind, friends nearby, and a short walk to school. For Divac, the provincialism and unfriendliness of Foca contrasted unfavorably with Sarajevo, and the insecurity of his family's accommodation made things worse. Even so, he insisted that he had adjusted and would not want to return to the city. Surprisingly, with the exception of Helena, it was native-born children in Foca who seemed less well. It was as if the displaced Serb children were determined to make the best of it and, perhaps, to show me that leaving the Federation had been good for them.

In Gorazde, Samir had no desire to go back to the now half-destroyed house in which his family had been held like prisoners. He preferred sharing one room with his family in a collective center until they could get something else. He said he had horrible memories every time he went near their old house. Admira, though, wanted to go home to her village in Republika Srpska, perhaps in part because it was closer to her father's grave.

Domestic Events

Horror is relative. Some children were quite clear that particular events in their personal lives far outweighed the misery caused by the war. Amela's life with her violent and alcoholic father meant that the coming of war was something of a relief because her father went away. She regarded 1994, when Gorazde suffered the worst offensive, as *the best [year] in my life,* because her father was on the front line, while she used her wits to help take care of the family and developed a close friendship with her mother. It was her father's return and his continuing violent behavior after the war ended that resulted in her attempt to kill herself by taking her grandmother's pills. Nina regarded her parents' separation at the end of the war as *more catastrophic* than the siege. For a brief period, she lost weight, cried all the time, and had suicidal thoughts, none of which had happened in that first terrifying year of war.

Children made clear distinctions between the different and sometimes contradictory feelings produced by different events. All of them, in both communities, saw death or injury of family members or friends as the worst thing that could happen. The impact was enduring, and was exacerbated if the child witnessed the event. Shelling frightened most of the children. But the fear was less if the bombardment could be interpreted as nonthreatening and if it became routine. Paradoxically, this was more likely in Gorazde, where shelling persisted for long enough to allow habituation, and occurred in the context of multiple other threatening events. One can get used to bombing unless, like R. J. Street, one endures a direct hit.

In Gorazde, where the whole community had been exposed to sustained violence, there did appear to be a dose effect: Children who had experienced more violence felt less well two years later. Children who lived in more central positions like Iris and endured repeated direct bombardments, and who repeatedly witnessed the deaths of others, like Elvira, had worse, more enduring symptoms than others who were less exposed.

In Foca, where most children had experienced less violence, the dose effect was if anything reversed. The displaced children, for the most part, had been more exposed to violence in places like Sarajevo, but it was local children who felt worse two years later. Children's personal interpretations of their current environment were more important than any objective reality.

For all the children, their subjective sense of safety seemed to matter more than the objective threat or how often danger occurred. Aerial bombardment that is intense and unexpected may feel much more frightening, even when of brief duration, than shelling that has become the background to daily life, unless one is reminded of one's vulnerability by a direct hit. Domestic violence and the breakup of family relationships can directly disrupt a child's security in a manner that more objectively dangerous events do not.

There were specific patterns of responses. As Nikola put it succinctly, *The saddest thing was the death of those people and most frightening is bombing.* Losses, especially of close relatives, were more likely to result in persistent sadness and depression. Bombing and seeing someone injured or killed produced immediate fear, nightmares, and intrusive imagery in some children. Yet these "traumatic" symptoms did not provide a guide to longer-term well-being. There were children who, like Nikola, were extremely frightened during the bombing yet had no symptoms and felt quite well two years later. Narcisa's flashbacks of bodies in the street were fading with time, and she felt happy and secure in her current life and did not regard such memories as an indication of ill health. Samir, who felt more insecure and fearful about the future, interpreted his memories in a more negative way and did see himself as unwell.

Children's memories of events and responses to them were not fixed. They shifted according to individual mood, what was going on in the community, and what purpose children thought the narration served. Ivana presented the NATO bombing as frightening in her written story: *I wanted to sleep, but it was impossible because planes were buzzing the whole night. I was really scared so I got close to my mother. I was wondering what will happen to us? Will we stay alive? I lost my grandmother in the war, so I was afraid I might lose somebody else from the family. I didn't close my eyes until almost dawn.* But in her interview, she did not mention the bombing at all; instead she focused on her Muslim friend Asra, and on witnessing Muslims being forced into prison. When I asked directly about the NATO bombing, she said, *I was not afraid then, I knew they wouldn't bomb us.* However, her mother believed she had been frightened and remained affected, and told me she still had a slight startle reflex to planes. I was with Ivana one day when NATO planes were flying overhead and saw no reaction at all. When I commented on the planes, she shrugged and laughed, saying they were boring.

Jovan told me that one of his most disturbing experiences was seeing dead bodies in the river, and that the picture came into his mind whenever he passed a particular spot on the bridge. In his first interview he said they were Serb bodies. A few weeks later he told me he thought they were Muslim bodies and clearly found this in some ways more upsetting, remarking spontaneously, *I saw people who are not my nationality, I'm talking about dead bodies. But it stresses me when I think how somebody could do that.*

I am not suggesting that there is one true version of events in either Ivana's or Jovan's case; rather that the details and emotions children remembered as significant two years later depended partly on the circumstances in which they were asked to remember, and who was asking. Ivana, when asked by a stranger from a NATO country ("the aggressor") to write about the war during class time, understandably emphasized the negative aspects of the NATO attack on her community and remembered the moments of fear. Many of her classmates did the same in their written stories, often using the formal and rhetorical language of adult public discourse. In interviews, as Ivana got to know and trust me, she focused on more personally significant events, such as her Muslim friend's experiences, and she remembered amusing details of the bombing. Jovan's ideas about the identity of the bodies in the river seemed to shift as there were arrests of war criminals in the community for actions against Muslims, and as there was more discussion in Foca about Muslims returning.

In exploring the effects of the children's experiences of war, I had discovered two things. First, specific events could produce quite specific feelings, but were hard to relate directly to longer-term psychological ill-health, except for personal bereavement. Second, there was some kind of dose effect evident in children in Gorazde. But there had to be other reasons for feeling less well in a post-conflict society because in Foca, the least exposed, native-born children were the ones who felt less well. If I wanted to understand this, I would have to look at the way in which the children made sense of the conflict as a whole.

10

MAKING SENSE OF MADNESS

Why were they attacking us? I always asked myself why. What reason could there be for this war which has given us so much pain and a scar on the heart that will never heal? I always ask myself that.

—Fourteen-year-old Muslim girl, Gorazde, 1997

Why was the war so cruel to us? Why did we have to experience this fate? These are the questions of the youngsters who lost their happy childhoods and their parents. We survived this war which left only graves, ruins, and sad memories. We try to get back to a normal life and to forget all the terrible things that happened. Why does it have to be that way? We still ask the same, same questions, even when we know they are difficult questions to answer and that no one tries to do so.

—Fourteen-year-old Serb girl, Foca, 1997

In 1942, seventeen-year-old Ina Konstantinova ran away from her home near Moscow to join a partisan unit and work as a saboteur behind German lines. Formerly a rather moody and restless girl, she wrote in an undated diary entry that year:

I have found my niche; here I am among friends. I am at peace with myself, and I'll definitely return victorious, but should something happen to me—believe me, I'll die honorably. This is how we all feel. Already many hardships have to be endured, but you should see me running about carrying out assignments. . . . In short, "life

is beautiful and wonderful!" Today the Germans carried out as
many as four air raids against our village. The bombing was awful
and their machine guns gave us a good thrashing. The bombs
exploded about 70 meters from us, and bullets whistled above our
heads (I lay in a ditch). But you see—I survived. Consequently,
nothing will ever happen to me; I believe this wholeheartedly.[108]

In contrast, fourteen-year-old Yitskhok Rudashevski, confined in the
Vilna ghetto with his family, wrote in his journal for June 24, 1941:

Our hearts are crushed witnessing the shameful scene where
women and older people are beaten and kicked in the middle of
the street by small bandits . . . Tears come to my eyes: All our helplessness, all our loneliness lies in the streets. There is no one to take
our part. And we ourselves are so helpless! . . . We are so sad, so
lonely. We are exposed to mockery and humiliation. A new feeling
of terror frequently overcomes the few neighbors of the yard. They
are looking for weapons. The courtyard is full of Germans. There is
a ring, the door is torn open and all hearts are pounding. Germans
in helmets rush in, their weapons resound. Meekly the cupboards
and drawers are opened to them. Cruelly they fling everything
apart, fling, throw, go away, and leave behind them a sad house
with things scattered all over. We stand around with pale faces. We
calm ourselves only when we learn that they have left. The mood
becomes worse from day to day.

But Yitskhok's mood changed completely when a school opened and he
joined a club that did "ghetto research" to document the details of ghetto
life. On October 5, he wrote, "Today we go to school. The day passed quite
differently. Lessons, subjects . . . There is a happy spirit in the school. Finally
the club too was opened. My own life is shaping up in quite a different way."
And on December 10, "I decided not to trifle my time away in the ghetto
on nothing and I feel somehow happy that I can read, develop myself and
see that time does not stand still as long as I progress normally with it. . . .
I do not feel the slightest despair."[109]

Both Ina and Yitskhok died in the Second World War. When Ina's unit
was surrounded by German troops, she sent her comrades toward safety

and covered their escape with machine-gun fire. Yitskhok and his family went into hiding after the Vilna ghetto was liquidated in 1943, but they were discovered and murdered in the slaughterhouse at Ponar.

What comes across from these young people's writing is their ability to endure horrendous and terrifying events because of their capacity to actively engage with those events and give their own lives meaning. Ina can find life beautiful while being shelled, and can deny the obvious risks because she has an active role in confronting the perpetrators. Even within the meaningless, brutal, and squalid confines of the ghetto, Yitskhok's helplessness and despair lift when he is able to study and decides to record and make sense of what is happening around him.

Being able to give meaning to one's experiences appears to be protective, both when terrible events occur and afterwards. In 1969, a comparative study of Israeli children living in two kibbutzim showed that those who were exposed to bombardment were no more anxious than those whose kibbutz was not shelled. The researchers believed that this was true not only because children accustomed themselves to shelling and so no longer saw it as threatening, but also because of their perceptions of their own roles in confronting it. The Israeli media portrayed them as brave and heroic, and this praise, combined with the kibbutz ethic of mutual solidarity, lessened their anxiety.[110]

Situations and the meanings given to them can change. In the late 1980s and early 1990s, black youth living in townships in South Africa were exposed to extraordinary amounts of violence on a daily basis. According to surveys done in Alexandra Township in both 1987 and 1992, more than 74 percent had witnessed an assault and more than 67 percent a killing. Many were subject to arrests, evictions, and intimidation. Yet when residents were interviewed and asked if they saw the violence as a problem, their answers changed from 1987 to 1992. The majority of young people interviewed in 1987 did not see it as a problem, while in 1992 the majority did. All regarded the violence as something abnormal, but in 1987, the youth saw it as positive because it was part of the liberation struggle with "clear political objectives and thus imbued with transcendent meaning." In 1992, they "no longer saw the violence as having a clear political objective" and felt unhappy because they saw the state as deliberately stirring up internecine violence. It was the changing political context and the way young people interpreted what was happening in their community that determined how distressing they found the violence to be.[111]

Many researchers, working in different parts of the world, have found that active engagement in or ideological commitment to political struggle seems to protect children from some of the psychological problems that can arise from exposure to political violence. In the first intifada of the late 1980s, Palestinian children who participated often showed greater stress at the time of involvement because of their greater exposure to the violence. However, in the period of peace that followed the Oslo accords, those engaged children had more self-esteem and looked back on the violence as less significant, while those who had been passive had more psychological difficulties. Developmental age played a role as well. Palestinian adolescents, who could view themselves as freedom fighters, coped better with police attacks than younger children who lacked the cultural knowledge to adopt an ideological position.[112] In a more recent study, the same research group found that the meanings given to one's role in a struggle can also counteract the dose effect of exposure to larger numbers of war-related events. In general, Palestinian children who experienced more military violence such as night raids, family members killed, injured, or imprisoned, or the destruction of their homes, had worse relationships with their peers than those who experienced less. However, above a certain level of violence, relationships actually improved. The authors suggested that those experiencing extreme violence in the context of a national liberation struggle got more social support and admiration, which strengthened them.[113]

When it came to interviewing the children of Gorazde and Foca I expected to find something similar. I thought there might be a relationship between the different ways children made sense of what had happened to them and how well they felt. I thought perhaps those who had the clearest, most "ideological" views, and who could provide themselves with explanations for the conflict, would feel better than those with none. But it was not that simple.

For a start, the majority of children had no overt ideological position. In both cities, *I hate politics* was a common response, and children had a very negative view of politicians. When I tried to get Svetlana to tell me what the word "politics" meant, she responded, *Awful [. . .] nothing [. . .] it just disturbs people.* Nikola said, *Somebody always wants to destroy somebody. In my opinion it is not good, I don't like politics, and I am not interested in that.*

Many children showed very little interest in questions like *How do you make sense of what's happened?* or *How will you explain this war to your own children?* They did not want to talk about the meaning of the war at all. As discussed in chapter 5, either they did not know and did not want to know, or they had explanations, but made clear when they shared them with me that the topic was boring. In both towns, it was the children who kept their distance from the conflict and avoided looking for explanations who felt psychologically well and secure. They were focused on their personal lives, good marks at school, friendships, sports, and the latest videos. The children who were curious about what had happened, who asked questions and did try to make sense of it all, were the ones who felt less well. Perhaps not surprisingly, this engagement in a search for meaning also had other costs. The engaged children disliked politics, but this did not stop them from being "politically sensitive." They were much more knowledgeable about current events than the distanced children, and more worried about the prospect of a future war.

The parents of the engaged children reported that they picked up on items of the news and asked questions like *Does that mean the war will start again?* In interviews, these children also spontaneously mentioned current local or national political events that concerned them. In Gorazde, this included issues like the city becoming an Open Town and the rumors that Gorazde might be "given up" to Republika Srpska if there was complete partition of Bosnia. In Foca, it was worry about the possibility of war in Kosovo, or the fights within the Republika Srpska political assembly. I had the sense that these young people were spending at least part of their time scanning their environments on the lookout for threats.

These distinctions between distanced and engaged children and the relationship to psychological well-being were true for both towns. However (as noted in chapters 5 and 6), there were other characteristics of both the distanced and engaged children that seemed to relate to the community in which they lived. In Gorazde, whether children were distanced or engaged was associated with how much violence they had experienced. The distanced children had been in a safer part of the enclave, and thus exposed to less shelling, or they had left the country as refugees. Gorazde refugee children were also among those who could be seen as least patriotic. They were not interested in fighting for their country in another war, or necessarily in living there in the future. Distancing in Gorazde also allowed for a more dispassionate, less partisan view of the conflict than that held by their more engaged and less-well contemporaries. Distanced adolescents attributed responsibility for the war more evenly to both sides, and they had no problem with the idea of Serbs returning to live in their town. What worries they did have centered on school and exams; they were mostly less aware of current political events, felt safe, and did not worry about another war.

Nedjad, for example, spent the war in the relative safety of a small village where there was little shelling. He was one of the few Muslim children to express complete empathy for Serb children in his written story: *I know many children from Republika Srpska who lost their dearest. They will suffer forever as well as children in BiH.* On two separate occasions, I asked him how he explained the war and each time his response was *Hmm . . . I don't know.* Nor was he interested in finding out. Although he acknowledged some symptoms in the checklist, in his case this method of assessment appeared to be misleading. It was clear in interviews that he was completely well, enjoying his life, doing well in high school, and planning to go to university.

In contrast, the children engaged in searching for meaning in Gorazde were those who had experienced the most violence. They tended to regard Serbs as more to blame for the conflict, a few of them were more ambivalent about Serbs coming back, and they felt much more anxious about the prospect of a future war.

Samir, whose story of his family's imprisonment in their own house is told in chapter 1, had suffered some of the worst experiences. On the checklist, he acknowledged having numerous symptoms, such as feeling frightened without reason, tense, panicky, and nervous, feeling sad, tearful, and worthless, having recurring memories of the imprisonment, feeling very jumpy, and avoiding places that reminded him of his imprisonment. In interviews, both he and his parents said he had become more fearful, withdrawn, and lonely since the war. They were concerned enough to be seeking help.

When I asked Samir how he made sense of the war, he was engaged and animated. He saw Serbs as responsible for the conflict: *Everything started because Serbs hated Muslims. [. . .] Serbs hated Muslims too much [. . .] they wanted to have Bosnia [. . .] so that Muslims wouldn't be there. They wanted to have only Serbia.* At a later point, he told me he was confused about

Serbs and politics and there were things he still could not understand. He wanted to know, *Why did they hate? Why did they want that? Why did they want to rule?* Being able to answer these questions would help him come to terms with his experiences. He was uncertain how he would respond to Serbs who came back to live in Gorazde, and he felt a bit insecure because it had been made an Open Town.

In Foca, I could not distinguish between distanced and engaged children based on how much violence they had suffered. They had all experienced significantly less violence than Gorazde children. However, they did differ in their attitudes about the return of Muslims and in their ideas about who was responsible for the conflict. In contrast to Gorazde, it was the psychologically well, and distanced, children who were most against Muslims returning and most convinced that Muslims were primarily responsible for the war. It was the less-well children, those who were searching for explanations, who were more evenhanded about responsibility and more open to the possibility of living with Muslims again. Radmila and Liljana illustrate the contrast.

Radmila had not had a good war. She fled with her family from a mixed village near Gorazde, got caught between the lines, moved back home repeatedly, and was frightened by NATO bombing (see chapter 6). However, she reported no symptoms on the checklist, felt completely well when interviewed, and was enjoying her life in the farmhouse near Foca. She had no interest at all in the reasons for the war.

Did you ever wonder yourself why it happened? I asked.
No.
You didn't think about it?
No.
Do you have any explanation?
No.
Do you wonder at all?
No.
What do you think the war was for?
I don't know.
Radmila was convinced that living together again was impossible because Muslims hated her. But she had no worries about the possibility of a future war. She did not think about it.

Liljana's war experiences were not as bad as Radmila's. She lived with her father's extended family in a large house built by her grandfather. Both her parents worked in business. She spent the first four months of the war in Serbia with an aunt. Her worst experiences of the war were worrying constantly for her father on the line, missing *friends who left*, and *bad living conditions*. The NATO bombing frightened her, as her home was close to the bridge. They all spent a night in the cellar and then retreated to the woods for the second night. Fortunately, no one in her family was killed.

Two years after the war she was one of the most unhappy girls whom I interviewed. She could not sleep and had frequent bad dreams, although these were not about the war. She said she ate too much, cried all the time, was worried, irritable, tense, and restless, and thought quite often of ending her life. She felt that these symptoms had nothing to do with her experiences in the war, but arose from her life now: the atmosphere and living conditions in Foca and the stress of her first year in high school, where her marks were poor and the workload felt overwhelming. She thought she had got in with the wrong crowd of new friends. In her story, she wrote eloquently of her wish to understand what had happened, her sadness at missing her old friends, and the current mood of the city:

> *War. Why war? I was always wondering that, but I never got an answer. Maybe I never understood why something awful like that happened because I was still a child, but I know that it marked me in some way. Four awful years, spent in fear, pain, grief for those we lost and for the nice childhood I never had. Wishing for fun, company, games, joy in everything that makes life beautiful, but unfortunately, there was none of that. God, I'm wondering why is the world so cruel, why dark forces made our destiny and brought the greatest misfortunes to children who are not guilty of anything.*
>
> *It was very difficult to part with best and dearest friends who had to go somewhere else and to leave their homes. Even now, after the war, it is not so nice or great. We all miss many things, we're all somehow depressed, tense, nervous, but it's like that and we have to carry on living. The most important thing is that people didn't die for nothing, and the rest will come with time. Even I know that to get back to the better life before the war, it will take a lot of time.*

She would have liked some explanations. When she was young she had pestered older people and eavesdropped on her father's conversations when he was home from the line, but she had not understood what she heard. *Now nobody is giving me answers,* she said, and she had stopped asking because of the fatalistic view that *What happened happened. We can't change anything.* But it was clear from her story and our conversations that she puzzled over it all. She read voraciously, *serious books* such as Vuk Draskovic's *Noz* (The Knife) that she hoped would provide explanations.[114] *I want to read to find out how was it in previous wars, how people felt, how they survived.* She watched television and discovered that *The war is over but nothing is solved. Everybody wants to come back to where they lived before. A lot of people died and it seems it was for nothing, because there was a lot of talking and it seems that we will still live together again. Not now, but maybe in a few years.*

Like many of her contemporaries in Foca she felt this made the war itself meaningless: *A lot lost their homes, and in the end it seems to be for nothing, to live together. What was the purpose of the war?* Given the sadness she had expressed about friends who had had to leave, I pushed her on this topic, and like Vesna (chapter 6), she was clearly ambivalent and uneasy about the contradictions in the situation. Her explanation for the war was:

> *We all wanted to be in power. Muslims wanted their power. They wanted us to be under them. Not in the real sense like it was before once under the Turks. In one way they wanted to be in power to have authority. And just in one way we wanted the same. But I think the other nationality, Muslims, wanted that more, Croats, and because of those political conflicts, war came. They just couldn't agree with each other, and that's why we decided to live separately. So that everybody could rule their own people.*

But she felt that separation was *not good,* and when I asked what should happen to those who wanted to come back, she paused for a long time and then said *If they think it will be better for them, it's their decision. Whoever wants to, he can come back, but in that way, we will all be mixed again.* She thought people who had lost someone would mind.

Would you like your old friends back?

Another long pause. *Yes, I would . . .*

So it's a contradiction, I started to say, and she interrupted, *Not so much . . . because a lot has changed. But I would like them to come back.*

Even though she thought the lessons for the future were clear— *There is no need to create hatred between people because they are all people of flesh and blood, it doesn't matter that we are different nationalities*—she was very pessimistic about anyone being able to learn from experience. And while she hoped people would come back, she knew, *We won't be happy.*

Will you be happier living separately? I asked.

I don't know, no.

So you're stuck then?

Exactly.

It is worth noting that after I discussed this same theme with Vesna, who expressed similar confused ambivalence about the forced separation and living together, she became slightly physically unwell. She and her mother talked with me about whether this might have been a result of the interview because Vesna had not thought or spoken of these matters before and the conversation had upset her. They then decided it was a "summer allergy." As she recovered quickly and wanted to continue, we did meet again without ill effects, although I avoided difficult topics in the second interview.

My findings contrasted with those of many studies of children in other countries: in Bosnia, the children who avoided looking for any meaning and distanced themselves felt psychologically more comfortable than those who tried to make sense of things. Looking for meaning was associated with psychological distress. So what was going on?

For the children described at the beginning of this chapter, the search for meaning led to active participation in the conflict and to greater self-esteem. In the ghetto in Vilna, Yitskhok Rudashevski began to feel less helpless and frustrated when he found an active way to challenge his circumstances by documenting them. Ina Konstantinova was active in the war as a partisan, with every minute of her life taken up in pursuit of a goal. South African and Palestinian children have lived through years of low-intensity conflict where active engagement means actual participation in demonstrations. In contrast, the war in Bosnia was a prolonged high-intensity conflict, in which children had little opportunity for active participation except in sharing the tasks of basic survival.[115]

In both towns, the children experienced long periods of anxiety about close relatives on front lines and about the threat of being attacked. In addition, the Gorazde children endured actual shelling and siege for nearly four years. After the war, both groups of children lived in relatively unstable political environments: Gorazde was a Muslim island within the Serb-controlled entity; Foca was at odds with the international community monitoring the peace accords and suffered the consequences. The presence of the UN Stabilization Force (SFOR) throughout the country was a constant reminder of the war.

Both groups of children also lived with the legacy common to all post-communist states: disenchantment with and alienation from politics, and a belief that politicians are corrupt and self-serving. And they were old enough to remember that the upsurge of political activism in their country in the early 1990s had been a prelude to war. They had no models of effective democratic political activism, or clear targets against which to act. Families on both sides talked of feelings of unimportance and powerlessness.

In this context, it was not surprising that activism and ideological commitment did not present themselves as effective means of coping. Rather than searching for the meaning of a conflict they could not control, many children focused on friendships and on personal achievement, such as good marks at school, sports, or music. Meanwhile the unwell children, who were engaged in looking for meaning, paid the price of a certain political sensitivity and awareness of threats to their security. Because of their powerlessness in the face of these threats, this sensitivity led to feelings of discomfort, which led to more alertness and more discomfort. Children who are sensitive to their political environment without being able to take action can find themselves as many described: sad, anxious, and restless.

Other studies have found that looking for an explanation of stressful events does not always prove helpful. In the fall of 1980, at a school soccer game in southern Illinois, a lightning bolt hit the field, knocking down all the fifth- and sixth-grade players and killing three. Steven Dollinger, a psychologist at Southern Illinois University, decided to look at the children's explanations of the disaster, and how these explanations related to their emotional upset. He expected that certain kinds of meanings might be more protective than others. What he actually found was that those who gave any explanation of what caused the disaster were much more upset than those who gave none. The content of the explanations did not seem to matter. Some blamed chance, some an act of God, some the team itself for wanting to play in poor weather. It was those who stuck with "I don't know" who had fewest emotional difficulties. Dollinger speculated that there were two ways of understanding these findings. One possibility was that the search for meaning followed from the degree of upset: those who were the most upset were those most in need of explanation. Alternatively, the meanings themselves led to becoming upset.[116] Both theories made sense to me in southeastern Bosnia.

In Gorazde, where children were exposed to years of shelling, it looked as if being more upset resulted in a greater need for explanations. Some (though not all) of the children who suffered more of the violence felt unwell; consequently, they were more engaged in trying to make sense of what had happened. They thought about questions such as, "Why did they want to kill me?" "Why can't I go home?" and "Who was responsible for destroying my home?" There were no easy answers, and plenty of nagging questions. Why were those identified as war criminals still at liberty? When could Muslims with homes in Republika Srpska safely return there to live? Posing unanswered questions does not bring psychological relief. In addition, their political sensitivity and insecurity made the prospect of living with returning Serbs, some of whom they saw as the aggressors, more alarming. Not surprisingly, they were more ambivalent about doing so, and more partisan in attributing blame. The Gorazde children who had been more protected from the violence were less troubled and more secure. They felt more distanced from the conflict and did not need to look for explanations, because the war had caused them less distress.

Seeking explanations had a different significance for children living in Foca. Here it looked as if it was the search for meaning that led to distress, rather than the other way around. For some children, searching for meaning increased their sense of victimhood and isolation. In some stories, the writers explicitly stated that the feeling that the world was against them had made the bombing of the town particularly traumatic: *The world was on their side and that's why many people from Republika Srpska are traumatized by NATO bombing.* Similar feelings echo through the unhappier texts:

Now I am here in Srbinje, but I don't feel good. I am with Serb peo-
ple, our brothers, but nothing can change my childhood. The war
stole everything I had; it took my lovely cousins and uncle. [. . .]
Why did war happen? That question will never get out of my head.
And I still wonder does Bil Klinton know how it is for us and what
he did to us. The whole world is always against us, everybody is on
the BiH side. They were always on their side, during the war and
now when it has stopped. They simply want to destroy us Serbs.
They want to eradicate us.

This girl's essay ends on a note of proud and lonely bravado, telling *the*
world to leave us alone because no one will *choke* the Serbs and *God is our*
only hope. However, she will never forgive anyone or reconcile herself to
the fact that she *cannot go home* to Sarajevo. One has no sense that her
ideological commitment to the Serb cause has helped her come to terms
with her losses. Instead, her interpretation of events has increased her feelings of abandonment and threat.

For some in Foca, trying to make sense of what had happened in the
town led to an awareness of injustice. These "engaged" children were more
open to the possibility of living with non-Serbs again, and less partisan
about who was responsible for the war. But their search for meaning also
exposed them to uncomfortable truths about their own community, which
contributed to their psychological discomfort. So Liljana felt *stuck* because
Muslims' return would make nonsense of Serb suffering in the war, but she
also missed her old friends, was unhappy with her new ones, and felt, as a
basic principle, that people should be able to live with one another. Svetlana had no explanations for what had happened, but she wanted some.
She did not blame anyone, missed her Muslim friends, and wanted them
back. She too had been nervous, restless, and irritated since the war ended.
She told me that things were not right because of *changes here since the war.*
I didn't feel like this before.

Children who chose to ask questions about what had happened in Foca
had to make sense of the sudden disappearance of large numbers of people,
visible destruction in a town that was not shelled, parental silence, large
spaces where mosques had stood that nobody mentioned, sudden arrests
by international troops, and the depressing stagnant nature of the community. These questioners were mostly children who had been born in

Foca and remembered what it was like before, and all made frequent references to how unpleasant the town had become. Marko told me, *It's not as it should be,* although he could not explain why. Tatiana, who had spent much of the war in Belgrade and had looked forward to returning to Foca, said *Everything is going wrong.* She disliked the atmosphere in town. At school she was so stressed by the workload that she thought of abandoning everything. Many native-born children identified living in a neglected and isolated community, worrying about school marks, and missing friends as their worst problems. Possibly, there was greater pressure to do well in school in Foca because scholastic achievement compensated parents whose side had lost the war and gave children a way out of an unhappy living situation through university.

Although the search for meaning in Foca could result in children's developing more moderate opinions, such views had a cost. They put these children at odds with the dominant public discussions in the town, where both political leaders and popular opinion as expressed in the local media accommodated themselves to (and even celebrated) the results of ethnic cleansing. Those children in Foca, like Susana, Milica, or Radmila, who avoided examining such issues, avoided any such conflict and had better individual psychological health. They were enjoying their lives and doing well at school.

Near the end of my first research trip to the Drina Valley, in the summer of 1998, Samir and his family decided that he should visit a traditional healer, a well-known woman who lived in a large apartment block near his house. She agreed that I might come with the family to learn about her methods, and so I spent an afternoon with Samir and his parents in her small, over-heated apartment while she *took away his fear.* It was overheated because the stove was on high in the middle of summer, with a fist-sized lump of iron melting in a pan. Once it was molten, she cast it into cold water and examined the pattern it made: a complex web of loops and whorls, all tangled together. *That indicates a great deal of terror,* she told Samir. Wrapped in a blanket and sweating profusely, Samir followed the healer's Instructions to hold the water and the iron and look at the mountains outside the window, while she said prayers over his head. Afterwards he drank some of the water, and the remains were cast away in a particular place far from his home. The session took an hour. At no point did his therapy involve any discussion of what caused the terror. It was simply named and symbolically removed, both digested and thrown away.

When the session was over Samir looked different. The tension had gone from his face and he seemed genuinely cheerful and relaxed. These feelings continued over the following weeks, and when I repeated the symptom checklists, he was almost symptom free. He felt much better. He was not frightened anymore. He said that if some of the fear came back he would just return to the healer. A Serbian girl in Foca, who had suffered nightmares and sleeplessness after the NATO bombing, also wrote of seeing *a woman who helped me and got rid of the fear,* which suggests that the tradition was common to both communities.

None of the other unwell children wanted individual psychological assistance, although I offered to put them in touch with professionals in their towns. What they thought would make a difference was better living conditions, stable places to live, or the possibility of returning home. They wanted more things for young people to do, like computers, movies, and clubs. They wanted to see their parents less stressed by poverty, unemployment, and grief. They wanted old friends back, more understanding and supportive teachers in school, an end to corruption, reparations, the arrest of war criminals, and security. The children knew that their recovery did not depend on individual therapy, but was intimately bound up with the recovery of their social and political communities. These responses and choices made me question the conventional approaches of the humanitarian aid community toward war-affected children.

It would be unwise to make generalizations based on a study of a small group of children in one war zone. However, there are implications that deserve further thought and are in keeping with findings by others.

First, trying to understand the psychological impact of a war solely through the use of symptom checklists can be misleading. In this context, it would have resulted in the unnecessary pathologizing of children who were well, while those who felt unwell, but could not express this as "symptoms" would have been missed. The only way to find out which symptoms matter is to ask children and spend time with them.

Second, war is long and complicated, and different events will affect different children in different ways. The dose effect—how much and how long—does seem to matter when the violence is severe and prolonged, but so do the children's interpretations of what is happening: How threatened did they feel? Were they frightened for their own lives, or for someone they loved? These interpretations also depend on the interpretations and behavior of those around them, particularly parents.

Third, overwhelming fear and the appearance of traumatic symptoms at the time of an event do not necessarily predict longer-term psychological distress. A researcher working in the Bosnian city of Tuzla at a time when the city was regularly bombarded found that 94 percent of the 364 displaced children he examined met criteria for PTSD as set out in the *DSM-IV*. However, he suggested that in that particular context, high levels of symptoms might be adaptive.[117] I also found that children who had been badly frightened during shelling or bombing were mostly doing well two years later. Any enduring impact seemed to be more closely related to how personally disruptive the event had been: Was their home or school directly attacked? What had happened to their family and friends and the landscape in which they lived?

Fourth, the worst thing that can happen is to lose someone you love. Thinking in terms of personal disruption also helps to explain the enduring effects of loss. Children who lost fathers and elder brothers had their whole worlds torn apart. This was especially the case in Bosnia, which is a patriarchal society in which families organize around male leadership. Young boys like Edin were pushed into more adult roles and given no space to grieve. Girls like Helena felt completely cast adrift.

Fifth, some things are worse than war for some children. Again, thinking in terms of personal disruption may explain why. Divorce and domestic violence can completely undermine a child's immediate world, while, as Amela's experience showed, war may actually be a liberation from abuse. In Eastern Sri Lanka one study found that poverty, child abuse, and witnessing parents fighting were just as likely to cause psychological distress and PTSD in youth as living through decades of civil war and experiencing the Southeast Asian tsunami. There are similar findings for children in Afghanistan.[118]

Sixth, it matters where you live. The difficulties of living in a politically isolated and materially neglected postwar community such as Foca outweighed the effects of bombing and shooting. Two years after the war ended there were more unwell children in Foca than in Gorazde, although Gorazde suffered much more violence during the war. The fact that most of these Foca children were more alienated than their contemporaries in Gorazde, and that half of them wanted to leave the country, suggests that the misery created by ethnic cleansing affects not only those who are driven away but also those who remain behind. The concept of personal disruption may be helpful here: The disruption of the town, the arrival of large numbers of new people, combined with a change in its name, left many local families feeling like strangers in their own community. Foca-born young people like Liljana and Tatiana made clear their sensitivity to this mood. Tatiana was miserable returning to a town that had changed beyond recognition. She wanted to get away from a community she no longer recognized. She felt more unwell than Radmila, who had suffered more during the war, but who was determined to adapt to new circumstances, and happy to start afresh in an attractive new house with her family around her.

Seventh, distancing is an effective means of coping for some children, in some situations. This challenges widely held assumptions about the psychological impact of stressful events. It suggests that we might do well to pay more attention to avoidance as a constructive rather than pathological coping mechanism.

Much therapeutic endeavor in Western contexts is based on the premise that all stressful experiences should be explored and reexamined to be assimilated. Some of those working with children have suggested that all children exposed to stressful events should be encouraged to reexamine the events at an early stage, and that to "foster mastery" of the associated distressing emotions the therapist should "overcome the efforts of the child to avoid and deny" what has occurred. Children can then be helped to a more realistic understanding of the event, reassured about their own responses, and educated as to what may occur in the future.[119]

Although the term is not always used, this is one form of "debriefing," a method of front-line psychological assistance for those exposed to traumatic events that became very popular in late nineties, particularly in humanitarian settings, perhaps in part because it was a treatment that gave psychologists a front-line role similar to those fixing broken bones and building temporary shelters.[120] In their essence, debriefing methods involve group work in which all those exposed to a stressful event are seen shortly after its occurrence. There is encouragement of emotional ventilation and exploration of what happened to gain understanding, combined with the provision of information and social support. This approach has been used indiscriminately with whole communities exposed to a particular event, on the assumption that it will avert later psychological disability.[121] Results with young people have been mixed: With some it has increased their distress; with others it has been shown to decrease unpleasant intrusive symptoms.[122] Over the last decade, a growing body of research has suggested that debriefing is ineffective when given to all those exposed to traumatic events, and in some circumstances, it may be harmful, resulting in an increase of distressing symptoms.[123] WHO issued a recommendation against the use of debriefing in 2003. It updated the evidence and retained this recommendation in 2012, stating that, "'Psychological debriefing should not be used for people exposed recently to a traumatic event as an intervention to reduce the risk of post-traumatic stress, anxiety, or depressive symptoms."[124] This may be particularly important with those whose personal coping methods rely on avoidance.

There is some research suggesting that more avoidant methods may be protective. Hanna Kaminer and Peretz Lavie studied long-term coping mechanisms in Holocaust survivors who had either been in concentration camps or spent long periods in hiding. They found that one group rarely talked about their experiences even with their close families. They had not forgotten these experiences, but they avoided thinking of them and had successfully repressed the unpleasant feelings of helplessness, anxiety, and depression they had felt at the time. This was particularly evident in sleep. They slept well and found it hard to recall their dreams. They were well-adjusted, had a positive outlook on life, were neither defensive nor easily aroused, had few physical illnesses, and were doing well in work and personal relationships. Those in the less adjusted group, meanwhile, were flooded with memories in the form of traumatic symptoms during the day and nightmares and sleep disturbances at night. They were more anxious and depressed and had far more physical complaints. They were also much more sensitive to their daily environments, particularly any aspect that could be seen as threatening. The researchers suggested that the ability to seal off memories of past atrocities and limit remembrance could be adaptive and that therapists should explore this possibility.[125]

Displaced people in northern Angola, who suffered four decades of war, advised those in their community who were bereaved and suffering to "abandon the thoughts and memories of war events and loss," accept the inevitability and universality of death and suffering, and get on with making a new future through the creation of new families. Bosnian Muslim culture similarly encourages stoicism in the face of disaster and loss. I was often told by more religious families of the importance of not expressing too much distress about death, as this might upset the dead. Mourning is expressed through formal and gender-divided rituals.[126]

Nerma and her mother invited me to a Tevhid to say prayers with other women for Nerma's grandmother a month after she died. I had seen few tears, but watched Nerma spend a whole day cheerfully scrubbing her grandmother's house in preparation. Avoidance and a literal throwing out of the symptoms was a central part of Samir's traditional healing session. But avoidance may sometimes have a cost. One man told me that he had never cried over his twelve-year-old daughter's death because parents' crying over children filled the grave with tears and prevented the children from being happy in paradise. For the same reason he preferred not to talk about his loss. This man suffered from intermittent chest pain, and we agreed that his heart "ached with grief," but he wanted me to find solutions other than the ventilation of emotions, solutions that did not run against the grain of his faith.[127]

I should make clear that distancing is not the same as the clinical concept of denial, in which the conscious mind actually denies that events have happened. Kaminer and Lavie pointed out that the well-adjusted Holocaust survivors were not denying their experiences and, significantly, had not forgotten them. Similarly, none of the Bosnian children who distanced themselves from the conflict denied the events or pretended that painful aspects had not taken place. Most of them volunteered quite detailed descriptions of their personal war experiences, and were animated, and sometimes visibly moved, in doing so. However, their normal choice was to avoid seeking explanations for the past. In addition, all were actively engaged in normal life, had plenty to say about it, and were functioning well. This was quite different from one of the children from Gorazde who had been exposed to a great deal of violence and could be described as "in denial." Although this child had been in Sarajevo during the siege and his father had been injured, he was unable to remember any detail of his war experiences, and he was withdrawn and monosyllabic throughout our interviews. He insisted he was alright, but he had done badly at school since the war because of poor concentration and was seen by friends and teachers as not really coping.

My clinical experience in the Balkans also suggested that if given the opportunity, the majority of children are good at judging for themselves which approach is right for them at a particular time. I worked with five related children after a horrifying massacre in Kosovo in the spring of 1999. Nineteen of their relatives, including their mothers, were machine-gunned in front of them and they themselves were left for dead. I watched them successfully piece their lives back together over three years. Each child chose a different method of coping. One needed to talk about the massacre at length and replay the whole experience. One wanted to tell the story to a journalist, but did not want to repeat it again. The others had no symptoms and did not want to discuss the subject at all. Two years later all of them wanted to tell their story when asked to give testimony to the International Tribunal and they saw that their accounts could contribute to gaining justice for their relatives. This family taught me that even children who are related and have shared a horrifying experience will not deal with their grief in the same way, yet the differences need not impede their recovery.[128]

The same children will use different methods at different times. The majority of the Bosnian children told me that they used distraction such as play or talking with parents and friends while actually in the shelters. Israeli children exposed to Scud missile attacks in the Gulf War used similar methods.[129] Nina and Elvira distracted themselves when bombs were actually falling, but also kept detailed diaries of events, another means of emotional processing. Some children threw their diaries away after the war; some kept them as a record that they reread.

Anna Freud noticed that children who had endured the Blitz usually did not talk about the events until they had emotionally processed them in other ways. Most children will find appropriate ways to express themselves when they want to do so if they are given a chance. Imposing discussion and exploration of events on a child who at that moment wants to avoid a topic may be as harmful as being unable to listen to a child who wants and needs to talk. This is not to suggest that those children who become trapped in an unproductive repetition of events, as revealed in their play, or dreams, or stories, should not be assisted to find a way out; rather that early *indiscriminate* intervention may prevent the emergence of more appropriate and natural methods of coping. Those children who are engaged in the search for meaning are clearly looking for their own recovery. The question is how they can be best supported in doing so.

Social and political interventions that rebuild the social world may have a far greater impact on emotional well-being than individual psychological ones. After I left the Balkans, I worked with displaced adolescents living in collective centers scattered across Northern Iraq. Many of the teenagers had lived through four or five wars. They did not want to discuss the past. What they wanted to talk about was the here and now. They hoped I could do something to change their horrific living conditions, which included a filthy, collapsing police station where Saddam had tortured their compatriots—the yard was full of toxic waste—and some sand-filled tents in the boiling desert where girls spent hours each day finding water and wood, but were otherwise confined. The children saw that their parents were sick; other children and teachers verbally abused them for being "IDPs" (internally displaced people) when they went to school. There was nowhere to play. All this bothered them far more than their memories of conflict. I had similar experiences talking to refugee children in South West Uganda in 2006. Their worries centered on poverty, and how to access or continue schooling.[130] Again and again, researchers have found that in the aftermath of conflict the first things people ask for are homes, school, health care, opportunities for recreation, and places people can go to socialize—the restoration of normal social ties and community life.[131] This is what the Bosnian children wanted most.

There is a need to recognize that both searching for meaning and distancing can have personal and collective political consequences that can be positive or negative depending on the environment. In the autumn of 2003, the Kosovar children were the first Albanian witnesses prepared to face one of the alleged perpetrators in a war crimes trial in Serbia. We traveled to Belgrade together, and while staying in the city the children made friends with the Serb hotel staff and the security police who protected them, and they told me how amazed they were at the kindness of everyone. Their search for meaning and justice had begun a process of reconciliation.

However, a commitment to a transcendent meaning in political struggle can lead not simply to the sacrifice of one's own life, but to a willingness to kill others, as exemplified by the young Palestinian suicide bombers of

238 • THEN THEY STARTED SHOOTING

the second Intifada. The ideological training for suicide bombers includes mytho-historical interpretations of the past, the destruction of empathy, the fostering of hatred of the other, and encouragement to value martyrdom, with its promise of both material (for the bombers' families) and spiritual rewards.[132] When the quest for heroic meaning is taken to the extreme, it can have horrifying consequences.

In Gorazde, engaging in the search for meaning created greater anxiety and fears about the threat from the other side, whereas disengagement allowed children to acknowledge the role of their own side in the conflict and to feel more open to reconciliation with former enemies. In Foca, in contrast, the children who used distancing could avoid contradictions in the story of what had happened in Foca and maintain better individual psychological health. They came across as well adjusted to their environment, but some of them, like Susana and Radmila, also demonstrated a disturbing lack of empathy. Avoidance and silence on issues such as what had happened to their classmates left unchallenged their implicit beliefs that ethnic cleansing was a defensive necessity and that security rested in living in an ethnically homogenous ministate. Neither of these beliefs seemed likely to promote the rebuilding of intercommunal relationships within the country, the long-term stability of the region, or their own security and well-being as individuals. Paradoxically, in Foca it was unwell children, who questioned the accepted version of events, who offered the best hope of communal recovery. But how easy was such a quest to sustain? And at what cost to themselves? Four years later, I went back to find out.

PART FOUR

THE ADULTS THEY BECAME

11

CRIMES AND PUNISHMENTS

There were Serbs living in a nearby village [who] did not want to go anywhere. They got along with others well. [. . .] Then the VRS told my father that they would destroy our village, so Father said, "Well we can take that Serb village." He wanted to use them as hostages if the Serbs from the front line started shelling. He planned to do that. But he would not kill and torture the Serbs in that village. [. . .] I don't know. Father had to do it, he had no choice.

—Fifteen-year-old Muslim boy, Gorazde 1997

Prosecutor: You knew, in fact, that none of those procedures in place for detaining these people legally were ever followed, isn't that true?

Krnojelac: And that is why, excuse me, I begged and asked not to be there and to be taken out of the KP Dom, so as not to be held responsible for it. . . . I was not pleased at all when I saw two people, my neighbors until then, the Muslims, at the KP Dom. I was not pleased to see them there, nor did I want to be the one who would be their superior. That is why I asked to be withdrawn immediately.

—Milorad Krnojelac, former warden of the KP Dom prison, 2001

I have now come to the belief and accept the fact that many thousands of innocent people were the victims of an organized, systematic effort to remove Muslims and Croats from the territory claimed by Serbs. At the time, I easily convinced myself that this was a matter of survival and self-defense. In fact, it was more. Our leadership, of which I was a necessary part, led an effort which victimized countless innocent people. Explanations of self-defense and survival offer no justification. . . . Why did I not see it earlier? And how could our leaders and those who followed have committed such acts? The answer to both questions is, I believe, fear, a blinding fear that led to an obsession, especially for those of us for whom the Second World War was a living memory, that Serbs would never again allow themselves to become victims. In this, we in the leadership violated the most basic duty of every human being, the duty to restrain oneself and to respect the human dignity of others. We were committed to do whatever was necessary to prevail. . . . In this obsession of ours to never again become victims, we had allowed ourselves to become victimizers.

—**Biljana Plavsic, pleading guilty to crimes against humanity, 2002**

I returned to the Drina Valley in the summer of 2002 and moved back into my old apartment looking out over the river. The view was much the same as before, apart from a widened footpath and a factory at the end of the road. The house had been newly plastered and the only shrapnel scars left were in the stairwell and a tiny reminder in my bedroom door. The biggest change was in Nerma herself. She had undergone that magical "duckling into swan" transformation that occurs between fourteen and eighteen. She looked stunning, had acquired a handsome boyfriend and a place at Sarajevo University to read economics, and was spending every night at the international rock festival that was taking place in the town that week. Everyone was on the street: whole families filled cafés and promenaded back and forth across the river, munching snacks and greeting friends. I went out partying with Lejla, my old interpreter, and Ana and Jelena, two sisters from Foca. All of them worked together for the International Police Task Force in Gorazde. It felt as if things were changing at last.

The houses next door to Nerma's were still empty shells, but these were now a minority. Changes in the property laws had made it easier to evict temporary occupants, and the slow trickle of returning Serbs had become a steady stream. Almost a thousand families had registered to come back, and many were in the process of rebuilding their houses with help from international donors.[133] In the suburb of Kopaci, two hundred Muslim families had taken matters into their own hands two years earlier and had camped out on the interentity boundary until the international community had bullied the reluctant Serb local authorities into giving them back their homes.

The Balkan world as a whole was changing. After the war and the NATO air strikes in Kosovo, Milosevic had been thrown out of power in Yugoslavia in a popular uprising and handed over to the International Criminal Tribunal at The Hague by his own people. Vojislav Kostunica was now president of the Federal Republic of Yugoslavia, and although an ardent supporter of Republika Srpska's right to independence during the war, he now apparently accepted the integrity of the Bosnian state. Negotiations between Serbia and Montenegro made it look as if the term "Yugoslavia," as well as the federal presidency itself, were about to be consigned to history. The other Balkan architects of Dayton were no longer on the stage. In Croatia, Franjo Tudjman had died and been replaced by the moderate pro-Western Stipe Mesic. Within the Federation, the nationalist SDA had lost heavily in the 1998 election to the moderate Social Democratic Party (SDP) and Alija Izetbegovic had retired, although hard-line nationalists retained allegiance among the Bosnian Croats and the Bosnian Serbs. It looked as if the entity structure itself might be weakened by a new constitutional court ruling that declared the dominance of any ethnicity, in either entity, unconstitutional and discriminatory. Political structures at every level would be obliged to have representatives from all three constituent peoples. Local administrations would be obliged to hire returnees according to national quotas based on the population of the last prewar census.[134]

Meanwhile the pursuit of international justice continued steadily at The Hague, if somewhat more erratically on the ground in Bosnia. The tribunal had shifted its focus from camp guards to political and military leaders and had indicted two former Bosnian Serb presidents, Momcilo Krajisnik and Biljana Plavsic, for genocide, crimes against humanity, and violations of the laws and customs of war. The indictment stated that to "secure control of various municipalities of Bosnia and Herzegovina which had been proclaimed part of the Serbian Republic of Bosnia and Herzegovina, the Bosnian Serb leadership . . . pursued a course of conduct involving the creation of impossible conditions of life, persecution and

244 ◆ THEN THEY STARTED SHOOTING

terror tactics in order to encourage non-Serbs to leave the area, deportation of those reluctant to leave, and the liquidation of others." Krajisnik had been arrested in his pajamas and awaited trial. Biljana Plavsic had handed herself over voluntarily.[135]

The slow-burning fuse of agony over Srebrenica was approaching some kind of resolution. Forensic examinations of mass graves had so far revealed more than two thousand bodies, the majority of whom appeared to be civilians killed in execution style. There were many more grave sites to be examined and every indication that the rest of the seven to eight thousand men and boys missing since the fall of the town were dead. General Mladic and Dr. Karadzic remained at large and occasionally visible. Karadzic had been the object of a number of bungled arrest attempts. He reputedly lived somewhere in the mountains near Foca. General Radislav Krstic, commander of the Drina corps, which had organized the transport for the forced expulsions of twenty-five thousand women and children and had assisted in some of the executions, was tried and sentenced to forty-six years for genocide.[136] A memorial meeting was held in Srebrenica that July. No politicians from Republika Srpska attended.

There were more arrests in Foca. My translator Gordana was on duty in the IPTF station in early 1999, when without warning French SFOR officers tried to arrest Dragan Gagovic as he was driving five little girls home from a karate tournament. There was an exchange of fire that ended with his death, and the children were taken into safe custody. Gordana found herself alone in front of the station, facing a large crowd of angry parents led by a drunken Tuta, the paramilitary gang leader, holding a grenade. She tried to explain that the children would be released very soon. The crowd, incited by Tuta, wasn't interested in explanations and broke into the barricaded station and severely beat up the international monitors, who narrowly escaped with their lives. A local police officer managed to save Gordana, who hid terrified at home for the next three weeks, receiving threatening phone calls.

Tuta blew himself up and injured two Germans when they tried to arrest him in October 2000. At The Hague, Dragoljub Kunarac and his colleagues, on trial for their mistreatment of Muslim women in Foca, received sentences of between twelve and twenty-eight years in the first convictions that defined rape and enslavement as crimes against humanity.[137] Krnojelac, Foca's former primary school headmaster who had been warden of the KP

Dom in the first year of the war, was arrested in the summer of 1998 and sentenced to seven years for aiding and abetting persecution, inhumane acts, and cruel treatment.

I wanted to see what had happened to the children. Did they know anything about these events, and did it matter? How had they grown up? Had they all recovered? How did they feel now about living with former neighbors, and what were their hopes for themselves and for their country? I managed to find more than half of the original forty children, ten in Gorazde and twelve in Foca.

I bumped into Samir and his family by chance. They had just moved into their new house on the steep hill above Gorazde's armaments factory. After nine years of sharing, all the children had rooms of their own. They made me coffee in the spacious living room while I admired their sheep, which were visible in the small orchard. They had finally got some help from donors and rebuilt the grandfather's destroyed house. Samir was unrecognizable. The shy, nervous, slight boy had grown into a fit, muscular youth. He was training as a welder, but his real interest was sports. His main worries and frustration were about the lack of work and decent training opportunities in Gorazde. He felt as if he had lost too much time and had not achieved anything, such as his ambition to be a football player. He dreamed of going to Germany, or at least Sarajevo, to work and train, although not permanently. He liked Gorazde, but it was a dead end. He now had a girlfriend. The fear and insecurity, sadness, nightmares, and flashbacks had all gone. He avoided going to the old house alone; if he did the memories of the family's imprisonment there returned and made him *feel bad in his soul.* Yet he no longer felt bothered about whether the neighbors who had imprisoned them would come back. *I wouldn't pay attention. They can come back.*

The ones who hurt you? I asked.

Yes, but you can forget all that. I don't need them punished. I don't think about the past, just the future. I want my children to have a good one.

He did want someone punished: *the ones who gave the orders.* He thought The Hague was *too good* for Milosevic. Anyway, he had heard that only Serbs who were *not afraid* stayed in Gorazde; the others returned just to sell their houses.[138] *I would like to live together, why not? There are good and bad people whatever nationality. If it's a good person, why not be friends?*

National elections were a month away and Samir was now eighteen, but he was not interested. *There are so many lies on our side. They promise much, but they steal and nothing changes.*

So what kind of politician would you like? I asked.

Someone who thinks of our well-being. There is still no party that can connect us. There has to be one that can connect people, connect Serbs and Muslims.

Admira was still living with her mother and sister in a flat formerly occupied by Serbs. No one had reclaimed it. Admira no longer wanted to go back to their village. She enjoyed life in town too much. She was getting top marks at medical high school and planned to go to Sarajevo to train as a physiotherapist. She felt no ill effects from the war. She still missed her father and felt sad at times like the anniversary of his death, but found it harder as she grew older to remember him clearly, although her mother sometimes talked of the nice life they had had.

She was more ambivalent than Samir about her Serb neighbors' return. She was glad Milosevic was at The Hague. He was *disgusting* and deserved to suffer as they had suffered. *But I can't forgive them; it doesn't make me feel better. Probably other children who lost someone feel the same thing. I can't get over it. I have nothing against them. They can return, but I don't feel comfortable with contact. It would be better if they said, "Yes we did it," but whether I would feel easier I don't know. I really didn't have a chance to talk with them. I haven't seen anyone I knew. I prefer not to think about it. I don't think about it.* Yet she still followed documentaries and the news. *It's hard, but I still do it. I want to understand the war.*

What is your understanding now? I asked.

They wanted a Greater Serbia. They failed and that is their loss.

Are all Serbs guilty?

There are good ones, but they're rare. They had an awful attitude to Muslims and I don't think it's changed.

Narcisa had decided studying law was boring. *Someone else can do it.* She had discovered a facility for math and had her future mapped out: do an economics degree at Sarajevo, marry her boyfriend, travel, and then come home and set up a business with her parents. She loved Gorazde and had no wish to live anywhere else; it was where all her family and friends lived. She noticed she was more emotional than before the war, but she had always been an intense person; she did not see herself as unwell. Recently, her mother had become ill. This had got them all talking about their experiences in Visegrad, and she thought her emotions were related to that. Thinking about the place made her uncomfortable. Despite this, she felt much easier about Serbs coming back than before. She and a friend had admired a new boy at school and gone over to talk to him. *When he said his name was Goran I had no reaction like . . . oh, he's a Serb.* They had become friendly. They did not discuss the past. *I don't see him as responsible. I had thought I would be bothered, but I wasn't. I think it's going to be good, there are some chances.*

It was the Serbs' leaders she held responsible, and to some degree her own as well, although she thought *Muslim and Serb behavior was very different in the war.* She had just seen a documentary about Srebrenica on television that had upset her: *When they ran out of bullets, they started burying people alive.*

All the young people I reinterviewed in Gorazde felt well. Their concerns and worries were the normal ones of relationships (almost all of them were in love) and future careers, exacerbated by the almost nonexistent work prospects in the town. Nina was already studying German in Sarajevo and hoped to be an interpreter. She had come to terms with her parents' separation, although her mixed feelings of love and anger toward her father still caused her confusion. Senad was going to Madrid to do computer studies. Nedjad wanted to teach history. Armin wanted to be a crime investigator. Elvira planned to be a pediatrician.

Most were not worried at the thought of living with Serbs again, and like Narcisa, had already had positive experiences. Elvira, though, shared Admira's ambivalence. She had met an old friend, a Serb, the previous summer. *She said to me, "Look what they did to us, how they separated us," as if she didn't blame Serbs, as if she was from a completely different planet! As if Americans had done it! She asked for my phone number, I told her openly I did not want contact. She cried and said "Am I guilty?" I said I was not accusing anyone, but her father did these things, then I left the room.* Elvira had not seen the friend since. *I don't mind if they all return, but I don't want contact with them.*

They were all disillusioned with politics and politicians; most of those old enough did not plan to vote. Narcisa thought all politicians were corrupt, self-interested, and untrustworthy. The few who did intend to vote wanted *tolerant* non-national parties that were *for all Bosnians.* Nedjad felt

Bosnia was becoming a *state of old people.* He wished the older people who had conspired to make the war would just get out of the country altogether.

My first impression of Foca, as I drove in over the brand-new bridge across the Drina, was that it had undergone a similar renaissance. There was a bustle in the streets, new rows of small boutiques, and new cafés. The international organizations, which had evacuated after the Gagovic incident, had come back more than a year earlier, bringing Muslim employees with them. I had been told that Muslim families had returned to live in some of the surrounding villages and even in the town itself. However, as in Gorazde, the festive feelings of a warm summer day masked the reality that unemployment ran at 75 percent. The main employer, the state-run wood-processing factory, had burned down the previous year, and more than fifteen hundred people had lost their jobs.[139] Rumors abounded that the fire had been deliberate, set on a Saturday when the works were deserted. Headmaster Mojevic thought it was not unrelated to the sudden emergence of a number of small private firms doing the same work.

Not much had changed in Mojevic's primary school, Sveti Sava. Dust and sunlight filled the unpainted empty corridors, and the picture of the saint still hung above Mojevic's chair. The Biljana Plavsic calendar had gone and a large map of Bosnia-Herzegovina covered half of one wall. *This is Bosnia,* Mojevic said, *and whoever thinks differently is wrong.* He wanted to tell me about the projects for interentity cooperation in which he had been engaged, including joint holidays on the coast with Federation children and the setting up of a mixed subschool in a village where Muslims had returned. He had finally left the Serb Democratic Party, fed up with its corruption and its failure to work with the international community in helping the town. *When dirty water is up to my ears, I get out.*

We had a drink on the terrace of the newly painted Hotel Zelengora. The refugees had all moved out. The headmaster's own house in Ustikolina had been rebuilt, and his sister went there often. He stayed away, feeling he might not be welcome. He lit a cigarette and apologized to me, saying he had quit, but the old accusations of war crimes had resurfaced and got him smoking again. As before, he was anxious to tell me his version of events. This time it was a complicated story of how he had convinced a fellow commander that forcing Muslim detainees to dig trenches on the front line was illegal and had gone to rescue them. On their return journey to the KP

Dom prison, other soldiers had taken them out of his hands, and while he had run to a phone to check orders, *a tragic accident* had occurred: They had all been killed. He was incensed that he should be accused of their deaths, he who had once gone to prison himself for four days for protecting Muslim prisoners. *A great writer from Montenegro said, "It takes courage to defend oneself from someone else, but greater courage and humanity to defend someone else from oneself."* His conscience was clear. *If war started again, I would again be with my people.* Despite his own anxieties, however, he thought things in Foca were getting better. *Those who wanted little states are now in a minority.*

Svetlana and her family had been evicted again. It took me some time to find them, living in a farmhouse left empty by fleeing Muslims just outside the town, which they shared with a widow and a disabled child. All of them were facing eviction in the next fifteen days and had no idea where they were going. They were very upset about this uncertainty and about Svetlana's uncle's sudden death earlier that week. Although their previous flat had been reclaimed by its Muslim owner, who had promptly sold it, the original owner of this house had not filed for repossession, but the municipality was evicting them anyway *and giving the property to someone else,* said Svetlana's father. He thought the municipality used the new laws to suit itself. Their old house was still in ruins and no one had offered assistance to rebuild it, although some neighboring Muslim returnees had received assistance for their houses. The municipality was supposed to provide alternatives for homeless people, but said it had none. He had actually helped build the flats that now housed the displaced people who had lived at the Hotel Zelengora, but they would only give him one if he paid half the mortgage immediately. How could he possibly do that on their tiny wages?

Svetlana was feeling pretty miserable at that moment. She wanted to scream and shout because everything was so awful. She felt particularly bad for her father. *He suffers a lot, but he cannot cry. This week he won't eat at all.* There were other problems as well. A few weeks earlier two men had stopped a car beside her and tried to grab her while she was walking home alone. The appearance of a neighbor had frightened them off. The incident had brought back familiar feelings. She had flashbacks and felt anxious much of the time. *Before that happened, I wasn't afraid of anything and could go anywhere; now I am really scared to go anywhere alone when it's dark.* We sat under laden plum trees looking down on the river and she said it was a pity that I had come just now because before all these things happened she had been having the best time of her life. She was learning to be a cook; she had made new friends and was really beginning to enjoy her life in Foca. *It's different with lots of friends, just totally different.* Like Admira in Gorazde, she did not wish to return to village life: *I can't even remember much about the village now.*

Unlike Admira however, Svetlana was no longer curious about the war and just thought it was stupid. Regarding the Milosevic trial, she did not want *to listen or to say anything about it.* She had heard there was some kind of killing at Srebrenica, but *I really don't have an opinion. I don't want to think about it.* She personally saw no problems with Muslims returning. She had seen quite a few families in Donje Polje, the Muslim section of town, and had a Muslim friend who had come back to Foca to take exams because it was easier than in Sarajevo, so she had helped her get textbooks. But Svetlana had lost her unequivocal wish to return to the way things were before.

They want theirs and we want ours. We can't live together because Muslims say Serbs were Muslims before and Serbs say Muslims were Serbs before. [. . .] I would be afraid if I had to go to a Muslim area.

Why?

That's a stupid question. Because they are Muslims and we are Serbs and we were at war. Because maybe they would hate me because I am a Serb.

So how does one get past the fear?

I don't know; I'm not sure. It would be good if all Serbs and Muslims went back to their homes, but the reality is that the Muslims get more help than the Serbs. If we were treated equally, it would be better. It was not a topic that interested her much. As before, politics bored her, and she was not going to vote. *In this country, we voted a hundred times without getting anything. I really don't see the point.*

I could not escape the feeling that Svetlana had distanced herself from the questions that had bothered her four years earlier, and that this distancing contributed to her feeling more at home in the community.

Some of the other Foca young people seemed to have made a similar adjustment. Tatiana, looking radiant from a holiday on the coast, also told me that the previous year had been one of the best of her life because of making new friends. She still hated *Foca. . . . The way they think and gossip.*

In this town, you have to watch how you walk, how you cross the street, whom you talk to. . . . I could never stay here; it's not good for young people or their careers. They don't like foreigners, don't like different cultures. I like different cultures and nations. People make barriers around themselves to keep the outside world out. She was eager to escape and had taken a year off from school to earn the money, working as an interpreter for French SFOR. She planned to go to France after a year at Novi Sad University in Serbia.

Why not Sarajevo? I asked.

My father is not a nationalist, but he wouldn't like me to go there, although it's probably better than Novi Sad. He wouldn't like his golden princess in the Muslim part of Sarajevo; it would lead to gossip and it's too risky.

This had nothing to do with any personal animosity toward Muslims, she told me. She was very pleased when the father of a Muslim friend greeted her in the street, and she felt sad that the girl herself had still not been in touch. *Probably because I wasn't here. I don't believe she doesn't want to see me.*

Regarding the return of Muslim people in general, she never discussed it. *I am indifferent,* she told me with a shrug.

It was such a contrast to her stated outlook that I commented, *You seem very detached?*

I don't have anything in common with the people returning. We live in our own apartment; we didn't occupy anyone else's apartment. There are more important things to think about.

She was not sure if she remembered the mosques in Foca, although she thought it was *stupid* to have knocked down something that had been there five hundred years.

What if there was an attempt to rebuild them?

I am indifferent. They will build it or not.

As to what had happened to Muslims in Foca or elsewhere, she had little information or curiosity. She was not sure if she believed any of it. *I don't know, I can't say it's impossible. It's possible of course.*

What about Srebrenica?

I don't know anything concretely; I heard a lot of people were killed.

Do you think it's true?

Maybe . . .

Stojan was also eager to get out of Foca. He had no ill effects from the NATO bombing, had done well in high school, and planned to go to

Belgrade to be a construction engineer. He did not see himself coming back. *There's no future here* in Foca. *Everyone wants to go.* He had given up basketball for lack of a team, but he still enjoyed his life. When I asked how he felt about his old neighbors and friends coming back, he said he didn't remember them, but *it isn't a problem.* His father had been given a new flat by his employer, so they had moved out of the neighborhood. He did not think many would come back to town, only the elderly. He didn't remember so much about the war. As for those things that were supposed to have happened in Foca, most people thought it was lies and he agreed.

But you told me you saw houses burning, I remarked.

Yes, that's not a crime, one house burning.

But the whole of Donje Polje?

True, but maybe the people who did it were angry.

He had not heard about any other crimes. *I am a patriot,* he explained.

As in Gorazde, the majority of the children I reinterviewed in Foca had grown into healthy young adults. Dusan had recovered from the death of his brother. He thought of him quite often but it was with pleasure rather than pain. Ivana wanted to go to Novi Sad to study psychology. Divac's family had sold their flat in Sarajevo. He still enjoyed visiting the city even though he found the *Muslim domination too strong.* He wanted to study literature, but thought doing economics in Pale had more prospects. Jovan fantasized about traveling to Greece, but chose to study dentistry in Foca to earn enough to help his parents. Muslims coming back did not affect them very much, as very few were returning to the town itself. They did not think about it.

There were exceptions. Helena, whose father was killed in the first month of the war, had not had a good time since I saw her last. Her family had been evicted from their apartment and moved to a collective center out of town. But they now lived in temporary accommodation, sharing one room between the three of them, while they waited for a flat. Helena would have liked to go back to Sarajevo, but that house had been sold. *I don't want to stay in Foca, but who asks me.* She looked exhausted, admitted that she was sleeping and eating poorly, and said she felt tense and miserable. She even had occasional thoughts of suicide, although they were just thoughts. Her grades had fallen to average and she no longer enjoyed high school, but she still read avidly at home. She had no idea what she would do next or where she wanted to go. *New Orleans,* she joked. *Good bars, good music.*

I wondered to what degree her unhappiness was related to missing her father. She felt sad whenever she thought about him, but said she did not think about him very often. Much of the misery seemed to be related to living in Foca, which was *awful and depressing.* She had some good friends, but could not talk to people in general. Given her rather different opinions from her contemporaries, I was not surprised. Despite not having lived in Foca during the war, she was much better informed than many others about what had happened in the town. She had heard that *a lot of Muslims were killed by Serbs, especially women and children,* and that *a big crime was committed against Muslims in Srebrenica.*

Sara still missed her Muslim best friend: *I used to dream she was here, every night.* She no longer worried about people coming back. *Muslims could be better friends for you than Serbs [. . .] maybe before I had some anger and hatred, now I know Serbs did some similar things to them also.* She had heard that *Serbs had occupied the town, imprisoned Muslims, and forced them to go away.* It made her feel awful. She had visited Sarajevo recently and loved it. In Foca, she felt trapped and hopeless, afraid that she would not get the grades necessary to escape.

Young people in Gorazde shared the continuing ignorance about crimes committed by their own side. They knew nothing about Josanice. Elvira responded to hearing about the massacre of elderly Serbs and children with the same indifference that I encountered in Foca when discussing Srebrenica. Her reaction was unusual, however. The others in Gorazde were shocked and upset that they had not known. *Do you want to know about it?* I asked Narcisa. *No, just as they don't want to hear about Srebrenica, but yes, it's important. It should be on our Bosnian TV.*

The Wounds of War

"The world has only just begun to realize that left untreated, the psychological wounds of war can be most damaging, as children grow up unable to function normally, often driven to perpetuate the violence they have experienced," UNICEF stated in their yearbook for 1994.[140] The implication—that those who suffer most will inflict their suffering upon the next generation—did not seem to fit the children I watched grow into young adults in the Drina Valley. In their stories, only a very few children in both cities wrote of the desire or need for revenge. In my first interviews, I had given the children the hypothetical moral dilemmas beloved of social psychologists, and was impressed by the maturity of their answers.[141] Almost all expressed principled objections to lying and stealing. These things were wrong because they damaged others, trust, and one's own good name; but they would put these principles aside to save a life, even the life of a stranger. Conflict situations such as someone occupying your desk or using your things should be verbally negotiated, with or without help from authorities. There were no ethnic distinctions in these responses.

Four years later, although some of my respondents felt anger toward those they perceived as the main perpetrators of the war and ambivalence about contact, these feelings did not manifest themselves as hatred for their contemporaries on the other side or a desire for revenge. It was striking that some of those who had suffered most, like Samir, Narcisa, Helena, and Sara, were the most open to the renewal of relationships. Apart from Helena, most had recovered remarkably from the war, although some like Svetlana had been very disturbed by new events. They all had the same worries and concerns over studies and relationships. Most were making "sensible" career choices, opting for security at the expense of other hopes. They all showed the same deep attachment and sense of responsibility for family. They all were frustrated with small-town provincialism and talked in identical terms of their alienation from politics and their suspicion of politicians.

Yet the wound to the community seemed wider than ever. Individual psychological health seemed to be sustained, at least in part, by means of damage to collective understandings. Bosnia and Herzegovina played football against Yugoslavia for the first time that summer. The match received massive publicity. Foreign dignitaries and the political elite from both entities attended the game in Sarajevo. Some hoped it would be seen as a symbolic acknowledgment of a mutual recognition of statehood. But the Yugoslav team captain walked onto the field with his hand in the Serbs' three-finger salute.[142] The more numerous Federation fans, mainly Muslims, whistled and jeered through the Yugoslav national anthem (once the anthem of the old Yugoslavia), waved the wartime Bosnian flag, and shouted provocative slogans such as *Allahu Akbar* (Allah is the Greatest) throughout the match. Fans of Republika Srpska (RS) and Yugoslavia, who for their own protection had been carefully segregated, waved Serb nationalist flags and shouted *Raso Raso* (the nickname of Radovan Karadzic). Both sides shouted *Ustasha* when unhappy with a decision of the Croat referees. The players themselves were sportsman-like, and the more experienced Yugoslav team prevailed. When Yugoslavia scored, the RS politicians joined in the applause, guiltily stopping at the horrified glances of their Muslim colleagues in the V.I.P. box. After the match, Yugoslav and Serbian fans and the police who tried to protect them were badly beaten up by supporters of the BiH team. Far from heal-ing wounds, the match had highlighted the wide gulf between the entities and the degree to which Bosnia was not yet a unified country.[143]

Nikola went to the match and rooted for Yugoslavia. He could not imagine anyone in Foca doing otherwise. Dusan too was delighted at the victory. He continued to resent the West's attempts at *forced reconciliation* and still hoped for independence for Republika Srpska. *No one can issue a document stopping Serbs from liking Yugoslavia.* He did not believe people wanted to live together, otherwise there would not have been a war, and he was glad to see so many house exchanges.

Although most of the Foca young people now knew that Republika Srpska was part of Bosnia-Herzegovina, and traveled without fear in the Federation, none saw Sarajevo as their capital. As their university choices indicated, they oriented themselves eastward toward Serbia. Stojan still preferred to be a Yugoslav, even though the term was on its way out. Jovan thought that if the entities disappeared he could always go to Serbia. Even Francophilic Tatiana, who was *indifferent to all of this* and wanted to get out of the Balkans altogether, did not want anyone to call her a Bosnian in case *they could think I was a Muslim.*

Why not say Bosnian Serb?

Serb is simpler.

I reminded her of her preference for the term "Muslim" as a little girl. *I wouldn't like that now. Simply, I am not a Muslim and I want them to know what I am. It's not so important; I'm not a nationalist. But if someone asked me what I was, I would say.*

The Bosnian government's attempt to substitute the term "Bosniak" for "Bosnian Muslim" had not helped. It made many in Foca feel that yet again Muslims were trying to prove that Bosnia was "theirs." *We always lived together in this area, so why do they now want to prove they were here first?* Mojevic asked me.

Helena supported Bosnia in the football match. She thought it really strange that people in her apartment block supported Yugoslavia, and even supported Romania when the Bosnian team played against that country. *It is our country,* she declared. Sara felt the same.

In Gorazde, Iris thought football matches brought out primitive behavior in everyone. Senad was furious. He had watched a Federation/RS match where *all the Serbs were wearing Karadzic T-shirts and shouting, "We love you, Karadzic, you are our greatest hero," and they wore those hats with the skull and crossbones. It's the symbol of a massacre. They are more like Nazis.* Members of the Bosnian Party for Democratic Action (SDA) were *like Nazis* as well, bullying people into religious observance. He hated the new Islamic center in town. *The guy who runs it has a beard now, but he sold tobacco and alcohol during the war instead of defending the city.* I often went in the Islamic center myself to use the Internet. It seemed to be largely occupied by small boys playing Counterstrike on the computers, talking loudly over the Arabic reading of the Koran piped over the speakers.

The other young people I talked to in Gorazde were more sanguine, feeling quite unbothered by and uninterested in the occasional covered young woman or bearded young man who had appeared in town. Most were still believers, but no longer attended mosque or mekteb. Nedjad thought people had stopped supporting the SDA. They saw themselves as Bosnian first and Muslim second. Narcisa completely agreed with Headmaster Mojevic about the word "Bosniak." *I hate the term, it's stupid! Our history professor said it's our national name. I am a Bosnian, like the Serbs and Croats. They're trying to create differences between people. They talk about getting along and forgetting everything and then they make up that name. None of my friends use it.* Like the others in Gorazde, she hoped the entities would disappear. *It's not called "Muslim Bosnia," we all live here.*

Another event brought the differences home to me. On September 11, the first anniversary of the destruction of the World Trade Center towers, Bosnian TV ran a documentary about New York. I watched it with Nerma and her brother Rijad, both of whom wept most of the way through. *If you experience something that is not good you always pray to God that no one else suffers like this,* Narcisa said of the September 11 attacks. She had been horrified and upset on the day itself, imagining how the victims felt, and angry at the way Osama bin Laden had *misused and misrepresented Muslims and Islam.* Most of the others in Gorazde felt the same. In Foca, rumors abounded: that it was the Mafia, or President Bush himself, prepared to sacrifice his own to launch a war near Russia, or possibly Karadzic had arranged it. Sara, Helena, and Ivana simply told me, *It was awful.* Most of the others had *no special feelings* and were not upset, although they felt sorry for ordinary people. Divac was pleased, just as he had been when Yugoslavia beat the United States at basketball. They all hoped the Americans would get the message that they should stop interfering in the affairs of other countries.

Memory and Forgetting

It was not just that most young people in Foca and in Gorazde continued to have contradictory views about their identity, the nature of their state, and their relationships with the rest of the world. They appeared to be dealing with memories of the past in quite different ways. In 2002, I gave all of them the same health measures I had used previously. For the most part their lifelines showed increasing well-being and optimism. All the symptom scales, except Helena's and Svetlana's, showed a marked fall. They all explained the small number of residual symptoms as part of their normal repertoire for coping with daily life. However, there were significant differences between the towns in the parts of the trauma questionnaire that dealt with memory and avoidance.

Often high scores in these two areas go together. When people have specific painful recollections, they try to suppress them or avoid triggers to the memory, like Samir avoiding his old house or Narcisa avoiding Visegrad. But I found that although young people in Gorazde had more-intrusive recollections, flashbacks, and nightmares than their contemporaries in Foca, they had less avoidance, and their avoidance scores were lower than in 1998. For the most part, they did not avoid the places, thoughts, and feelings associated with traumatic events, or find themselves unable to remember them. Nina told me she still had the same dream every month: of Serbs coming after her in a helicopter or a plane, shooting or bombing. She would try to escape; once she got killed. She said she was not bothered by the dream. Armin said he regarded his flashbacks of the siege as normal. This made sense, given that four years earlier some children in Gorazde had felt an obligation to hold on to their memories to some degree despite the discomfort the recollections caused.

In Foca, in contrast, some avoidance scores had actually increased, although all the other scores, including those referring to intrusive memories, had fallen. Jovan no longer worried about whose dead bodies he had seen in the river. He told me he was forgetting a great deal. Ivana had some memories of Muslim apartments being looted: *It was awful to see. I can't remember it clearly. The best thing is to forget everything that happened. I have almost forgotten.* It seemed as if in these young people the symptoms of avoidance and forgetfulness referred to the war as a whole rather than specific traumatic events. Nikola had no particular memories that troubled him, but gave himself the highest possible avoidance scores. Thinking about the past was *negative,* and he was trying to *forget everything.* He became quite irritated with me in the interview, saying he never discussed questions about what had happened.

Are they important questions? I asked.

No, I don't think so. The most important thing is to have a sports hall, we don't.

Marko was not irritated. I had got into the habit of interviewing the young people in Foca at a café with a terrace overhanging the river. In the early evening the mist rose, hiding the water and giving the valley a translucent, ethereal feel. Despite the chill Marko lingered after I finished my questions, asking me to tell him more about the book I was writing. I mentioned how children in Gorazde had responded to four years of shelling.

Who was shelling Gorazde? he asked in a surprised tone.

Well, it was besieged throughout the war, by Serbs, did you not know that?

Yes, he had known. His father, like most Foca fathers, had been on the front line there, *and I think we took the town. Well, not completely, but almost.*

Then he asked me what I thought about Foca. I told him that it was hard to see people in the town struggling, that my perceptions were also colored by listening to the experiences of those who had lived here before, and that the ruins in Donje Polje made me sad. He nodded impassively, seeming neither bothered nor curious.

How do you feel about the destruction here? I asked. He shrugged. His indifference made me push a little further. *Does it make you sad?*

No, he said blandly. *I am not sad. I am not bothered.* And he smiled his charming smile.

I thought about this knowing and not knowing. It was almost as if the war had been a football match and the knowledge retained was about what *our side* had won or almost won, whereas the knowledge avoided or dismissed was about what winning or almost winning had cost. As a child, Marko felt the town was *not as it should be.* Now grown up, he no longer noticed such a problem, or if he did, it had no effect on him.

As I said in chapter 10, this distancing practiced by the young people is not the same as the clinical concept of denial. Stanley Cohen has tried to rescue the word "denial" from the clinicians and classify it in more literary terms. He describes three kinds of denial in political contexts: literal (the facts themselves are not true), interpretive (the facts have been misunderstood), and implicatory (the facts are known but their moral or political consequences are regarded as minor or nonexistent).[144]

I saw all these kinds of denial in defendants from Foca on trial at the International Criminal Tribunal at The Hague. Kunarac and his colleagues argued that there was no attack on non-Serb civilians in Foca—that their suffering was unfortunate "collateral damage" incurred during a legitimate military operation. The defendants did not deny having had sexual intercourse with a number of Muslim women and girls. However, Kunarac argued that a woman identified as FWS-50 could not have experienced severe mental pain or suffering when he had intercourse with her as she had been raped on previous occasions by other perpetrators.

Radomir Kovac, one of Kunarac's codefendants, believed his victims had consented to intercourse because they did not continuously and forcefully resist throughout the act and because, he claimed, he was in love with one of them. Moreover, they could not be considered to have been enslaved in his house, when they had the key and could have escaped at any time. He did not clarify where teenage Muslim girls could have gone, with no money and only the clothes on their backs, in Serb-controlled Foca in 1992.[145]

Krnojelac did not deny that abuses had occurred in the KP Dom, but claimed that as *prisoners of war* the prisoners were *legally detained.* He argued that the prosecution had misunderstood his position. As warden, he had had no authority over or responsibility for prisoners detained by the military. He had worn a military uniform at work because he had nothing else to wear after his house burned down. The prisoners who had sent him requests for help had done so because he was an old friend, not because he was their boss. His desk was arranged so he could not look out and see the prisoners, and he did not remember "ever casting a deliberate look" into the yard. "Whatever I learned, I learned from other people. I did not see anything with my very own eyes. It was known that people were brought in, but I did not see anything with my very own eyes. I would have to remember had I seen it, but really, I had so many other obligations." He even denied some of the assistance prisoners said he had given them because admitting it would have implied that he had known about their plight. The judges did not accept these arguments and stated that the combination of knowledge and a failure to act, when he had some power to do so, made him guilty of aiding and abetting the principal offenders.

In the dock, Krnojelac came across as a mild-mannered, inoffensive man, certainly not a nationalist ideologue. He was married to a Croat and had Muslim neighbors who still spoke well of him. The defense and prosecution psychologists described him as completely normal, if somewhat passive and lacking in initiative. He described himself as someone who would feel duty-bound to finish assigned tasks to the best of his ability. Yet even if one does accept his defense of lack of responsibility, as did all my Foca respondents, the question remains as to *why* he did not stand up and look into the yard to see what was happening to the good neighbors he knew were there. The implication is that he felt it had nothing to do with him.[146]

Personally, I and my family have no connection with those things, Jovan told me. He was right. None of this *war generation,* as Divac described them, those whose childhoods were consumed by the conflict, had any responsibility for the horrors that occurred. Their wish to distance themselves seemed in many ways sensible, and even a key to their personal resilience. It did not seem surprising that by 2002 far more of the young people had adopted this strategy than before. The possible consequences of not distancing seemed evident in Helena.

Yet this aspect of their resilience left me worried. I was glad to see them happy and well. But I felt, as I had four years earlier, that the cost in empathy was high and that underneath the detachment, the implicit understandings that had led to war in the first place remained unchallenged and intact, even in those who said they rejected nationalism. Tatiana was sure that *Serbs suffered the most.* When I asked if the people who were driven out suffered any injustice, she assumed I referred to Serbs evicted from Muslim-owned apartments because of the new property regulations, which she felt were unfair. When I said that I meant Muslims driven out during the war, she gave me the explanation I heard from so many in Foca: *Someone had to go. If they had been organized like the Serbs were organized, Serbs would have had to go. Muslims were planning to organize themselves and if they had succeeded, the Serbs would have had to go.*

So Serbs were organized?

No, Serbs were not organized, it's only by accident that Serbs took the town. Foca will always be a painful point for Muslims because of that stupid journalist who said lots of Serb soldiers came from Serbia and that Muslims ran away.

Sitting in a café in Nuremberg while attending the war crimes trials in 1946, the journalist Martha Gellhorn had a conversation with a young German. He told her that Germany "made war because England was ready to attack her. The Allied bombings . . . were not correct; they could not be forgotten: What did innocent women and children have to do with war?" He could not explain why Germany bombed Warsaw, London, and Coventry first. "Talk about the concentration camps was exaggerated and propaganda;" he "had seen people returning from 'protective custody' . . . fat and sunburned. . . . It was wrong to kill the Jews; it was a mistake. On the other hand, you could not help hating them because they never did any real work. . . . Now Jews were returning to this town, and German families had to give them back their houses and sit in the street. No one spoke to Jews." At the end of the war, he continued, "people hated Hitler because he had lost the war," but now they could see that he had not been so bad.[147]

Others who were children in Germany during the war later remembered "the collective silence" that followed in the post-war period. Families never discussed the war at home. Hitler and the Nazi years did not exist at school. History stopped in the previous century. Dan Bar-On, a psychologist who interviewed these children in middle age, thought this emotional and physical distancing beneficial. It allowed them to approach the truth in their own way when they were ready. Not all of his interlocutors agreed. "That's why you have this situation where one guy believes it and the other one doesn't. Hitler just didn't exist. We didn't learn anything except that the war started. That was all . . . that was a big mistake because as a result nobody—well very few, anyhow, became concerned about the matter."[148]

The silence after the war in Germany followed a war that had definitively come to an end, and in which one side was defeated. It was *Stunde*

Null (zero hour), as the Germans called it, and everything had to start over.[149] I had no such sense of history having stopped in Bosnia in the summer of 2002. On the contrary, the conflict seemed to be continuing, not only on football fields, but in classrooms. The only harmonized action that had taken place in the education system was the removal of "objectionable" material—as defined by an international team of experts—from textbooks. This was done by the simple measure of blacking it out or adding a stamped annotation that read, "The following passage contains material of which the truth has not been established, or that may be offensive or misleading. The material is currently under review." One immediate effect of such outside intervention was that some schools exhibited the unchanged pages on their notice boards.[150] Meanwhile the entities continued teaching contradictory and divergent histories in what they insisted were quite separate languages. Divac assured me *Serbian and Bosnian are not the same,* although he had grown up speaking the same language as his Muslim neighbors. The war also continued in the offices of petty bureaucrats—such as those who told one of my friends, when he finally got his home back in Kopaci, that if he wanted electricity he had to apply on the other side of the country in Banja Luka—and in the speeches of politicians. In the week I arrived, Kostunica, Yugoslavia's president, declared that Republika Srpska was "part of the family, temporarily separated from the Serbian motherland" (although he later claimed he had been misrepresented and had only meant unity within the European Union).[151] *This war after the war is worse than the real one,* muttered my friend. The war was also being fought through memorial sites. Foca mourned its dead with a phallic monstrosity by the new bridge surrounded by flags and fountains; Gorazde maintained one of the Serb tank positions that had bombed the town, adding swings to the defunct military hardware so that children could play among the guns.

And the war continued in Foca's museum, once Tito's temporary headquarters in the Second World War, now containing a large memorial room dedicated to the recent conflict. Here a wall plaque informed the curious that Serbs "were among the most chosen nations in the world." In this area they had always "fought for survival" and been obstructed by the great powers: "the aim of Serbs west of the Drina had been the preservation of Yugoslavia as a country where all Serbs lived. . . . The Muslims, advised by the great powers, started the war against the Serbs. In Foca they had started sniping from the minaret." Now Serbs were "again under pressure" because the international community "wanted to remove the statehood Republika Srpska had gained by political and military means and make it disappear into a unitary Bosnia-Herzegovina." The International Criminal Tribunal at The Hague was yet another proof that "those who began the war are not yet satisfied with its results."

This is really stupid, Ana said at the museum, almost refusing to translate in her exasperation. She was fourteen when the war began, and she found our interviews with young people in Foca perplexing because her own memories and experiences, which remained clear in her mind, were somewhat different. The war started for her the day she went to school and found it closed with some twenty bewildered Muslim children and only a handful of Serbs in the yard. They were all sent home. Her mother's boss was amazed that their own family had not *left already.* Ana spent most of the war evacuated to Montenegro, completing high school and university there.

She came home intermittently to an increasingly alien town. The first time was just after the fighting ended, when she was horrified to see the house opposite hers burning, and even more upset when her Serbian friends said, *Well, it's nothing, a house being burned . . . nothing.* She found it odd that they all now seemed to have video players when no one had owned one before the war. That was the moment when she realized Serbs were stealing, and she felt awful. The municipal authorities had issued a telephone number citizens could call if they saw anyone looting. Once when she and friends saw two Serb ladies going into an abandoned Muslim apartment; they called the number, but nothing happened.

The Serb authorities drove around town with a loudspeaker telling Muslims they must stay indoors and could not even go shopping, so her mother went to buy essentials for their neighbors. Their best Muslim friends hung onto their house in Donje Polje for some months, but finally had to leave because of death threats. Her father helped them pack in tears, unable to speak. He also argued with others in their apartment block to allow their Muslim neighbors, women and children, into the shelter during the fighting. He was threatened with court action for protecting Muslims.

Her parents cried each time they visited her, telling of neighbors arrested or forced out. Her grandmother, once a partisan herself, was devastated. Ana spent much of that first summer in Montenegro listening to accounts on the radio of Sarajevo being shelled by *Serbs, Chetniks, killers, and monsters.* She felt sickened and miserable that her father could be seen like that when she knew he was not. He had simply felt unable to abandon home, country, and identity. Ana knew the reports were true because her aunt had stayed in the city and her uncle was injured by a Serb grenade. *It was the worst period of my life, just sitting in the house listening to the news. For three months, I destroyed myself, didn't eat, didn't sleep . . .*

I puzzled over what made Ana so different from the Serb children I had interviewed. She was older, and had a longer period of shared life with Muslims before the war, including her own Muslim best friend and her parents' close friends and neighbors. Indeed, because her family was not churchgoers, her first experience of visiting a religious building was a school trip to the Aladza mosque when she was eight years old. She thought it was beautiful. Also, she came from a Serb family who believed in and lived the Yugoslav ideal of brotherhood and unity: partisans on one side, a grandfather on the other who had donated money for the building of mosques in nearby villages. Like Nina, Ana was proud to be one of Tito's pioneers. But many of Ana's Serb contemporaries had similar experiences and did not share her views. Perhaps two differences were most significant: First, she and her family were inoculated against Milosevic and his propaganda because one of their relatives knew him and had suffered at work from disagreeing with him; second, they had relatives in Sarajevo whose firsthand accounts of wartime events challenged the Serb official version.

Ana's depression in that first year of the war again indicated the cost of empathy and openness for young Serbs in Foca, and her mental health during the war was certainly helped by learning to distance herself. She turned off the radio after that first summer, got into the local high school in Montenegro, made sympathetic friends, and immersed herself in her studies. When she returned to Bosnia she accepted a job in Gorazde, where she had friends of several nationalities (a number of Serb translators now worked there), and felt no need to identify with Foca's Serb community. So accurate remembrance carried little cost, although she was aware that many in Foca saw her as a traitor.

Trials and the Truth

One afternoon I found myself caught up in the largest SFOR convoy I had seen since the end of the war. Tank after tank was followed by dozens of armored personnel carriers with soldiers in full battle gear. Helicopters buzzed overhead. The apparent aim was to destroy Karadzic's support network of safe houses. Dusan's father thought it a bad joke. *I know where Radovan is,* he told me. *We all do. Ninety-nine percent of Serbs support him.* He and his wife were in a militant mood, furious at attempts to *divide Serbs* by strengthening the border between Bosnia and Serbia. *September 11 is only a warning; we are going to destroy America with the help of Saddam Hussein.*[152]

A Serb-Arab alliance? I asked in some bewilderment. *Is any frontier worth going back to war?*

Should we allow Bosniaks as a minority to tell Serbs what to do? Dusan's mother responded. *The only thing left free so far is that we don't have to attend mosque!*

Tatiana was deeply upset by the helicopters and angry at the International Tribunal for *making stupid actions in Foca, hunting a person who does not exist.* She did not think Karadzic or Mladic was guilty. *Some crimes were committed by real psychopaths and they couldn't control them. Normal men would not have done it.* Most of the others felt similarly. They were *patriots, and nationalists, fighting to create a country for Serb people.* Milosevic also had their sympathy and support. He too was a *patriot,* unable to control the irresponsible actions of others. They admired his ability to defend himself and felt he had been betrayed by his own people. Dusan thought the trial was a circus. *Ordinary people don't support handing him over.*

Summing up the case for the prosecution in Radislav Krstic's trial at The Hague, the prosecutor Mark Harmon expressed his regret that a certain witness for the defense, a well-educated Serb journalist, still "could not believe" the facts of what had happened at Srebrenica, despite overwhelming evidence. He went on to argue:

> Purposeful ignorance of these terrible deeds and an unwillingness to confront them in a responsible way can only create fertile grounds for future misunderstandings between Bosnian Serbs and Bosnian Muslims and may poison the future for the people of Bosnia who deserve a respite from the ethnic strife that has characterized this conflict. The nations of the world created this tribunal in an effort to ensure peace in the region, and part of our mandate is to ensure that evidence of crimes is objectively

presented, tested in a court of law to ensure that the wrongs committed in the former Yugoslavia do not go unpunished, and to permit future generations to have access to the objective record of these events so that they may be inoculated against the calculated deceptions that thrive in the milieu of chauvinism, blind ethnic pride, and ignorance. The truthful record of these events can assist in the recovery of the victims and also in the future reconciliation of the peoples of Bosnia.[153]

In passing judgment on Krstic, Judge Almiro Rodrigues emphasized the importance of individual attribution of guilt because "to associate this evil with Serbian identity would be an insult to the Serbian people and would betray the concept of civil society."[154]

The hope of those who set up the International Criminal Tribunal was that trying the architects and main perpetrators of war crimes in the former Yugoslavia would relieve societies as a whole of collective guilt. In Gorazde, it seemed to be having the desired effect. Residents were universally delighted to see Milosevic in The Hague, although Senad felt he was *too comfortable* and wanted him to suffer. The arrests and trials of the major criminals made it easier for Samir, Narcisa, and others to be friendly to *ordinary* Serbs whom they did not hold responsible, although some like Admira were not so forgiving. *The best way is to try the guilty ones, no matter which side, and then you can forget the past,* said Samir. Nor did they object to the idea of criminals on their own side being arrested. *There is no question that many of ours did things that were just as bad,* Senad told me.

It is always easier to discuss the possible criminality of your own people in the context of your side's generally acknowledged victimhood. The problem in Foca was the feeling that the Serbs' victimhood, and need to defend themselves, had never been understood or acknowledged. The Hague was unjust, I was told repeatedly, *because only Serbs are there and only Serbs are punished for genocide, only Muslim women were raped, and I know Serb women were raped and Serb children killed. No Muslims there, just a few for some crimes, but no one for genocide!*

Were Muslims trying to wipe out Serbs? I asked.

Probably . . . Tatiana sat twisted up in her chair, tapping her foot repeatedly against the floor in the distress this topic was causing her.

What will people think about us and our country if they see only Serbs

there and no one else? If other people of other nations were there [fighting]
they should be there also!

What about Mladic and Karadzic?

It is stupid and awful to blame only one side!

All the young people in Foca, including Helena, agreed with this last
sentiment. And they had another concern. They could accept that some on
their own side had committed abuses, and they wanted those individual
perpetrators tried, preferably by national courts rather than a biased international community. *Maybe there are some Serb criminals,* Stojan told me,
*but I don't think the authorities could have ordered the crimes. The people
who did it had to choose to do it. Individuals have responsibility.* But trying
Mladic, Karadzic, and Milosevic would not liberate Serb society, as those
at The Hague might wish.

On the contrary, trying their leaders would, symbolically, put their
whole society on trial because many of them still believed in those leaders and the project in which they had been engaged: the *patriotic defense
of the Serbian people.* These young men and women astutely understood
the implications of Milosevic's indictment. If Republika Srpska was not
the result of a valiant struggle for liberation in which, unfortunately,
some horrors and excesses had occurred, as in all wars and on all sides;
if the Serbs had not endured bombing, and losses, and deprivation for
something honorable and worthwhile; but if instead their entity had been
brought into being through a collective *criminal enterprise* that involved
among other things "genocide; persecutions; extermination, murder,
unlawful confinement, tortures; deportation; and wanton destruction,"
as Milosevic's indictment claimed,[155] and if all these acts had actually
been sanctioned or ordered by Milosevic, Karadzic, Mladic, and other
leaders, where did that leave these young Serbs and their families, who as
decent people could not condone such actions? Completely homeless for
a start—no wonder they could not believe the charges and preferred not
to think about the actions underlying them.

War crimes trials have a reputation for attempting to be too many things
to too many people. Not only are they intended to uphold and develop
international law and ensure that leaders and states are as accountable for
crimes as individual criminals; the punishment they exact is intended to
vaccinate society against future wrongdoing. They are a forum for victims

to recount and exorcise their experiences, a history lesson, and a means of arriving at objective truth, which supposedly will assist recovery and reconciliation. How to combine these aims? In The Hague the pressure of time and the pursuit of facts—Did this gun position actually fire these mortars? Was the defendant present when this killing took place?—meant that only selected witnesses were called to recount their journeys through hell. History lectures designed to show the "context" in which the atrocities had occurred were often cut short. As the judges explained, the criminality of any particular attack upon a civilian population was not diminished by the defendants' belief that the civilians were members of an ethnic group that was responsible for starting the conflict, or that that ethnic group might have carried out similar attacks in other places or at other times.[156]

Nor do such trials end the historical debate. In Japan today there are young nationalists who argue that the version of events promoted by the war crimes trials in Japan at the end of the Second World War, the "Tokyo Trial" view of history, is wrong and undermines morale. The Japanese did not plan or wage an aggressive war in Asia; it was "a tragic and noble struggle for national survival and the liberation of Asia from Western colonialism. The Chinese and Korean Wars were regrettable errors." A hundred thousand people including babies and the elderly were not mutilated, raped, and massacred in a few weeks by Japanese soldiers in Nanking in 1937. Some soldiers acted with excessive zeal in the heat of battle and some innocent civilians got caught in the crossfire. Hiroshima, planned in cold blood, was a much greater crime. Japanese schoolbooks treat these matters with discretion, mentioning only that in "December 1937 Japanese troops occupied Nanking" with a footnote stating that reports of the killing of Chinese civilians resulted in international criticism. In contrast, Japanese junior high school students petitioned the Peace Museum in Hiroshima, which commemorates the victims of the atomic bomb, to provide an "aggressors' corner": They wanted an explanation of Japanese responsibility for the war to complement the gruesome horrors suffered by the Japanese in August 1945.[157]

These matters are debated in Japan half a century after the end of the Second World War. Is it necessary to wait that long in Bosnia? Is it possible? Narcisa felt secure for the moment, but she worried that if SFOR left, *war might start again. I think we would attack each other, goodness knows who first.* Admira worried that the Milosevic trial was failing to teach the Serbs that the quest for a Greater Serbia was wrong, and that they might try again. Nikola thought there was bound to be a war in fifty years because the international community had interests in Bosnia, and they always intervened.

The Balkans is a barrel of gunpowder; it just looks like peace at the moment, Dusan's mother told me. *When NATO goes it will be destroyed or divided, you cannot stop people from doing what they want.* She asked if I had seen Danis Tanovic's *No Man's Land,* which had won the Oscar for best foreign-language film of 2001. In the film, three soldiers from Serb and Muslim military units are trapped in a trench in no-man's-land. One Muslim is lying on a mine. He was placed there while unconscious by a Serb soldier (now dead), who explained to his young colleague that when Muslims came to remove the body, the mine would explode and kill them all. All three soldiers want to get out, but neither side wishes the other to leave, knowing that the other's presence is what keeps them safe. They call for help from the international community, to defuse the bomb and to rescue them all, and while waiting, argue over the causes of the war. There are flickers of a human relationship. The international community, reluctantly intervening because the media are there, cannot remove or defuse the mine. Their presence exacerbates the relationship between the soldiers and their distrust of one another ends fatally. The film ends with the surviving Muslim soldier still lying on the mine as darkness falls. *That's Bosnia,* said Dusan's mother, *a body lying on an unexploded bomb.* Tatiana liked the scene *where one is asking the other who is guilty and he says "We are guilty because you have a gun pointed at me."* I agreed with her that responsibility established at gunpoint meant nothing, but I thought both she and Dusan's mother missed what I saw as the central metaphor of the film: the real danger to all the people of Bosnia came from the failure to discuss and defuse the brutal crimes that lay hidden beneath the bodies of their victims.

Could it be done? I heard a Bosnian Serb politician on the radio calling for "a thick line" to be drawn under the past. That had also been Tito's approach, which was one reason why the new history plaque in Foca's museum singled out communism for its anti-Serb characteristics. Many Serbs now felt that Tito's emphasis on "brotherhood and unity" had led to a denial or minimization of their suffering at the hands of the other ethnic groups in the Second World War, a denial that had contributed to the conflict today.

In Sarajevo, a consortium of one hundred NGOs from all three ethnic groups in both entities agreed. They had decided to establish a "truth commission." It would draw on the experiences of previous commissions such as the South African and Latin American ones, but it would not be identical. Respected citizens from all three ethnicities would travel from community to community and hold public hearings whose aim would be to allow all citizens to speak freely about their experiences as victims, and to encourage those who had acted with moral courage to help and protect their neighbors to speak up.

This was not about forgiveness and apology. *Eighty percent would say an apology was insincere because mistrust between ethnic groups is so deep,* explained Jakob Finzi, a Jewish civic leader from Sarajevo who was one of the commission's main advocates. He continued, *People are not just victims of war, they are victims of propaganda. Many don't know what happened on the other side. Unfortunately, there were crimes on all three. It is clear Muslims were the greatest victims, but they have to recognize their crimes against the other side. In this region, everyone is ready to be a victim and no one is able to take responsibility. If we can show we are all victims, and there are some perpetrators, it will be easier to live together.* The main aim of the commission would be to establish the actual truth of events, what had happened and why. Finzi envisaged a database and eventually a joint historical commission. This was not a substitute for justice. The commission would work in cooperation with The Hague and have no power to grant amnesty for war crimes. Remarkably, the project had the support of every political party and all religious groups. It hoped to embark on hearings in the coming year. *Truth is not always healing; it can be a bitter pill, but it's better to swallow it now,* Finzi warned. The alternative was *three Bantustans or three ghettos,* a disaster for everyone.

In Foca, opinions were divided. Many argued that it was better to forget crimes than to engage in endless discussion. Tatiana did not think the commission was needed, nor did she want to find anything out for herself. She had met a couple of boys from Gorazde in SFOR, and they had all agreed it was unnecessary to look at the past when you were having a good time. Most of the others in Foca felt similarly. Divac was fed up with Srebrenica. He thought it was important to find out what had happened there *because whenever you say Bosnia or Republika Srpska, people think immediately of Srebrenica.* But he was sure the commission could not work. *Serbs*

(2)(2)(2)(2)(2)(2)(2)(2)(2)(2)(2)(2)(2)(2)(2)(2)(2)(2)(2)(2)(2)(2)(2)(2)(2)(2)(2)(2)(2)(2)(2)(2)(2)(2)(2)(2)(2)(2)(2)(2)(2)(2)(2)(2)(2)(2)(2)(2)(2)(2)(2)(2)(2)(2)(2)(2)(2)(2)(2)(2)(2)(2)(2)(2)(2)(2) father, who wanted to report that his son was being beaten up by two of the Serb boys. The three antagonists eyed one another angrily and sat as far apart as possible.

We left the children together and discussed the problem in the corridor. The father was adamant that it was nothing ethnic. His house had been burned down in 1992, but he had returned two years ago and not had any problems. *Why not come back? It is my home.* He got along fine with everyone, indeed it was Serb neighbors who told him what was happening to his son because the children in question bullied everyone—their father was a well-known radical. He just wanted it stopped. The schoolteacher was reassuring. He would call all the parents to a meeting to discuss all the children's behavior and it would be resolved.

The teacher was a serious and soft-spoken Serb who had lived in Sarajevo. He thought the school was going well. Some of the Serb parents had refused to let their children go to school with Muslim children at first, but now they accepted it. They all learned both Cyrillic and Latin, and he taught the Serbian curriculum, but he adapted it. There were sections on "The Battle of Kosovo" and "slavery under the Turks" which he thought inappropriate, so he ditched them. The main problem was that a neighbor had hijacked their water supply so the children had to pee in the schoolyard, and also they needed books. The OSCE had promised, but none had yet appeared.

Back inside the classroom, things had settled down, and I was given permission to speak to the children. Yes, they all liked the school, and they enjoyed all the classes except math, and they wanted a toilet. *What's the capital of Bosnia-Herzegovina?* I asked. *Banja Luka,* said half of them cheerfully; *Sarajevo,* said three others somewhat shyly. The teacher smiled. *They still have to learn these things,* he said. All the children politely stood up together to say goodbye.

I spent my last morning in Foca visiting the museum with Ana. It was built as a hotel by the Austro-Hungarians and had the best location in the city. Today there was glass missing from the front doors, cracked plaster, and cobwebs. All the downstairs rooms were locked. Two women came down to greet us. They were extremely apologetic. They were fighting with the municipality, which had taken over the building at the beginning of the war; for now their twelve thousand objects were confined to a handful of rooms upstairs.

The municipality even destroyed a plaque on the wall which stated that President Tito lived here in 1942, said one of the women, who seemed to be a curator.

Why did they do that?

Because they thought history began in 1992.

She was happy to show me everything. She unlocked the rooms dedicated to the partisan war, unchanged since Ana's childhood. We looked at large maps of shifting front lines and photos of the Central Committee (*all famous, all dead,* Ana commented), homemade partisan boots, and a Remington typewriter used for issuing directives. Then we were taken to the room where the curator kept her mobile exhibition: "A History of Foca from Prehistory to Today." There were Turkish pipes, a Roman vase, an Austro-Hungarian cupboard and gilded mirror, a German 1944 banknote exhorting the local population to "Come to our side before it is too late. Save your life, then liquidate your commissars and then come. This banknote guarantees a hundred people freedom, life, and bread."

There were domestic objects that looked Ottoman. *Are these Muslim?* I asked.

No, that is the most common mistake. These things were in Serb, Croat, and Muslim houses.

So people in this town had a common culture?

Only in part because they did not wear the same clothes, but material objects were the same.

She showed me a display of postcards of schoolchildren in a variety of ethnic dress, and all the different cultural associations that had existed in the 1930s. There were photos of nineteenth-century Foca, a graceful, multispired town, in its fork of the river. *This is only part of what we have. There is no room to display it all.*

You have no pictures of the Aladza mosque? I asked. She became slightly flustered. She said she would look.

Meanwhile, I wanted to see the memorial room for the recent war. She seemed curiously reluctant, but unlocked the door, revealing blown-up photos of burned and horribly disfigured dead children from Josanice. The curator shook her head. Ana translated the history lesson from the plaques on the wall. As she did so, the curator, increasingly distressed, kept interrupting. She told me repeatedly that it was not the view of the people who worked there; it was just one man's opinion. If you asked her for an explanation of why neighbor ran from neighbor, she would not be able to give one. She was not sure if anything written there was true. Her personal opinion was that it was a mistake to write any historical explanations at present. It needed time for the truth to come out.

We went into the next room and looked at photos of the 647 men and boys who had died for Srbinje. Then we headed down the uncarpeted stairs. The other woman caught us before we left and pressed something into our hands. It was two small guidebooks to "Foca." The covers showed an unrecognizably smart museum, behind which was the spire of an intact mosque and the clock tower. There were also two postcards of the Aladza mosque, serene in winter sunlight. Someone had cared enough to preserve them.

12

WHAT THEY DID NEXT

They want to continue with the experiment called "Bosnia-Herzegovina" regardless of how many times it has proven a failure. We are sick and tired of being some sort of chemical elements that foreigners put in test tubes and shake up in an attempt to get a result that is impossible. Our chemical elements do not combine.

—Milorad Dodik, president of Republika Srpska, October 2011

My political dream is to expel the hatred from Bosnia. [. . .] There is no way to separate the country into two entities and three nationalities. No separation of the country. Whoever talks about separation is inviting another war and people are being lied to. It is not in the Dayton Agreement.

—Zdravko Krsmanovic, mayor of Foca, July 2012

People died for nothing, the war was a waste.

—Mirko, twenty-eight years old, Foca, July 2012

The older generations have the hate because they died; they were fighting for their lands on both sides. But the younger generation, we were just kids; we don't remember anything and we want to have fun. It is not important; it does not matter if your name is Milan or Ibrahim.

—Varis, eighteen years old, Gorazde, July 2012

Foca, July 2012

Early morning: I stand on a rattling wooden bridge across the Drina. SFOR took their Bailey one with them when they left, and local people built this shaky-looking structure to replace it. But it is not the obvious precariousness that captures my attention; it is the slim white shaft of a minaret rising over the newly renovated houses of Donje Polje. And looking upriver to where the main part of the town clusters on its spur between the Cehotina and the Drina, there is the bright turquoise flash of a new swimming pool, complete with sunshades and deck chairs, glistening invitingly in the morning sunlight.

My Gorazde friends told me the town was different. For one thing it is called Foca once again. In 2004, the people elected a new mayor, Zdravko Krsmanovic, a Serb politician without any ties to any national party. He handed over the remaining war criminals, cleaned up the town, built a sports hall and a swimming pool, and went to Sarajevo to invite Muslims back, promising that the town was safe and he would rebuild their mosques. To date some four thousand have returned, mostly elderly people to the surrounding villages. Meanwhile, young people come from all over Gorazde canton to use the pool, go shopping and go to discos, and there are regular sports matches between the communities. I drive into town, park my car on the main street, buy a freshly baked croissant from a new takeaway, and go for a walk. Across the river in the tatty public park where the scratched monument thanking Tito for liberating Foca used to stand, a large, beautiful Orthodox church is nearing completion. I walk back down a busy main street and stand outside the town hall, housed in an elegant Austro-Hungarian building. There on the flagpole is the blue and yellow flag of Bosnia and Herzegovina, just across the road from the monolith commemorating the deaths of all the young men who died fighting to avoid living in that very state.

As always, the contradictions of this small country leave me bewildered and confused. It is hard to come to any conclusion as to which way things are going. In 2002, Biljana Plavsic, one of the architects of the ethnic cleansing of Republika Srpska, pleaded guilty to crimes against humanity. At the time she made a dramatic apology (see chapter 11), in which she acknowledged the terrible suffering of Muslims and Croats caused by organized ethnic cleansing and condemned the Serbian leadership for "provoking fear and speaking half-truths."[158] Just before her release from jail in

2009, Plavsic retracted her apology stating, "I have done nothing wrong; I pleaded guilty to crimes against humanity so I could bargain for the other charges."[159] Milorad Dodik, president of Republika Srpska and once the darling of Western diplomats for his seemingly moderate views, provided her with a hero's welcome, and promised a lifetime pension.[160]

Meanwhile, the ethnic straitjacket imposed by the Dayton Agreement continues to foster fragmentation rather than cohesion. The education system provides a good example. All thirteen local ministers of education finally agreed on guidelines for writing history textbooks in 2005.[161] These stated, among other things, that the state of Bosnia and Herzegovina should be the "main reference point"; that the three constituent peoples and national minorities should be presented in an impartial manner; that "diversity" should be seen as a "factor of enrichment"; and that textbooks should be scientifically based, objective, and "aimed at building mutual understanding, reconciliation, and peace." However, Muslim children study the "arrival of the Ottomans," while some children in Republika Srpska continue to study "the Turkish conquest and the fall of Bosnia under Turkish power" and are told to "identify the forms of resistance (rebellions and uprisings") to the Turkish power."[162] Some Republika Srpska textbooks suggest Bosnia's multiconfessional, multiethnic make-up is actually the problem and a danger, the recent war being proof that peaceful coexistence is impossible.[163] Even preschools are not free from contentious debate. In 2008, Sarajevo education authorities banned Santa Claus from the city kindergartens and introduced Islamic religious instruction, a move opposed by most parents in the city. When the Social Democrats won control of the city in 2011, they reversed the policy and fired the director responsible.[164]

The political arena is little better than the schoolyard. After elections in 2010, it took another fourteen months to form a government. This fell apart after only two months, in May 2012, because of conflict between the two main parties in the federation. In 2009, the European Court of Human Rights ordered Bosnia to amend its constitution because national minorities like Jews, Romas, and anyone who chose not to define themselves as one of the three main ethnic groups were barred from running for president or high office.[165] But three years later the necessary constitutional changes have still not been made. In fact, Bosnia's seventeen ethnic minorities are ignored and invisible in many aspects of Bosnia's public life. President Dodik regularly makes clear his dissatisfaction with the state of

Bosnia and Herzegovina and his wish that Republika Srpska might secede. Only a month previously he said in an interview that as far as the Serb entity was concerned, Bosnia and Herzegovina was "just a stop along the way, where it has stayed for too long."[166]

What do you think? I asked Divac. We were back at the café beside the Drina. Gordana was translating and Divac looked very much as he had a decade earlier, just slightly more tired. This was not surprising as he now had a wife and a son of two and a half years and ran his own café in town.

I see things differently from when we last spoke. I see everything from an economic perspective, not nationalities. It's more important to me to have a good life here in Foca than whether I am Serbian and have a lousy life. I prefer to have a decent life rather than a divided Bosnia.

Divac went on to explain how he felt he belonged to Republika Srpska and wanted the entity to remain *because of what happened to our nation*, but he wanted a united functioning state of Bosnia and Herzegovina. *I feel that I belong to Bosnia-Herzegovina rather than Serbia. I see it like this: in Bosnia—Serbs, Croatians, Muslims, all nationalities, they are Bosnians; in Serbia, they are Serbians; in Montenegro, all Montenegrins.*

That's a big change from when I last talked to you, I said, remembering sitting in the same café with the ardent young Serb nationalist who regarded Karadzic as a hero.

There have been some big changes in my life also. I look at the world with different eyes. He had worked in an office in Gorazde for eleven months and made some very good friends. *I can see now there are good people in Gorazde and there are good people in Foca, and there are bad people in Gorazde and bad people in Foca. But still I think people deserve to have Republika Srpska and defend their rights to be Serbian, to respect your own victims and to live a normal life.*

The last decade had not been easy for Divac. He studied economics in Pale, but now regretted that choice *because we don't have enough jobs for so many economists.* In any case, he had been unable to complete his degree because economic difficulties meant that he had to return to Foca to help his father support the family. Things improved in 2007 when he got a job with a microloan bank. He loved the work, particularly because it took him all over the country. *But I lost my job in 2009 because of the economic crisis. People could not get loans and we all got fired.* He had married three months previously and his new wife also lost her job—it was a very low point in their lives. Fortunately, he had already set up the café as a small family business two years earlier. This was now their main source of support. *It's not a brilliant income, but we are making more money than losses. I have some big obligations, but I hope in some two to three years I will have paid off the loans.*

The most striking thing about Divac was his maturity and optimism despite all the difficulties. At the beginning of the interview, we repeated the symptom checklists and the lifeline. Divac was almost symptom-free. He still looked back on his childhood in Sarajevo as the happiest period in his life and the war as an "unpleasant" experience, but he felt completely well.

The war had had no enduring psychological effects on any of the other young people I met up with in Foca. Mirko was doing national service in 2002, so we had not met on that visit. He thought about the war sometimes, but felt untroubled by the memories because *I was not in the war,* even though there was shooting around his village in the first two years. Now he was a full-time farmer, helping his elderly and frail parents with tending fifty sheep and a cow, and growing fruits and vegetables. It was very hard work, but *we survive.* Jovan did not make it to Greece although he did go on university trips to Austria, Italy, and France. He was a dental technician at the university and in private practice at home. He also worked as a waiter—*You have to do two or three jobs in order to have a normal life*—but still did not earn enough to move out of the family home and marry his girlfriend. His father unfortunately had cancer, but Jovan felt *completely well.* The intrusive images of the drowned woman beneath the bridge never came back; although he remembered the experience when I brought it up, he told me, *I press that issue somewhere deep inside and I have no problems with that. I don't think about it. I have a lot of obligations and that helps me not to think about problems in general.*

Nikola came home after obtaining a degree and a master's degree in banking in Belgrade, and went into business with his father, marketing timber to Serbia. He too felt *completely well, but rich from that experience. I try to ignore war and everything that happened, but I see the war here as I see the wars which I read about around the world. I see the war as rain. It is something that happens and I cannot influence it, millions of people have experienced it.*

The biggest change was in Svetlana. She was now the married mother of a four-year-old boy and finally living in her own home. Her husband had swapped his Sarajevo apartment for a large house in Foca, which they shared with extended family. On her lifeline, she described herself as 120 percent well. Her depressive and anxiety symptoms had diminished to half of what they were in 2002.

Are you happy? I asked, looking around the well-furnished living room, as she cuddled her son, thinking of the cramped apartment in which we first met.

Yes very! She replied as tears came to her eyes, *I am emotional—when we talk about sentimental issues I always weep, I hope you will not mind because everything is OK.* She saw her emotional reactivity as part of whom she was, and her residual symptoms as mostly related to economic anxieties about the future. Sometimes these made her feel hopeless and worried. She had worked as a cook at the hospital, but lost that job two years ago. Her husband was a car mechanic, but could only get temporary contracts a long way from Foca, so they only saw him a few days a month. This separation was the most upsetting thing in her life.

Helena was also transformed. The anxious, miserable, and troubled teen-ager of 2002 had evolved into an intelligent young adult. She was back in Foca briefly to visit her mother, who finally had her own apartment in one of the high-rises in the center of town. Helena did not like Foca any better than the last time we met: *The only nice and pretty thing here is nature. There are no possiblities, no theaters, no movies, no people, no work.* She thought her symptoms of a decade ago were just connected to puberty. When I asked how the war had affected her, she laughed: *I cannot judge, I don't know what I would be like if everything was alright. Maybe I would be a little bit better; I hope I would not be worse.* She still worried about things sometimes, and felt tense and nervous, but like Svetlana, she saw these symptoms as related to current circumstances and as part of her own personality rather than the war. *I don't think I am optimistic in general. I always think the worst thing can happen. That's the way I am; I was always like that.*

What do you worry about happening?

It's not that I expect something horrible to happen, but I think things will just continue in the same way. What is frustrating is that you don't have so many possibilities here. You cannot change your job, move, travel. If you get one job, one apartment you should be happy, that's it. Everyone lives like that, most people.

She did think the loss of her father had permanently affected her. *I did not have an authority figure in the family. I did not have the same opinions as my mother. We always argued about everything and I did not see her as an example. I became stubborn and didn't want to respect anything. The same in society; I did not see any worthwhile values or people that I could admire.* Helena found those values in art and science at university, while getting her degree in world literature at Pale. Her heroes were *people who create something. I mean artists from all over the world, it does not matter where they come from or which period.* Recently illness and some operations had kept her unemployed for two years. But she now worked in a library, taught Serbian language and literature to high school students in Doboj, and had a boyfriend in Belgrade.

The only person who saw herself as unwell was Tatiana, who put the final dot on her lifeline at zero. *Neither side of my life is fulfilled. There are people with relationships, job, degree, I cannot say I have any one of these things. I have definitely started thinking it's to do with my character.* She went to Novi Sad University, as planned, to study French, but still had not obtained her degree because of a perfectionism that made it difficult to complete assignments, and what she felt was Serb prejudice on the part of her professors towards Bosnian Serbs. She felt insecure and missed her family. Recently, she had returned to live in Foca and complete her studies from there. She did see some relationship between her current state and the war. She thought her years evacuated to Belgrade as a child, living away from her parents, contributed to her current insecurities. By returning to live with her family in Foca, *I am filling in holes. I am trying to make up what I missed.*

But when you came back before, you hated Foca? I remarked.

Now I am organized in another way. I go to the gym; I only drink coffee with people who don't make me nervous. I choose what I am going to do in one day. [. . .] I won't give up! I want my degree. I would like to reform education. It's really ambitious; I don't know if it's possible . . . but . . . reform it from the beginning to the end.

Gorazde, July 2012

In the evenings I wound my way back down the Drina to Gorazde. The Adzovic family had welcomed me back. So I sat on the familiar balcony and watched a heron fly low across the water. Nerma's two-year-old daughter played with her grandfather in the garden. Nerma had finished her degree, married her handsome boyfriend, and now lived in her grandmother's old house. Her older brother Rijad and his wife Medina had converted my old rooms into a beautiful apartment. They insisted I take over the living room and dining room to sleep and work. A Slovenian had bought and renovated the Serbian neighbor's house next door as a holiday home. There were renovations and new buildings all over the city, including an enormous new mosque donated by the Turkish government, and a riverside hotel with a terrace by the central bridge. *Angelina Jolie and Brad Pitt stayed there,* I was told repeatedly. As always on summer nights, every café was full and the central street packed with strolling people. The biggest change was that there was now full employment. Vitkovici had become an industrial zone with two new factories employing Serbs from surrounding Republika Srpska. The munitions factory had restarted, and Samir and Armin both worked there.

It's not very interesting, but it is a job. Armin worked on the assembly line producing detonators for coal mines and was paid less than $300 a month, *not enough, as it is a very dangerous work* and insufficient to get his own place or marry his girlfriend. So, like Jovan, he still lived with his parents. He had studied journalism at Sarajevo University, but dropped out of the course when he got a semiprofessional contract playing football for the Sarajevo team. He had had a few very happy years *traveling and earning good money* until injury forced him out. But even after this blow to his ambitions, he was upbeat. As far as he was concerned, the only lasting effect of the war was the massive change in family circumstances. They had had a comfortable income before the war, but now you *simply cannot afford everything that you were used to earlier.* He thought that living in Gorazde throughout the siege and *barely surviving [. . .] maybe made me stronger because you know what you have been through.*

Samir worked at the same plant and described himself as *super-well*. He looked as cheerful and fit as he had at 18, and put his lifeline at 120 percent. This was despite ticking some of the old symptoms on the checklist, such as worrying about things a lot, feeling worthless and blaming himself, and often feeling anxious, shaky, nervous, and having palpitations. *That's standard for me,* he said, when I asked about them. *It's usual. I always have symptoms; I see them as part of who I am. They don't bother me because I can control myself and I can control them.* He had also had his share of hard times. He had survived an explosion at the plant in 2010, a car accident the following year, and his parents, with whom he still lived, had just decided to separate. As in the past, he went to the traditional healer for treatment whenever he felt stressed and he found it just as helpful. He was no longer troubled by any wartime memories. The site of the old house had been sold and completely disappeared under a new driveway. *I remember sometimes that there was something there one time in my life, but there are no hard feelings. The memories I have are of small children playing there, nothing else.*

Narcisa was doing everything she planned. She had obtained her degree in economics, worked as an accountant, and hoped to start her own business the following year. But in 2007 her father had died of a stroke at the age of fifty-five. The loss had devastated her and it took two years for her to feel normal again. She still missed him. *It wouldn't matter if he was seventy or eighty years old, it would be the same. I really miss him; I miss talking with him; I miss joking with him.* However, she had married her childhood sweetheart and was now blissfully happy, on maternity leave, after the birth her first baby.

Admira, who had lost her father in the war at seven years of age, found that as she got older she missed her father more and more. *Every event—for example, when my nephew was born or when we have some holidays, then I miss him very much. It's a feeling of emptiness. You miss someone when you expect them to share what happened.* I ask her why she too put her lifeline at 120 percent. *I do miss him but I have accepted that. He is gone and I have to live my life [. . .] all the symptoms have gone. Now I am good! I feel good!* She looked great, sitting playing with her nephew in the sunlight on the top floor apartment of a house she had bought with a shared mortgage with her mother and sister. She had qualified as a nurse, but *to be a nurse here in Gorazde you need connections. There are so many of us.* So she worked as a quality controller for a German firm. She liked her job: *I earn a good regular salary, much more than I would as a nurse.*

The only person who had some residual symptoms connected to the war was Elvira, who told me that *almost every day some sound or some situation reminds me of what happened.* When she had heard the fireworks at the annual International Friendship festival the previous week, there was *the feeling inside myself that things are happening again, I don't get images, only the feeling of fear. The visual memories don't happen anymore. Now I only get actual images if I choose to remember and summon them.* She still avoided particular places like a small street where many people were killed, or a couple of memorial sites. *From time to time, I pass through those places, but I avoid them as much as I can because if I go I feel very sad.* But like Samir and Admira, she insisted that she was 120 percent well. *I actually don't see them as problems at all. In some way, I am glad these symptoms exist because it is proof I did not forget. I would not like to forget those things because it is something that I have experienced, it is a part of me and I was part of that. It's not like I remember every day or talk about it every day.*

She was engaged to be married and her obvious happiness was connected to another significant event: regaining her hearing after suddenly losing it completely two years earlier. No one was sure if the deafness was related to an earlier fall or treatment with the wrong antibiotic. Either way, Elvira had found the period of deafness as devastating as the war. She was obliged to give up much loved work as a pediatric nurse and *was really depressed and sad.* But she was lucky enough to have a cochlear implant. She then had to learn to hear from scratch. *That is why I put this year as a great year because this was the year I could hear again.* And she was back at work in the local hospital, working in an administrative position in intensive care.

As I listened to all the things that had happened to these young people, it was clear that life trumps war. I felt both astonished and impressed at their capacity to cheerfully deal with all the difficulties thrown at them in the last decade. Their reaction to economic downturn was to work harder, taking on extra or dangerous jobs. Between them, they had faced unemployment, disappointed expectations, personal injury, serious illness, and bereavement. Not one of them had been dragged down. The most striking feature was that whenever they had to cope with adversity, they did so with courage and maturity. Those who had any continuing symptoms accepted these as part of their temperament and personality. None of them interpreted such symptoms as an indication of pathology or feeling unwell. They were almost all optimistic about their personal futures.

One of the debates in the research literature is whether the accumulated experience of numerous stressful events makes you more vulnerable to the next one that comes along, or more resilient.[167] For these Bosnian young people, wartime experiences had in some way inoculated them and made them better able to cope when things went wrong. *I value my life more. I think that's it*, Narcisa explained. She thought that because her generation lost their childhoods to the war they felt much older than their actual years, and thought and acted accordingly: to paraphrase both Nikola and Armin, this generation was *rich* with this experience and it had made them *stronger*.

Their resilience was beautifully illustrated by their lifelines, as was their changing perspectives on their war experiences. When I interviewed Narcisa at fourteen, she looked on the war, particularly the family's entrapment in Visegrad, as the worst thing that had happened in her life, although she was happy and well at the time of interview. She felt well in 2002, although her mother's cancer cast a slight shadow, while her memories of the awfulness of the war were slightly moderated. On this occasion in 2012, her lifeline showed that the impact of the wartime memories remained the same as a decade ago, but that she now regarded the personal loss of her father in 2007 as the greatest source of distress in her life. Although with marriage and the birth of her baby, her lifeline had bounced back and she was the happiest she had ever been.

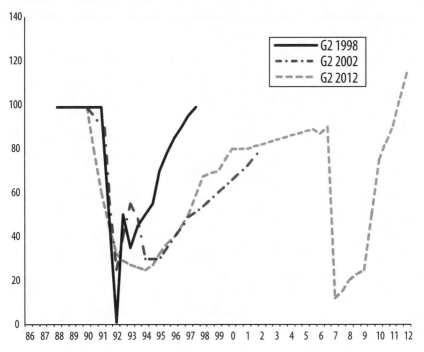

Narcisa's lifelines illustrating her subjective view of her well-being:
1998, 2002, and 2012

Apart from Tatiana, none of my respondents felt worse. There was an interesting difference between communities: all the Gorazde respondents put their lifelines at 120 percent, which is better than their remembered prewar state. In Foca, with the exception of Svetlana and Mirko, they all put it at 80 percent, lower than their prewar state, perhaps reflecting the differences between living in a community with full employment and one that was still struggling.

How had they coped so well? The most obvious thing was that none of them felt isolated. They all had the supportive families and communities with shared values that I discussed as protective in chapter 8. They were all still closely connected to their parents, either living with them, working with them, or caring for them. Many were living in the traditional Bosnian way with houses split into apartments occupied by extended family, or with family very close by. *The secret is my mother*, Admira told me when I asked her directly what had helped. *I don't know what she did. She was always there for us and she led us through life like no one else. She supported us in everything, and even now when we are adults, she is always there for us. She works as a cleaning lady in one school. She is very hard-working.* In addition, most had successful relationships with partners; three of them were now parents themselves.

There was also the wider community. Apart from Helena who was just visiting her mother, they had all actively chosen to live in Gorazde or Foca and found pleasure in doing so. This was as much the case for those displaced by the war as the others. Svetlana was completely happy in her big family home. Divac did not miss Sarajevo *because I am in Sarajevo every few days.* He enjoyed the *thrill of a bigger city with more opportunities,* but it did not feel like his hometown any more: *I don't feel that sense of connection.* He now loved living in Foca. He no longer talked of getting out of the country, but took me back to the apartment he and his wife had bought with a loan. It was in a dilapidated high-rise, where neither paintwork nor wiring appeared to have been fixed since it was put up in the early eighties. But from their balcony, there was a stunning view: across to the forested mountain sides, out over the heart of the town, and west down the silver line of the Drina. *When we came here, we went to the balcony and said we like it here. [. . .] I feel very good here in this town. I know all the people. Nature is beautiful, so whenever I am angry, I can get into nature in my own world or with friends. Also people are changing because the economic situation is getting better. It's getting better and better.*

Admira felt the same about Gorazde. Her mother had rebuilt their old home in Republika Srpska as a summer house and Admira could now visit her father's grave in the local cemetery close by, but she loved living in Gorazde and could not imagine leaving. *I feel best here.* Armin told me he *would not go anywhere else. I enjoy it 100 percent. I was in Sweden and I could scarcely bear a month there, wherever I go, it's difficult to stand being away a long time.* And Tatiana made clear that returning to live with her parents in Foca was central to her strategy for recovery.

I did wonder if some of Helena's residual tensions were partly due to her feeling that there was still no specific local community to which she belonged. When I asked her, *Where are you from?* She groaned and told me she had a problem with the question. *A few days ago, I started to cry because of that question.* She explained that she had been in Belgrade with her boyfriend when someone asked her where she was from. She answered "Bosnia." *But for this guy, it was not enough and he started asking questions and I did not feel pleasant answering because I really don't know where I come from. I was born in Sarajevo, but I cannot say I am from Sarajevo. I lived in Foca; I lived in Pale; now I live in Doboj. I don't have a feeling that I come from some place, that I have some connections to some town. Some people have connections, they feel like they have their own town. . . .*

Do you have a sense of coming from Bosnia?

Yes, yes.

What about Republika Srpska?

Huh, these are artificial divisions, I live in Republika Srpska, but I move all around Bosnia-Herzegovina. I meet different kinds of people. I come from Republika Srpska, but that's . . .

She did not finish the sentence, clearly dissatisfied with the state of things. Helena still felt homeless. Luckily, she had intelligence, family, boyfriend, and work—all of which compensated.

Samir, Edita, and I walked around Gorazde together on a sunny Sunday morning. The river was a bright greeny blue, foaming in a brisk wind. From the center of the bridge, if you stood and then turned in a circle, you could take in the whole community, clustered along both banks and piling up the hills on both sides of the water. The ruins had gone; there were no visible signs of war except the one beneath our feet: the old pedestrian footbridge—built to protect people from snipers and still preserved as a monument. Outside the cultural center was a large new tourist map of the canton with enticing pictures of all the things one could do: people rafting and swimming in the river, the festival of International Friendship, the new mosque, hotel, and ancient monuments in the mountains. Samir had not noticed it before and thought it was great. He felt there was *development and progress* all around. We had coffee in the garden outside the center and Samir explained that feeling okay depended on one's outlook

In Bosnia we have a saying: When it is hardest for you, you have to laugh.
Is it hard? I asked

No, it's not hard now; everything is fine, but even when there are hard moments I remember that and then they pass. Of course, every man has some sad moments in his life, but I am satisfied because my health is very good and I can see on TV there are a lot of sick people, so I am very thankful. I am really happy that I can live normally and play sports.

It struck me that both Svetlana and Samir could in some way be seen as the sensitive children I discussed in chapter 8, those whose constitution makes them more vulnerable in adverse conditions, but more sensitive to better times and able to make the best of them.

One of the things that helped Elvira to cope was religious belief. Given that she came from a mixed household with a Catholic mother, I asked, *Why Islam?*

I was reading about the other religions as well. [. . .] I had some situations when I was really sad and I needed something, and then I started to believe in God and then it was only believing in God that helped me pass through these bad things that were happening to me. I was not listening to other people and their interpretations of religion, I was just reading and learning by myself.

Political Well-Being

This personal well-being and optimism was in marked contrast to a shared pessimism about the state of the country in general and a shared disgust with those they held most responsible for the continuing mess. When I asked Narcisa if her obvious happiness in her personal life extended to Bosnia she laughed. *With our politicians? I don't think so. They lie and cheat and deceive people. Because they are still trying to make people hate each other, so they can stay and rule and take money. On all sides, trust me. Maybe there are one or two individuals who are trying to make something better and think like us normal people, but it's hard. Because when you see the political parties here like the SDA, they are here for twenty years and what happened? Nothing! Nothing! And on the other side there is the SDS. It's all the same, the same people holding the hand of power for twenty years and in all of those years they make money.*

The political alienation that I discovered in most of the children when I first interviewed them was even stronger than before. Almost all my respondents in both towns agreed with Narcisa that politicians were corrupt, self-serving, interested only in hanging onto power, and deliberately using national politics to stir up tensions and maintain the status quo. Helena thought *politicians on both sides like to keep this situation because they like these closed communities.* A dangerous game in times of hardship, Divac pointed out, because *politicians can start a fire between people.* Jovan told me life experience had made him realize *politicians are not honest or decent people.*

Narcisa became quite passionate discussing it: *Politicians on all sides are still living in the time of war and they are still trying to amplify those things that were important in war and I don't like that. What most people want is jobs and a future and that's it. Nobody really cares about each other's names and religion.* Despite her cynicism, Narcisa voted, as did Divac: *You have to make a choice whatever it is. You must vote to make changes. If you don't vote, you won't make a change.* But many of the others didn't bother. Svetlana had voted for Dodik in the past because he promised jobs, but as he did not produce any she no longer cared.

I don't vote, never, because nothing will change, Admira told me.

Helena took an identical view:

Never. I have never voted in my life. I don't know for whom I should vote and I know it will not help to change anything.

What about changing the politicians?

The problem is that politicians did not come out of the sky, they are from here, so you would have to change all the people. Helena explained, *young people join politics in order to get a job and then when they get a job they become the same. Not because they have some ideas or they want to change something because nobody has ideas.*

Armin agreed. *A politician is a thief, if I take his place I will turn into a bigger thief because I will learn from him. That cannot be overcome; it just goes on and on. All of them are only concerned with their own interests, but not interested in the country at all.*

I moved between the two cities and heard identical voices and identical complaints. The exception was Nikola. *I forgot to mention, I am politically active,* he told me with a smile near the end of our interview. He had joined the SDS (Serb Democratic Party). *You can vote for me in the next municipal elections.* He could see I was astonished. I remembered him as a boy telling me he did not like politics because *somebody always wants to destroy somebody,* and he was not interested.

People around me expect me to be politically active. If you want to get a job, you should be politically involved.

But you have a job in a family firm?

If you want to succeed in your business ideas, you must be politically engaged.

And if you are not, you cannot go forward?

No. Basically, the majority can't get a job, but it is easier through politics.

Through a particular party?

It's probably easier if the party is in power. That's normal. With business, it is much better to be in the party that is already in power. In this way, you can easily reach your goals.

But why the SDS?

Most of my friends are there and they literally forced me to join them.

But this party is particularly associated with the national politics of the war that you and your family criticized, I said, remembering his father explaining to me how national parties were to blame for the conflict. He responded like a practiced politician:

We would like to make it clear to whole world and Europe, there are more mature political views based on coalitions with other political parties with different opinions in it. We have one goal: to have a better standard of life for people.

But then why is it called Serb Democratic Party?

Anyone can join. It got its name at beginning of the war when nationalism was in force, but I have Muslim friends who will vote for me.

So why not get rid of national names?

I would change it now! I think it is for marketing: a matter of recognition.

As always, there was a disarming straightforwardness about Nikola. He was completely frank about political engagement being the best way of pursuing business interests. But I was depressed at his willingness to join a party that used its historical association with creating an ethnically pure Serb state to market itself.

I decided to consult some actual politicians. There was no shortage of them. The constitution imposed by the International Community at Dayton created a federal government, two entity governments, and ten cantons within the Federation entity, as well as the internationally administered Brkco district. So this small country of four million people had fourteen parliaments, five presidents, thirteen prime ministers, one hundred forty ministers, and seven hundred members of parliament. There were more politicians per capita than any other country in the world; it apparently cost 60 percent of the gross domestic product. *When you say "Minister" in Sarajevo, everyone turns around because everyone was at one time a minister!* Krsmanovic told me.

We were sitting around a long oak table in the meeting room in the mayor's offices besides the river. Krsmanovic thought that Bosnia's direct transformation from a communist authoritarian system to multiparty democracy allowed national parties, dominated by *criminal and mafia elements*, to take control. *They pursued their interests through national speeches. Young people see this and that's why they hate them.*

So, how do you change this?

With a new politics, with new social and democratic parties. Not like the Serbian Social Party and the Bosniak Social Party, then you will have fascism. He had established the nonethnic New Socialist Party (NSP) and was forming alliances with other nonethnic parties like Nasa Stranka in Sarajevo, whose president was Danis Tanovic the Oscar-winning director of *No Man's Land*.

In 2014, we expect political changes in BiH and we expect to change the leadership. He wanted to replace Dodik as president in the federal government. He planned to *improve Dayton* by abolishing the cantons and entities: *Now you have thirteen countries in one country*; by transferring power to local authorities: *90 percent of the time people solve their problems at the local level;* and by strengthening the power of the state *to meet European Union standards*. His plan would remove large numbers of privileged positions with the stroke of a pen. I could not see the current powers voting in their own execution.

It was impossible not to be both charmed and impressed by Zdravko Krsmanovic, but I was astounded that the people of Foca had voted for him in 2004.

People were very afraid of the indicted war criminals that were still in the town. I gave them a personal example because I was speaking without fear. And when you give an example to the community they try to do the same.

That is my candidate. I have voted for him three times because I like his attitude and opinions in everything, Headmaster Mojevic told me. *He is smart and a good man, the others are not even up to his knees.* Gordana and I had joined him at our old meeting place: the terrace outside the Zelengora Hotel. Disco music was blaring and I could not help but notice that on a weekday morning it was packed with young people drinking coffee. Krsmanovic brought in an Egyptian businessman to open a new timber plant, but as yet it only employed fifty people although a hundred jobs were planned. Mojevic was now retired and struggling financially like everyone else, having had an expensive heart operation. But he was as friendly and forthcoming as always.

He was as disgusted with most politicians as his former pupils: *Only the thousand people who are cronies of Dodik live well. The rest of us are all at the edge of existence. Those currently in power do not give any hope to the young people. [. . .] It's not normal that someone who works in parliament has 6,000 to 7,000 KM when half a million people in BiH, both the Federation and Republika Srpska, are not working! They just survive and I doubt that they have more than one meal a day. On the other side, those who work in parliament have good cars, good salaries, they have everything and poor people are hungry and not working.*[168] Headmaster Mojevic had moved back to Ustikolina in the Federation, *to my own field, to my own house.* The war crimes charges had been dropped. He got on well with his old neighbors: *They often come to see me. They call me for celebrations and picnics.* He could not see the logic of being *closed in your own community. That's the ghetto, that is not life.* Krsmanovic envisioned a future where Foca and Gorazde municipalities were joined together.

Every person in Bosnia has the same problems: they have to eat, they have to work, they have to travel, and go for holidays so they need money for all that, it doesn't matter if you are Bosniak or Serb, you have all the same problems, Dr. Emir Guso told me. Emir was a doctor at Gorazde hospital and a city councilor for the Social Democrats. At twenty-eight, he was the same age as my respondents and shared all their criticisms of politicians. He did not see himself as one. He got involved in politics because he did not want to sit around allowing bad leaders to do what they liked. *I'm someone who won't sit and wait for something to happen. To put it simply, I want to make some changes myself.* He felt the old guard had the wrong perspective to lead his generation: *We have a lot of problems, a lot of issues and baggage from the past and I think it is the right time to get rid of all of them.*

Emir's story was as painful as any I had heard. Born in Visegrad, the war began when he was six. He and his brother were separated from their parents; his mother was killed by the Serbian army. The boys were placed in an institution for the mentally ill. Then they were transferred to another institution in Belgrade. Emir managed somehow to regularly escape; he met an Albanian family who fostered both brothers until the war was over. The brothers returned to Gorazde in 1995 to be reunited with a father who thought they were dead and who had also remarried. Not surprisingly, Emir passed a rebellious adolescence, but then fulfilled a childhood dream to study medicine. Interestingly, it was empathy with Palestinian children that had motivated him. *During war in Belgrade I was watching TV and I saw a lot of children and people wounded and bleeding in Palestine.* He wanted to do something to help, so *I kind of figured out that that I should become a doctor, and one day go there and try to help.*

He had not made it to Palestine. In Bosnia, he had got involved in the Helsinki Committee for Human Rights. *I went to summer school and I liked it. Then there was a competition for young leaders and I was chosen by the United States State Department to go to their youth leadership program for Bosnia-Herzegovina in 2002.* After one month in the United States he returned to Bosnia and s*tarted doing a lot of work in the human rights area.* In 2008, he became the youngest candidate elected to the city council. Like Krsmanovic, he wanted to reform the constitution. Bosnia is *fractured* and *locked by a national key: We don't ask, who is clever? Who is the right man for the job, the main question is: What is he? Is he Serb, is he Bosniak, is he Croatian? [. . .] It has to be changed. I want to do it. I believe there is a growing mass that will cut it one day. It has to be a whole country.*

Perhaps it was possible. Emir's view challenged Dodik's insistence that Bosniaks *are stubbornly trying to prove their national identity, which they can only do by destroying the nationality of others—primarily, of the other constituent ethnic groups of Bosnia.*[169] National identity was much less salient and fixed in all my respondents than it had been a decade ago and religious belief was still characterized by moderation and tolerance.

However, concerns about the growth of Islamic fundamentalism in Bosnia persisted. In 2011, a Bosnian follower of Wahabi Islam, Mevlik Jasarevic, fired an automatic rifle at the U.S. embassy. He was arrested and was on trial that summer.[170] Saudi Arabia had spent more than $1 billion on "Islamic activities" in Bosnia between 1992 and 1998, all in support of Wahabi Islam. At least one community in Bosnia practiced Sharia law. In early 2010, an international Wahabi group launched a conversion campaign that attempted to bring Catholics, Orthodox, and Bosnia's persistently secular Muslims into the Wahabi fold.[171]

It was spectacularly unsuccessful in the Drina Valley. The mere mention of Wahabis produced smiles and groans from all the Gorazde respondents. Admira roared with laughter when I brought them up. *I really don't know. They are not sane! They are turning religion around and they are untidy; they are not very clean. They wear those trousers! They have no impact in Gorazde for sure.* Her sister agreed: *We all know how to pray in the mosque; we learned it from our grandparents who leaned it from their grandparents, so we all know how to pray in the mosque. We don't need them to come and change that and tell us there is another way of praying. No one will accept that.*

We are European Muslims! Our culture is a European culture. Arab countries have their own culture and we are different, Nerma said firmly. Narcisa was angry that they had completely misinterpreted Islam and made it look bad. *It's wrong; you are not supposed to live your life like that. It all comes back to hatred. You are not supposed to raise your children or live your life hating someone because they are Serbs because they are black; it is not healthy. Wahabism is not my religion. It has made Islam look dirty everywhere in the world. Look at the Taliban, look at Osama Bin Laden, Afghanistan, or Iraq. It's the same; they live their religion in some strange way.* She had been in Ireland in 2007, uncovered, and dressed as usual in her western jeans and T-shirts. *When I said I was Muslim they all looked at me, Where is your covering? Are you supposed to be alone? And is anyone with a sniper gun around you? That is not Islam!*

Religion continued to be important to Narcisa. *I am a Muslim; it is part of my life. I want to raise my children like Muslims, but it doesn't consume me on all sides. Because I know what I believe. I believe in God and I believe God is one and I believe it in that spiritual way; like every religion in the world, you should be good. You should try to do good things. If you are a Muslim, do good, if you are Orthodox or Catholic, do good. It does not matter if you praise your God one way or the other.*

Elvira was the only Muslim I met who told me she was "covered." I say, "told me" because I did not immediately notice. I took her turquoise cap as a fashion statement that matched her close-fitting cardigan and glamorous long skirt. Elvira regarded the Wahabis as *a completely new religion that has nothing to do with Islam.* She thought people joined because they were paid to do so. A friend of hers had covered herself for two years while she received an income and had then uncovered herself when it stopped. The Wahabis had also offered her Catholic mother a substantial sum to convert and put on a Niquab. *Of course, she did not accept! Never, not my mother; she would not give it a thought.* What all my Gorazde respondents had in common was a belief that religion was a very private matter between them and God, and that privacy and moderation allowed for tolerance and respect for others.

For the same reasons, they continued to despise government attempts to turn Muslims into "Bosniaks." When I asked Admira where she was from, she gave me her family name.

And how do you identify yourself?

I am a Muslim. I don't like the term Bosniak. Because the Serbs are called Serbs, the Croats, Croats. So I want to be Muslim. Bosniak means people who live in Bosnia—all nationalities.

So it looks like government attempts to create a Muslim national identity have failed?

For me they failed completely. I am Bosnian; I am from Bosnia.

So is Muslim a political term or cultural and religious?

I am not nationalistic. I don't know. . . . I do believe but I am not fasting and I don't go to mosque, but I do believe. . . . Many people are like me here. Most I think.

Being Muslim for my respondents was about culture and belief, not ethnicity. Samir identified himself as a *human being* and *I am from Bosnia, I wouldn't say to anyone I am a Muslim. I am a believer, but I don't want to be labeled. [. . .] I am a normal Muslim; I need to respect other religions as well.*

I heard a similar language of moderation and tolerance in Foca, where most saw themselves as nonpracticing believers. Jovan thought *religion is a good thing because people should believe in something, but it should be kept as an individual private thing. Everyone has the right to think about it in their own way.* He personally saw himself as *less religious* than in the past. He now told me he was *a man from Foca and a Bosnian.* Helena was no longer the only "Bosnian" in the town. Divac now shared the Gorazde view that all nationalities were Bosnians. Tatiana told me she did not have a national identity because she could not identify herself. Even Nikola, who now described himself as an "Orthodox Serb" and wanted to keep Republika Srpska to allow *Serbs to express their national and religious tendencies,* thought complete separation would not work economically. *What would we do with Gorazde? We would have to have a border crossing through Gorazde to get to Visegrad!* Divac pointed out.

The trouble was that there was still no agreement over whether people could actually live together again. Nerma wanted *a united Bosnia and Herzegovina. I don't see another way to be; we are multicultural and mixed and always will be.* Armin agreed it would be *100 percent better* if there were no entities. *It is one country.* Narcisa actually lived in Republika Srpska. Her husband's family home was in the suburb of Kopaci, now called Novo Gorazde. She commuted to work in the center of Gorazde.

But in Foca, most still worried that mixing completely might be dangerous, even though none of them had any personal animosity toward people on the other side. Helena often met Muslims in Doboj, which straddled the entity boundary like Gorazde. *Basically, we all agree what happened was wrong; we did not need this and it moved us back. So, you wonder who actually started this if we all have the same opinion.* But still *because of everything that happened, because we had a war, because we don't like each other . . . I don't know. Maybe separation is better. When we lived together, we started to fight. That's not good. It's possible we could fight again.* Nikola thought keeping a majority Serb population in Republika Srpska and a Muslim majority in the Federation was the only way to ensure permanent peace *because we don't know when some stupid people will start thinking in a stupid way.*

And when I reminded Svetlana of her wish, as a fourteen-year-old, for people to live together again, it was the one moment in our reunion when she was a little angry with me.

Now I am a grown up and understand our situation. I am sure we cannot live together. I don't know; I am not against, but I cannot see any chances for it.

Why is that? I asked

Because of everything. Because they think we are guiltier than they are, and I think actually it was the same from both sides. The guilt is equal. She did think Muslims *suffered more* during the war, but she was fed up with them *because they talk more about it than we do and we cannot forgive that.* This remained the heart of the problem. There was still no consensus on who was responsible for the war or how the past should be remembered.

Looking Backward

Tatiana spontaneously told me she had thought about this topic for a whole year after our last meeting. *I said it should be forgotten, full stop.* Recently, she had watched two commemorations on television: the red chairs for all the victims of the Siege of Saravevo, followed one month later by a commemoration for the first Serb couple who died in the city. It confirmed her opinion. *I think if we continuously commemorate those things, we will never come to the point where one will accept the other.* She believed ordinary people were being manipulated. *Suppose we imagine Serbs and Muslims are a married couple and they had a fight . . . even physical . . . if you are going to make it up and stay together, the only way is to forget.* How could they remain together if every year each commemorated the various blows inflicted by the other party, she asked? It was a clever metaphor, but it depended on seeing both parties as equally guilty. *It is not important who started it first, it just happened and everybody is guilty.* Mirko agreed. *What happened, happened. Maybe if you repeat it all the time you cause more hatred.*

But in Gorazde, some did not want to forget. Elvira still felt her memories were central to her sense of identity. *I don't want to forget. I want to hold onto the memories. I am satisfied with myself and I think those memories are part of what made me the person I am now.* She told me she still had a shivery feeling of fear when she met Serbian men who might have been involved in the war, and acknowledged that *memories and reconciliation do not go together—I would be forced to forget about one.*

Isn't it a bit sad that you would rather have memory than reconciliation and pass that onto your children? I asked.

298 ♦ THEN THEY STARTED SHOOTING

It is not hatred and I don't think that fear is a bad feeling at all. Maybe for you it sounds sad, but for me it would be sad if I forgot everything and was just to be with them as if nothing happened. I think that I sufficiently forgive and forget that I am able to communicate normally, when I meet them in the street or when I meet at work. I can say good day and good afternoon. That is enough and nothing more.

Sometimes she felt angrier with her own community: *They do not remember anything and they don't want to remember. They are better neighbors to the Serbs than to us. I think we need to have fair and proper nice relationships, but to forget . . . this kind of lying and pretending does not make sense to me.* She was astonished that after a silence on July 11th to remember Srebrenica, life returned to normal on the 12th as if nothing had happened. *Every day we Bosniaks and Muslims need to think about Srebrenica and to remind ourselves what happened there and pray to God that such things never happen again to anyone.*

Those who lost someone close cannot forget, Admira told me, *but most people have forgotten. There was a poll on TV and they asked people in the streets what happened on May 4, 1992 and they did not know! Older people in Gorazde did not know that was the day war began here in Gorazde. Even if one person did not know, it would be significant for me.*

Narcisa was ambivalent about remembering the past. A decade earlier she had felt she should hold onto images of the dead women and children in the street. But now they had *kind of gone; I remember what happened, but the clear images in my head are not so clear.* In any case now she was older. *I don't need the memories, I really do understand where I was and what might happen. [. . .] Sometimes I think I should never forget what happened and sometimes I think I just want to live my life and not live it in the past. Honestly, I don't know.* It was evening. She moved between rooms in the family apartment, made us coffee, fed her daughter and rocked her to sleep. *I am not saying "forget it all," I am just saying try to live your life the best you can and don't think about . . . that way . . . like everyone was thinking during the war . . . try to get a job, have a family, have a baby or . . . you know . . . make some good in your life. It's not all about politics; it's not all about religion. Because every religion—Catholic or Muslim or Buddhism—they are all about doing good and if you follow that you cannot go wrong.*

And while everyone agreed that the political leadership on both sides was responsible, rather than ordinary people, most of those in Gorazde regarded it as an unequal conflict where prime responsibility lay with the Serbs. The war crimes trials continuing at both the ICTY and in the newly created court in Sarajevo did not resolve these issues. Elvira thought those on trial would not get *the sentences they deserve. It is a very nice life there.* She wanted *all of those who pointed guns and canons at people* to be treated in the same way. Admira thought it was too late. *Maybe they will die soon.*

It's not too late, said Narcisa, *it's never too late for that. People need to know the truth and people need to hear it. Because there were war crimes on both sides on the Bosnian Muslim side and Serbian, so it's important.*

Divac thought *everybody should be responsible for their acts and if they are guilty they should go on trial.* Unlike a decade ago, no one I talked to in Foca defended Mladic or Karadzic, even if old graffiti still decorated the walls of apartment blocks. But Divac still felt the process was unjust and biased against Serbs.[172] He was a *little bit angry* that the sentences for Serb war criminals were so much longer than those given to Muslim and Croatian war criminals. *Not that they did not deserve it, but I think Serbian war criminals get in total around a thousand years while all others get a total of thirty years.* The years were *not proportional to the crimes committed by those sides.*

Do you think the crimes were equal?

Not equal, but not as different as these sentences suggest.

Krsmanovic regarded this perception of unequal justice as a major stumbling block in relations. *Why the Bosniaks trust me is because at the beginning of my mandate, I went on Gorazde TV and said what happened in Foca, in the sports hall—there is no justification. I don't justify it and there are no excuses and no justification. But for this crime, you have ten people who are sentenced, while on the other hand you have people who were killed; you have small babies two years old burned in a stove and nobody has been tried for this crime; and children in Foca feel there is no justice.*

He was referring to the massacre at Josanice and I felt some sympathy for this position. If no one in the Drina Valley was accountable for crimes committed by Muslims, it was much harder to discuss crimes committed against them. Tatiana told me she watched a TV documentary about crimes committed against Muslims in wartime Foca, when she was in France in 2005. *I switched it off; I could not watch it. I <u>know</u> what they were going to say about the crimes that happened here. I didn't see them, so I cannot say "it happened, yes I saw it with my own eyes," but I would never say it did not* *happen. [. . .] But if we made a documentary movie about individual crimes committed by Muslims, they would not show it on French TV, not even for a million dollars.*

The only way to solve this issue is to present the truth—only the facts of what happened without ideology, said Krsmanovic. *Everyone should know what happened, everywhere.* But such an independent accounting had still not occurred. The truth commission suggested by Finzi never materialized because all the national parties regarded it as too threatening. In schools, the subject of the last war was considered too difficult and controversial to be tackled at all. The Council of Europe had recommended a moratorium on teaching the period between 1992 and 1995 until there could be some agreement upon what should be taught.[173] So the silence in school was filled in by parents. *At age three, children are educated to know what they are and that they should hate the others,* Tatiana told me. Narcisa agreed: *When you give birth to your child you breastfeed it with nationalism. I am trying not to raise my children that way, [but] we are still teaching the old stories.*

Meanwhile, tit-for-tat memorial ceremonies grew increasingly politicized and the arguments over genocide continued. Elvira was incensed that the Serbs in Srebrenica held a concert on the same day as the Srebrenica memorial. Headmaster Mojevic assured me that a Muslim neighbor moved his father's bones from a local cemetery to Srebrenica to increase the body count, and that probably many others were doing the same.

In some way, I wished I had not brought up these issues. My respondents answered my questions, but I sensed that this part of the discussion wearied them. And the views they shared with me did not help me make sense of their actions in the way they did ten years ago. Quite the opposite, often the realities of the lives they described contradicted their rhetorical positions. Helena taught both Muslim and Serbian children in class together in Doboj and told me children from both entities studied and played together, and had good relations in and out of school. She met Muslims at parties and concerts and was friends with a Muslim colleague in school. *I don't think about a person's nationality.* Nikola traveled and had business colleagues and friends all over the country. Mirko traveled to the Sunday car market in Sarajevo, where no one cared if he was a Serb. He had an aunt and cousin living there and thought the city was *great.* Divac did not see the interentity border any more. *I just pass it.* Living in Gorazde had completely changed his attitude to the "other side." He understood how hard the war was there: *Not easy at all; it was much better here in Foca.* He thought it was *harder for them to accept the fact of living together* and was amazed that they did. Now he and friends spent weekends in each other's towns.

Jovan regularly went to work in Sarajevo and his father was treated there for cancer. He felt quite happy about Muslims returning to Foca. *I meet them everywhere in coffee bars, relationships are normal.* As far as he was concerned, *people are people* and *there are good and bad people in every nation.* In Gorazde, Samir felt exactly the same: *I don't divide people according to nationality, just according to their humanity.* Samir had met up with old Serb neighbors: *We spoke and I just see them as any other people, normal people, I don't blame them. [. . .] They were really happy to see me the first time because they knew me when I was little and I accepted them as good people.* Armin wanted to meet an old school friend with whom he shared a bench for two years.

There seemed to be a mutual decision to agree to disagree and simply not to talk about the past. Divac thought *most people can live without remembering every day.* There was no need, Samir explained, *We don't talk about that, we want to be good friends, and to have a better future than the past.*

Admira, one of those most opposed to Serbs returning in 2002, now worked alongside them: *I cannot say that I like them, but—I don't know how to explain—I have normal relations; I don't mind normal communication—I work with them, but I don't love them.* I watched her thinking aloud: *There are Serbs in my office. . . I am not sure. . . I think they were on the other side, but we don't talk about that. I went to visit a Serb colleague at Christmas and it was nice. I do have one friend who visits; actually, my sister's friend from work, so we always congratulate her on her birthday and on holidays, and she visits us. Actually I like her; I love her.*

Admira explained to me how "not discussing" and "not forgetting" should not be seen as mutually exclusive activities. Both were needed. *It should not be forgotten, to avoid repetition. We can forgive, but we cannot forget.* But the war was *something that happened and is in the past so there is no need to talk about it.* Reconciliation and normal relationships depended on this agreed silence because otherwise both sides just defended their positions, which created tension.

Even Elvira had regular contact with her Serb relatives and took a similar approach. Her uncle and his family were Serb. He fought on the other side and they had returned to live in Novo Gorazde. Her father did not allow them in the house, but she visited the family frequently. *He is my uncle. I love him, although I know he was there.* Her solution was *never discuss any subject related to the war because we are aware our feelings are completely different on that subject.*

I could no longer see any relationship between these attitudes and the quantity or quality of war experiences my respondents had suffered. Samir and Elvira both had horrible wars, but differed markedly in their attitudes to the other side. What seemed to make the difference was simply spending time with people from the other side. Almost everyone I talked to had to do so because of family or work. When people met regularly they often discovered they liked one another. Actually living with the other community could be transformative, as in Divac's case. This was why the politicians of the national parties, who depended on interethnic hostility to maintain their base, worked so hard to maintain separation.

Another encounter made me hopeful. My translator in Gorazde, Edita, had lost her husband in the first year of the war. Her son Varis, born in 1993, had never known his father. Now he was 18 and enjoying his last weeks of vacation before going to University in Sarajevo. He thought his "generation" was quite different from those a few years older. The hatred was much less, even for boys like him: *Okay, the war took my father; I have his blood. But I don't want all Serbs dead. When I was a little kid of five or six there was some kind of hate towards Serbs, but now I know that on both sides people lost their fathers and sons.*

What had made the difference? An intelligent mother who had told him what happened on both sides, and a shared life with other children from other ethnic groups, in which the past was openly discussed.

I have Serb friends here in Gorazde, in school with me.

How do you get on?

Nice, really nice, we drink coffee, go out together, party . . .

Do you argue about what happened?

We don't argue. I say something my parents told me. They say the same, and there's a bit of talking. It's not arguing. There's no fighting; it's just relaxed.

Are there different views on what happened?

Yes, both sides have their stories of what happened and it's not like one side is right, the other is not; it's more like 50–50 percent because everyone hears lies.

What about Srebrenica? Do they have different perspectives on that?

No, they say, okay Srebrenica happened, but Josanice also happened.

Varis knew all about Josanice because his mother had told him. *It was important he know* she said simply. But discussions about the past did not take up much of Varis' and his friends' time. They were much more interested in having fun. Varis traveled freely and without fear all over the country. He had been on a European Union sponsored reconciliation project in which a mixed group of children from towns in both entities had all visited each other's communities, learning about what had happened, setting it in the context of other wars, like Cambodia *because it is something similar. [. . .] Now I can go to Visegrad and sleep. I have a friend there and he can come here.* He was optimistic for the country, particularly because there was a good, free, higher education system. The main block to reconciliation was politicians.

If it comes together, the number of politicians will decrease because the number of entities and cantons will decrease and they don't want that. All they want is big salaries and a secure job.

What's to be done about that?

I don't know; I am just a kid! He laughed. He and his mother were off to the coast in Montenegro for a holiday.

Varis was not alone in his views. Despite divided schools and manipulated curriculums, there were many his age who felt the same. Various studies carried out with young people across the country found that young people had less negative perceptions about other ethnicities than their parents, were keen to mix, and wanted to learn about the past even though they recognized it might be difficult.[174] In a test census run in October 2012, a surprising 35 percent, mostly young people, described themselves as Bosnians and Herzegovinians and refused to give themselves an ethnic identity. Clearly, country meant more than ethnicity for a substantial proportion of the population.[175]

I used my last day in Foca in the same way as I had ten years earlier. I went to the museum. The plaque commemorating Tito's occupancy in 1942 had been put back, but the glass doors were still cracked. The lobby still felt abandoned and dilapidated. The doors to the rooms were all still locked. Gordana and I went up the stairs and banged on the office door. Dragiza, the curator who had shown me around before, opened it, smoking a cigarette and pushing back disheveled reddish hair. She remembered me and was delighted to show us around again. I wanted Gordana to see Tito's typewriter where he wrote the regulations for the 110 day Foca Republic. Although, when I asked to see the memorial room for the recent war, Dragiza was even more reluctant than before to let us in.

You have a good memory, she remarked, as she unlocked the door. And as Gordana looked at the pictures of the horrors of Josanice and read the historical explanation on the wall, Dragiza interrupted with even more emphasis than on the previous occasion: *This is not a proper way to write history. Basically, when someone is writing a history about war—any war, civil war, First or Second World War—both sides should be consulted. It should be examined in a proper way in order to write an agreed history.* This room belonged to the veteran's association and they did not encourage children to visit it. What she wanted to show us was her new exhibition, downstairs in one of the rooms they finally had back from the municipality.

This is "Foca in the Past," starting from the first photo of Foca, which was taken in 1888. It was an expanded version of the collection she had shown me in 2002. This time pictures of the Aladza mosque and others were clearly visible. *I tried to show Foca through a different time, the way that people in Foca lived some time ago; and how people from Foca knew how to organize their cultural life. . . . These mosques were built out of wood and they were destroyed by time, not by people. . . . I liked these pictures, that's why I put them up. . . .* She walked us around, explaining how she had collected pictures and objects from local families. There was the first steam train from Austro-Hungary; city girls hanging out and smoking cigarettes in the 1920s; rafting on the river in the 1930s. *This is the first Serb school in 1864. . . . Here is the first medical doctor in Bosnia. He was from Foca. He finished medicine in Vienna.*

She took us to a cabinet in the center. *This is interesting to see here: These are the jewels the craftsmen made.* Dragiza pointed to a jeweled belt: *This was a belt that men used to wear, and the signs of all three nationalities are in this belt. You see in the middle: Croat, Serb part, and Muslim part— you see in the middle?* It was a lovely belt, with three distinct gemstones in the center.

And all in one belt. So it is really about the unity of the three cultures in some way?

Yes, yes!

After leaving the museum, Gordana and I drove over to Donje Polje. The young imam had agreed to meet with us. We walked up the small cobbled street between restored villas to the mosque. It was an extraordinarily beautiful Ottoman building, with slim, graceful, wooden pillars holding up the portico and lovely arched windows and doors. There was a graveyard around the back, where old turbaned pillars mixed in with new graves. Two men were there. They smiled and greeted us. The younger one explained he was originally from Foca and now lived in Sarajevo. He was back to visit his father's grave as it was Ramadan.

Is it comfortable to visit?

The first time people come back there is a little tension, but the second and third time they realize its okay.

So how is it?

It's really not complicated. People think it is very complicated, but it is not so complicated. People live together: Muslim, Orthodox Serbs, people live together. The reason not so many were coming back to Foca was simply that having moved to the capital or even abroad to the United States or Sweden, not so many wanted to come back to a city with no jobs. It was economics, not politics.

The imam agreed. Fifty people had come back to the town itself, but as yet no young people because of the lack of work. Also, *every community was attached to the mosque. We had eleven mosques, so I hope when we manage to build all the mosques then more people will return.* Imam Jancic was in his twenties. He told me he had decided to come of his own accord in 2007, after completing his studies at Faculty of Islamic Science at Sarajevo. *I just came. I got a call from my professor at the madrassa who said Foca was left without an imam.* Jancic had been there five years and had a wife and new baby. He missed having a young congregation, but relationships with the town were good. There had been some graffiti on the mosque two years earlier, but it was done by drunk teenagers who were being prosecuted. He got on well with the Orthodox Church. They had an annual "Dialogue between Faiths," *so we communicate like real neighbors.*

I drove back to Gorazde and spent my last evening there with Nerma, Rijad, and Medina, watching the opening ceremony of the Olympics, including its extraordinary parade of the athletes of the world. According to Krsmanovic, Bosnia-Herzegovina had sent *eight members from both entities: judo, athletics, shooting. We have no chances of medals, but it's good to compete; it is the presentation of the country, when you take the flag.* He had lit up when discussing sport, describing how he had been at a handball match in Gorazde between Greece and BiH and had woken up the whole audience: *Whenever BiH is playing, I am a fan. The mayor of Gorazde, who was sitting next to me, he gave me a scarf. I can make an atmosphere, I jumped, I started to wake the audience, to call the players, and then we won!*

Dragiza was a big fan of Krsmanovic. Like the man at the mosque, she told me things were much more normal than they appeared. Young people moved freely between towns for matches and concerts. Yes, her Muslim friends had moved to Sarajevo, but that was normal: *economically it's better,* but they visited often and the friendships had endured over years. *You don't hear it on the media, they don't tell you.* Nerma agreed: *The political situation does not reflect the real situation as it is in Bosnia, and does not give a picture of how people could live together and how we live. Politicians just live in their own world and don't show what is really happening between ordinary people.*

Sarajevo

The following day I drove back over the mountains to Sarajevo. I had forgotten the astonishing beauty of the country and the drama of the entrance to the capital city as you came down the road from Pale and through a narrow gorge straight into the oldest part of town. The bombed library and city hall were still clad in scaffolding, their restoration incomplete, but otherwise there were very few signs of war, just the Sarajevo roses, and the plaster-filled bomb craters painted red to mark the spot where people died. I had a meeting with Nina. She had moved here a decade ago to study German and was now working for an international NGO. Economic difficulties had meant she had still not quite completed her degree because of going part-time. But she had certainly had some interesting jobs, as a weather girl on national TV, as the assistant manager of a rock band, and now as a health project manager combating tuberculosis across the country. She explained all this as we wandered in search of a quiet café. However, instead of finding one, we got swept up by a walking tour of the city and decided to tag along.

The tour guide was a nineteen-year-old student of international relations who charmed us all by serving up a mixture of historical facts, funny stories about the war, and toffees, handed to any tourist who gave a correct answer to his questions. He planned to be mayor of the city within a

decade. We learned that Sarajevo was the first city in Europe to have a cof-
feehouse in 1534, predating London and Paris by more than a century. We
heard how the Sephardic Jews had come to the city from Spain in 1492 and
that the Haggadah was saved from the Nazis by the simple ruse of telling
them that other Nazis had already taken it.

Welcome to European Jerusalem, the guide said. standing in front of the
Serbian Orthodox church, the second biggest in the Balkans, built in 1868,
during the time of the Islamic Ottoman Empire, with contributions from
Muslims, Catholics, and Jews. *Only here in Sarajevo are Allah, Yahweh, and
Jesus so close, [. . .] even in my building we have people of different religions,
it is a unique city, a special city. All Europe should live like this.*

It was clever and entertaining, but it left me feeling slightly depressed.
In fact, the city's non-Muslim population, as the guide had acknowledged,
was still less than 20 percent, much reduced from the prewar 45 percent.[176]
Although I was pleased to discover Gordana was living here again; she was
married to a local Serb, and had a four-year-old son. But for how long was
so much of Sarajevo's identity going to rest on living through the longest
siege in history (1,925 days) with glossy maps illustrating key points, tours
of the secret tunnel under the airport, and a special museum dedicated to
life in wartime?

For Nina, her war was something to be put behind her. The only enduring symptoms were a slight feeling of claustrophobia in crowded elevators
that reminded her of being crushed and breathless in the transport truck
during their escape. And she still had the helicopter dream: *It's flying in
front of me; one man comes out, opens the door, puts a gun to my head, and
kills me, always.* Sometimes the location varied, but she always died. Now
the dream came only once or twice a year and did not frighten her too
badly. *It doesn't cause problems. I know it is because of the war. I live a normal life.* She regarded herself as *lucky. So many people suffered more than
me.* She had suffered no terrible losses or injuries and acquired a second
family in Germany. Looking back, that first year of war in Gorazde *was
sometimes like a game for me: Okay, I am going to help the medicine people
or with the water. I was young; I was eight or nine; I was aware and I did
not understand it.* Life was not perfect today. Sometimes she felt *lost* and
somewhat lonely, but that was related to current relationship difficulties
and her continuing sadness over her parents' divorce. She had to some
degree healed her relationship with her father.

Nina shopped at Zara and prayed five times a day. Sitting there in her skimpy sundress, she struck me as a much better symbol of Bosnian multiculturalism than the religious monuments we had just visited. She explained how as a devout young Muslim woman, she had no difficulty working for an equally devout Orthodox Serb boss, alongside 120 others from all over Bosnia. She had the same approach as her compatriots. There was no need to talk about the past. *We have the same goal: to have a better future for all people in Bosnia-Herzegovina. I know there are innocent people everywhere and this is the most important thing. We have a good heart and we want to make things better.*

Maybe it is as simple as that. One encouraging story I read in all the twentieth anniversary reviews and prognostications on Bosnia's future was Julian Borger's account of war veterans helping each other out across entity lines. When the Serbian entity failed to pay pensions to its veterans, it was their former enemies, veterans from the Bosniak-Croat side, who fundraised to help them out. "Who better than those who were in the trenches, the people who were shooting each other, to lead the way?" Semsadin Pojata, a former Bosniak sergeant from Gorazde, said, "If we can do it, why not students, why not governments?"[177]

Why not indeed? As I went over all my interviews, I realized three things were particularly striking about everyone I had talked to. One was the desire to grab life by both hands and make the best of things, whatever was thrown at them. A second was the complete lack of personal animosity to anyone on the other side, and a third was a Clintonesque "the economy, stupid" hanging over almost every conversation. I thought of Svetlana's passionate response when I asked her what might make the country function.

Give people work and jobs; give young people some perspective so they can get married and have kids! We don't ask much, just to earn enough to support our children and to have a modest normal life, is that asking much?

Elvira told me at that although her personal life was great she knew *there are so many who are not employed or who work fifteen to eighteen hours a day, and their directors treat them like slaves and they have very low salaries. They need to do something, to protest.* And if they did, she would join them on the line. Perhaps that moment that Dr. Emir talked about—the one where a growing mass of people will just cut off the burden of the past and take action—is not so far away.

CHRONOLOGY

The chronology is drawn from the following sources: Ivan Lovrenovic, *Bosnia: A Cultural History* (Saqi Books, London, UK; 2001); Joe Sacco, *Safe Area Gorazde: The War in Eastern Bosnia, 1992–95* (Fantagraphics, Seattle, WA; 2000); Laura Silber and Allan Little, *The Death of Yugoslavia* (Penguin Books, London, UK; 1995); The Bosnian Institute's regular *Bosnia Report* (London, UK, 1993–1997); the BBC World Service;[178] and interviews in Foca and Gorazde. It is not comprehensive, but highlights the key historical events that are relevant to the narrative at international, national, and local levels.

1908   Austria-Hungary annexes Bosnia-Herzegovina.

1914   Gavrilo Princip, a Bosnian Serb student, assassinates Austria's Archduke Franz Ferdinand in Sarajevo.

       First World War begins.

1918   Kingdom of Serbs, Croats, and Slovenes founded, incorporating Bosnia-Herzegovina (BiH).

1929   Renamed Kingdom of Yugoslavia.

1939   BiH divided between Croatia and Serbia.

1941–1945   Second World War.

       BiH incorporated into the quisling Independent State of Croatia.

       The Drina Valley changes hands repeatedly, coming under Fascist, partisan, and Chetnik control.

1945   BiH becomes one of six republics within Tito's highly centralized Socialist Federation of Yugoslavia (with Serbia, Croatia, Slovenia, Macedonia, and Montenegro).

1974   New decentralizing constitution attempts to counter Serb hegemony with strong federal institutions and regional autonomy for Serbia's provinces of Vojvodina and Kosovo. Each of the six republics and two autonomous provinces has its own parliament and a representative in the federal presidency.

1980 Tito dies.

1981 Unrest in Kosovo: Albanian demonstrations in favor of granting Kosovo republic status are suppressed by the federal army.

1983 Communist authorities in BiH sentence Bosnian Muslim activist Alija Izetbegovic to fourteen years for counterrevolution, conspiring to create a "Muslim state," and calling for multiparty democracy. (He serves five years.)

1984 Winter Olympics held in Sarajevo.

1985 Serbian Academy of Arts and Sciences declares that under communism, Serbian sacrifices in the Second World War have been rewarded with economic and political discrimination and with genocide in Kosovo, and recommends territorial unification of the Serbs as the solution to these problems: "The full national integrity of the Serbian people, regardless of which republic or province it inhabits, is its historic and democratic right."

1987 April: Serbian Communist Party official Slobodan Milosevic begins his rise to power as "defender of Serbs" in Kosovo.

September: Milosevic takes full control of the Communist League of Serbia.

1988 June: The bones of Prince Lazar, the canonized Serbian ruler killed in the Battle of Kosovo in 1389, are displayed at large gatherings in Serbia and Bosnia, encouraging Serbs to "return to their religious and national roots."

October: Provincial government of Vojvodina is deposed and replaced by Milosevic loyalists.

1989 January: The government of Montenegro is deposed and replaced by Milosevic loyalists.

February: Albanian miners' strike, demanding respect for Kosovo's autonomy.

March: New Serbian constitution revokes Kosovo's and Vojvodina's autonomy but retains their representatives in the federal presidency. (Milosevic now controls four of the eight federal presidency votes.)

June: On the six-hundredth anniversary of the battle of Kosovo, Milosevic tells more than a million Serbs at the battlesite: "Serbs through two world wars . . . liberated themselves and when they could they also helped others to liberate themselves . . . Six centuries later we are again in battles and quarrels. They are not armed battles, though such things should not be excluded yet."

The Croatian Democratic Union (HDZ) is founded in Croatia with Franjo Tudjman as president of the party.

December: Milosevic is elected president of Serbia.

1990 January: Fourteenth Extraordinary Congress of the Communist League of Yugoslavia rejects proposals for a more decentralized Yugoslav Federation.

Slovene and Croatian delegations walk out, ending the conference and Yugoslavia's Communist Party.

February: Serb Democratic Party (SDS) is founded in Croatia.

Milosevic declares a state of emergency in Kosovo.

May: In Zagreb, football riots between Belgrade Red Star and Zagreb Dynamo supporters.

Croatia's first democratic elections: HDZ wins a majority and Tudjman is elected president of the republic.

Yugoslav People's Army (JNA) orders all territorial defense units in Yugoslavia to disarm except those in municipalities with Serb majorities.

Party for Democratic Action (SDA) founded in Sarajevo, with Izetbegovic as president of the party.

July: Kosovo assembly declares Kosovo an equal and independent republic within the Yugoslav Federation; Serbian assembly annuls Kosovo assembly and government, takes over its powers.

Serb Democratic Party (SDS) founded in Sarajevo, with Radovan Karadzic as president of party.

August: In Croatia, Serb nationalists, supported by the JNA, clash with Croatian police.

November–December: First democratic elections in BiH: SDA (26.6%), SDS (23.5%), HDZ (14.4%) form coalition government, with Izetbegovic (SDA) as president of presidency, Momcilo

Krajisnik (SDS) as president of assembly, and Jure Pelivan (HDZ) as president of government.

December: Communists retain control of Serbia and Montenegro in multiparty elections.

1991   February: Serb minority in Croatia form Serb autonomous regions of Krajina, committed to remaining within Yugoslavia "with Serbs from all other nations, including BiH, that accept a common state."

March: Serb autonomous regions of Krajina declare independence.

Milosevic and Tudjman secretly propose to divide BiH between Serbia and Croatia.

June: Council for National Defense of Muslim Nation founded in Sarajevo, with Patriotic League as military wing.

Slovenia declares independence and leaves Yugoslav Federation after ten-day war.

Croatia declares independence.

July: War between Croatia and Serbian autonomous regions, which are supported by JNA. Non-Serb recruits and officers start to leave JNA. War lasts six months, involves ethnic cleansing and attacks on civilians, and displaces 500,000 Croats and 250,000 Serbs.

Serb irregular forces and JNA occupy one-third of Croatian territory. SDA and SDS hold nationalist rallies in Foca, attended by respective political leaders.

Strike at the Foca Trans bus company ends with formation of ethnically divided bus companies in Foca.

September: Serb autonomous regions begin to be declared in BiH.

UN imposes arms embargo on all of former Yugoslavia, thus allowing JNA to retain military superiority.

October: JNA shells Dubrovnik and other Croatian towns.

BiH assembly declares BiH a "sovereign and indivisible state of equal nations."

Karadzic warns that Muslim nation could "disappear" if BiH seeks independence.

Assembly of Serbian Nation founded in BIH.

European Community (EC) proposal that Yugoslavia becomes a community of sovereign states with joint institutions, protection of minorities, and possibility of dual citizenship is rejected by Serbia and Montenegro.

November: SDS-organized Serb-only referendum in BiH; Serbs who vote support remaining in Yugoslavia.

December: EC accepts Badinter Arbitration Commission findings that Yugoslavia is in dissolution, invites the republics to request international recognition.

Serbia and Montenegro reject commission findings.

Serbian autonomous regions in BiH, including most of Sarajevo, declared to be Serbian Republic of Bosnia-Herzegovina with Radovan Karadzic as president.

Serbs and Muslims in Bosnia arm themselves; JNA and territorial defense forces provide Serbs with larger supply including heavy weapons.

1992　January: Ceasefire in Croatia; UN troops deployed in Serb-controlled areas; JNA troops pull back into BiH.

SDS proclaims Republic of Serbian Nation in BiH; Karadzic declares: "united Bosnia-Herzegovina no longer exists."

EU recognizes Slovenia and Croatia.

February 29/March 1: Referendum in BiH; 64 percent vote for independence.

March 3: BiH government declares independence; Serb paramilitary units attack in some areas of BiH.

April 3: Serb paramilitaries and JNA occupy Bijeljina; Five hundred Muslims killed, the rest driven out.

April 4: Bosnian presidency orders general mobilization; SDS sets up barricades in Sarajevo.

April 6: EU and USA recognize Bosnia-Herzegovina; Serb snipers kill four antiwar protesters outside BiH parliament.

April 7–17: In Foca, Muslim militia defeated by local Serb forces and paramilitaries from Serbia; attacks on non-Serb civilians in town and nearby villages continue throughout the year.

April 10: Zvornik occupied by Serb forces.

April 13: Visegrad occupied by Serb forces.

May: Gorazde attacked by Serb forces, beginning four-year siege of city.

May 12: Sixteenth Assembly of the Serbian People in BiH; Karadzic announces six strategic objectives, including eradication of the Drina River as a border between Serbian states; General Ratko Mladic of JNA warns that attempting to separate Serbs from non-Serbs and have the non-Serbs simply leave the territory would not be possible and would amount to genocide.

May 15: UN Security Council Resolution 752 calls for withdrawal of JNA from BiH.

Bosnian Serb Army (VRS) formed, with Mladic as commanding officer.

May 20: Armed Forces of Republic of Bosnia-Herzegovina (ARB-H) formed.

May 27: VRS shells civilians in bread queue in Sarajevo: twenty dead, one hundred injured.

May 30: UN Security Council imposes sanctions on Yugoslavia for failing to respect Resolution 752.

June: UN approves humanitarian airlift into Sarajevo; VRS hands over airport to UN.

July: Western media report widespread atrocities against non-Serb civilians in BiH, including forced deportations and organized killings within camps.

August: Serb Republic of Bosnia-Herzegovina renamed Republika Srpska (RS).

September: Forces from Gorazde push back VRS troops, enlarging besieged area; mule train over mountains keeps enclave supplied.

UN authorizes UN Protection Forces for Bosnia.

October: 7th Muslim Brigade of ARB-H formed in Zenica, declaring its aim to be a "fight for the faith"; volunteers from Arab countries terrorize local Serbs, Croats, and Muslims.

1993   January: Vance-Owen Plan proposes ethnic cantonization of Bosnia.

February: Fighting between ARB-H and Bosnian Croat forces (HVO); attacks on Muslim and Croat civilians.

March: First airdrops of food supplies on Gorazde.

May: UN declares Sarajevo, Zepa, Tuzla, Gorazde, and Bihac to be "Safe Areas."

VRS offensive takes remaining Bosnian government territory in Drina Valley, tightens siege on Gorazde, closing mountain route to Sarajevo.

Muslim soldiers massacre sixty-five Serb civilians in village of Josanice, near Foca.

UN founds International Tribunal for War Crimes Committed on the Territory of the Former Yugoslavia (ICTY), with headquarters in The Hague.

June: UN authorizes use of force to protect Safe Areas.

1994   February: Shell from Serb position kills sixty-eight people in Sarajevo market.

ARB-H and HVO agree to a ceasefire.

Serb forces begin to withdraw heavy weapons from around Sarajevo after NATO ultimatum.

April: VRS intensifies shelling of Gorazde and advances to town center on right bank of Drina.

NATO bombs Serb positions around Gorazde.

VRS takes one-hundred fifty UN personnel hostage; British jet is shot down.

VRS shelling continues as international community disputes use of air strikes; three-hundred thirteen killed and more than a thousand wounded in Gorazde in less than three weeks.

April 24: VRS retreats three kilometers from Gorazde center, agrees to demilitarization of Gorazde area and UN-monitored ceasefire.

1995   May: VRS shells Sarajevo marketplace and Tuzla, killing seventy-one civilians.

After NATO ultimatum to stop shelling Sarajevo, VRS takes three-hundred fifty peacekeepers hostage and uses them as human shields at military targets.

July: VRS occupies Srebrenica: Deports twenty-five thousand Muslim civilians and executes seven- to eight-thousand men and boys.

London conference warns that VRS attack on Gorazde will be met with substantive and decisive airpower; UN withdraws monitors from enclave.

VRS occupies Zepa, expels and kills non-Serbs.

July: Karadzic and Mladic indicted for genocide, crimes against humanity, and violations of the laws or customs of war.

August: Croatian army retakes most of Croatian territory (Operation Storm); mass exodus of Serbs, atrocities against those remaining.

Croatian army and ARB-H lift siege of Bihac.

VRS shells kill forty-one civilians in Sarajevo market.

NATO begins air strikes on VRS positions.

September: Croat ARB-H forces advance to within twenty-five kilometers of Banja Luka; local Serbs flee to Serbia.

October: Ceasefire supervised by NATO.

November: Negotiations begin in Dayton, Ohio.

December 14: Dayton Peace Accord signed in Paris; BiH divided into two entities: Republika Srpska and the Federation of Bosnia-Herzegovina.

1996　First violence against Serbian security forces by newly formed Kosovo Liberation Army (KLA).

June: Karadzic forced to resign presidency of SDS; Biljana Plavsic becomes president.

November: Opposition alliance (Zajedno) wins elections in Serbia; Milosevic annuls results and holds new elections.

Massive street protests begin, continue until original results reinstated in February 1997.

1997　July: Milosevic elected president of Yugoslavia.

November: Gorazde declares itself an Open City committed to facilitating the return of Serb citizens, in return for increased international aid.

1998 January: With Plavsic's support, moderate Milorad Dodik becomes prime minister of RS and transfers administrative authority from Karadzic stronghold of Pale to Banja Luka.

February–March: Serbian security forces massacre civilians in Drenica area of Kosovo.

March: In Foca, Dragoljub Kunarac hands himself over to the ICTY, charged with rape as a crime against humanity.

July: KLA steps up offensive against Serb forces, which respond with brutal counterinsurgency campaign.

Milorad Krnojelac, primary school headmaster and former warden of KP Dom prison in Foca, arrested and sent to The Hague.

October: Bosnian elections return nationalist parties in both entities.

Holbrooke Agreement with Milosevic arranges ceasefire in Kosovo, averts air strikes, and permits international civilian monitors in the province.

1999 January: Massacre of forty-five Albanian men at Racak, Kosovo.

March: NATO bombs Serb targets in Kosovo and Serbia, including Belgrade; Serbian security forces expel eight hundred thousand Albanians from Kosovo.

May: Milosevic indicted for genocide in Kosovo.

June: Milosevic agrees to withdrawal of Serbian forces and UN administration of Kosovo; NATO air strikes cease.

December: Franjo Tudjman dies.

2000 January–February: In Croatia, HDZ loses parliamentary elections; moderate Stipe Mesic elected president of Croatia.

April: Biljana Plavsic indicted for genocide and crimes against humanity.

July: Constitutional court of Bosnia and Herzegovina rules that both entities in BiH should amend their constitutions to ensure the full equality of the three "constituent peoples" throughout the country.

October: BiH elections return moderates to power in the Federation and nationalist hard-liners in RS.

Vojislav Kostunica elected president of Yugoslavia; Milosevic at first refuses to accept the result, but steps down after popular demonstrations supported by the army and police.

December: BiH and Federal Republic of Yugoslavia establish diplomatic relations.

Milosevic is arrested on charges of corruption and theft in Serbia.

Milosevic handed over to the ICTY and sent to The Hague.

2001   February: The ICTY sentences three men from Foca for mass rape as a crime against humanity.

April–May: In Banja Luka, foreign visitors and hundreds of Muslim returnees, attending the laying of foundation stone for the reconstruction of the Ferhat-Pasha Mosque, are trapped in Islamic center by several thousand Serbs; riots leave thirty injured, one dead.

August: Bosnian Serb General Krstic found guilty of genocide for his role in the massacre of over seven thousand Muslims at Srebrenica in 1995, sentenced to forty-six years in prison.

Three high-ranking Bosnian army officers indicted for alleged crimes committed in central Bosnia in 1993–1994.

September: Milosevic indicted for war crimes and crimes against humanity in Croatia.

October: Izetbegovic resigns as leader of SDA.

November: Milosevic indicted for genocide in BiH between 1992 and 1995.

December: In RS, SDS bans indicted war criminals from membership, including party founders Karadzic and Krajisnik.

2002   January: Bosnian authorities hand over six suspected al-Qaeda members to the United States.

February–March: NATO fails in two attempts to capture Karadzic.

March: Yugoslavian president Kostunica, Serbian prime minister Zoran Djindjic, Montenegrin president Milo Djukanovic, and EU foreign policy chief Javier Solana sign an "agreement in principle" to replace Federal Republic of Yugoslavia with a new union called "Serbia and Montenegro."

Krnojelac sentenced to seven years for aiding and abetting crimes against humanity at the KP Dom in Foca.

No Man's Land (Nicija Zemlja), written and directed by Sarajevo native Danis Tanovic, wins Oscar for best foreign-language film.

April: Dutch government resigns after publication of official government report on the role of Dutch peacekeeping forces in Srebrenica massacre.

October: BiH elections marked by low turnout and success of nationalist parties in both entities; votes of non-Serb returnees entitle Federation parties to 17 percent of seats in RS assembly.

Bosnian Serb company found guilty of exporting military hardware to Iraq in violation of the UN arms embargo.

December: Biljana Plavsic pleads guilty to one charge of crimes against humanity at the ICTY. The remaining seven charges are dropped. She receives an eleven-year prison sentence.

2003 January: The UN hands over policing duties in BiH to the European Union (EU).

February: The term "Yugoslavia" is dropped in favor of "Serbia and Montenegro" and disappears from the map of Europe.

March: Reformist prime minister of Serbia Zoran Djindjic is assassinated.

April: Mirko Sarovic, Serb member of presidency, resigns after being implicated in illegal military exports to Iraq and spying on international officials.

High Representative Paddy Ashdown abolishes Supreme Defence Council of Bosnian Serb Republic and alters constitutions of both entities to remove all references to statehood.

October: Alija Izetbegovic dies.

2004 October: Zdravko Krsmanovic wins local elections to become mayor in Foca.

November: After conducting an official inquiry, the Bosnian Serb government of Republika Srpska issues an official apology for the massacre at Srebrenica, acknowledging that "enormous crimes were committed."

December: EUFOR (an EU-led force) takes over peacekeeping duties from NATO in BiH.

2005   October: The European Commission opens talk with BiH on taking first steps to EU membership.

Muslims arrested in Denmark and Bosnia are suspected of planning terrorist attacks in Europe.

October: Entity and central parliaments back establishment of unified police force.

2006   March: Milosevic dies in his cell at The Hague.

May: Montenegro is recognized as an independent state.

October: Ethnic politics dominate general elections. RS leadership threatens to secede if there is any attempt to abolish RS autonomy.

December: Bosnia joins NATO's Partnership for Peace premembership program.

2007   January: Bosnia's state court jails three men for planning a suicide attack in Europe.

February: The International Court of Justice rules that the 1995 Srebrenica massacre constitutes genocide, but clears Serbia of direct responsibility.

2008   February: Kosovo declares independence.

July: Radovan Karadzic is arrested in Belgrade and transferred to the ICTY. He is charged with eleven counts of genocide, war crimes, crimes against humanity, and other atrocities.

October: In local elections nationalist parties do well among all three ethnic groups.

2009   March: Austrian diplomat Valentin Inzko becomes high representative.

October: Trial of former Bosnia Serb leader Radovan Karadzic begins at the ICTY.

December: European Court of Human Rights rules that the constitution of Bosnia and Herzegovina violates Article 14 of the European Convention on Human Rights because it does not allow people who are not Bosniaks, Serbs, or Croats to run for the presidency.

2010   February: Republika Srpska passes law making it easier to hold referendums on national issues, including a referendum on independence.

April: RS government revises 2004 report on Srebrenica, stating that numbers were exaggerated.

October: In general elections, the SNSD led by Republika Srpska Premier Milorad Dodik and SDP multiethnic party led by Zlatko Lagumdzija are the main winners.

2011   May: Ratko Mladic is arrested in Serbia and handed over to the ICTY. He is charged with genocide, crimes against humanity, and violations of the laws or customs of war.

July: Goran Hadzic, the last indictee of the ICTY still at large, is arrested in Serbia; 161 indictees have been arrested.

October: Mevlid Jasarevic opens fire with an automatic weapon outside the US Embassy in Sarajevo. He is from the northeastern village of Gornja Maoca, which is dominated by a Wahabi sect that refuses to recognize the Bosnian state.

December: After fourteen months of deadlock, Bosnia's Muslim, Croat, and Serb political leaders agree on the formation of new central government.

2012   May: The trial of Ratko Mladic opens at the ICTY.

June: Newly elected President Tomislave Nikolic of Serbia declares that the massacre at Srebrenica was not genocide.

July: Thirty thousand attend the mass funeral of some five hundred newly identified victims of the Srebrenica massacre.

October: Dodik proposes that Bosnia's unified armed forces should be abolished.

October: The Bosniak SDA, Serb SDS, and Croat HDZ are the main winners in local elections. These are the three parties that led the country at the outbreak of the war in 1992. Krsmanovic loses the election in Foca.

November: Unemployment in Bosnia and Herzegovina is 44 percent.

December: Jasarevic is sentenced to eighteen years in jail for terrorist acts.

December: Bosnian Serb ex-general and aide to General Mladic Zdravko Tolimir is sentenced to life in prison by the ICTY for genocide over the Srebrenica massacre.

NOTES

Introduction

1. Kofi Annan, *Report of the Secretary General pursuant to the General Assembly Resolution 53/35* (New York, NY, 1998), para. 503.

2. BBC Europe, "Serbia's new president, Tomislav Nikolic, has said the Srebrenica massacre of 1995 was not genocide," June 1, 2012. On April 25, 2013, BBC Europe reported that Nikolic had apologized on Bosnian TV for "the crimes committed by any individual in the name of our state and our people." But although he said "I kneel and ask for forgiveness for Serbia for the crime committed in Srebrenica," Nikolic still did not call it genocide.

3. Dodik stated in an interview that "Indeed no genocide happened in Srebrenica [...] those individuals have answered for it. Why then should an entire people be bullied with that story?" B92 Radio "Dodik believes RS is Serbia's top priority," June 8, 2012.

4. Valentin Inzko, *42ⁿᵈ Report of the High Representative for Implementation of the Peace Agreement on Bosnia and Herzegovina to the Secretary-General of the United Nations.* OHR, Office of the High Representative, Sarajevo, Bosnia-Herzegovina, November 11, 2012. Available at: http://www.ohr.int/other-doc/hr-reports/default.asp?content_id=47611. Accessed February 20, 2013.

5. "Millions of children inside Syria and across the region are witnessing their past and their futures disappear amidst the rubble and destruction of this prolonged conflict." Anthony Lake, UNICEF CEO quoted in *Syria's Children: A Lost Generation? Crisis Report March 2011–March 2013,* UNICEF, New York, NY. Available at: http://www.unicef.org/infobycountry/files/Syria_2yr_Report.pdf. Accessed March 30, 2013.

6. "All these children tell you these stories in a matter of fact way and then you realize that there are layers and layers of emotional trauma there," Justin Forsyth, CEO of Save the Children, quoted in Oliver Holmes, *Syria's Children Shot At, Tortured, Raped: Charity Report* (Reuters, Beirut, Lebanon, March 13, 2013).

1. Fighting Begins

7.   The four Cs (Cyrillic for S), displayed around a cross, stand for the phrase "only unity can save the Serbs."

8.   Alija Izetbegovic was president of Bosnia-Herzegovina at that time.

9.   The word "Balija" probably comes from the Turkish term used to describe someone living on the edge of a town. In the past, Muslim villagers sometimes used it about themselves. It is now a term of abuse used by non-Muslims about Muslims. Many Serbs connect it with "Ballist," the name of the nationalist Albanian organization, whose members Serbs regarded as collaborators with the Nazis in the Second World War.

2. The War Goes On

10. "Brotherhood and Unity": the slogan introduced by Tito after the Second World War to encourage loyalty to a unified Yugoslav state. For some, the phrase later came to symbolize an attempt to submerge ethnic distinctness.

4. Why Did We Fight?

11. Norman Cigar, *Genocide in Bosnia: The Policy of "Ethnic Cleansing"* (Texas A&M University Press, College Station, TX, 1995), 121.

12. Noel Malcolm, *Bosnia: A Short History* (Macmillan, London, UK, 1996). Ivan Lovrenovic, Bosnia: A Cultural History (Saqi Books, London, UK, 2001).

13. Tone Bringa, *Being Muslim the Bosnian Way: Identity and Community in a Central Bosnian Village* (Princeton University Press, Princeton, NJ, 1995), 156.

14. Josip Zupanov, "Research Shows Beyond Doubt, Intolerance and Media Propaganda Did Not Cause the War" (1995). In Mark Thompson, ed., Forging War: *The Media in Serbia, Croatia, and Bosnia Hercegovina* (University of Luton Press, Luton, UK, 1999), 317.

15. Norman Cigar, *Genocide in Bosnia: The Policy of "Ethnic Cleansing"* (Texas University Press, College Station, TX, 1995), 122.

16. *Merhaba:* an informal nonreligious greeting of Turkish origin, meaning "you are among friends"; used primarily by Muslim men and older people. Tone Bringa, *Being Muslim the Bosnian Way: Identity and Community in a Central Bosnian Village* (Princeton University Press, Princeton, NJ, 1995), 56.

5. What Became of Our Neighbors?

17. Human Rights Watch, Bosnia and Herzegovina, *"A Closed, Dark Place"*: *Past and Present Human Rights Abuses in Foca* (New York, NY, 1998).

18. Ibid., 11.

19. Ibid., 12, 15, 16.

20. International Criminal Tribunal for the Former Yugoslavia, Indictment, Gagovic and others, Foca case nos. IT-96-23, IT-96-23/1 (The Hague, The Netherlands, 1996), paras. 6.2–6.5.

21. Human Rights Watch, *"A Closed, Dark Place,"* 15–16.

22. Helsinki Watch, *War Crimes in Bosnia-Hercegovina*, vol. 2 (New York, NY, 1993), 254–255.

23. International Crisis Group Report, *War Criminals in Bosnia's Republika Srpska: Who Are the People in Your Neighbourhood?* (Brussels, Belgium, 2000).

24. Helsinki Watch, *War Crimes*, 355, 272–273.

25. Human Rights Watch, *"A Closed, Dark Place,"* 25.

26. Mark Thompson, ed., *Forging War: The Media in Serbia, Croatia, and Bosnia Herzegovina* (University of Luton Press, Luton, UK, 1999), 89–96.

27. The *Bosnian Book of the Dead*, published jointly by the Sarajevo-based Research and Documentation Centre and the Humanitarian Law Centre in Belgrade in January 2013, puts the total number of casualties at 95,940 named dead (with 5,100 whose circumstances of death must still be clarified.) "Roughly half the dead were civilians, while 82 percent of those were Bosnian Muslims (known as Bosniaks). Some 10,000 women were killed, again the majority Bosniaks. Of 24,000 Serb dead, 20,000 were soldiers." Daria Sito-Sucic and Matt Robinson, Reuters News Agency, Sarajevo/Belgrade, February 15, 2013.

28. Helsinki Watch, *War Crimes*, 7.

29. Joe Sacco, *Safe Area Gorazde: The War in Eastern Bosnia* (Fantagraphics Books, Seattle, WA, 2000), 155–160.

30. Ibid, 155–160.

31. Savo Heleta, *Not My Turn to Die: Memoirs of a Broken Childhood in Bosnia* (AMACOM/American Management Association, New York, NY, 2008), 18, 154, 44, 171, 96–97.

32. Laura Silber and Allan Little, *The Death of Yugoslavia* (Penguin and BBC Books, London, UK, 1995), 215.

33. Zlatko Dizdarevic, *Sarajevo: A War Journal* (New York, NY, 1994), cited

in Mark Thompson, ed., Forging War: *The Media in Serbia, Croatia, and Bosnia Hercegovina* (University of Luton Press, Luton, UK, 1999), 230–231.

6. What Country Is This?

34. Many young people in Foca thought of the newly formed Federal Republic of Yugoslavia (Serbia and Montenegro) as exclusively Serb. According to the 1991 census, however, 10 percent of Serbia's population was not Serb, and in the autonomous provinces of Vojvodina and Kosovo this rose to 45 percent and 90 percent, respectively.

35. Bosnia and Herzegovina is the formal name of the country. However the term Bosnia-Herzegovina is often used, or Bosnia on its own, both in coversation and writing. I have used all three terms here, following use by my respondents.

36. Lawrence Weschler, "Letter from Republika Srpska: High Noon at Twin Peaks," *New Yorker,* August 18, 1997, 33.

37. Jonathan Steele, "The Phantom Voters of Eastern Bosnia" *War Report,* October 1997.

38. Brcko had had a majority Muslim population before the war and had been taken by Bosnian Serbs. They did not wish to relinquish control of the town because of its strategic position in the corridor of land connecting eastern and northern RS. In 1999, a final agreement established a special demilitarized district for the entire Brcko prewar district under the exclusive sovereignty of Bosnia-Herzegovina, belonging simultaneously to both entities with a unified multiethnic government. Brcko District Office of the Higher Representative, *History and Mandate of the OHR North/Brcko* (2001). Because of noncompliance with different aspects of this final agreement by both entities, most recently by RS, the Office of High Representative has maintained various aspects of international supervision up to the present time. Valentin Inzko, *42nd Report of the High Representative for Implementation of the Peace Agreement on Bosnia and Herzegovina to the Secretary-General of the United Nations.* OHR, Office of the High Representative, Sarajevo, Bosnia-Herzegovina, November 11, 2012. Available at: http://www.ohr.int/other-doc/hr-reports/default.asp?content_id=47611. Accessed February 24, 2013.

7. Where Do They Come From?

39. All textbook quotations in this chapter come from books in use in Foca and Gorazde schools in 1997–98. These were the textbooks being used by the individuals in this study.

40. In Ivo Andric's novel, *The Bridge over the Drina,* a story is told that a

mason walled up infant twins in the central pier to ensure the successful completion of the bridge. Ivo Andric, *The Bridge Over the Drina*, (Harvill Press, London, UK, 1995).

41. Dusan's father echoed Serb intellectuals like Miroljub Jevtic who stressed the historical treachery of Bosnian Muslims in the popular press. "Those who accepted Islam accepted the conquerors de facto as their brothers, and the crimes of the latter as their own. That means their own hands are also covered with the blood of their own ancestors, the former Bosnian non-Muslim population." "Rezervisti alahove vojske" (The Reservists of Allah's army), *Duga*, December 9–22, 1989, cited in: Norman Cigar, *Genocide in Bosnia: The Policy of "Ethnic Cleansing"* (Texas A&M University Press, College Station, TX, 1995), 29.

42. Gavrilo Princip was a Bosnian Serb nationalist whose assassination of Austrian Archduke Franz Ferdinand in Sarajevo in 1914 was one factor contributing to the outbreak of the First World War.

43. Noel Malcolm, *Bosnia: A Short History* (Macmillan, London, UK, 1996), 51–81. Norman Cigar, *Genocide in Bosnia: The Policy of "Ethnic Cleansing"* (Texas A&M University Press, College Station, TX, 1995), 14–15.

44. Bogoljub Kocovic, *The Victims of World War II in Yugoslavia* (London, UK, 1985), 102, 174, 182, cited in Norman Cigar, *Genocide in Bosnia: The Policy of "Ethnic Cleansing"* (Texas A&M University Press, College Station, TX, 1995), 9. Noel Malcolm, *Bosnia: A Short History* (Macmillan, London, UK, 1996). Ivan Lovrenovic, Bosnia: A Cultural History (Saqi Books, London, UK, 2001), 192.

45. Noel Malcolm, *Bosnia: A Short History* (Macmillan, London, UK, 1996), 174–192. It was only by considering the Second World War that I could make sense of the frequent Serbian references to a German-Vatican-Islamic conspiracy against them—although this historical underpinning fell apart when the CIA was also included.

46. Ibid., 177.

47. Bajram: The day of ending the Ramadan fast and the most important festival in the Bosnian Muslim calendar, celebrated by all the Muslims I knew, whether they were believers or not, with visits and food.

48. Tone Bringa, *Being Muslim the Bosnian Way: Identity and Community in a Central Bosnian Village* (Princeton University Press, Princeton, NJ, 1995), 83. I am indebted to Bringa, whose detailed analysis of Bosnian Muslim life in central Bosnia before the war has increased my understanding of this aspect of Muslim identity.

328 ◆ THEN THEY STARTED SHOOTING

49. Ivan Lovrenovic, *Bosnia: A Cultural History* (Saqi Books, London, UK, 2001), 177.

50. This practice had been common in the past and still existed in some rural areas. Tone Bringa, *Being Muslim the Bosnian Way: Identity and Community in a Central Bosnian Village* (Princeton University Press, Princeton, NJ, 1995).

51. Ivan Lovrenovic, *Bosnia: A Cultural History* (Saqi Books, London, UK, 2001), 209.

52. The group based in Zenica was not made up of "Arabians," as Fikreta calls them, but of young Muslims who identified with particular reformist tendencies in the wider Islamic world. Their presence helped to sustain Serbian fears of an Islamic "threat," but their non-Bosnian form of worship was rejected by all the families I interviewed.

53. Maja Povrzanovic has described a similar process of war-induced ethnic recognition and crystallization in Croatia in "Children, War and Nation: Croatia 1991–4," *Childhood* (1997): 4, 81–102.

54. Vesna Pesic, "The War for Ethnic States," in N. Popov, ed., *The Road to War in Serbia: Trauma and Catharsis* (Central European University Press, Budapest, 2000), 34–38. Petar Njegos, *The Mountain Wreath of P. P. Nyegosh, Prince-Bishop of Montenegro 1830–1851*, trans. J. Wyles (Allen and Unwin, London, UK, 1930), 209.

55. Henri Tajfel, *Human Groups and Social Categories* (Cambridge University Press, Cambridge,UK, 1981), 255.

56. Miroslav Radovanovic, "O Potrebi donosenja nacionalnog programa" (On the Need to Draft a National Program), *Glas Crkve* 4 (1991); Bozidar Mijac, "Mir, da, ali kakav?" (Peace yes, but what kind of Peace?), *Pravoslavlje*, March 15, 1992, both cited in Norman Cigar, *Genocide in Bosnia: The Policy of "Ethnic Cleansing"* (Texas A&M University Press, College Station, TX, 1995), 31–32.

57. Piete Kuhr, *There We'll Meet Again: The First World War Diary of a Young German Girl* (Walter Wright, Gloucester, UK, 1998), 1, 4–5, 13.

58. M. Sherif and C. W. Sherif, *Groups in Harmony and Tension* (Harper and Row, New York, NY, 1953).

59. Henri Tajfel, *Human Groups and Social Categories* (Cambridge University Press, Cambridge,UK, 1981), 269–287. Once separated: Muzafer Sherif, O. J. Harvey, B. Jack White, William R. Hood, and Carolyn W. Sherif, *Intergroup Conflict and Cooperation: The Robbers Cave Experiment* (Institute of Group Relations, Norman, OK, 1961).

60. Patrick Quinn, "Offer to End Sanctions Fails to Sway Serbs on Peace

Plan," *Washington Times,* July 15, 1994, cited in Norman Cigar, *Genocide in Bosnia: The Policy of "Ethnic Cleansing"* (Texas A&M University Press, College Station, TX, 1995), 63.

61.   David K. Shipler, *Arab and Jew: Wounded Spirits in a Promised Land* (Penguin, Harmondsworth, UK,1986), 183, 195.

62.   As Arab children in Israel learned from Arabic-language books following an Israeli curriculum, these images were mostly found on the West Bank and in books smuggled from there. David K. Shipler, *Arab and Jew: Wounded Spirits in a Promised Land* (Penguin, Harmondsworth, UK,1986), 199, 201.

63.   Piete Kuhr, *There We'll Meet Again: The First World War Diary of a Young German Girl* (Walter Wright, Gloucester, UK, 1998), 314.

8. War and Well-Being

64.   Frank Bodman, "War Conditions and the Mental Health of the Child," *British Medical Journal,* 2 (1941): 486-488,.

65.   Anna Freud and Dorothy Burlingham, *Infants without Families: Reports on the Hampstead Nurseries, 1939–1945* (International Universities Press, New York, NY, 1973), 169, 172–173, 178, 193–207, 195. Freud acknowledged that her nursery had a selected population: children who did well when evacuated would stay in the country; the less successful evacuees were more likely to return to London and appear at the nursery. Her point is that these unhappy evacuees were more disturbed than children who had remained in London during the Blitz.

66.   Charlotte J. Carey-Trefzer, "The Results of a Clinical Study of War Damaged Children Who Attended the Child Guidance Clinic, the Hospital for Sick Children, Great Ormond Street, London," *Journal of Mental Science,* 400 (1949): 35-44.

67.   Dirk Van der Heide, in Laurel Holliday, ed., *Children in the Holocaust and World War II: Their Secret Diaries* (Washington Square Press, New York, NY, 1995), 35–40, 52, 53.

68.   Psychological genocide: R. M. Fields, *A Society on the Run: A Psychology of Northern Ireland* (Penguin, Harmondsworth, UK, 1973). Lost generation: H. A. Lyons, "Violence in Belfast: A Review of the Psychological Effects," *Community Health* 5 (1973): 163-168. Delinquency rates: K. Heskin, *Children and Young People in Northern Ireland: A Research Review* (Open Books, Shepton Mallet, UK, 1980).

69.   E. P. Benedek, "Children and Psychic Trauma: A Brief Review of Contemporary Thinking," in S. Eth and R. S. Pynoos, eds., *Post-Traumatic*

Stress Disorder in Children (American Psychiatric Press, Washington, DC, 1985), 4, 5.

70. On the emergence of PTSD, see Allan Young, *The Harmony of Illusions: Inventing Post-Traumatic Stress Disorder* (Princeton University Press, Princeton, NJ. 1995); Ben Shephard, *A War of Nerves* (Jonathan Cape, London, UK, 2000).

71. Wilbur J. Scott, *The Politics of Readjustment: Vietnam Veterans since the War* (New York, NY. 1993), cited in Ben Shephard, *A War of Nerves* (Jonathan Cape, London, UK, 2000). Dickens: Allan Beveridge, "On the Origins of Post Traumatic Stress Disorder," in Dora Black et al., ed., *Trauma: A Developmental Approach* (Gaskell, London, UK, 1997), 3-10. Shell Shock: Ben Shephard, *A War of Nerves* (Jonathan Cape, London, UK, 2000), 357–359.

72. P. Hodgkinson, "Technological Disaster-Survival and Bereavement," *Social Science and Medicine,* 29 (1989): 351-6, cited in Ben Shephard, *A War of Nerves* (Jonathan Cape, London, UK, 2000), 386. Social movement: B. Raphael, L. Meldrum, and A. McFarlane, "Does Debriefing after Psychological Trauma Work?" *British Medical Journal,* 310 (1995): 1479-1480.

73. UNICEF, *The State of the World's Children* (Oxford University Press, Oxford, UK, 1996).

74. F. Arbuthnot, "Sanctions Are Making It Harder to Forget the Trauma of War," *Guardian,* December 30, 1994.

75. Lynne Jones, "On a Front Line," *British Medical Journal,* 310 (1995): 1052–54. Counseling programs: Lynne Jones, "The Question of Political Neutrality When Doing Psychosocial Work with Survivors of Political Violence," *International Review of Psychiatry,* 10 (1998): 2.

76. R.J. McNally, "Progress and Controversy in the Study of Posttraumatic Stress Disorder," *Annual Review of Psychology,* 54 (2003): 229–52.

77. D. Summerfield, "A Critique of Seven Assumptions behind Psychological Trauma Programs in War-Affected Areas," *Social Science and Medicine,* 48 (1999): 1449–62.

78. A. Argenti-Pillen, "The Discourse on Trauma in Non-Western Cultural Contexts," in A. Y. Shalev, R. Yehuda and A. C. McFarlane, eds., *The International Handbook of Human Response to Trauma,* (Kluwer Academic/Plenum Publishers, New York, NY, 2000), 87–102. Vietnam veterans: Ben Shephard, *A War of Nerves* (Jonathan Cape, London, UK, 2000), 392–96.

79. A. Young, "An Alternative History of Traumatic Stress," in A. Shalev, R. Yehuda, and A. MacFarlane, eds., *The International Handbook of Human Response to Trauma* (Kluwer Academic/Plenum Publishers, New York, NY, 2000), 51–68.

80. D. Silove, S. Ekblad, and R. Mollica, "The Rights of the Severely Mentally Ill in Post-Conflict Societies," *Lancet,* 355 (2000): 1548-9. L. Jones, J. Asare, A. Mohanraj, M. El Masri, H. Sherief, M. Van Ommeren, "Severe Mental Disorders in Complex Emergencies," *Lancet,* 374 (2009): 654-61.

81. Rwanda study: R. Neugebauer, P.W. Fisher, J.B. Turner, et al., "Post-Traumatic Stress Reactions among Rwandan Children and Adolescents in the Early Aftermath of Genocide," *International Journal of Epidemiology,* 38 (2009): 1033-45. Critique: D. Rodin and M. van Ommeren, "Commentary: Explaining Enormous Variations in Rates of Disorder in Trauma-Focused Psychiatric Epidemiology after Major Emergencies," *International Journal of Epidemiology,* 38 (2009): 1045–48.

82. D. Rodin and M. van Ommeren, "Commentary: Explaining Enormous Variations in Rates of Disorder in Trauma-Focused Psychiatric Epidemiology after Major Emergencies," *International Journal of Epidemiology,* 38 (2009): 1045–48; and P. Bolton and T. Betancourt, "Mental Health in Postwar Afghanistan," *Journal of American Medical Academy,* 292 (2004): 626-28.

83. A. Kleinman, "Anthropology and Psychiatry: The Role of Culture in Cross Cultural Research on Illness," *British Journal of Psychiatry.* 151 (1987): 447–54.

84. S. Weine et al., "Adolescent Survivors of 'Ethnic Cleansing': Observations on the First Year in America," *Journal of the American Academy of Child and Adolescent Psychiatry,* 34 (1995): 1153–58.

85. A. A. M. Thabet, Y. Abed, and P. Vostanis, "Emotional Problems in Palestinian Children Living in a War Zone: A Cross-Sectional Study," *Lancet,* 359 (2002): 1801–04. On the earlier Intifada: A. Thabet and P. Vostanis, "Post-Traumatic Stress Reactions in Children of War: A Longitudinal Study," *Child Abuse and Neglect,* 24 (2000): 291–98.

86. W.E Copeland, G. Keeler, A. Angold, & E.J. Costello, "Traumatic events and posttraumatic stress in childhood," *Archives of General Psychiatry,* 64 (2007): 577–584. A number of community studies in the high-income countries have suggested that around 80 percent of adults are exposed to traumatic events in their lifetime but less than 10 percent develop PTSD. See for example, G.A. Bonanno, C.R. Brewin, K. Kaniasty, and A.M. La Greca, "Weighing the Costs of Disaster: Consequences, Risks, and Resilience in Individuals, Families, and Communities," *Psychological Science in the Public Interest,* 11(2010): 1–49; D.J. Stein, S. Seedat, A. Iversen, S. Wessely, "Post-Traumatic Stress Disorder: Medicine and Politics," *Lancet,* 369 (2007):139–44.

87. Z. Steel et al. "Association of Torture and Other Potentially Traumatic Events with Mental Health Outcomes among Populations Exposed to Mass

Conflict and Displacement. *Journal of American Medical Academy,* 302 (2009): 537–49.

88. A. Bonanno, C.R. Brewin, K. Kaniasty, and A.M. La Greca, "Weighing the Costs of Disaster: Consequences, Risks, and Resilience in Individuals, Families, and Communities," *Psychological Science in the Public Interest,* 11(2010): 1–49; E.G. Karam et al., "Community Group Treatment and Outcome of War Trauma in Children." Paper presented at the 47th Annual Meeting of the American Academy of Child and Adolescent Psychiatry, New York, NY (2000).

89. L. Jones, A. Rrustemi, M. Shahini, and A. Uka, "Mental Health Services for War Affected Children: Report of a Survey in Kosovo," *British Journal of Psychiatry,* 183 (2003): 540–46.

90. E. Cairns and A. Dawes, "Children: Ethnic and Political Violence: A Commentary," *Child Development,* 67 (1996): 129–139.

91. P. Smith, S. Perrin, W. Yule, and S. Rabe-Hesketh, "War Exposure and Maternal Reactions in the Psychological Adjustment of Children from Bosnia-Hercegovina," *Journal of Child Psychology and Psychiatry,* 42 (2001): 395–404.

92. S. Qouta, R. Punamäki, and E. El Sarraj, "Child Development and Family Mental Health in War and Military Violence: The Palestinian Experience," *International Journal of Behavioral Development,* 32 (2008): 310–21.

93. A.S. Masten and A.J. Narayan, "Child Development in the Context of Disaster, War, and Terrorism: Pathways of Risk and Resilience," *Annual Review of Psychology,* 63 (2012): 227–57.

94. Ibid.

95. M.W. Gilbertson et al. "Smaller Hippocampal Volume Predicts Pathologic Vulnerability to Psychological Trauma," *Nature Neuroscience,* 5 (2002): 1242–47.

96. B.J. Ellis et al. "Differential Susceptibility to the Environment: An Evolutionary-Neurodevelopmental Theory." *Developmental Psychpathology,* 23 (2011): 7–28.

97. See, for example, J. Garbarino and K. Kostelny, "The Effects of Political Violence on Palestinian Children's Behavior Problems: A Risk Accumulation Model," *Child Development,* 67 (1996): 33–45; M. S. Macksoud and J. L. Aber, "The War Experiences and Psychosocial Development of Children in Lebanon," *Child Development,* 67 (1996): 70–88; P. S. Jensen and J. Shaw, "Children as Victims of War: Current Knowledge and Future Research Needs," *Journal of the American Academy of Child and Adolescent Psychiatry,* 32 (1993): 697–708.

98. T.S. Betancourt and K.T. Khan, "The Mental Health of Children Affected by Armed Conflict: Protective Processes and Pathways to Resilience," *International Review of Psychiatry*, 20 (2008): 317–28.

99. X. Wang et al., "Longitudinal Study of Earthquake-Related PTSD in a Randomly Selected Community Sample in North China." *American Journal of Psychiatry*, 157 (2000): 1260–66.

100. C. Fernando, *Children of War in Sri Lanka: Promoting Resilience through Faith Development*. Doctoral Dissertation, University of Toronto (2006) as cited in T.S. Betancourt and K.T. Khan, "The Mental Health of Children Affected by Armed Conflict: Protective Processes and Pathways to Resilience," *International Review of Psychiatry*, 20 (2008): 317–28.

9. Day after Day

101. Diary of Krystyna Stankiewicz, Department of Documents, Imperial War Museum, 83/10/1, 23, 193, 267.

102. *I Was There,* Diary of R. J. Street, Department of Documents, Imperial War Museum, 82/24/1, 10, 17.

103. These checklists have also been used and validated in other populations exposed to chronic violence: see R.F Mollica et al., "Effects of War Trauma on Cambodian Refugee Child's Functional Health and Mental Health Status," *The Journal of the American Academy of Child and Child Psychiatry,* 36 (1997): 1098–1106. I am grateful To Professor Mollica for permission to use his translations in Bosnia.

104. M. Gergen, "Narrative Structures in Social Explanation," in C. Antaki, ed., *Analysing Everyday Explanation: A Casebook of Methods* (London, UK, 1988), 94–112.

105. This process is fully detailed in Lynne Jones and Kostas Kafetsios, "Assessing Adolescent Mental Health in War Affected Societies: The Significance of Symptoms," *Child Abuse and Neglect,* 26 (2002): 1059–80.

106. For more details see Lynne Jones and Kostas Kafetsios, "Exposure to Political Violence and Psychological Well-being in Bosnian Adolescents: A Mixed Method Approach," *Clinical Child Psychology and Psychiatry,* 10 (2005): 157–76.

107. A. Dyregrov and M. Raundalen, "The Impact of the Gulf War on the Children of Iraq." Paper presented at the International Society for Traumatic Stress Studies World Conference, Amsterdam, The Netherlands, 1992.

10. Making Sense of Madness

108. Ina Konstantinova, in Laurel Holliday, ed., *Children in the Holocaust and World War II: Their Secret Diaries* (Washington Square Press, New York, NY, 1995), 256.

109. Yitskhok Rudashevski, in Laurel Holliday, ed., *Children in the Holocaust and World War II: Their Secret Diaries* (Washington Square Press, New York, NY, 1995), 161, 172.

110. Avner Ziv and Ruth Israeli, "Effects of Bombardment on the Manifest Anxiety Level of Children Living in Kibbutzim," *Journal of Consulting and Clinical Psychology,* 40 (1973): 287–91.

111. G. Straker, M.F.M. Mendelsohn, and P. Tudin, "Violent Political Contexts and the Emotional Concerns of Township Youth," *Child Development,* 67 (1996): 46–54.

112. S. Qouta, R. L. Punamaki, and E. E. Sarraj, "The Relations between Traumatic Experiences, Activity, and Cognitive and Emotional Responses among Palestinian Children," *International Journal of Psychology,* 309 (1995): 289–304. Developmental age: K. Kostelny and J. Garbarino, "Coping with the Consequences of Living in Danger: The Case of Palestinian Children and Youth," *International Journal of Behavioral Development,* 17 (1994): 595–611.

113. S. Qouta, R.L. Punamäki, and E. E. Sarraj, "Child Development and Family Mental Health in War and Military Violence: The Palestinian Experience," *International Journal of Behavioral Development,* 32 (2008): 310–321.

114. Vuk Draskovic's 1982 novel portrays Serbs as long-suffering, heroic, and virtuous (particularly the Chetniks in the Second World War), and Muslims as treacherous murderers who turn on the Serbs throughout history without understanding that they are betraying the nation from which they are descended. Vuk Draskovic, *Knife* (Serbian Classics Press, New York, NY, 2000).

115. Brian Barber found a similar difference between Palestinian activism and Bosnian passivity in his comparative study of Bosnian Muslim adolescents who were under siege in Sarajevo and Palestinian youth who experienced the first intifada in Gaza: B. K. Barber, "Contrasting Portraits of War: Youths' Varied Experiences with Political Violence in Bosnia and Palestine," *International Journal of Behavioral Development,* 32 (2008): 298-309.

116. S. J. Dollinger, "The Need for Meaning Following Disaster: Attributions and Emotional Upset," *Personality and Social Psychology Bulletin,* 12 (1986): 300–10.

117. R. D. Goldstein, N. S. Wampler, and P. H. Wise, "War Experiences and Distress Symptoms of Bosnian Children," *Pediatrics*, 100 (1997): 873–79.

118. See G.A. Fernando, K.E. Miller; D.E. Berger, "Growing Pains: The Impact of Disaster-Related and Daily Stressors on the Psychological and Psychosocial Functioning of Youth in Sri Lanka," *Child Development*, 81 (2010): 1192–1210. Similarly Catherine Panter Brick and her colleagues interviewed a thousand adolescents in Afghanistan. They discovered that while exposure to military violence predicted PTSD, the more common mental health problems of anxiety and depression were caused by family-level conflict and domestic violence, which related to everyday life in conditions or poverty, overcrowding, and displacement. C. Panter Brick, A. Goodman, W. Tol, M. Eggerman, "Mental Health and Childhood Adversities: A Longitudinal Study in Kabul, Afghanistan,"*Journal of the American Academy of Child & Adolescent Psychiatry*, 50 (2011): 349–62.

119. R. S. Pynoos and S. Eth, "Witness to Violence: The Child Interview," *Journal of the American Academy of Child and Adolescent Psychiatry*, 25 (1986): 306–19.

120. Beverley Raphael suggested one reason psychological debriefing was so popular despite the lack of evidence that it worked, was that it met a need for helpers to assist suffering and show concern. B. Raphael, L. Meldrum, and A.C. McFarlane, "Does Debriefing after Psychological Trauma Work?" *British Medical Journal*, 310 (1995): 1479.

121. Z. Solomon, Y. Neria, and E. Witztum, "Debriefing with Service Personnel in War and Peace Roles: Experience and Outcomes," in B. Raphael and J. Wilson, eds., *Psychological Debriefing: Theory, Practice and Evidence* (Cambridge University Press, Cambridge, UK, 2000), 161–73. For example, the New York Police Department received this form of assistance after September 11, 2001. Members of the department told me that some found it extremely helpful, but others perceived it as an unhelpful imposition.

122. Mixed results: P. Stallard, "Debriefing Adolescents after Critical Life Events," in B. Raphael and J. Wilson, eds., *Psychological Debriefing: Theory, Practice and Evidence* (Cambridge University Press, Cambridge, UK, 2000), 213–44.

123. See G.A. Bonanno, C.R. Brewin, K. Kaniasty, and A.M. La Greca, "Weighing the Costs of Disaster: Consequences, Risks, and Resilience in Individuals, Families, and Communities," *Psychological Science in the Public Interest*, 11(2010): 1–49; and S.C. Rose, J. Bisson, R Churchill, and S. Wessely, "Psychological Debriefing for Preventing Post Traumatic Stress Disorder (PTSD)," *Cochrane Database of Systematic Reviews*, 2 (2002). The authors made no changes to their 2002 conclusions in a 2009 update,

stating, "There is no evidence that single session individual psychological debriefing is a useful treatment for the prevention of post traumatic stress disorder after traumatic incidents. Compulsory debriefing of victims of trauma should cease."

124. WHO Guidance 2012. Available at: http://www.who.int/mental_health/ mhgap/evidence/resource/other_complaints_q5.pdf. Accessed March 30, 2013.

125. Hanna Kaminer and Peretz Lavie, "Sleep and Dreams in Well-Adjusted and Less Adjusted Holocaust Survivors," in M. S. Stroebe, W. Stroebe, and R. O. Hansson, eds., *Handbook of Bereavement: Theory, Research and Intervention* (Cambridge University Press, Cambridge, UK, 1993), 331–45.

126. C. Eyber and A. Ager, "Conselho: Psychological Healing in Displaced Communities in Angola," *Lancet,* 360 (2002): 871. Muslim culture: Tone Bringa, *Being Muslim the Bosnian Way: Identity and Community in a Central Bosnian Village* (Princeton University Press, Princeton, NJ, 1995), 184–96.

127. L. Mastnak, "Diary," *London Review of Books,* 19 (1997): 28–9.

128. Lynne Jones, "Notes for Thinking about Attachment, Grief and Loss in Societies Subject to Political Violence," in D. Southall, B. Coulta, C. Ronald, and S. Parke, eds., *International Child Health Care* (London, UK, 2002). Revised edition in press.

129. M. Weisenberg, J. Schwarzwald, M. Waysman, Z. Solomon, and A. Klingman, "Coping of School Age Children in the Sealed Room during Scud Missile Bombardment and Postwar Stress Reactions," *Journal of Consulting and Clinical Psychology,* 61 (1993): 462–67.

130. L. Jones, "'Responding to the Needs of Children in Crisis," *International Review of Psychiatry,* 20 (2008): 291–303.

131. See for example, P. Bolton and T.S. Betancourt, "Mental Health in Post War Afghanistan," *Journal of American Medical Academy,* 292 (2004): 626-28; T.S. Betancourt and K.T. Khan, "The Mental Health of Children Affected by Armed Conflict: Protective Processes and Pathways to Resilience," *International Review of Psychiatry,* 20 (2008): 317–28. International consensus guidelines to address mental health needs in emergency settings now include social support and community mobilisation as essential interventions. *IASC Guidelines on Mental Health and Psychosocial Support in Emergency Settings* (IASC, Geneva, Switzerland, 2007).

132. Anne Marie Oliver and Paul Steinberg, cited in R. J. Apfel and B. Simon, "Mitigating Discontents with Children in War: An Ongoing Psychoanalytic Inquiry," in A.C.G.M. Robben and M.M. Suarez-Orozco,

eds., *Cultures under Siege: Collective Violence and Trauma* (Cambridge University Press, Cambridge, UK, 2000), 102–30.

11. Crimes and Punishments

133. Briefing note, UNHCR, Gorazde and Visegrad office, Bosnia-Herzegovina January 2002.

134. International Crisis Group, *The "Constituent Peoples" Decision in Bosnia and Herzegovina* (Sarajevo, Bosnia-Herzegovina, 2002).

135. International Criminal Tribunal for the Former Yugoslavia, case information sheet, Krajisnik, case no. IT-00-39 (The Hague, The Netherlands, 2002). Plavsic made a dramatic guilty plea and show of repentance, but later stated that these were false and made in order to gain a lighter sentence (see chapter 12). I have retained the quote at the beginning of the chapter because it contributed to the context of my discussions with respondents in 2002

136. International Criminal Tribunal for the Former Yugoslavia, Judgment, Prosecutor v. Radislav Krstic, Srebrenica-Drina Corps case no. IT-98-33 (The Hague, The Netherlands, 2001), paras. 73–84.

137. International Criminal Tribunal for the Former Yugoslavia, transcript, Prosecutor v. Dragoljub Kunarac, Radomir Kovac, and Zoran Vukovic, Foca case nos. IT-96-23-T, IT-96-23/1-T (The Hague, The Netherlands, 2002).

138. A recent change in the property laws had made this much easier: Returnees only had to wait six months rather than two years before selling their houses.

139. International Crisis Group, *The Continuing Challenge of Refugee Return in Bosnia and Herzegovina* (Sarajevo, Bosnia-Herzegovina 2002).

140. UNICEF, *The State of the World's Children* (UNICEF, New York, NY, 1994).

141. I used the Heinz dilemma to assess moral reasoning. L. Kohlberg, *The Psychology of Moral Development: The Nature and Validity of Moral Stages* (Harper & Row, San Francisco, CA, 1984).

142. Serbs told me that the three fingers signify the eternal unity of Kosovo, Vojvodina, and Serbia, and thus the unity of all Serbs together.

143. I am grateful to Patrik Svensonn, then first secretary at the Swedish embassy in Bosnia-Herzegovina, for his firsthand account of events.

144. Stanley Cohen, *States of Denial: Knowing about Atrocities and Suffering* (Polity Press, Cambridge, UK, 2001), 7–9.

145. International Criminal Tribunal for the Former Yugoslavia, Appeals Judgment, Prosecutor v. Kunarac, Kovac, and Vukovic, Foca case nos. IT-96-23-PT, IT-96-23/1-PT (The Hague, The Netherlands, 2002).

146. International Criminal Tribunal for the Former Yugoslavia, Transcript, Prosecutor v. Milorad Krnojelac, Foca case no. IT-97-25-T (The Hague, The Netherlands, 2001), 7554ff.

147. Martha Gellhorn, *The Face of War* (Granta, London, UK, 1998), 230–31.

148. Dan Bar-On, *Legacy of Silence: Encounters with Children of the Third Reich* (Harvard University Press, Cambridge, MA, 1991), 329, 33.

149. Ian Buruma, *Wages of Guilt: Memories of War in Germany and Japan* (Vintage, London, UK, 1995), 49.

150. Ann Low-Beer, "Politics, School Textbooks and Cultural Identity: The Struggle in Bosnia and Herzegovina. Minorities in Croatian History and Geography Textbooks." In *Minorities in Textbooks: South-East Europe. International Textbook Research*, 2/23 (2001): 215-23.

151. Milanka Saponja-Hadzic, "Kostunica Remarks Frighten Bosnia," *Institute of War and Peace reporting, Balkan Crisis Report*, 368, (Amsterdam, The Netherlands, 2002).

152. It seems this was not an idle boast; see Nicholas Wood and Ian Traynor, "FRY Arms for Saddam," *Guardian*, November 25, 2002. I knew nothing at that time of a connection in arms dealing between Bosnian Serbs, Yugoslavia, and Iraq.

153. International Criminal Tribunal for the Former Yugoslavia, transcript, Prosecutor v. Radislav Krstic, Srebrenica-Drina Corps case no. IT-98-33 (The Hague, The Netherlands, 2001), 9836, 9837.

154. International Criminal Tribunal for the Former Yugoslavia, judgment, Prosecutor v. Krstic, Srebrenica-Drina Corps case no. IT-98-33 (The Hague, The Netherlands, 2001).

155. International Criminal Tribunal for the Former Yugoslavia, indictment, Prosecutor v. Slobodan Milosevic, Bosnia case no. IT-01-51-1 (The Hague, The Netherlands, 2001).

156. Elizabeth Neuffer, *The Key to My Neighbor's House: Seeking Justice in Bosnia and Rwanda* (New York, NY, 2001). Judges explained: International Criminal Tribunal for the Former Yugoslavia, Appeals Judgment, Prosecutor v. Kunarac, Kovac, and Vukovic (The Hague, The Netherlands, 2002).

157. Ian Buruma, *Wages of Guilt: Memories of War in Germany and Japan* (Vintage, London, UK, 1995), 161, 119, 114, 107.

12. What They Did Next

158. International Criminal Tribunal for the Former Yugoslavia, Sentencing Hearing Transcript, Biljana Plavsic, case no. IT-0040-I (The Hague, The Netherlands, 2003), 611–12.

159. Daniel Uggelberg Goldberg, "Plavsic Retracts War-Crimes Confession," *The Local* (Stockholm), January 26, 2009. Reprinted in *Bosnia Report*, February 4, 2009. Swedish original with photo available at: http://www.vi-tidningen. se/templates/ArticlePage.aspx?id=10784.

160. Nenad Pejic, "*A Land Where War Criminals Are Heroes*," Radio Free Europe, October 31. 2009

161. Commission for the Development of Guidelines for Conceptualising New History Textbooks in Bosnia and Herzegovina, Guidelines for Writing and Evaluation of History Textbooks in Bosnia and Herzegovina (2005). Available at: http://www.coe.ba/web2/en/dokumenti/cat_view/46-education--obrazovanje/87-published-in-2005--objavljeno-2005.html. Accessed February 15, 2013.

162. For example, curricula in Republika Srpska were still focused on Serbs, Serbian literature, and history and geography, and scarcely acknowledged the existence of space shared with other cultures and ethnicities within a common state. See Office for Security and Cooperation in Europe, Sarajevo, Bosnia- Herzegovina, *Primary School Curricula in Bosnia and Herzegovina: A Thematic Review of the National Subjects* (December 2009). Available at: http://www.zapravicnoobrazovanje.ba/Istrazivanja//1.%20Curricula%20 Analysis%20OSCE.doc. Accessed February 15, 2009.

163. Clare Magill, *Education and Fragility in Bosnia and Herzegovina* (International Institute for Educational Planning, Paris, 2010) 38. Available at: http://www.iiep.unesco.org/fileadmin/user.../Bosnia-Herzegovina.pdf. Accessed February 15, 2013.

164. See Center for Investigative Reporting (CIN), *Kindergartens: A Control Issue*, CIN online publication, (CIN, Sarajevo, Bosnia- Herzegovina March 23, 2009). Available at: *http://www.cin.ba/newsletter/pdf/CIN_12_2009-03-24.pdf*. Accessed February 14, 2013. *Santa Claus Wins Victory in Sarajevo as Public Kindergarten Director Fired*, (CIN, Sarajevo, Bosnia-Herzegovina February 3, 2011) Available at: http://www.isaintel.com/2011/02/03/santa-claus-wins-victory-in-sarajevo-as-public-kindergarten-director-fired/. Accessed February 14, 2013.

165. Lucy Claridge, *Discrimination and Political Participation in Bosnia and Herzegovina: Sejdic and Finci v. Bosnia and Herzegovina* (Minority Rights Group International, London, UK, January 2010).

166. B92 Radio, "Dodik Believes RS Is Serbia's Top Priority" June 8, 2012.

167. A.S. Masten and A.J. Narayan, "Child Development in the Context of Disaster, War, and Terrorism: Pathways of Risk and Resilience," *Annual Review of Psychology*, 63 (2012): 227–57.

168. KM is the Bosnian Convertible Marka coded as BAM: 6,000 KM are approximately $4,000

169. Radio Free Europe/Radio Liberty, "Republika Srpska's Dodik Says He's 'Only Supporting the Constitution'" October 14, 2011.

170. Jasarevic was jailed for eighteen years for terrorism in December 2012.

171. Nenad Pejic, "The Suicide of Multiethnic Sarajevo," Radio Free Europe/Radio Liberty, April 25, 2010; Dzenana Karabegovic, "Wahabi Group Launches Conversion Campaign in Bosnia," Radio Free Europe/Radio Liberty, April 2, 2010.

172. The International Criminal Tribunal for the Former Yugoslavia has indicted 161 people. Thirty-six have had their indictments withdrawn or are deceased. Of the remaining, ninety-four are Serbs, twenty-nine are Croats, and nine are Bosniaks. Available at: http://www.icty.org/sid/24. Accessed February 20, 2013.

173. H. Karge and K. Batarilo, *Reform in the Field of History in Education Bosnia and Herzegovina Modernization of History Textbooks in Bosnia and Herzegovina: From the Withdrawal of Offensive Material from Textbooks in 1999 to the New Generation of Textbooks in 2007/2008* (Braunschweig, Germany, 2008), 8.

174. Clare Magill, *Education and Fragility in Bosnia and Herzegovina* (International Institute for Educational Planning, Paris, 2010), 48.

175. E. M. Jukic, "Proud to Be Mincemeat in Bosnia," *Balkan Insight,* November 23, 2012. Available at: http://www.balkaninsight.com/en/blog/proud-to-be-minced-meat-in-bosnia. Accessed February 23, 2013.

176. According to the 1991 census, the city of Sarajevo had a population of five hundred thousand including 50 percent Bosnian Muslim, 28 percent Serb, 13 percent Yugoslav, and 7 percent Croat. Proportions today are estimated at 80 percent Bosnian Muslim, 12 percent Serb, and 8 percent Croat.

177. Julian Borger, "Bosnian War 20 Years On: Peace Holds but Conflict Continues to Haunt," *The Guardian*, April 4, 2012.

Chronology

178. Some details taken from BBC World Service, Bosnia-Hercegovina Timeline: A Chronology of Key Events. Available at: http://news.bbc.co.uk/2/hi/europe/1066981.stm. Accessed February 1, 2012.

ACKNOWLEDGMENTS

My thanks to the William T. Grant foundation for the funding to conduct the research that lies at the heart of this book, to Peter Filkins for permission to quote his translation of Ingeborg Bachmann's poem "Every Day," to the *British Medical Journal* for permission to quote Frank Bodman's 1941 paper on the war experiences of children, and to Savo Heleta for permission to quote from *Not My Turn To Die: Memoirs of a Broken Childhood in Bosnia*. Interviews with some of the respondents in 2012 were made for "Outlook" on the BBC World Service.

This book has been a long time in the making. First of all thanks to Professor Ian Goodyer of the Department of Developmental Psychiatry, Cambridge University, who permitted an unorthodox path during my child psychiatry training, and encouraged me to return to Bosnia after the war to do the research; and Professor Martin Richards, Sally Roberts, Gill Brown, and all the members and staff of the Centre for Family Research, also at Cambridge University, who provided academic guidance and friendship for a decade.

The idea grew out of conversations with Bosnian children during the war in Sarajevo in 1994 and 1995, and in Gorazde in 1996. I continued to live intermittently in Bosnia until 2002. I am indebted to all of the following for their support, friendship, thoughts, and for facilitating my work in innumerable ways during those years: the local and international staff of Catholic Relief Services in 1994–95; the local staff of MSF Gorazde 1996; British ambassadors to BiH, Robert Barnett, Brian Hopkinson, Charles Crawford, and the staff at British Embassy and British Council in Sarajevo; and the staff in the UNHCR offices in Sarajevo, Banja Luka, and Gorazde and the OSCE office in Foca. Particular thanks to Goran and Amela Simic, Kris Janowski, Matthew Newton, Dejan Balic, Elisabeth Tomasinec, Edin Culov, Aida Lakovic, Nerfisa Medosevic, and Amer Sijercic. Patrik Svensonn, Izeta and Mirsad Purivatra, and Narcisa and Semir Beslija made me welcome in Sarajevo at different times. Mirsada, Miralem, Rijad, Medina, and Nermana Adzovic have made me part of their family in Gorazde for 15 years.

I am completely indebted to all my translators, especially Edita Beslija, Gordana Matic, Lejla Sudic-Hendo, Vedrana Vukovic, Jasmin Kuljuh, and Ana Elez-Radcliffe, who did much more than just translate. Their understanding and enthusiasm for the project, their empathy and sensitivity with the children, their administrative and diplomatic skills made my fieldwork possible. Their friendship is one of the things that made it so enjoyable.

The staff of the document collection of the Imperial War Museum gave suggestions as to manuscripts worth reading as well as providing working space in one of the loveliest libraries in London. I am grateful for their permission to quote from the diaries of Krystyna Stankiewicz and R. J. Street.

Thanks also to Noel Malcolm, Brendan Simms, Quintin Hoare, Vanda Vucicevic, and all the staff at the Bosnian Institute for patience with historical and factual queries and suggestions as to source material. Any inaccuracies remain my responsibility. Thanks to Mark Cousins, Dave Hansen, Nicholas Humphrey, Gill Moreton, Ben Shephard, Cornelia Sorabji, Jon Swain, Richard Vogler for reading early drafts and Asmamaw Yigeremu for reading later ones; Erica Jones and Jurg Honegger for providing quiet sanctuaries in which to write.

I am grateful to my agent Katinka Matson, and Elizabeth Knoll and Camille Smith at Harvard University Press, who midwifed the first edition; Sue Waldram at the BBC World Service who found the funds to send me back to Bosnia in 2012, and Erika Goldman at Bellevue Literary Press, who believed in this book from the start, and has adopted the second edition.

Finally, my thanks to the headmasters and teaching staff and psychologists of all the schools in which I worked in both Foca and Gorazde, for allowing me into their classrooms and for sharing their thoughts and opinions. My deepest thanks go to my respondents and their families, children at the outset, young adults now, who welcomed me into their homes and lives and gave me so much of their time. I hope they will find their thoughts and feelings accurately reflected even when our interpretations of events differ. My hope is that this book may be one step along the path to mutual understanding.

INDEX

Bosnian, as language, 27, 262
Bosnian Entities. *See* Federation of Bosnia
    and Herzegovina; Republika
    Srpska
Bosnian Serb Army, 117
Braco, 271–72
Bradford, England, 187–88
Brankovic, Vuk, 151
Bratunac, 112
Brcko, 71, 291
Bridge over the Drina (Andric), 151
Bristol, England, 181
bulas, 162–63
Burlingham, Dorothy, 182–83
Bush, George W., 257

Cajnice, 118
Cancar, Petko, 104
Carey-Trefzer, Charlotte, 183
Celebici concentration camp, 112, 116
chauvinism, 161
Chetniks
    as disparaging term, 157–58
    Muslims and, 39–41
    Narcisa and, 39–40
    Nina and, 49–51
    random searches by, 55
China, war with Japan, 268. *See also*
    Nanking, China
citizen groups, 93
Cohen, Richard, 81
Cohen, Stanley, 259
combat stress. *See* post-traumatic stress
    disorder
communism, 87–88
    as anti-Serb, 269
Communist Party, 96
concentration camps, 105
    at Celebici, 112, 116
    Croats and, 152
    Human Rights Watch reports on, 112
    during World War II, 152
Congress of Berlin, 155
Constantinople, 97
Copeland, William, 193
coping strategies, in children, 183, 286–87.
    See also memory, war and
    activism and, 227
    Freud on, 236–37
    during Holocaust, 234
    play as, 211
    resilience and, 194
Coventry, England, 261
Croatia, 38, 94
Croats
    in BIH, 17–18, 130
    concentration camps and, 152

separation of, from other ethnic
    groups, 71

Dayton Peace Agreement, 129–31
    BIH after, 24, 68–70, 175
    BIH constitution after, 291
    ethnic cleansing after, 133
    exclusion from, 23
    Foca after, 21, 135–37
    Gorazde after, 133–34
    home reclamation in BIH after, 69–
        70, 135–36
    Muslims under, 129
    political fragmentation as result of,
        277
    Serbs under, 130
    Western sponsors of, 130
death, witnesses to, 206–8
debriefing, 233–34
denial, distancing compared to, 235
*Diagnostic and Statistical Manual of
    Mental Disorders*, 186, 189
Diana, 60
Dickens, Charles, 155, 187
displacement. *See* evacuation and
        displacement, during wartime
distancing
    denial compared to, 235
    psychological impact of war and, 233
    for war memories, 259–61
Divac, 110, 138–39, 169–70, 213
    postwar life for, 278–79
    war memories for, 260
Dizdarevic, Zlatko, 124
Djozo, Husein Efendija, 155
Dodik, Milorad, 24, 275, 277
Dollinger, Steven, 227–28
Donje Polje, 98, 250, 258, 263, 305
dose effect, 214, 231–32
Dragiza, 303–6
Draskovic, Vuk, 225
Drina River, 17, 97
DSM-III. *See Diagnostic and Statistical
        Manual of Mental Disorders*
DSM-IV. *See Diagnostic and Statistical
        Manual of Mental Disorders*
Dubrovnik, Croatia, 97
Dusan, 46–48, 58–59, 64–65, 87, 91–92
    ambivalence towards Muslims, 139,
        141–42
    on loss during wartime, 205
    on Muslim-Serb conflict, 152
    return to Foca, 70–71

Edin, 209, 232
    on loss during wartime, 204
Edita, 287–88, 302

BELLEVUE LITERARY PRESS has been publishing prize-winning books since 2007 and is the first and only nonprofit press dedicated to literary fiction and nonfiction at the intersection of the arts and sciences. We believe that science and literature are natural companions for understanding the human experience. Our ultimate goal is to promote science literacy in unaccustomed ways and offer new tools for thinking about our world.

To support our press and its mission, and for our full catalogue of published titles, please visit us at blpress.org.

BELLEVUE LITERARY PRESS
New York